UNLEASH
YOUR
PSYCHIC
POWERS

BY EMBROSEWYN TAZKUVEL

Celestine Light Magick Series

ANGELS OF MIRACLES AND MANIFESTATION
144 Names, Sigils and Stewardships to Call the Magickal Angels of Celestine Light

WORDS OF POWER AND TRANSFORMATION
101+ Magickal Words and Sigils of Celestine Light
to Manifest Your Desires

CELESTINE LIGHT MAGICKAL SIGILS OF HEAVEN & EARTH

Secret Earth Series

INCEPTION (BOOK 1)
DESTINY (BOOK 2)

Psychic Awakening Series

CLAIRVOYANCE
TELEKINESIS
DREAMS

AURAS
How to See, Feel and Know

SOUL MATE AURAS
How Find Your Soul Mate & "Happily Ever After"

UNLEASH YOUR PSYCHIC POWERS

PSYCHIC SELF DEFENSE

LOVE YOURSELF
Secret Key To Transforming Your Life

22 STEPS TO THE LIGHT OF YOUR SOUL

ORACLES OF CELESTINE LIGHT
Complete Trilogy of Genesis, Nexus & Vivus

Published by Kaleidoscope Productions
1467 Siskiyou Boulevard, #9; Ashland, OR 97520
www.kaleidoscope-publications.com
ISBN 9781494722760

Book layout and design by Sumara Elan Love
www.3wizardz.com

Copyright © 2013 by Embrosewyn Tazkuvel

All rights reserved
This book including the cover illustration, may not be copied except for personal use by the original purchaser. The book may not be reproduced or retransmitted by any means in whole or part, or repackaged, resold, or given away for free as a download, in whole or part, in any form.

Distribution
Only legally available to be purchased as a paperback book through retail or online bookstores, or in eBook format through major online retailers and their affiliates.

PLEASE DO NOT PARTICIPATE IN PIRACY.

UNLEASH YOUR PSYCHIC POWERS

EMBROSEWYN TAZKUVEL

In Appreciation

Endless thanks to my lovely wife Sumara for her professional book formatting. How wonderful it is to be able to work and collaborate each day with my multi-talented Soul Mate.

Many thanks to my daughter Angeline for her great illustrations.

And special thanks to Skye for her diligent work proofing and checking the flow of the manuscipt.

TABLE OF CONTENTS

Part I: The Foundation
- Chapter 1: **You Have Amazing Abilities**...13
- Chapter 2: **What's Different About This Book?**...................................17
- Chapter 3: **My Own Journey of Discovery**...21
- Chapter 4: **Short History of Psychic & Paranormal Abilities**............39
- Chapter 5: **What's the Science? Are the Skeptics Ever Right?**........43
- Chapter 6: **Sex in Seances and Paranormal Experiences**..................51
- Chapter 7: **Categories of Psychic & Paranormal Abilities**................55
- Chapter 8: **Connect Your Senses to Unleash Your Supernatural Gifts**..59
- Chapter 9: **Focus is Essential…Usually**..69
- Chapter 10: **Psychic Self-Defense**..79

Part II. Personal Experiences, Including Discovery & Training Insights
- Chapter 11: **Empathy & Intuition**..119
- Chapter 12: **Seeing, Feeling, & Reading the Aura**..........................125
- Chapter 13: **Animal Whisperer**...137
- Chapter 14: **Lucid Dreaming**..141
- Chapter 15: **Disrupting Electrical Devices**.....................................149
- Chapter 16: **Earth Energy Sensitive**..159
- Chapter 17: **Precognition**..177
- Chapter 18: **Divine Intervention**..195
- Chapter 19: **Ki Force**..197
- Chapter 20: **Astral Projection**..211
- Chapter 21: **Biblioelucidation**..219
- Chapter 22: **Faith, Spiritual & Auric Healing**.................................223
- Chapter 23: **Dreams & Dream Interpretation**.................................229
- Chapter 24: **Dowsing & Pendulums**...247
- Chapter 25: **Clairvoyance**...257
- Chapter 26: **Insight Card**s...271
- Chapter 27: **Channeling**..279
- Chapter 28: **Automatic Handwriting**...289
- Chapter 29: **Telepathy**...295
- Chapter 30: **Telekinesis**...301

Final Thoughts..317
Appenidix
Appendix A: **Celestine Light**..321
Appendix B: **The Inquisition**..323
Appendix C: **Salem Witch Trials**..329
Appendix D: **Marvelous Margery**..335
Appendix E: **Mistress of Levitation Eusapia Palladino**...343
Appendix F: **Mastering Your Brain Waves of Power**...353

Part I
THE FOUNDATION

Chapter 1
YOU HAVE AMAZING ABILITIES

Every single person has psychic abilities. I guarantee that you also have paranormal powers. This book is all about helping you to discover and develop the unique psychic and paranormal gifts that were your birthright. Plus, it will teach you how to develop many additional psychic and paranormal abilities you are interested in mastering. Skeptics may scoff at the statement that everyone has supernatural abilities, and even those who believe in them may seriously doubt that they possess such gifts, but everyone does. It is like a person who never opens their eyes and claims and maybe even believes that they are blind. The reality is their eyes are present. If they just open them they will be able to see. It is the same with your psychic and paranormal abilities. They only are called 'super" natural because most people do not realize they are in fact a 'natural' aspect of all humans.

One of the big disconnects and a large part of the misconception problem is many people from scoffers to believers, think of paranormal powers as some type of magic or mystical abilities. Despite all the books and movies that depict paranormal abilities in such light, the reality is they are simply normal aspects of your senses and innate mental and physical abilities that you do not use and maybe are not even aware that you possess.

In the fantasy world, such as in the Harry Potter books and movies, there are only a few people who possess magic powers. The majority of the population who do not, are the "Muggles." In real life, there are relatively few who know about their paranormal abilities, and most people either deny their existence or deny it in themselves. But neither ignorance or denial change the reality.

Paranormal and psychic gifts are only considered "special" because so few people tap into and unleash their hidden powers. Most people live and die never realizing they were far more than they knew. Don't let this be you! I want to help you learn to develop your wonderful paranormal gifts. I know you have them! I can do this best by sharing with you the techniques and experiences that helped me discover and develop mine. In classes I have taught during the last twenty years, I have been overjoyed to find that most people can quickly discover and begin to use paranormal gifts that have been laying dormant and unknown within them for all of their lives. Yours are about to come out! You are so much more than you know. I am humbled, and it is an honor for me to be able to help you discover and unleash the magnificence that is truly you.

For more than twenty years I have been teaching people to see the bio-electric energy aura that exists around every person. In my aura classes and in my book *Auras: How to See, Feel & Know*, I help people begin seeing the aura within 5 minutes. It's that easy! The techniques I use quickly bring out this "psychic" ability in any person that has vision in both eyes. It doesn't matter whether they are ardent believers in paranormal abilities or adamant disbelievers. If they follow the simple instructions, their body will almost immediately reveal a wondrous new ability to them. It's not magic, but it is magical. Being able to see auras, like every other psychic or paranormal ability, is simply learning how to tune in and develop incredible innate abilities that have been patiently waiting inside for their owners to learn the secret keys to unleashing their magnificent power.

The same opportunity exists to uncover a myriad of psychic abilities and paranormal powers simmering inside of you. Or, if you have already discovered them, to vastly increase what you can do with your supernatural gifts. The greater you, has been waiting patiently to be unleashed. Now is the time.

Though all people have psychic and paranormal abilities, they do manifest easier with certain types of people, who because of their nature, have an affinity for tuning into subtle energies both within and outside of themselves. Here's a quick little test I give my new students to apprise how easy it will be for them to discover and develop their special powers and abilities. Everyone has them and everyone can develop them, but it is easier for people with these characteristics.

1. On a scale of 1-10 how imaginative are you?

Imagination is a vital trait for developing supernatural abilities. It is an elemental aspect of dreams, daydreams, vision and creativity. It is your bridge between the world of your 5 physical senses and the perceptions of your psychic senses. If you are unsure of how to rate your imaginative abilities, close your eyes and draw a rose in your mind. Create as many details as you can from the shape, color and texture of the flowers. Can you go to the next level and call up a rose aroma? Can you go one level higher and imagine feeling the prick of a thorn?

2. Rate your ability to focus, without distraction on a scale of 1-10.

As one consideration of the score, include the length of time you can typically focus before you get distracted. The ability to focus on a single thought or action is essential to manifesting most psychic and paranormal abilities at anything other than a beginners level. The longer you can focus without deviating from your task and despite distractions that may occur around you, the more powerfully and fully you will call forth your supernatural powers.

3. On a scale of 1-10, rate how much you trust and act on your intuition.

Intuition is the most common form of psychic ability. Everyone has experienced something inside them guiding them to do or not do something, contrary to what their conscious mind is telling them. As this is a direct link to your psychic abilities, accessing how much you listen to your inner voice, gives a good benchmark to know how far along the path you are to more fully developing your supernatural abilities.

4. On a scale of 1-10, rate how empathetic are you to the challenges other people have in their lives.

Empathy is another easily accessible and essential psychic ability. At first empathy may be all in your conscious mind. But as you open up to it, your aura interacts with the other person allowing you to truly feel what they are feeling. If they are crying, you probably will be too.

5. How sensitive are you to energy of both people and electrical devices?

Psychics tend to be very sensitive to energy of all types. Because they are so affected, it can be uncomfortable or overstimulating for them to be in large crowds of people because of the cacophony of energy coming at them from all directions. Group activities, even with friends, can leave them physically drained, unless they have learned to shield themselves from other peoples energy when they are in groups or crowds. They also tend to be more affected by electromagnetic radiation from things like overhead power lines or any electrical device emanating a large electromagnetic field.

Now add up your score. The higher it is, the easier, quicker and more powerfully you will be able to manifest your psychic abilities and paranormal powers.

45-50 You are already very psychic. Amping up your abilities will be easy.

39-44 You have all the right traits and have probably already had some strong psychic experiences. With just a little regular practice you should be able to develop several supernatural abilities.

30-38 You have certainly had some psychic experiences but you may not have recognized them for what they were at the time. Practice is important for you, particularly practice focusing and using your imagination and creativity.

20-29 You probably have not given a lot of thought to psychic and paranormal abilities, at least not as gifts you might have yourself. But if you dedicate yourself to learning about the supernatural and practicing the techniques necessary to develop the abilities, they can become as strong in you as anyone. Give extra emphasis to developing your ability to see, know and feel auras.

0-19 You are very grounded in the "real world." But as you learn to accept that there is also a vast unseen world out there, you will be able to tap into it with psychic abilities as well as anyone. Developing a deeper empathy for other people is a key to developing your powers.

You will also need to not just look at psychic abilities from a mental perspective, but develop an emotional passion for learning more and bringing forth your own supernatural gifts.

Chapter 2
WHAT'S DIFFERENT ABOUT THIS BOOK?

Looking into the future and receiving answers to life's questions, from the gypsy palm reader to the Ouija Board, from the astrologer to the psychic clairvoyant, is one of the most enduring interests of humankind. Sometimes it's fun and games like young teens using a Ouija Board to discover who will get the first kiss. Other times, especially when people are paying money going to professional psychics, it's more serious and the answers more detailed.

In ancient times divination was a far more essential affair for everyone from the peasants to the kings. It was an intricate thread woven inextricably into the tapestry of humanity. Seeking answers to the future, the farmer looked to affirm the most auspicious day to plant, the miller the optimum time to grind the grain, while the merchant sought signs that he should seal a deal. Kings grand and petty, equally looked to diviners and signs in the wind and the flame to know how to rule and proceed. Alexander the Great committed to battle only after consulting the Oracle at Delphi as had his father King Philip of Macedonia. While many variations and methods of divination and paranormal powers are still used today, most of those from earlier eras are lesser known or have been quietly forgotten and covered in the dust of years gone by.

I have always been drawn to the mysterious and unknown. From an early age I have been aware of my own unique qualities and wondered how I could learn more about them. For many years I thought of myself as the only "purple person." Not that my skin was purple, or that I thought I came from the Planet Purple, or the 4th dimension of purple; I was just different. So different in the perception of the world around me that I while think of myself as a purple person I began assigning various different colors, based upon the predominant color in their aura, to everyone else. During my youth, paranormal abilities were part of my everyday life. I had at first assumed that seeing auras and being able to communicate with animals were just normal human traits. But being called a liar by my mother and laughed at by my childhood friends when I tried to talk about these abilities, led me to the opposite conclusion - that I was the only one that had them!

It wasn't until I was in my early twenties and began to read books in the library about psychic and paranormal abilities that a wonderful light went on in my head and a warm glow spread in my heart as I realized I wasn't alone. There were others with abilities just like mine! I had simply never met any yet. Probably because I had been hanging out with friends who lived in very limited worlds of their comfort zones, instead of seeking out friends with greater horizons and a more unlimited way of thinking.

Yet for all my excitement generated from realizing I actually wasn't the only purple person in the world, it still took many more years to work through my redneck upbringing and scientific education that continued to limit my acceptance of my abilities. I couldn't deny them because I lived them everyday. But neither did I fully embrace them. And I certainly didn't understand them. I fervently wanted to be able to explain these strange gifts by science or reason, but for the most part I could not. And I was still haunted by the rejection of my mother and friends when I had tried to talk about them.

As I write this, I am now in my 59th year. I have had many, many amazing psychic and paranormal experiences in my life. Some of the most profound I will share with you in this book. As you read through it or glance at the Table of Contents, you'll recognize many of the paranormal gifts I will be talking about. You'll also notice a glaring absence of some that are commonly written about or depicted in books and movies. Lastly, you'll see some you have probably never heard of before. Commonly known or obscure, I have chosen psychic abilities rooted in my own life and research. Experience with others seeking to develop their psychic and paranormal gifts, has proven that by sharing the techniques I've used successfully myself, I can most quickly and easily help you bring out the unique and awesome psychic and paranormal gifts in your life.

Part I contains foundational information about psychic and paranormal powers to help you understand the context and evolution of supernatural abilities, and provide a firm platform to launch the safe expansion of your supernatural gifts.

The psychic and paranormal abilities elaborated upon in **Part II** are those in which I have had significant personal experiences. For the most part, they appear in the order that I became actively aware of them for the first time in my life. Empathy /Intuition is at the head of the list because that is the first ability I had a conscious understanding of in the same way I understood I could see with my eyes and hear with my ears. Until it is driven out of them by painful experiences or dogmatic indoctrination, all children have an innate and powerful empathetic ability. If you are a young child and your mother or father are sad about something, even if they don't express their sadness to you in any overt way, you still innately know they are sad. Psychic empathy is as natural and instinctual as breathing, until it is turned off by repeatedly ignoring it.

You'll find quite an extensive **Appendix**. Appendixes B-E were originally intended to be

What's Different About This Book?

chapters in the book as I was writing it. Upon final assembly of the manuscript, I realized that while the subjects of those chapters are interesting to me, they might not be to some readers, so I stuck them at the end as appendixes. Those who have an interest, will likely find them fascinating, and those who don't, can end their read at the last chapter, hopefully greatly fulfilled and motivated.

In my life journey, I have not been exposed much to the thoughts, experiences, writings or teachings of other paranormal practitioners or psychics, other than in a few instances, beginning with the trip to the library in my early twenties when I discovered I wasn't the only purple person. I've never attended a psychic seminar other than my own classes, and have only read or even glanced through, very few books on the subject. I did attend two psychic fairs many decades ago. Some parts were interesting, but I was also disappointed by what I perceived, based upon my scientific background and own psychic experiences and abilities, to be a fair amount of self-delusion and in some cases deception. It's not that I don't have an interest in the experiences of others, or give credence to the authentic, but more that I prefer to not be influenced by what other people have experienced, be it real or imagined. That is one way I insure myself of the authenticity of my own experiences. Hopefully, this means everything I present to you in this book will be new and fresh, giving you perspectives and techniques you haven't had or heard before that will help you to call out your own paranormal gifts quickly and powerfully.

In our modern age it seems everyone wants to have instant or at least very quick gratification. It is not uncommon for me to receive emails from people wanting to know how they can immediately or very quickly, acquire mastery of one particular paranormal gift or another. There are some psychic gifts or paranormal abilities you can manifest for the first time by applying correct techniques after just a few minutes of practice, such as seeing auras. But if there is a path to mastery of any psychic or paranormal ability after just a few minutes or even days of training and practice, I do not know it. However, there are shortcuts that I have discovered, not only special techniques, but also helpful habits such as treating your body as a temple, abstaining from mind or mood altering drugs, and not partaking of food or drinks that harm your health or addle your mind.

Overall, bringing out and mastering your personal supernatural abilities is not unlike the journey of your school years: to excel you need to study, focus, and apply yourself to practice with consistency and continuity. But the effort is so, so worthwhile. Discovering and mastering even one special gift will expand your consciousness, horizons and possibilities more than you can imagine. And I hope as you read and apply the teachings in this book, you will bring forth a great array of psychic abilities and paranormal powers. I know they are inside you clamoring to come out!

Chapter 3
MY OWN JOURNEY OF DISCOVERY

There once was a time when I was a politically conservative, overly religious, fairly red-necked, student of geophysics. I had been raised in an American Southern family full of bias and prejudice against people that did not hold the same values or make the same choices in life. Majoring in a science field in college I gradually adopted science as an alternative path to my upbringing. I wanted to make choices and decisions based upon facts, not supposition, personal preference or simple emotional desires. Not that I didn't still maintain my own closet full of biases. That was especially true for the unscientifically founded New Age movement. I frequently voiced my opinion that anyone that believed *(insert any New Age belief)* had marbles for brains.

Yet behind my science facade I was deceiving and being untrue to myself. Since my earliest childhood years I had spontaneously manifested psychic and paranormal abilities. When I was younger and naive, things like seeing auras around people's heads weren't paranormal, they were just normal. It was only as I grew older and realized everyone else didn't see what I saw that I came to understand that maybe they were paranormal abilities after all. The reality was I had experienced numerous paranormal events. And I continued every year of my life to manifest multiple psychic abilities. To my great frustration, I couldn't explain any of the things I could see or do with the precepts of science, so I very unscientifically finally just accepted that they were inexplicable. I tried not to think about that aspect very much.

In most cases my special abilities didn't just pop into existence full-blown. They most often began with something small that barely caught my attention. Over the years, in addition to focus and regular practice, I developed many techniques and exercises to help strengthen and expand the psychic and paranormal abilities I discovered within myself.

Discovering Myself Alone In the Swamps

Looking back, I think it all began with my love of the outdoors and walking and exploring alone in the forests and swamps I grew up around as a kid. From the earliest days of childhood and into my youth and later adulthood, I loved spending time alone in nature. I felt one with everything around me and far beyond. I would come home from school, quickly change my clothes, say "hi" to my mother, then be out the door heading for the woods and swamps. I spent dreamy hours every day, especially during the long, warm days of summer, learning by wonder-filled observation about the plants and the animals. I knew where the muskrats denned, where the fish gathered in deep pools, where the snakes and turtles sunned, where the skunks slept in the day, and the best places to find juicy wild berries and the tiny, tasty licorice ferns. Communing with nature as I did, in silence, alone with no other person to speak with, my normal senses, sight, sound, touch and smell all became more acute. But the channels to perceiving more beyond those senses also opened up in ways I'm sure would have been less likely if I had been at home watching TV or playing games with my friends. I also enjoyed the company of people and was not by any means shy. But I gained deep fulfillment and personal growth whenever I wandered alone among the myriad creations of nature; wonders which never ceased to leave me spellbound.

As an adult, when I had young children at home, my family attended church regularly. But during the languid days of summer, it was often without me, as the vixen allure of the wild woods always beckoned with a call too strong to resist. When I was absent from church on Sundays, because I had instead chosen to commune with nature in the woods, mountains, or on a wild beach, I would tell people that inquired where I had been, that I had simply been worshiping in the cathedral built by God. I came to know the majesty of God and appreciate my own uniqueness in many ways during the countless hours I delighted alone in nature.

Animal Whispering

It's interesting how there are some things you just seem to innately know, even when you have never previously seen it or heard about it elsewhere. Being able to communicate with animals telepathically and through body language was one of those innate understandings I was blessed with from my earliest age. I knew with firm conviction that of course animals could understand my thoughts and benign intentions. Any doubts about that reality simply never entered into my head.

I spent innumerable hours quietly alone in the woods and swamps observing animals of all kinds from birds to beavers. Stealthily hidden away in the foliage, downwind so they could not detect my scent, I would remain unmoving for hours at a time watching the cycle of animal life unfold before me. I learned the body language of animals that showed when they were happy or sad, playful or melancholy. I gained an understanding of when their ferocity was merely defense posturing and when it indicated true intent to attack in moments unless I backed away.

Spring, with all the new births, was always my favorite time of year. I especially enjoyed observing the myriad of bird species, from the crows nesting in the top of the tallest tree, which

My Own Journey of Discovery

I climbed up to see, to the quail hidden on the ground in a dense thicket. And I would challenge the most callous heart to not melt at the sight of a tiny newborn baby deer laying on the ground fresh out of the womb, bravely struggling to stand on wobbly legs for the very first time next to its mother.

With every encounter, with both wildlife and domestic animals from dogs to horses, I learned how to convey my own loving intentions with my body language. But with every step and every movement I was also speaking aloud to them in my mind. No words came out of my mouth, but I could tell by their reactions, even when I was physically not moving, that they were sensing the intent of my silently spoken thoughts. I knew they did not understand the words spoken silently in my mind, but was sure they understood the peaceful, loving, calming assurance of my telepathic mind speak. Over time, I began to have a knowing about their feelings and desires. I say 'knowing', because it was an understanding in my mind that was created by a combination of their body language, aura and paranormal perceptions of their thoughts and feelings.

In **Chapter 13**, *Animal Whisper*, I will share more about my experiences communicating with animals and how you can begin to have this emotionally very fulfilling ability as well.

Assburn Hill

My senior year of High School was certainly eventful in many ways, none more so than the expansion of my paranormal abilities and a big part of that occurred free flying off a cliff. My family lived in Spain near some steep cliffs overlooking the ocean, made entirely of clay, which were about 150-200 feet tall. The upper two thirds of the cliff was nearly vertical rock hard clay. The lower third was a thick talus slope of little clay balls that had dried and fallen down from the cliff above. If you tried walking on the talus you would sink up to your calf in the dried clay balls.

There was one particular section of the one mile long cliff, locally called *Assburn Hill*, where the top was uniformly flat, with no trees or significant vegetation. This allowed the very brave, or very stupid, to get up a head of steam, run full blast off the edge of the cliff, then fly through the air falling for 100 feet or more, landing in the talus slope below. A jumper needed to land on the talus slope with a perfect 5 point landing to not get hurt; both hands, both feet and the jumpers bottom all had to hit at the same moment. If done correctly, the jumper would then slide very fast, but safely, down to the bottom of the hill. This caused a lot of friction on the posterior, hence the name of the hill. If a jumper landed with anything less than all 5 points they would often go head over heels and end up injured.

Feeling my athletic oats at age 17, I was one of the brave/stupid people who made this jump. I ended up doing it several times over a period of days. I can unequivocally say it was the most exhilarating thing I have ever done, especially as it became an unforgettable spiritual and paranormal experience.

The first jump was the most difficult. The massive cliff face was stone hard clay. Hitting it would be like hitting concrete. As the cliff was not exactly vertical, the top edge of the talus safety zone at the bottom of the cliff actually was about 15 feet away horizontally from the top edge of the cliff where a jumper flew out into empty space. If a jumper didn't travel 15 feet horizontally during their descent from the top of the cliff, they would not land in the talus slope, but would first make contact with the hard clay cliff, which would inevitably cause them to bounce and twist, sometimes even spinning and flipping before they hit the talus slope on their second bounce. I had seen and heard of some very bad accidents.

I could jump over 15 feet in the long jump, so I figured I should be able to easily make the talus with the added horizontal distance gained during the vertical fall. But understanding that point of physics did little to qualm my trepidation as I looked over the edge to the bottom of the cliff 200 feet below and the top of the talus slope that looked so far down and so far away horizontally. It sure appeared a lot further than 15 feet.

I thought a lot about whether I really wanted to make the attempt, because with Assburn Hill there were no second chances; no practice runs. You either succeeded or you failed, and if you failed, it was inevitably very painful.

I came to the precipice, to look over the edge of the cliff at the talus slope far below every day for about a week, trying to convince myself that I could do this. Every time, I instead convinced myself that it was too risky, with nothing to be gained for success, and a great deal that might be potentially lost in failure. And the record of success had not been good with other jumpers. Only about 2 out of 10 of the people who attempted the jump made it to the talus slope on their first attempt and most never tried a second leap.

Even great long jumpers failed. There is just something very intimidating about running and jumping off of a cliff without a parachute, when the only thing you can see below you is a steep dirt slope, and beyond that, the ocean stretching far into the distance. I think the many first-timers that failed would speed toward the edge of the cliff thinking they had the needed courage, but inside they were still shaking with fear. Their unacknowledged fear prevented them from exerting their full athletic power to propel them as far as possible into space to reach the relative safety of the talus slope.

At last, I concluded that the risk was too great and the reward non-existent. But that night when I knelt down to say my nightly prayer, something wonderful happened. I was praying about my future, as I was considering which college to attend, when suddenly I was interrupted by a vivid vision. I saw myself leaping into space off the top of Assburn Hill. It was a beautiful, sunny day. The ocean was so blue. I clearly heard a voice in my mind say, "**Do not lose the expansion of spirit you can gain for failure to make the attempt.**" In my life-like vision, it seemed as if I was flying with my arms outstretched and not falling at all. It felt as if I was in the air for minutes not seconds, as I took time to look around at people on the beach below and to watch a falcon flying at eye level nearby. Finally I began to fall through space and it also seemed to take a long time. Then I softly landed in the talus quite far down the slope, and slid safely to the bottom. In my heart, there was a feeling, even in the vision, that having done that, I could do anything.

I finished my prayer exuding euphoria. I knew with firm resolution that when the sun rose high in the sky on the following day, I would conquer Assburn Hill.

This was a major turning point in my life. The details of my multiple jumps off of Assburn Hill are in **Chapter 19,** *Ki Force*. My entire attitude about life was transformed from mundane into something wonderful once I jumped off that forbidding cliff. I knew and have known ever since that day, that if I believe in something with all of my heart, if I believe in something without doubt or fear or hesitation, there is nothing that is impossible. In that one glorious moment when I conquered the unknown danger of Assburn Hill and my own inner fears, I realized for the first time in my life, that I was much more than the box I had lived my life within. My heart and mind opened much wider to the unlimited possibilities of my future and burned with a greater willingness, even eagerness, to learn more about my psychic and paranormal abilities, and who I really was and could be.

Discovering the Ki Force

Beginning in 8th grade, I devoted myself to the study of martial arts. After long meditation and practice, I had perfected the ability to call in an astounding force, we call the Ki Force, whenever my life was in danger or when I was in a tournament. For brief moments it imbued me with far greater strength, speed and reflexes than I normally possessed, as it did for any expert practitioner of my style of marital arts. You've probably heard stories about old ladies who lift a car off the victim of an auto accident. That's the Ki force at work. The difference between her action and those of a martial artist is she had no idea how she did it and in martial arts we train to learn how to call it in on command.

In **Chapter 19,** *Ki Force*, I'll go into detail about my experiences with the Ki Force and how you can call in this marvelous force to aid you in emergencies. I mention it briefly in this chapter because it was an essential contributor to helping me develop my paranormal gifts. It was a mysterious force spoken about by most as if it was a myth, that became an indisputable reality for me when it first saved my life.

In martial arts the great masters were said to devote themselves to learning how to call this amazing force of power to them whenever it was needed. I never gave it much thought as I was decades of experience away from being a martial arts master. But it came unbidden to me once in a tournament. From that day on I was intensely interested in this mysterious power.

My opponent had just head clapped me. He first punched me hard in the stomach and when I bent forward a bit in pain he slapped me savagely with open palms on both ears. That stood me up in shock. He then roundhouse kicked me in the chest sending me flying backwards landing hard on my back and knocking the wind out of me. That should have been an end to the competition. I should have just been laying there in a daze. But from somewhere deep inside me a ferocious beast was unleashed by the Ki Force. Energy surged through me with an astounding power I had never felt before. It seemed to me that I flew up off the mat into a standing position, snarling in rage like an angered animal. I let out a bloodcurdling growl sounding for all the world like a raging tiger and charged my opponent.

He startled by my recovery, but quickly took a strong defensive stand. But his efforts were fruitless. It seemed to me that my every move was in hyperspeed, while every one of his was in slow motion. In a span of a couple of seconds I must have hit him with at least a dozen blows of both fists and feet. He never even had time to move and fell from the spot he was standing into oblivious unconsciousness. The moment he hit the mat the fury inside me vanished and I was as calm as a languid summers morning. It was only later, speaking with my Sensei who had been standing on the sidelines in awe-struck amazement at what he witnessed, that I learned that the Ki Force had come to me.

After pondering the events I realized there was a special action that had triggered the Ki Force filling me. During the next several years I learned to call in the Ki Force at will using this trigger and two other keys. Lucky for me I did, as being imbued with the Ki Force literally saved my life on at least two subsequent occasions.

Mind Over Matter

Another ability I learned in martial arts was how to use my mind to physically control my body and make it do things it shouldn't be able to do, like slow down or turn off my pulse in specific locations in my body. As I spent endless hours during my youth walking alone in the woods and mountains and along the beaches, I had a lot of time to practice the meditations and techniques necessary to perfect these abilities. They came in quite handy on multiple occasions.

One beneficial time was during my freshman year of college. A couple of years earlier I had trained myself to regurgitate a mouthful of food upon the command of my mind. I know that sounds really gross, but I ended up making a tidy sum on wagers with people who didn't know I had that ability. The bet was that once they snapped their fingers I had 10 seconds to regurgitate at least a half a cup of anything, but not more than a cup. I never lost.

In my late 20's, I learned to refine it so if I ate something with a fat content like a steak with fat around the edges (this was before I became a vegetarian), I could after a few minutes of digestion, call up and expel just the fat. And no, this was not a sign of anorexia or bulimia. I have never had a problem with my weight. I mention this ability despite its grossness, because I do feel in a strange way it is a paranormal gift, as it demonstrates the ability of the mind, which I believe is an integral part of the spirit and psychic prowess, to have dominion over the physical body of this life.

Another major use of this ability came when I desired to get out of the Coast Guard earlier than my contracted enlistment time. I had foolishly joined when I was in my late teens, when I couldn't find a regular job and really needed some money. I knew on the first day of boot camp that the military, with all of it's ridiculous rules and requirements to obey the orders

My Own Journey of Discovery

of imbeciles, wasn't for me, and nothing that happened in the following months gave me any reason to change my mind.

After boot camp I was sent to school at Governors Island in New York, right off of the tip of Manhattan and adjacent to the Statue of Liberty. I was rooming on base with a man named Dan whom I had met on the plane going to boot camp, and we were subsequently sent together to Governors Island for further training.

On the day I made my decision to get out, I came into our room and announced it to Dan. He got a great kick out of it and laughed himself silly, telling me there was no way I could get out early with an honorable discharge. I told him, "watch me."

The next day I went to the infirmary and complained of illness due to having to breathe cigarette smoke from all the smokers, especially in the chow hall. Claiming to get ill from cigarette smoke wasn't a great stretch for me. I had always hated to breathe second hand smoke and it did irritate my eyes and throat. If I did not use the power of my aura to create a protective shield around my body, having to breathe that much smoke would actually make me nauseated. This was back in the mid 70's when smoking was still freely permitted and common in both the workplace and any public place, especially in the military.

The doctor told me there wasn't much he could do and I would get used to it. I could see he needed some more evidence. The next five dinners in a row at the chow hall, I used my ability to call up the contents of my stomach on the command of my mind and made sure I made a mess of it all over the place. I went back to the Coast Guard doctor with my new symptoms and they were strange enough that he decided to run some tests.

This was where I really got to have some fun. For the next 30 days I was subject to all kinds of tests and whenever possible I skewered them by commanding my body to do inexplicable things. The two that come most readily to my memory are my blood pressure and hearing tests.

For blood pressure they had the standard wrap around the upper arm, blow up with air, blood pressure tester. There was a tube filled with mercury on the wall that showed the numbers, which served my purposes well because I could see exactly what was happening. At various stages of the testing I just shut my blood pressure off. I simply commanded my pulse to cease on the arm with the blood pressure cuff.

The technician was very confused. He thought his machine was malfunctioning so he ran the test again; same results. Then he thought I might be affecting it by clenching my muscles or pressing my arm against my body, so he had me stretch my arms diagonally out in front of me on a table, and also had me stretch out my legs just to insure I couldn't be using any physical actions to impede my blood flow. It didn't matter. "I think you are a walking corpse," he said. "You have almost no blood pressure."

I just smiled and said, "Well, I guess that is something the doctor would be interested in knowing about."

Later, they tested my hearing on one of the standard machines that make very quiet little sounds. You are supposed to raise your hand when you hear a sound and raise it with either the right or left hand, depending upon which ear the sound was heard in.

As I knew that the technician was aware of exactly when the sounds were initiated, I figured it would be a simple matter to tune into his aura and know when a sound was being made even if I couldn't hear it. It worked perfectly. I was tested twice to make sure they hadn't made an error as I was able (to the techs understanding) to hear every sound the machine made.

That was so unusual that they had me go off island the next week to a clinic on Staten Island that had a super machine with a far greater range of sounds. Once again, I tuned into the technician. Auras can be sensed and felt as well as seen. Feeling the interaction of his aura with mine it was once again easy to know when a sound was being generated. Even though I heard only the first dozen or so, I continued to raise my hand every time the techs aura indicated a sound was being made. When the test was done he told me the results were impossible.

The end result of all this effort was good for me, as I was given an honorable discharge for medical reasons after just 6 months in the Coast Guard. Their diagnosis for discharge was surprisingly accurate: "psycho-physiologic reaction to cigarette smoke". In other words, my brain was making my body react in physical ways, which in essence was a correct diagnosis. They told me if I waited another 30 days I could get lifetime disability payments based upon a percentage of disability to be determined by a hearing. But I waived my right to disability and got discharged a few days later, as it would not have been fair to the taxpayers to take disability payments. Plus, I wanted out sooner rather than later.

Electrical Suppression

Inexplicable occurrences seemed to follow me like a shadow sometimes, ever reminding me that mysterious forces swirled in and around me. I knew from a very early age I was different and was continually reminded of the fact every time something would happen that I knew did not occur with 'normal' people. One of those inexplicable occurrences was a profound effect I had, and continue to have, on many electrical devices.

My first inkling that my presence could sometimes affect electrical devices was walking under street lamps, or even driving by them in a car. Sometimes nothing at all would happen. However, more often than not if the street lamp was on, it would go off as I passed near it. If it was off, it would come on. I'll never forget one time in 8th grade, I was visiting my friend Bobby V. It was a warm summers night and we had been down the block playing with some of his friends. As we returned to his house for the night, we passed a darkened street light. As we walked beneath it flickered to life casting an eerie yellow glow.

Bobby looked up with a quizzical expression. "That's weird," he said in a surprised tone. "That light has been burned out for over a year. I guess the city finally got around to replacing it."

We didn't give it a second thought until we got to his door and were about to go in the house and the street light went off again. Street lights going on and off when I passed was nothing new to me, but it sure weirded Bobby V. out. He told me later that the street light never came back on again after its one brief moment of resurrection.

As I got older and gained more knowledge of science and engineering, I thought during the early part of the night, when the lights were just switching on, those with weak ballasts might be struggling to ignite the lamp and subsequently came on later than the others, coincidentally just when I was passing by. Later I concluded there was some truth to the weakened lamp theory as there were certain street lamps I could easily affect at will. Command it to come on, and on it flashed; command it to go off, and it was lights out. But others just down the road I could not seem to control. My conclusion was that weakened bulbs nearing the end of their life or with old starting ballasts, were more easy to influence from whatever mysterious energy seemed to emanate from my body and affect them.

Affecting the EKG Machine

When I was twelve, we went with my Mom, Dad and sister, to visit my Aunt Shirley and Uncle George in New Jersey. Uncle George was an amateur astronomer and scientist. He had some research scientist friends at nearby Princeton University that were doing some type of experiments measuring brain waves. They were looking for volunteers and Uncle George suggested to my Dad that my sister and I go in as test subjects as they were paying $5.00 each to volunteers. That was a lot of money to a kid in the sixties!

We came into a room with a bunch of monitoring equipment. My younger sister went first. She lay down on a hospital type bed and we got to watch while they stuck several electrodes on her forehead that had long wires running from them to a large portable machine beside the bed. She just lay there comfortably for about 10 minutes, doing absolutely nothing, while the machine scratched out a never ending series of jagged lines recording her brain waves on a large scroll of paper.

I could hardly wait for my turn. $5.00 for just lying in bed for 10 minutes! If I remember correctly they stuck 4 electrodes on my head. I just closed my eyes and started daydreaming about where I was going to go exploring in the swamp when I got back home. After about a minute on the machine I was jolted out of my reverie by a quiet beep beep that must have been some kind of alarm as the two research scientists conducting the experiments rushed over to their machine. I opened my eyes to see looks of bewilderment and alarm on their faces.

One of them came up to me with his face close to mine and shined a light in my eyes. "How do you feel?" he asked.

"I'm fine," I replied.

"What were you thinking about?" he inquired.

"Exploring the swamp by my house," I answered nonchalantly.

"What kind of feelings were you feeling," he asked.

I just shrugged my shoulders. "I don't think I was really feeling anything in particular."

"Well Jesse, I want you to think of something that makes you very mad or worried or upset. Can you do that?" he wondered. I thought about it for a moment and remembered when I had been walking recently through a field and stepped on a 3-foot piece of old plywood that was lying flat on the ground. I hadn't noticed the rusty 16 penny nail sticking point-first up through the board. It was so sharp it went through the sole of my sneaker and completely through my foot with the point popping through the top of my foot and the top of my sneaker! I didn't even know it had happened until I went to move that foot in my walking stride and was bewildered as to why a board was suddenly stuck to it.

Seeing the tip of the nail sticking through the top of my sneaker I sat down on the ground in disbelief and pried the nail out of my foot by grabbing my foot and pulling up on it forcefully until the board popped off. I immediately walked back home, gingerly favoring my injured foot and worrying the whole way home that I was going to get tetanus from stepping on a rusty nail. Remembering that experience was my upset thought for the brain wave experiment.

I hadn't been thinking about that experience for more than a few seconds before the beep beep alarms started going off again on the machine. The two scientists were holding their chins and talking excitedly with each other. My Dad, sister and Uncle George were curiously peering over their shoulders trying to see what all the excitement was about. As I did not receive any new instructions I just kept thinking about my bad experience with the rusty nail impaling my left foot. After a few more minutes their monitoring machine just shut off. They checked the plug at the outlet, pushed buttons on the monitoring machine trying to restart it, but all to no avail.

Apparently they were prepared for potential breakdowns. They simply unplugged the electrode connections, rolled the dead machine away, rolled another just like it into place beside the bed, then reinserted the electrode connections that were attached to my head. The scientist told me to be calm and clear my mind of all thoughts. I did this and everything was fine with their machine. Then he told me to think an upsetting thought once again. Accommodatingly, I revived my anger about having a nail go through my foot. Within a minute their backup machine also went dead and there was nothing they could do to revive it. Now it was the scientists that were upset. Apparently those were the only two machines they had and there were many more people scheduled to be tested that day. But my sister and I were paid our $5.00, so we were happy.

It didn't occur to me at the time that I might have had anything to do with the brain wave machines shutting down. But over the years that followed, with many other examples of curiously failing equipment, it became more than obvious that my energy at times disrupted electrical devices. So many light bulbs have popped and computers and other electronics have failed around me that it has become a running joke in my family. It's sometime quite exasperating, especially when my computers shut down. At times I just want to scream, but I've learned to laugh instead and just take it all in stride. I'm thankful for my gifts, even when the ramifications aren't always planned or desired.

My Own Journey of Discovery

Even this quirky skill of disrupting electrical devices, I discovered was one that could be taught, practiced and acquired by others, as I detail in **Chapter 15 *Disrupting Electrical Devices***. My wife and youngest daughter first learned the technique to turn on and off street lamps when my daughter was about 6 years old. We had a two acre field beside our house and at the far end was a street with three street lamps in view. We had great fun together, standing on our front porch looking at the high street lights, combining our paranormal energy to focus on a single street lamp to make it go off or come on as we desired. After one light went off it was reluctant to come back on right away. Rather than just wait for it to fully cool off, we would look down the street to the next one and turn it off, then further down to the last one in view and turn it off. This took about 5-10 minutes and with another 5-10 minutes of waiting, we could return our focus to the first one and turn it back on, and then turn on the next two in succession.

The Dampened Years

I have always been very spiritual, but not too inclined toward living within the bounds of organized religion. I attended various churches from time to time simply because I enjoyed being around the community of friendly, most often positive people. This did not impinge in any way on explorations of my paranormal abilities, because for years I was never officially a member of any church and subject to their dictates, rules and beliefs. That all changed in my senior year of high school when I joined the Church of Jesus Christ of Latter-day Saints (Mormons). I was excited to find a church that answered many of my unanswered questions about Christian beliefs, but unprepared for the gauntlet of rules and expectations that came with that church.

I was active in the church for about ten years. During that time I went on a two year mission that was aborted at six months, got married to a sweet LDS lady from France, had three wonderful children, and immersed myself in the Mormon culture. It ended in divorce, separation from my kids who lived in France with their mother, becoming inactive in the church, and subsequently asking to have my name removed from the records as a member, which they were kind enough to do.

I still highly respect Latter-day Saint members and admire them for the many good personal traits they have and that their church instills in them. I look back on those thirteen years, not as lost, because there is something gained in all experiences, but as a time when I had to dampen and hide my psychic gifts because they were not understood by church members and often even opposed by the teachings of the church. If I was confused when my science background had conflicts with the concept of paranormal abilities, I doubled down on that challenge when my church did as well.

It was somewhat ironic, as I had a singular experience, my very first astral travel, when I was earnestly seeking to answer the question within myself as to whether I should join the LDS church. It was one of the most memorable and profoundly exciting experiences of my life, as I detail in **Chapter 21 *Astral Projection***. Still ignorant of the actual intolerance of the church toward psychic and paranormal activities, I was thrilled, mistakenly thinking that in joining the church I must be associating with a group that was going to help me expand my psychic and paranormal abilities. Why else would I have one of the most amazing paranormal experiences of my life at that time? How ignorant I was of the reality.

I attended church every Sunday in those early days and went to youth activities on Wednesday nights. I was so pumped about my astral travel that I enthusiastically recounted my experience with many LDS members and friends. They all gave me very odd looks. I was very surprised that none of them had similar experiences. With a smile of humor for the enthusiasm of a new member, many people thought I was a little daft. So, as I learned to do in my youth with my ability to see auras, I just stopped sharing my experience with anyone. Then one day the leader of the congregation called me into his office for a visit to talk about my astral travel moment. With warmth and kindness, and tolerance for the ignorance of a new member, he explained that Mormons did not believe in astral travel and I needed to not speak about it anymore with the church members. He told me it must have all been in my imagination.

I couldn't believe it. I was devastated. One of the most cherished moments in my life had just been officially erased. For months a part of me remained missing and greatly missed. One day I couldn't take it anymore and I prayed aloud to God asking for an explanation of how something so wonderful and real to me could be seen by the church as being imagined. I told God I was going to open the scriptures at random and point to a verse and would that verse please be the answer I was seeking. At the time I had what was known in the Mormon world as a "Quad," which is the Christian Bible together with the Book of Mormon and two other books the Mormons consider scripture, all in one bound book. The verse I ended up opening to and laying my finger upon was Alma 29:16 in the Book of Mormon. What was written was a first person account, where the person telling the story related how his spirit had been lifted out of his body. He explained, "*Now, when I think of the success of these my brethren my soul is carried away, even to the separation of it from my body, as it were, so great is my joy.*" It was an excellent description of astral travel. I had my answer! Though the Mormons of today may not believe in astral travel or paranormal abilities, the ones 2000 years ago certainly did! Rather than cause a hullabaloo by pointing out the discrepancy between today and yesteryear to church members, I simply kept the good news to myself.

Auric Healing with a Big Assist

Not long after getting out of the Coast Guard I decided to go on a religious mission for the LDS church. I was sent to the Pennsylvania Pittsburgh mission. After I had been on my mission for about 2 weeks my companion and I were called by a hospital to come and give a blessing for the sick to a lady who was receiving care. This was new territory for me. I had not grown up in the Mormon church. Not only had I never participated in a blessing, being a new member, I had never even seen one! What happened next was the greatest miracle and display of supernatural power I have ever been a part of. I share the details in **Chapter 22: Faith, Spiritual & Auric Healing**.

This event was a major epiphany in my life. Prior to this experience I looked at psychic and paranormal gifts as interesting and mildly useful in life. After this, I realized and never forgot that true miracles of a very significant nature can occur when these astounding powers course through you. I realized from this moment onward that supernatural gifts were not a game, but a great and powerful stewardship requiring forethought and prudence, as well as the courage to use them.

The Ki Force and the Church Do Not Mix

While on my mission for the LDS church I fell strangely ill. For weeks I could not keep any food down and I lost considerable weight and I hadn't had any spare weight to lose. During the last few days of my mysterious affliction I couldn't even keep water down. Tests run by the doctors left them baffled. Two blessings to be healed by my fellow missionaries had not effect.

Seriously beginning to wonder if I was going to survive, I asked three of my fellow missionaries to take me to the tallest nearby hill. I had decided to call the Ki Force to save me as it had multiple times in the past. High pointy hills almost always had positive energy vortexes shooting out of the peak. I knew it was on a spot like that I had my best chance of calling in the power of the Ki Force.

What happened next was a great miracle. But it also directly led to not completing my mission and going home the very next week. It was a major turning point in my life. I realized clearly that not only did the church not have all the answers, but they didn't even understand all of the questions. My experience with the Ki Forse that sunny day on a hill in Pennsylvania reoriented me onto my own path of psychic and paranormal discovery. What happened that day saved my life in more ways than one. You can read the details of the event in **Chapter 19: Ki Force**.

First Experiences with Telepathy

I had never given much thought to telepathy before I experienced it for the first time. I had never practiced it or had a desire to do it. That was likely because I had no one to experiment and practice with that would give it any credence. That all changed when I went to France to marry my first wife in my early 20's. I would like to say that my first experiences were with her, but unfortunately they were with her younger sister by 16 months, which made for a decidedly awkward situation. I'll share the details of that particular story in **Chapter 29: *Telepathy***.

The interesting result for me was that after my encounter with her sister, the first person I had ever picked up a telepathic thought from, both strangers and friends thoughts would occasionally slip into my head unbidden. It was like I could hear them talking to themselves.

I did not care for the experience as it seemed more noise and interference in my own thoughts and was thankful that it began to occur less and less often, until finally rarely at all.

Telepathic abilities did return to me more frequently many years later, once I met and married Sumara in the mid 90's. Today, it is not uncommon for me to spontaneously pick up snippets of her thoughts and the thoughts of others who are my family or friends. She has the same ability with me, which can be quite fun and interesting at times. I'll share more of the details in the chapter on Telepathy.

Involuntary Auric Trances

After returning prematurely from my mission, I continued as an active LDS church member still enthralled by other aspects of the religion, especially the concept of eternal marriage. I married my French sweetheart in the Mormon temple in Zollikofen, Switzerland. We had three wonderful children and lived lives as active Mormons during all of our 9 years of matrimony. But I was a most unusual Mormon and my strange ways were disturbing and incomprehensible to her.

As the years passed, I remained stifled within the doctrinal confines of the Latter-day Saint religion, which made no room and had no tolerance for so many of my most important life experiences. My wife was not sympathetic to my predicament. Paranormal experiences were so alien to her that she began to think I must be crazy. I didn't help my cause when occasionally during our 9 year marriage, I fell into spontaneous, involuntary auric trances. This really freaked her out and shook her up. I will admit they were strange, but for me, also very wonderful.

These unusual trances, which once spontaneously initiated I had no way to stop, first began when I was 16 years old and would come upon me suddenly. I haven't had one for many years, but during the time I was in my first marriage, in my twenties and early thirties, they usually occurred about once a year, sometimes less often and occasionally more. The trances would typically last 15 - 30 minutes, but sometimes longer.

Before the trance initiated, I would be just going about my normal life, thankfully always at home or out in the wilderness, and never at my place of employment. I could be in the middle of a conversation with someone, without a single thought in my head about anything paranormal. With a simple casual glance, I might stare out the window or up at the ceiling, or across a mountain valley while hiking. Suddenly without any warning, my aura would begin rapidly expanding immensely and connecting to so many other energies that I quickly disconnected from my immediate surroundings.

With astounding rapidity my auric field would begin to expand in and out, without any intent or control on my part. Each expansion would push it out further. And with each contraction, which was much smaller by a factor of thousands than the expansion wave, I would slip further into a trance state. In less than a minute, usually within just six or seven cycles of expansion and contraction, my aura expanded to a diameter of about a kilometer. Within the first 10 seconds

My Own Journey of Discovery

I would have slipped down onto the ground, laying down looking up at the sky or ceiling, knowing what was coming and looking forward to it with immense joy.

I never went into a complete trance, and what I did go into was nothing like trances I would experience years later when I was channeling or revelating. My conscious thoughts remained present and aware. For instance, when I was at home, my eyes were open and I could see my wife standing above me, trying to hold back tears of confusion and fright and begging me to get up. But I could not move at all.. I never could at those moments and was overcome with almost complete paralysis. My aura continued to expand beyond my town, and then beyond my state, and then beyond my country until it seemed to cover the Earth. Meanwhile, my body remained immobile and incapable of moving even a finger.

During the semi-trance, I would be in two existences at once. My physical body remained immobile on the ground in a lightly conscious state, vaguely aware of what was happening around me and the conversations of people, but unable to move or speak. Meanwhile my aura was touching everything and everyone in the world. It was exhilarating beyond description! And though there might be chaos around me from people standing beside me in a frenzy of confusion, I was experiencing an unearthly calm and melodious peace.

Imagine when you have felt your greatest passion, your deepest sorrow, or your most sublime joy. Now imagine feeling all of those emotions at the same time multiplied a thousand fold. Through their auras interacting with mine, I felt the emotions of billions of people and uncountable multitudes of animals of every description. Throw in having a billion streams of thought simultaneously running through your mind, to the point it is just indecipherable noise, and you'll have a small understanding of this profound experience.

A typical paralysis trance happened in my home in Washington State in 1981. My wife and two young children were present. We had been laughing and playing a game together, having fun, when suddenly I felt the trance coming on. I did not ask for it, but neither did I push it away. I accepted it.

Right where I was standing, I slowly laid down on the floor. My body was already semi-immobile and within another minute completely immobile. I could not get up no matter how hard I tried, nor could I do anything other than stare straight ahead. The energy overwhelmed me. It was more than I could process or understand, but it felt marvelous.

I could dimly see and hear my wife standing over me, telling me I was scaring her and to please get up, but I couldn't. My body was incapable of moving other than to breathe and mutter slightly that I was fine. Although it might have looked like I had suffered a heart attack or stroke, I was in no pain and not experiencing any kind of medical problem. Only my aura moved, and it went everywhere. I felt as if I was touching God.

Just as suddenly as it began it would quickly end. One moment my auric field was ever expanding and sensing all life, then in a breath, like a thunderclap, it was suddenly rushing back to my body. Thousands of miles out it had stretched and in a blink it snapped back to a normal size. As soon as it did I could move again and in moments stand up, albeit a bit unsteady for a minute or two. Gingerly I would feel my body for a moment confirming I was still all there. The experience would leave me with a non-stop natural high for at least the next three days, even in the face of my wife's upset or my church leader's disapproval when they subsequently heard of the incident.

My first wife and I ended up divorced after 9 years of marriage. Other than the church and our three beautiful children, we simply had nothing else in common. When I drifted into inactivity in the LDS church and began to focus more on my psychic gifts and paranormal abilities, I'm sure it seemed to her as if she might as well have been married to a martian. One summer her father who lived in France was ill and she went with the kids for a two month visit while I stayed in the USA to work. She filed for divorce while she was over there and never returned. I was very sad and lost for the following two years, being so unexpectedly separated from my children. I had wonderful parents and my noblest desire as a young adult was to be able to become as great a parent to my children as I had been blessed to have when I was a kid.

All of my children ended up coming to live with me as teenagers and I'm very grateful for those years. But as difficult as it was to be separated from them for some years, it was also a very fruitful time for me. Without the time consuming daily responsibilities of family and children, and no longer doctrinally or emotionally connected to the LDS church, I became much more receptive to new thoughts and possibilities. This became all the more so when I got together with a beautiful, cheerful New Age lady named Skye. We became fast friends and bonded adventurers in life together for the next 9 years. I learned a great deal from her and she was one of two people who became an indispensable catalyst to truly opening up the expansion of my psychic and paranormal abilities.

New Age Nonsense?

Skye was the very first New Age person I had ever met. During our early years together, it was all I could do to not laugh out loud whenever she would spout one of her New Age beliefs. Looking through the lens of my scientific training and knowledge most of her beliefs seemed patently absurd. For the first several years we were together we thoroughly enjoyed sharing life and adventures, but she had to keep pretty mum about her New Age conceptions because I would just shoot them down as being ridiculous if she brought them up. I'm referring both to many psychic and paranormal abilities people purported to have, and to a wide range of what I considered looney-toon beliefs that circulated in the New Age arena, such as the world was going to have three days of darkness and was then going to be reborn. I also gave no credence to her belief in channelers: people who supposedly could communicate with higher realms and purvey enlightened knowledge to us ignorant savages still here on Earth in a physical body. That, and much more about my belief system would soon change.

Despite all of my personal supernatural experiences I was still a contradiction within myself. My training had been in science and the scientific method of evaluation. Even though I had manifested many types of psychic and paranormal abilities, I still was uncomfortable and did not accept them in many ways because I could not scientifically explain them. And I was highly skeptical of the purported psychic abilities exhibited by anyone else, because they were often described or manifested very differently from mine.

About this time Skye asked me to attend a semi-trance channeling with a very well-known channeler in Seattle, Washington, named Evelyn Jenkins. Now of all psychic abilities people claimed, I put channeling up there at the top of the least likely. I had two sessions with Evelyn, about one week apart. After the first she never wanted to see me again, and after the second she told me I was the person she had been channeling for the last 10 years seeking to find, and now that she had found me she could stop channeling. My own evolution between those two extremes was a major turning point in my life.

In **Chapter 27,** *Channeling*, I'll share the details of my encounters with Evelyn and my subsequent almost daily experiences channeling the wisdom of higher beings, as well as the steps you need to take to begin channeling yourself if you desire. My life has been profoundly affected and benefited from channeled knowledge and advice. I'm sure it is a gift most people can find within themselves if they seek it and are prepared to receive it.

Sumara

After my encounters with Evelyn, though I was open to receiving valuable information through people who were channels, I never channeled myself, nor personally explored any new paranormal abilities until Sumara Elan McGoff came into my life. Like Skye, she was a catalyst for unlocking my gifts and abilities.

Skye and I had been together for 9 years. We both always knew with our psychic sense, that there was another woman coming into our lives that would be a key to our future. We had no idea how long we would need to wait, but in the fall of 1995 Sumara appeared and we both instantly knew she was the one. I knew by sight and the astounding, immediate Soul Mate auric connection we had on every one of our energy centers. Skye knew just from hearing her name that she was the fulfillment of a precognitive communication she had with one of her 'Guides' the previous year.

That first meeting with Sumara was 18 years ago as of this writing in 2013. We were married 1 year after we met and she, Skye and I continued to resonate in a wonderful reverberating harmony. A lot of magical experiences have occurred in all three of our lives since Sumara created the 'power of three.' We have been wonderful catalysts for each other's growth and expansion, and continue to be to this day. You can read more about it in **Chapter 17:** *Precognition*.

Unleash Your Psychic Powers

Chapter 4
A SHORT HISTORY OF PSYCHIC & PARANORMAL ABILITIES

Specific psychic and paranormal abilities go in and out of vogue from one era to another. For much of history various forms of divination were the predominant psychic power called upon or known by the average person. It is only in modern times with the preponderance of movies, books and television shows that other paranormal gifts have received widespread recognition.

Today's entertainment media are good indicators of the paranormal gifts that are currently the most popular with the general public. Recent shows such as *Charmed* (1998-2006) had main characters with powers of **telekinesis**, **astral projection**, **divination**, **scrying**, **apportation**, **levitation**, **past vision**, **energy healing**, **teleportation** and **auric energy power**. Multiple shows during the last 15 years have highlighted **psychometry** where the psychic receives flashes of past events by touching an object that was involved in the event.

Late 1800's to Early 1900's: Going back a few generations to the first decades of the late 1800's and early 1900's, **spiritualism** and **afterlife communication** were very popular, as were spiritualist churches where contacting the spirits of the deceased through a medium was the central part of the service.

Middle Ages: In the Middle Ages there was a fascination with fire. Even peasants paid attention to the movement of the flame from an oil lamp or torch (**lampadomancy**) and looked for signs and portends of the future in the smoke rising from cooking fires and the crackle of pockets of pitch as logs burned (**libanomancy**).

Wizards of the early Middle Ages would often cast salt onto the floor and interpret the patterns, or use a mixture of various types of mineral salts cast into a fire and interpret the colors (**halomancy**). Casting pebbles or small rocks into a still pool or running stream and noting the pattern of the ensuing ripples (**hydromancy**) was another popular technique of the professional diviners. A more advanced form of *libanomancy*, predicting the future based upon the reaction of incense cast upon hot coals, was also a popular form of divination with the professionals.

Talisman or **Lucky Charms** have probably been popular since the dawn of time, but became particularly popular during the early Middle Ages when it was not uncommon to purchase an enchanted Talisman from traveling wizards.

Another common form of divination during the Middle Ages that has fallen out of favor in modern times is **Mirror Gazing** and related methods using reflective surfaces, collectively known as *catoptromancy*. The psychic Nostradamus, from the 1500's, still heralded today for predictions of many of the world's great events he made that many people feel came true, was said to favor the use of a bowl of ink to exhibit a reflective surface from which he could divine his prophecies.

The paranormal power imbued in a mirror has been a central theme in a couple of key modern and early modern stories, including 'Snow White', where the wicked witch sought an answer by asking, "Mirror, mirror on the wall, who is the fairest of them all?" It was also through the paranormal qualities of a 'Looking Glass', known today as a mirror, that Alice journeyed to Wonderland in Lewis Caroll's fanciful story.

Roman Period: From Julius Caesar to King Philip of Macedonia, history remembers the leaders and the history changing actions they took. But forgotten in the annuls of history are the psychics they consulted before they took the actions. It was common throughout both the Greek and Roman periods for kings, generals and landowners to consult esteemed psychics before going to war, planting crops or seeking ways to appease the gods for errors they might have made.

During the Roman Empire, observations of natural phenomenon was popular, particularly *augury*, which studied the reactions of birds and domestic animals during thunder and lightning storms. Romans were also big star gazers and often combined the arrival of celestial meteorites with terrestrial thunder and lightning storms to divine the future (*meteoromancy*). Romans also had far less inhibitions about the human body than many cultures and often viewed one another naked in the common Roman baths. Perhaps the frequent viewing of naked bodies led to the popular form of divination know as *moleosphy*, which made predictions based upon moles, birthmarks and skin blemishes.

Greeks and the Oracle of Delphi: One of the most famous paranormal abilities of all time were the cryptic prophecies issued by the Oracle of Delphi in ancient Greece. The location of the Oracle was considered a sacred shrine by Greeks. For most of its history, every kingdom honored the independence of the Oracle grounds, making the shrine available to all Greeks and visitors from other lands. The shrine was built around a fissure in the ground from which issued spring water and an always burning flame of ethylene gas. It was considered by many Greeks to be the sacred center of the world.

Archeologists say that the site of Delphi was inhabited beginning in the 14th century B.C.,

A Short History of Psychic & Paranormal Abilities

during the Mycenaean times, by small settlements revolving around the worship of Mother Earth as a deity.

Over the centuries the shrine grew in importance and wealth. As it was only open a few days each year during a nine month period, and closed for three months every winter, long lines of pilgrims would form weeks before the opening. Wealthy supplicants would donate great treasures and works of art for the privilege of cutting to the head of the line and being graced with an oracle of the future.

The shrine espoused no particular religion and had allegiance to no particular kingdom, though it did have protection of various kings from time to time. Coupled with its geographically central location in Greece, it became a gathering spot for intellectuals and a neutral ground for adversaries to discuss treaties.

By the 8th century BC the Oracle of Delphi had become well-known throughout the countries bordering the Mediterranean Sea and far beyond due to the accurate oracles of the shrine priestesses, particularly one named Pythia. Leaders of almost every kingdom bordering the Mediterranean had absolute faith in the accuracy of Pythia's visions of the future. For many leaders, any major decisions of consequence was only made after consultation with the Oracle of Delphi.

The famous Greek historian Plutarch, was born in a small town only 20 miles from Delphi and for a time served as a priest of the Oracle. It is from his account that we have a description of the inner sanctum and the procedures. Plutarch records that the priestess Pythia would enter a chamber in the inner sanctuary and sit on a tripod that spanned a chasm in the earth from which issued small amounts of hydrocarbon gas (ethylene) which were always burning in flame. Under the mind-altering influence of the gas, Pythia would fall into a trance and begin speaking in a language incomprehensible to mere mortals. Priests such as Plutarch would understand her words and interpret them for the supplicants.

The oracles were famously difficult to decipher, which allowed people to assign their desired meaning to the cryptic words, or assign the ensuing events to coincide with the prophecy, thus insuring a very high accuracy of the oracles. An example of the common dual meaning open to interpretation, would be "***You will go you will return not in battle will you perish***." Depending on where one adds a single comma the meaning will be exactly opposite. "You will go you will return, not in battle will you perish." Great news! You can go to battle and the Oracle has prophesied that you will not perish but will return home. Or, "You will go you will return not, in battle will you perish." Bad news; you will go away to war but will not return and will perish in battle.

In 356 B.C. The temple grounds were captured by an alliance of Phocians, Athenians and Spartans. Its vast treasures accumulated from supplicants over many centuries, were carted off and sold to finance their war. King Philip of Macedon soon liberated the shrine and it fell under the protection of his victorious empire.

In 191 B.C. the temple was taken over by the Romans and in 86 B.C. it was once again pillaged for its treasures to finance a war. Three years later, now only a shell of its former glory, the temple was thoroughly destroyed by a Thracian named Maedi who is the infamous person that according to legend filled in the fissure and extinguished the sacred flame that had been burning uninterrupted since the memory of man.

Ancient Times: In the more primitive world, any paranormal ability exhibited is likely to have been a significant event and led to the psychics becoming priests, priestesses, shamans and medicine men.

Casting pebbles or bones and predicting the future based upon how they fall and arrange, is a form of divination known as ***cleromancy*** that began in very ancient days and continued to be used in related forms through every subsequent era.

Another ancient form of divining that would find no acceptance in the modern world is ***cephalomancy,*** which would entailed severing the head of a donkey or goat, then tossing it onto hot coals and making predictions based upon how it burned and smelled.

Interpreting the death throes of living human and animal sacrifices, and studying remnant body parts, seemed to be popular forms of divination in ancient times as well. ***Extispicy***, ***Haruspication***, ***Hieromancy*** and ***Hieroscopy***, all which were prophetic techniques based upon the study of the entrails of sacrificed animals. As purchasing animals for sacrifice was beyond the means of common people, they sought their signs of the future by noting the severed heads and entrails of fish (***Ichthyomancy***).

The Old Testament / Torah dating back over 3,000 years, records Joseph using his psychic abilities to interpret the dreams of the Egyptian Pharaoh. ***Dream interpretation*** continued to be a paranormal gift relied upon by kings and leaders through the Greek and Roman times as well, and still holds some fascination with people today.

Chapter 5

WHAT'S THE SCIENCE?
ARE THE SKEPTICS EVER RIGHT?

"I am attacked by two very opposite sects – the scientists and the know-nothings. Both laugh at me, calling me 'the frogs' dancing master'. Yet I know I have discovered one of the greatest forces in nature". Galvani, discoverer of electricity

Having been trained in a scientific education myself, majoring in geology and geophysics in college, I can assure you that most scientists give very little if any credence to the concept of paranormal powers or extrasensory perception (ESP). I'm sure there are far more scientists that are willing to accept the possibility of UFO's, than there are to accept that humans may have senses and abilities that so far have not been effectively measured by scientific testing procedures.

In addition to the scientists, professional skeptics have long derided anyone claiming paranormal abilities and have what would seem to be an excellent track record of debunking claims of psychic, paranormal or occult ability. James Randi and his associates are currently well-known and have tested many claiming to have supernatural abilities. They have a standing offer of a $1,000,000 prize to anyone they could not prove to be a fraud. After many years their offer is still unclaimed. From the unknown to famous paranormal celebrities like Sylvia Browne, all have failed to pass Randi's controlled testing. Randi also wrote a book meticulously exposing Uri Geller's amateur magician methods of key bending and spoon melting. And live on the Tonight Show with Johnny Carson, Geller was unable to perform a single paranormal demonstration under controlled conditions.

In contrast, I know unequivocally from my own experiences that psychic and paranormal abilities are very real, and that miracles and paranormal phenomenon happen that have no explanation by the measurements of science that have heretofore been employed. Despite my own skeptical, scientific nature, I have undeniably had amazing physical paranormal experiences that current science can offer no credible explanation whatsoever to account for or explain.

That doesn't mean I think psychic abilities are some type of magic, because I do not, though the effects can be magical. I believe they are based upon scientific principles, which like so many modern scientific principles that were once derided but are now established as fact, the foundations of the paranormal are unknown and scoffed at, and will continue to be until they are discovered and proven.

However, in many instances the skeptics are right. The psychic and paranormal fields are filled with charlatans and hucksters who charge a lot of money and give nothing of concrete substance or useful specifics in return. I have seen good and trusting friends duped by purported psychics. The worst part is many people want so much to believe that they don't even know or care that they were duped. In many instances, like fervent believers of any religion, they don't want to hear anything negative or contrary to what they believe. Joseph Dunninger, a famous mentalist of the early 20th Century, summed up the conundrum of helping the believers to be more skeptical and the doubters to be more open to the possibility of truth: *"For those who believe, no explanation is necessary; for those who do not believe, no explanation will suffice."*

Certainly there are also many well-intentioned and good-hearted psychics and paranormal practitioners, who truly believe they have a special gift. They match it with a compassionate desire to use it to help others, often for little or no compensation. Some have real and tangible psychic gifts, while others may just imagine they do. But in both cases, they are not doing what they do for fame or fortune, but simply to help their fellow travelers of life, in the way they honestly feel they can.

Sony's Investigations Into the Psychic & Paranormal

Perhaps one of the most credible, scientifically guided studies of psychic and paranormal powers was conducted by the Sony corporation. Though it was an under the radar program and is not even well known in the psychic/paranormal community, it was a fully funded research conducted over seven years by a team of five scientists and researchers.

The Sony Paranormal Lab, as it was known within the company, was headed by Yoichiro Sako. Sako joined Sony immediately after graduation from the prestigious Tokyo University, with degrees in computer science and mathematics. Prior to his work in the Sony Paranormal Lab, Sako seems to have had little interest in the ESP arena. But after successful stints in the departments for CDs, CD-ROMS, 8mm video, voice recognition technology and artificial intelligence, he was looking for new challenges.

It was well known in the company that Masaru Ibuka, one of the two founding fathers of Sony, had an interest in ESP and traditional herbal medicine. In 1988, he created the Pulse Graph Research Department to develop a device to identify health problems by deviations in the human pulse.

What's the Science?   Are the Skeptics Ever Right?

Based upon Ibuka's known interests, Sako approached him in 1989 and proposed creation of a new department to study human bioenergy, known as "Qi" in Chinese, "Ki" in Japanese and "Chi" in the western countries. The Ki Force that dwells within us is an integral aspect of many Eastern spiritual beliefs. Mr. Ibuka was receptive to the proposal and by the next year Sako was working in the Sony Corporation Research Laboratory, measuring physiological changes such as pulse and skin temperature, when Ki Masters exerted mental/psychic force to alter the test subjects Ki energy.

Sony believed there was marketable potential in Sako's research. In 1991, the corporation added four assistants to the staff and established a separate laboratory, code-named "ESPER" (Extrasensory Perception and Excitation Research), where Sako could continue to expand his research into the Ki Force and a wider range of ESP and PSI phenomena, including clairvoyance, synchronicity, mind-body interactions, consciousness and other supernatural phenomena.

ESPER was almost a clandestine operation. Barely anybody in the Sony corporation was aware of its existence and even less people if any, outside of Sony. That is why it was such a shock when its existence and purpose was made known to the public in 1998. On that fateful day, without pomp or fanfare, in a jaw-dropping announcement, Sony confirmed it had verified the reality of extra sensory powers, but also announced they were closing the ESPER program as they had been unable to discover a marketable use for ESP. "We found out experimentally that yes, ESP exists, but that any practical application of this knowledge is not likely in the foreseeable future," Sony spokesman Masanobu Sakaguchi told the South China Morning Post. Sako had published a paper on 'Clairvoyance and Synesthesia' in Journal of International Society of Life Information Science the previous year, in March 1997, but it seemed to have escaped the attention of the media or even the psychic community. Sony's official announcement in 1998 went virtually unnoticed as well, despite it's significance.

So what did the Sony researchers discover about psychic and paranormal powers? Two years after the announcement of the closing of the ESPER project, the lead researcher Yoichiro Sako, spoke at a meeting of scientists in Las Vegas, Nevada. That Sako was still completely vested in his research was evident by one of his first poignant and amusing comments, "If it is difficult for you to understand my talk due to my poor English," he began, "please understand my talk using telepathy."

Sako stated that the greatest success of the ESPER project was the astounding verification of clairvoyance. Unlike the high tech, hands-off approach taken by parapsychologists in the Western countries, Sako's team utilized low tech tests and fraternized freely with the test subjects. They found children to be the best test subjects. Like other paranormal researchers, they found kids to be more open to their abilities than adults.

One series of tests for clairvoyance had an astounding ***97.1% success rate!*** That is a number scarcely believable to Western psychic researchers who are thrilled when they hit a 70% success rate. Sako explained the goal of this clairvoyance test was to prove the test subjects could "see" letters, numbers and drawings written on a tiny piece of paper 1.5 inches (3.8cm) square. After writing the image, number or drawing on the paper, the experimenters would fold it three times and then crumple it into a tiny ball. They would then place the ball in the test subjects ear or hand it to them to tightly pinch between two fingers. Out of 35 test subjects 18 had perfect matches for every mystery paper including one that had the equation "1+2=5." As Sako commented light-heartedly, "It's wrong, but they were right." There was only one failed response subject. The remaining 16 were so close to describing the hidden writing that less rigorous researchers would have also scored them as perfect. Single letters or simple numbers or drawings were easier to sense according to Sako.

Though the test subjects were allowed to use any method they desired to determine the contents of the hidden letters, numbers or drawings, Sako said most of the children employed a similar method that involved the following 9 steps:

1. Close your eyes
2. Do not be distracted. Focus on discovering what is hidden.
3. See the ball of paper. Imagine unfolding it.
4. See a light appearing in the middle of your forehead.
5. See the light expand as the surroundings darken.
6. See letters, numbers, or the image appear in the light.
7. Brighten and move the light as necessary to clearly see the image or numbers.
8. Memorize what you see.
9. Write down what you have seen.

This is just one example of successful scientifically based tests that have given strong evidence of the existence of unexplainable psychic powers. My purpose in writing this chapter is not to debunk the skeptics, but to bridge the gap between the believers and the disbelievers and help each side see that the other has some areas of validity. It seems each side is firmly entrenched in their beliefs and positions and gives no credence to the other sides point of view. I hope we can change that way of thinking at least with some people. My desire is simple: to the believers I say, it is true that there are a lot of psychic frauds out there. Especially egregious are those who charge a lot of money for a bunch of nebulous nothing that anyone can interpret to be applicable to them. If you understand how deception has been unveiled by the skeptics, you will be well on your way to only having helpful and authentic experiences.

To the skeptics I say, too many of us have experienced paranormal and psychic events that are so physically tangible and completely unplanned, unexpected and unexplainable, to be anything but very real. Please keep an open mind while you hold onto your skepticism and don't be looking just to disprove the paranormal. Thank you for ferreting out the frauds, but be brave enough to also expand your methods and sincerely search for the authentic. Paranormal gifts most likely will require alternative means of investigation other than the standard scientific methods. Sony Corporation seems to have blazed that trail well. Please seek out and be open to genuine psychics and those with real paranormal gifts, because they are out there.

Modern debunkers of psychic phenomenon tend to give a single test and make their conclusions. Investigators from earlier eras conducted far more exhaustive tests, often running several months in length. Looking back on some of the more noteworthy paranormal examinations of earlier eras will shed some light on the question of whether paranormal, supernatural abilities are frauds or genuine.

Randi's group is far from the only one that has offered rewards for scientific proof of extrasensory, psychic, or paranormal ability. In the early 1920's, Scientific America magazine made two offers of $2500 each. The first was for anyone that could create an authentic spirit photograph under observable controlled conditions. William Hope in the 1920's, was one of the most famous spirit photographers. But neither he, nor any other man or woman ever won the prize.

The second prize was for anyone who could demonstrate an authentic "visible psychic manifestation." Though several people were tested for both prizes, nobody was ever awarded either prize. That does not mean however that they were all frauds or tricksters. Nor were the testers completely honest in their testing procedures. Harry Houdini, the foremost illusionist of his time, was on the board of the testing committee. It was revealed by the channeled entity during a challenge of the medium Margery, that Houdini had sabotaged the devices the medium was supposed to effect so they would be incapable of working. Upon investigation by other members of the committee, the accusations of sabotage proved to be true.

Factoring in inflation, the $2500 prize in 1922 would be the equivalent of $34,000 in 2012. The amount of the prize continued to rise as the sponsors hoped to attract more famous psychics to be tested. Joseph Dunniger a famous mentalist of the 1920's – 1960's and friend of Harry Houdini, offered three additional $10,000 prizes, and continued to offer them throughout his career, to add to those put up by Scientific America.

1. $10,000 to any medium who could reproduce by psychic or supernatural means any physical phenomena that he could not reproduce by natural means or explain in materialistic terms.

2. $10,000 to anyone who, with the aid of 'the spirit world', could disclose the translation of a

Spirit photograph by William Hope

secret coded messages entrusted to him by Harry Houdini and Thomas Edison.

3. $10,000 to anyone who could introduce him to a real ghost.

$10,000 in 1922, was the equivalent of $137,000 in 2012 purchasing power.

Elizabeth Allen Tomson was the first person who proclaimed herself ready to be tested by the Scientific America committee. But she was disqualified from the actual testing procedure after a preliminary inspection uncovered 20 yards of gauze taped to her groin, flowers concealed under her breasts and a small snake hidden under her arm pit.

The first person to actually undergo a testing procedure with the Scientific America committee was a well-known spirit medium named George Valiantine. He sat in a chair in a very dark room for a séance. During the séance a trumpet appeared in the air and floated around the room while a disembodied voice spoke out of it. Certain he had undeniably passed the test, Mr. Valiantine must have been crestfallen when the committee revealed they had secretly wired his chair to have a light in an adjoining room, where some committee members sat, come on every time he got up from his chair, and go off every time he sat back down. They noted that each time the trumpet and voice appeared, coincided with when he got out of his chair. And each time the trumpet disappeared, coincided with when he sat back down in his chair.

Nino Pecoraro *(1899–1973)*

A young Italian man named Nino Pecararo became prominent among Spiritualists in the early 1920's. Nino claimed to bring in the spirit of Eusapia Palladino, who had herself been a very famous medium of deceased spirits. As she was no longer among the living, Nino claimed she had become his spirit guide. Sir Arthur Conan Doyle, the writer of the popular Sherlock Holmes detective stories, was an ardent believer in Spiritualism and supported the authenticity of Nino.

Nino was born in Naples, Italy and traveled to the United States after some success as a spirit medium in Europe. Conan Doyle first attended one of Nino's seances while he was on a tour of the United States in 1922 to lecture on spiritualism. During the séance, Nino was tied with picture wire and sat inside a darkened cabinet. During the séance a toy piano sitting on the table in the room had tinkling keys and shrieks were heard from the cabinet in which Nino sat unseen by the others in the room.

Nino's first investigations by the Scientific America committee proved baffling to the observers. He was tied to a chair with over 60 feet of rope, but unexplained phenomenon from a tipping table to knocking sounds and disembodied voices at various places around the room continued to occur.

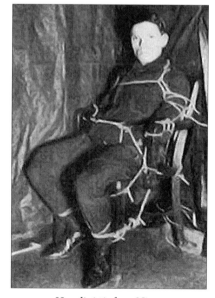

Houdini tied up Nino

What's the Science? Are the Skeptics Ever Right?

Hearing that the committee was giving credence to the young medium, Houdini returned for a séance. As an escape artist himself he understood how a person wrapped with a long lengths of rope or wire, could take a lung full of air and flex their muscles while being tied. Afterward, simple letting out breath and relaxing muscles would create enough slack in the rope to escape. A freed medium in a pitch black darkened séance room would then be able to freely move about, tipping tables, knocking on walls and articulating disembodied voices from various locations in the room.

Houdini took the rope with which Nino had been tied and cut it into several small pieces. He then used each piece to tie the various parts of the medium's body to the chair in which he was sitting. One for his left ankle, one for his right. One for his left hand, one for his right. One for under his arms, another for across his belly. One for behind his right knee, one for behind his left. Thus tied up there were no spirit manifestations of any kind during that séance and Nino became another medium deemed a cheat and a failure.

UNLEASH YOUR PSYCHIC POWERS

Chapter 6

SEX IN SEANCES AND PARANORMAL EXPERIENCES

Through many centuries, sexual ambiance has often been associated with the use of psychic and paranormal powers, a fact that has been used by debunkers to discredit those claiming psychic gifts by painting the participants in a morally disapproving light. It is undeniable that sex and nudity in some form or other, from subtle to blatant, has often played a part in the use and exploration of paranormal gifts by some practitioners since the days of the early Pagans. However, sex in in any form, even the slightest innuendo, is certainly not a prerequisite for discovering, or a requirement for using psychic and paranormal gifts.

As a whole, the people that embraced Spiritualism during the late 18th and early 20th centuries, and paranormal abilities through many centuries, tended to be open-minded to alternative possibilities and methods of discovering truth. If this included some nudity they often had no qualms. Many were simply free spirits who did not feel constrained by the bounds and decrees of church or society, and were willing to employ what others would consider questionable means to achieve their goals.

Also, many people involved not just in Spiritualism, but any form of paranormal gifts, believe or have discovered, that some level of nudity or sexuality enhances the power of their paranormal abilities. This makes sense if you consider that each one of us is a bioelectric entity. Bioelectrical impulses control virtually every aspect of our bodies from our movement to our thoughts. It is not farfetched to consider that clothes, particularly synthetic clothes, could affect and dampen essential bioelectrical impulses required for certain psychic or paranormal manifestations.

Many adherents of Spritualism during the late 19th and early 20th century felt sexual stimulation in one form or another made their psychic powers more acute and powerful, hence they were fairly uninhibited. Though they may have been prim and proper while out on the

Unleash Your Psychic Powers

town, in the privacy of their seances and paranormal activities they did not hide from their sexuality in shame, but embraced it as an important element of their psychic practices.

In modern times, the Chakra system of India has become well-known in most countries of the world, as has the similar Root Ki system of Celestine Light. Both teach about the energy centers; swirling vibrant bio-electric power locations in the body that relate to specific bio-energies and have important harmony and symmetry with each other. (Insert energy center Lotus man image)

The top center, located above the head, is considered the energy location for psychic abilities, while the lowest energy center, found in the groin area, is the bio-energy center for sexual and creative energies. Because these two energy centers are the bio-electrical bookends of the body they have an essential symbiotic relationship with one another. Stimulation of one stimulates and expands the other in a reciprocal and expanding reverberation. This understanding has led many sincere and modest people from Pagans of bygone eras, to Spiritualists of the last centuries, to modern pursuers of their psychic gifts, to put aside some of their modesty in hopes of enhancing their psychic power.

Sex in Seances and Paranormal Experiences

The Sexual-Psychic Intrigues of Mina and Eusapia

In recent times there really has not been much of a scientific nature occurring in the field of psychic research. But during the late 19th and early 20th centuries it was a prominent field of study. Many respectable scientists, including multiple Nobel laureates, invested considerable time methodically investigating psychics, particularly those who were Spirit Mediums that exhibited telekinetic powers, as they sought to determine if there were unknown forces or laws of physics at work. Magazine articles about ongoing psychic research were common in prominent publications such as *Scientific America*.

None of the Mediums were more exhaustively tested than Mina "Margery" Stinson Crandon and Eusapia Pallidino. As we look to determine whether there is any validity to the debunking claims of skeptics, the record of these two women and their cadre of investigators, some whom supported them and others that opposed them, is very enlightening. As accusations of using sex to influence the investigators was one of the claims against both women, a quick look at the record in that regard will clear the air before we delve more deeply into the actual research and results of investigations into their paranormal abilities. (*The detailed accounts of their lives can be found in the Appendixes at the end of the book.*)

Most mediums were women and these two women epitomized many of the qualities, both good and bad, attributed to mediums by their supporters and opponents, and to women mediums in particular, during the time period of the late 19th and early 20th centuries. Both women produced outstanding physical paranormal phenomena. Both had notoriety and careers spanning decades and were investigated by eminent scientists and investigators over one hundred times. Both had ardent supporters and equally vocal opponents. And during their younger years, they were also both accused of using their feminine charms to beguile certain investigators to report the results of their seances favorably. Houdini and other opponents went as far as accusing some of the investigators of acting as collaborators with the mediums to aid in producing fake paranormal phenomena.

In Margery's case, the sexual perception was encouraged when her husband, during seances at their home in Boston, would proudly show nude photographs of his wife while she had been in trance at previous seances, to the sitters of the one about to begin.

Eusapia seemed to openly embrace her sexuality and several of her male séance attendees and investigators admitted to having sexual relations with her.

Part of the investigation procedure of spirit mediums included pre-seance clothing and body searches to insure they were not hiding anything in their clothes or on their person that would enable them to fake manifestations during the séance. Female mediums often were naked under their dress to facilitate the search. Even when the search was conducted by a woman, there certainly must have been a voyeuristic atmosphere pervading the room as the several male investigators carefully scrutinized the proceeding to insure it was thorough.

Eva Carriere, a medium of the late 1800's, ostensibly to insure she wasn't hiding hidden aids, would strip completely naked during the pre-seance search, and then submit to a probing vaginal search by her mistress and sponsor, Mademoiselle Bission, all under the watchful eyes of the male investigators. As extra evidence of her authenticity, she would often insist on another vaginal search after the conclusion of the séance.

Though there are several reports of Eusapia's sexual antics, the only one I found in my research about Margery, was told in the 1970's by a patent attorney to his friend who was a collector of Houdini artifacts. "I am telling it to you now", he said, "because she's dead and gone and I'll be going soon anyway."

Whether it is true or simply a fanciful story cannot be verified, but the attorney claimed he had attended a séance with Margery many years earlier at her home in Boston. He had been directed to sit in the place of honor on her left, holding and controlling her left hand to insure she did not use it to create manifestations. The attorney related: "As soon as the lights went out, in the dark, Margery took my hand and put it between her legs. She was naked under her robe. She tried to make me masturbate her but I was embarrassed and pulled back. She pulled me in again and finally I just pulled my hand away and froze. I was very embarrassed."

Chapter 7
CATEGORIES OF PSYCHIC AND PARANORMAL ABILITIES

Although the words psychic and paranormal are almost always used interchangeably and synonymously, I prefer to classify them as two very different type of abilities, as in my experience they are quite different by nature. However, a person with paranormal or psychic abilities will usually manifest both types, often in multiple forms, especially once they have opened themselves up to discovering and developing their gifts.

Someone with psychic powers has a sensitivity to energies and perception of people and events beyond common scientific instruments ability to register and beyond the capabilities of the normal five senses to perceive. Psychic abilities are receptive, non-intrusive and non-forceful. Though exhibited by both men and women, psychic abilities are a feminine energy and are most easily manifested by those with peaceful, loving dispositions.

Paranormal abilities are a male energy involving the exertion of auric energies to forcefully produce a physical effect or manifestation. Though both men and women can produce paranormal effects, they are created most easily by people with a strong sense of self and confidence in their abilities.

Psychic is perception, paranormal is projection. Psychic pulls in, paranormal pushes out.

I believe that everyone is born with psychic and/or paranormal abilities that will begin to manifest spontaneously at some point in their life. Everyone I have ever met that has seriously looked inward, seeking to find unknown lands within themselves, has always discovered they were blessed with one or more of these special gifts. But most people are too busy in their day to day life to take time for inward journeys.

Unleash Your Psychic Powers

They simply remain ignorant of their blessings because they have either never looked for them, or they repressed them when they spontaneously manifested because of the disapproving religion or culture in which they were raised.

In many cases, both paranormal and psychic abilities can be learned and magnified with practice. You'll find many opportunities within the pages of this book to discover and empower your own special gifts and abilities.

Some of the More Well-Known Psychic Abilities Include:

Aura Reading

Automatic Writing

Card Reading

Clairsentience

Clairvoyance

Divination

Dowsing

Empathy

Intuition

Lucid Dreaming

Non-trance Channeling

Precognition

Psychometry

Remote Viewing

Scrying

Spirit Communication

Telepathy

Some of the More Well-Known Paranormal Abilities Include:

Apportation

Astral Projection

Energy, Faith or Reiki Healing

Exorcism

Full Body, Full Trance Channeling

Ki Force

Levitation

Categories of Psychic and Paranormal Abilities

Pyrokinesis
Teleportation
Telekinesis

UNLEASH YOUR PSYCHIC POWERS

Chapter 8
CONNECT YOUR SENSES TO UNLEASH YOUR SUPERNATURAL GIFTS

We tend to think of our senses in an isolated individual way. Even though we use them together all of the time we most often separate them in thought and discussion, such as "What did you see?", "What did you hear?" and "What did you feel?" instead of using an all encompassing phrase such as "what did you experience?"

Making choices, reasoning deductions, or taking actions based upon just one sense is not always reliable. What you think you saw, may have actually been something else. What you think you heard, may have misinterpreted. The most accurate results come from noting the input from all of your senses, then making a conclusion that takes all of them into account.

The same requirement applies to the use of your sixth sense powers, if you want to have reliable consistency using your psychic and paranormal abilities. It's actually often (though not always) quite helpful to also consider the incoming signals from multiple physical senses when using a psychic gift. Most people use their psychic senses far less than their raditional five senses, so the psychic senses are much rustier. A little extra input from the physical senses can help activate and expand the psychic ones.

Psychic senses are by nature revealing of that which is obscured from the traditional five physical senses, but that doesn't mean the physical senses should be completely ignored or cannot help the psychic sense draw correct conclusions. Based upon the erroneous assumption that the psychic senses are separate from the physical ones, many people when attempting to tune into their psychic senses purposefully try to tune out input from their physical senses. My experience over five decades has come to an opposite conclusion and demonstrated that not ignoring the physical five senses, but instead paying close attention to them, can enhance and facilitate the use of many psychic and paranormal abilities.

The challenge is knowing how much to tune in to your physical senses. Psychic senses can be very subtle and easy to overlook if the physical senses are too overwhelming. If there is too much sensory information coming in from the physical senses - sounds that are too loud, visual input that is too noticeable, aromas that are too strong, too much of anything physical - then those sensations become large enough distractions that the incoming signals from the psychic senses are not sensed!

The merging of sensory inputs, both psychic and physical, is anathema to many people hoping to call out their psychic abilities. Yet despite the prevailing attitude to the contrary, the "sixth sense" was meant to often be used in conjunction with the other five, just as each of them are often used together. How many times have you first heard a sound and then looked up and visually identified what was making the sound? How many times have you smelled a delightful aroma and then looked around until you found the source? How many times have you felt a sensation such as a bug bite, and quickly reacted to simultaneously bat it away and also visually identify what it was that was biting you?

Your physical senses work together to help you navigate the world you live in. But there is much more to the life than what you see, feel, hear, touch and smell. The hidden parts of the world and of people are vast. Psychic and paranormal abilities tap into, reveal, and to some degree influence these obscured vistas and energies. Though the sixth sense may be the primary engine to enter and navigate the supernatural world, it is still aided and further empowered when it can call upon the powers of one or more of its sibling physical senses.

The best personal example I can give you is "Aura Projection." As I'll go into in greater detail in **Chapter 12:** *Seeing, Feeling, and Reading the Aura*, when you are in conscious control of your own aura, you are master of a very powerful force. I have used the power of my aura many times for a wide variety of applications. But without recognizing and utilizing the mundane sense of physical sensation, I would never have been able to use my aura as a physical, emotional and mental force. If I did not recognize and learn to harness the associated physical sensations in my body as my aura projected with power, there never would have been any power or any projection.

It is very easy for skeptics to discount psychic and paranormal abilities by coming up with plausible, alternative, non-supernatural means by which the incident could have occurred. With that in mind, they will have a challenge coming up with another explanation for the incident I am about to relate. This occasion of "Aura Projection" demonstrates how vital the link can be between the physical senses and successful use of the psychic senses and manifestation of your paranormal powers.

This is a deeply personal story so please respect it as such. I am sharing with you a very private event in my life that heretofore have been shared with very few. I have changed the name of the sister in this retelling of the event to protect her privacy.

Decades ago, before I asked to have my name removed from the records and as I've already mentioned, I was a member of the Latter-day Saint religion. Though I was happily married to a lovely LDS lady, I had a powerful psychic attraction to her sister, Susanne; one such as I had never felt so strongly with anyone before. Unfortunately, just knowing I had any kind of special connection with her sister that I didn't have with her, drove a wedge between me and my wife that eventually contributed to breaking us apart.

The most intense feelings Susanne and I had for each other occurred during a two week visit one Christmas. It was just a couple of months prior to her getting a mission call when she was 21 years of age, to serve as a missionary for a year and a half in France. She called us on the day she received her mission call from the 'Prophet', the supreme head of the church. It is a similar position of authority to the Pope with the Catholics. Mormons believe that mission calls, where a person is called to serve as missionary in a specific location, are given to the Prophet by revelation from God. Except in the most extraordinary circumstances that allow no other recourse, mission calls, because of their revelationary nature, are never changed.

We lived near Seattle, Washington, USA at the time. When I heard that Susanne was called to a place so far from me, beyond the width of the USA, across the Atlantic Ocean and on another continent, I just could not bear the thought of not seeing her at all for the next year and a half. I vowed with an intensity and passion such as I had never had for anything, that her mission call would not stand! I was terribly upset. I was passionately intense, steadfastly intent that she would ***not*** be going to France on her mission!

I *felt* auric power swirling inside me with hurricane intensity, unlike anything I had ever felt before in my life! The intense feelings tingled in every cell of my body imbuing me with utter and complete confidence in my ability to change what could not be changed. I was indomitably sure of myself and of my paranormal abilities to accomplish my will that day. There was never any doubt, not even the faintest thought that I would not succeed doing something that had never been done before – forcing, by auric power, the prophet of the Mormon church to undo what he had decreed.

That night under the light of the stars and the dim glow of distant city lights, I went for a walk alone until I arrived at the track field of the local community college. As I approached it I sent angry energy and thoughts to anyone that might be present to leave before I arrived. I projected my aura out before me so that anyone present on that field would feel an angry foreboding force and leave out of fear for what they could feel but not see. I normally could not manifest such a potent auric projection no matter how much I might want to. Until this moment the study and use of auras had been more a function of my mind and had little to do with my heart. On this day, for the very first time, my heart and my mind, my feelings and my thoughts, were united in a very powerful union. As I thought in my mind to project my aura outward, I felt a force physically moving inside my body as if a river was rushing in a torrent right through me.

I walked out to the center of the track field in the early hours of the night. I stood with head slightly bowed, eyes tightly closed and fists clenched in front of me held at waist level. I flexed the muscles in my arms tightly. In my mind I willed my aura to come in very close so its power would be bottled up in a smaller space. Then I began to swirl it around and around in a rapid, whirlwind, omnidirectional spin. I did this by first creating a mental image of being enclosed inside an omnidirectional spinning sphere of white light. My perspective was from the inside looking out. My teeth were gritted in undaunted determination. I had a burning intensity that my will would be done. But the most powerful thing I *felt*, physically *felt*, was my auric energy swirling like a tornado inside of me. I *felt* this force everywhere: from the roots of my hair, to the tips of my toes, and every cell in every inch of my body inside and out. It was a euphoric feeling of rapidly moving supernatural energy filling me completely.

After less than a minute I had concentrated the power enough. Opening my eyes wide, **with my physical sight**, I could see my auric field swirling close around me and faster, so much faster than I had ever seen an aura swirl before. I was inside a tornado made from a billion jewels of colored light. I now released and expanded my aura in a sudden explosion! In my mind I willed it outward. **With my eyes I watched** it explode outward in a gigantic, circular, horizontal ripple. Though my physical sight was limited to a short distance around me, I continued to psychically see the auric force field expanding outward. I saw it envelope my city, then my state. I saw it roll over the mountains of NE Oregon, across the desert of Idaho, the plains of the Great Salt Lake and come to rest with glowing scintillating power over the city of Salt Lake City, Utah, the location of Spencer W. Kimball, prophet of the Church of Jesus Christ of Latter-day Saints.

Pushing both arms up above and in front of me with my fingers splayed wide apart, I declared with authority and in a loud, voice of conviction that would not be deterred, "Spencer Kimball, you will change the mission call of Susanne LeBlanc from the Paris, France mission to the Seattle, Washington mission, immediately!" Pounding one of my fists into my other hand I said it again, "Spencer Kimball, you will change the mission call of Susanne LeBlanc from the Paris, France mission to the Seattle, Washington mission, immediately!" As I said it I could **physically feel** my aura connecting to his, even over a distance of thousands of miles. A third time I uttered the words with absolute insistence that my will be obeyed. "Spencer Kimball, you will change the mission call of Susanne LeBlanc from the Paris, France mission to the Seattle, Washington mission, immediately!"

As soon as I let out the third utterance of my demand a great calm washed over me and I knew without doubt that my will would be done. I had *felt* Mr. Kimball's aura and I had aurically *felt* him agree to my demand. I mentally called my aura back to me and it came back in a sudden rush that took only a few seconds. As I walked home I felt a great conflict of emotions. I was amazed and overjoyed to realize the power I had wielded and to know without doubt the effect that had transpired. I also had a heavy remorse and a great pang of guilt, a sentiment I seldom felt. I realized immediately after the deed had been done that it was an immature and selfish action, not worthy of the person I aspired to be. It was wrong and I shouldn't have done it. But I had, and now I needed to wait to see how great the repercussions would be. My wait would not be long.

The very next day Susanne called us to tell us that the most amazing thing had occurred. Her mission call had been changed by the Prophet! Instead of going to the Paris, France mission

Connect Your Senses to Unleash Your Supernatural Gifts

she had been recalled to a new mission in Seattle, Washington. Everyone was baffled and abuzz about how this could be! Mission calls were never changed except for extraordinary circumstances. Even then, it was against church policy for young missionaries to be called to serve in locations where they had close family as that was deemed to be too big of a distraction. So even if her mission had by some unlikely circumstance been changed, it would never have been changed to Seattle, Washington where her sister and brother-in-law lived.

These unprecedented events were too much for Susanne. She sincerely wanted to focus on her missionary work and knew close proximity to me could end up being more than just a distraction. She went to her local Bishop and confessed our relationship. Because of our relationship, being close to me while trying to serve her mission was the last place she wanted to be, or the church would want her to be! But as the mission call had come by revelation to the Prophet, it was not going to be changed again. However, events dictated it was now time for me to be called into the woodshed for punishment.

I got a telephone call from the clerk of my local church for a hastily arranged interview with my Bishop, the ecclesiastical leader of my local LDS congregation. At the interview the next day, he wanted to know about my relationship with Susanne and for me to confess to my sins which his aura plainly said he had already determined had to include adultery. The fact was, my relationship with Susanne was strictly psychic. Though in our own confusion at what we were experiencing and how to express and manifest our relationship, there was some innapropriate physical contact, it was completely non-sexual, But question after question from the Bishop clearly showed he did not believe it. Giving up in frustration at my unwillingness to admit to his preconceived beliefs, he arranged an interview the next day for me with the Stake President, the ecclesiastical leader of a large geographic area around Seattle.

His interview was pretty much the same as the Bishop's. Blunt, probing, and insistent upon getting me to confess to adultery. Instead I told him the full account of what I had done with my aura to influence the Prophet and get Susanne's mission changed to be close to me in Seattle. He thought that was the most preposterous claim he had ever heard anyone make. His primary argument was it would violate 'free agency', which is one of the foundational beliefs of the Mormon faith, that everyone is free to make their own choices in life rather than be compelled. His second argument was even if 'free agency' could be subverted, God would not allow anyone to be able to dictate to the Prophet.

I countered with some simple facts that he could neither deny or explain. First, as new missionaries get a letter from the Prophet himself calling them by revelation to their mission locality, how is it possible that Susanne's letter would be voided and the revelation changed, within 48 hours to a completely different mission? Did God or the Prophet get it wrong the first time? Second, it is strictly against church policy for a young missionary to serve a mission in the same area where they have close family. So, of the hundreds of mission locations on the planet Earth, why would Susanne's mission that should never have been changed in the first place, be abruptly changed to the exact place on the planet where I happened to live? His only reply was that he didn't know the answers to those questions other than he knew I couldn't have had anything to do with it.

To any skeptics out there who also doubt that paranormal powers exist, I would pose the same challenge to you that I did to the Stake President: given the facts of the events and the beliefs and policies of the LDS church at the time, what other reasonable explanation can be postulated?

The point of sharing this story with you is to give you a firm understanding of how beneficial and sometimes even essential, the melding of one or more of your physical senses with your sixth psychic sense is, to successfully utilize your psychic and paranormal abilities. Not applicable in every instance, and more so with your paranormal powers than your psychic abilities, but still a vital connection between physical and psychic that should not be overlooked or dismissed.

If I had not been aware and open to feeling my aura swirling inside of me, I would never have even slightly been able to harness and direct its power. It is only because I could ***physically feel it*** that I knew when the power had built sufficiently, like a jet revving its engine with its brakes locked before takeoff. Just before I exploded my aura out across the states I looked with my physical eyes at the swirling bejeweled sphere of light I stood within, and my eyes and body turned to point toward the geographic Southeast to visually guide the leading edge of the first exploding ripples headed for Salt Lake City.

The most important and indispensable physical connection came years before the fateful day on the track field under the stars. You see, I had met the Prophet, President Spencer W. Kimball and his wife Camille a few years before in New York City when he had come to dedicate the new church building near the Julliard School. It was a short but very profound private meeting in a room full of people. In fact, it was in the middle of a news conference. The only reason I was in the building is my LDS employer had asked me to go to there to prepare flowers for President and Sister Kimball's arrival. When I came into the room where he was speaking to a throng of reporters with his wife Camille at his side, he saw me enter. Though we had never before met or communicated, he looked right at me and there was an undeniable spark of auric recognition and connection for both of us. He looked away from me for a moment and asked the media people if they would excuse him for a few minutes as someone had just entered the room to whom he had to speak. They were dumbfounded as they had been right in the middle of a question and answer session. They looked at one another perplexed and just milled around seemingly at a loss for what to do. But they quickly became non-existent in my mind.

President Kimball beckoned me over where he, Camille, and I could stand a good distance and out of earshot from the group of media people. For the next 5 minutes it was as if he and I were the only ones in the room. We shook hands and then held both hands firmly together for a long time, reveling in each others auric energy and reluctant to let go. We had an amazing conversation, the most profound I've ever had with anyone, and one I will never publicly share. I walked away somewhat in a daze, but with an auric connection to Spencer W. Kimball inscribed inside of me.

Connect Your Senses to Unleash Your Supernatural Gifts

If we had not physically met on that day in New York City, if we had not physically shaken hands and shared both physical and auric touch, I would never have been able to connect to him strong enough over such a geographic distance, to have sufficient influence to shake him to his core and get him to change Susanne's mission from France to Seattle, Washington. In fact, if we had never met in person, I would not have known his aura. If I hadn't known his aura, I would have never found him in Utah and never been able to establish any auric connection at all. Susanne LeBlanc would have gone to Paris, France as she had been originally called, and there would have been nothing at all I could have done about it despite all the passion and desire I might have mustered.

As this event illustrates, there is a very potent connection between the physical and psychic senses. You would do well to cultivate and not ignore it if you want to expand your psychic and paranormal abilities. What you *feel* is a HUGE connection to your psychic senses and paranormal powers. If you are not physically feeling sensations inside of your body when you are calling upon and using your supernatural gifts, then you are only catching a glimmer of your true potential.

When intentionally using and incorporating your physical senses with your psychic ones, the first step is to consciously become more aware of your physical senses. To be aware requires consciously thinking about the input your senses are giving to you. The normal human habit is to tune out virtually all sensory input. What song played on the radio 5 minutes ago? What was the plot and story of the TV shows you watched last night? It's not that we forgot these events. It's that we never mentally acknowledged them enough to have put them into our memory. We can't remember what is not there.

How many people have you just been introduced to whose name you could not remember 5 minutes later? Although many people will claim they simply cannot remember names, the true reason is they heard, but did not mentally acknowledge, the other person's name. With unconscious vanity, when they were introduced the only name they heard was their own. The name of the person they were introduced to was never inscribed into their memory. It's as if they never even heard it.

One way to help with names is to vocally say the other person's name after the introduction. That helps inscribe it in your memory. For example, if you are introduced to Tom, you don't simply say, "glad to meet you." You say, "Glad to meet you **Tom**." Without conscious effort to acknowledge his name, what you heard is forgotten. Without the little extra effort to transcribe the name in your memory, the next time you meet Tom, you will have lost his name because you never really had it. With a little embarrassment you will only be able to ask, "how are you?"

The same is true of recognizing and giving a moments thought in your mind to the signals sent by your other physical senses, because they often are secondary indicators of something your psychic senses are telling you. Maybe there is a slight breeze blowing across your bare arm on a warm summer's day that suddenly turns cold when you are approached by a stranger. Did the weather suddenly change, or is this a physical sense that is warning you along with your psychic intuition to beware of this unknown person?

Perhaps you get a psychic mental flash of an injured loved one that is confirmed by input from an out of place physical sense, such as hearing a distant cry, or smelling a peculiar odor, or seeing a whiff of smoke at a place there should be none, or hearing the bark of a dog or the scolding call of an upset bluejay. Not only can the physical senses help to confirm what the psychic senses are indicating, they can often help pinpoint and define that which the psychic senses only vaguely hinted.

To aid your quest to have a synergy between your psychic and physical senses, simply develop a new habit of tuning in more alertly to each of your senses during your daily activities. When a formerly sighted person becomes blind, they quickly learn to become much more aware of the sensory input of their other senses to compensate for their loss of sight. It is not that their other senses such as hearing, suddenly become better. They simply become more keen as they start paying greater attention to the information their other senses are telegraphing. Like the blind person, if we start paying more attention to the sounds, skin sensations, aromas and tastes that surround us, our appreciation for the value of our often ignored senses rapidly increases and the world quickly becomes a far more fascinating place.

I consciously work at training all of my senses, including my psychic senses to work more acutely and in unison each day during my normal activities. There is nothing elaborate involved and no preparation is necessary. Simply think about the sensory input from each sense one at a time, and then be aware of them all in unison, or more correctly in immediate very rapid succession.

As an example, today I made a trip to a home improvement store. From where I parked it took about 30 seconds to walk into the building. As I walked toward the store, I mentally asked myself, "ears what are you hearing?" As much as possible I ignored any input from my other senses and just listened. I heard cars on the freeway about 100 yards behind me that I hadn't been aware of before. I heard the whistles and chirps of multiple species of birds that I had been oblivious to just moments before. I heard a truck down the aisle in the parking lot starting up, and the clank of metal as a person outside the store dropped the lid of a barbeque he was looking at.

Continuing my approach to the store I mentally asked myself, "skin what are you feeling?" Immediately I felt the cuffs of my long-sleeve sweatshirt gently rubbing my skin as it moved slightly up and down on my wrists as my arms swayed back and forth while I walked. I also relished the feel of the warm sun on my face and hands.

Getting closer to the store I mentally asked myself, "mouth what are you tasting?" With a bit of disappointment I tasted my own dragon breath and realized I had forgotten to brush my teeth after breakfast. Yuck! I had to be careful not to get too close to anyone and blast them with bad breath!

Passing into the entrance of the store I mentally asked myself, "nose what are you smelling?" That became a bit of a sensory overload. When you consciously think about noticing the smells,

Connect Your Senses to Unleash Your Supernatural Gifts

there are a lot of unpleasant ones in home improvement stores. I'm not sure how anyone can stand to work long-term in places that have such strong chemical odors.

Then, I consciously thought about my psychic senses, specifically my aura. With my eyes I saw it glimmering in front of me and inside and out I felt its energy coursing through me and all around me. I expanded it out and asked, "aura what are you finding out there?" Immediately I felt all the auras of the people within 50 feet of me and there was nothing unusual. Though there was a wide range of human dramas from people feeling happy to others feeling sad or sick, there were no malevolent or angry auric signals.

Lastly, I mentally called out to all of my senses, quickly one after another, "eyes-see, ears-hear, nose-smell, skin-feel, tongue-taste, aura-interact." I tried to be simultaneously aware of the input from all 6 senses. The reality is we can only focus on one thought at a time. But if done in very rapid succession it is as if you are aware of every one of them at the same moment. The entire exercises lasted not more than a minute, took no special equipment and cost no money. Nor did I discover anything particularly interesting. But in that single minute I did grow stronger in my ability to receive information from my senses and to use them together.

Whether lifting weights to improve your physical body strength, doing mental calisthenics challenging your mind to increase its capabilities, or employing techniques to expand your awareness and psychic senses, regular exercise is a key to success and improvement.

Unleash Your Psychic Powers

Chapter 9
FOCUS IS ESSENTIAL...USUALLY

Attention and focus on your intent to manifest a desired psychic ability or paranormal power in a specific manner is usually an essential action for success. But sometimes it's not and the opposite is more effective. As strange as it seems, some supernatural phenomena manifest more quickly and fully if they are not thought about much after setting a focused intention.

In most cases you will need to experiment on your own with the various powers and abilities. Focus or non-focus that works for you, may be the opposite of the method that works for someone else. Most abilities will manifest easier for you with concentration. With others you may find more success by setting your intention and then not thinking much about it. Your personality, current level of abilities with any psychic powers, and interest and desire, are some of the factors affecting which method works best for you.

Focused Disinterest Technique

Spoon bending is an example of a paranormal power that works for most people with the focused disinterest technique. Anyone who focuses on bending the spoons and forks will have little success short of brute strength, with any part other than the thin easily bent shaft, unless they use the focused disinterest technique.

The focused disinterest method is similar for any psychic ability or paranormal power you want to apply it to. Here's an example of how to use it for spoon bending. You can use either a spoon or a fork for this exercise.

1. Hold the spoon in your hand in front of you where you can comfortably look at it.
2. Focus all of your attention on the spoon.
3. Observe the shape of the spoon, the design on its handle, the heft of its weight.
4. Become one with the spoon. Feel it merge into your hand. It's as if it is a part of you,

an extension of your hand. Mentally and physically swirl your auric power inside your body. Send it swirling down your arm and into the spoon. Become one with the spoon.

5. While looking at the spoon with total focus, say aloud, "spoon, you are going to bend and contort as soft and easy as putty." Say it aloud 3 times.

6. Now forget about the spoon. Lower your hand so you are no longer looking at the spoon. Hold the spoon in both hands and begin moving your hands all around applying slight pressure in various directions. Do this while striking up a conversation with the person sitting nearest to you about any topic you wish not related to spoon bending or psychic powers. Make the conversation interesting so that you completely forget about the spoon in your hand as you continue to move your hands around it applying slight pressure. If you don't have a person to talk with, go ahead and turn on the TV and watch a show.

7. When your conversation has a stopping point take a look at your spoon. It will likely look like a pretzel.

How to Focus and Stay Focused

It is so easy to get distracted. In everyday life this makes us inefficient but it isn't a great impediment. With psychic abilities and paranormal powers it is a significantly more serious handicap and will likely prevent you from manifesting your powers, except in instances when disinterest is the modus operandi.

Lack of ability to hold a focus is a lifelong bad habit for most people. As an example, my teenage daughter is often doing her homework, texting with multiple people, talking with others on Skype, and playing a group online video game on her computer, all at the same time! She can be commended for multitasking. But though she still accomplishes everything she hopes to, it takes her 6 hours to do 2 hours of homework because of all the distractions. Multitasking like this may work for tasks of everyday life, but it eliminates the possibility of intentional, controlled, manifestation of most psychic powers and paranormal abilities. They are still there and may manifest spontaneously on their own, but the incident will be erratic, unpredictable, undependable and usually unhelpful.

Breaking the lack of focus bad habit and replacing it with an ability and beneficial habit to focus and concentrate continually on the task at hand, is an essential skill to increasing your psychic abilities and paranormal powers far beyond the average the average psychic.

It really is as simple as forming a new habit to replace an old one. Lack of ability to continually hold a focus without distraction is the old, bad habit. Staying focused, for a continual period of time on a single item, thought or effort, is the new, good habit. Bad habits do not just go away. To successfully banish them you must replace them with a new, good habit. You can establish this habit and ability by regularly doing concentration exercises. Your mind and

Focus is Essential...Usually

psychic abilities are both strengthened by mental exercises, just as your body is strengthened by physical exercises.

Focus Exercise #1 The Half Dollar Flip
1. For this exercise you will need a United States Kennedy 50 cent coin. This coin is used because it has a very memorable image on the reverse side. If you are in another country, obtain the largest or most distinctive coin issued in your country. You are not going to use the side with a face of an ex-president or ruler. You want a coin with a striking image on the reverse side.
2. Once you have your coin go to ***http://www.random.org/coins***. This an excellent Random Number Generator.
3. Select the coin from their list that you are holding.
4. Enter '1' in the flip box. You are going to make 'tails' come up, one flip at a time.
5. Click 'Flip Coin(s).'
6. An image of the coin you flipped will appear. It may show heads or it may show tails. If it shows heads, flip it again until the image on your computer is tails, which should match the coin you are holding in your hand.
7. Now you are ready to begin the exercise. Look at the coin in your hand. Focus on the image on the reverse side. Look at it in detail in all parts. Think 'tails' in your mind or even say it aloud.
8. Click the button on the website that says 'Flip Again.' The image will come up with your coin, either 'heads' or 'tails.'
9. Focus once more on the image of the coin in your hand. You are only using the reverse side of the coin. You will be choosing 'tails' 100% of the time. Never alternate and choose 'heads.'
10. When you have focused strongly, and stated 'tails' aloud or in your mind, click 'Flip Again.'
11. Once more the site will show you heads or tails. Continue to focus on tails and flipping the coin.
12. Keep a mental or written record of the number of times tails comes up compared to the total number of flips.

The Law of Averages predicts you will have 50% tails and 50% heads. I tried this just flipping a coin without thinking about which side would show and it came up exactly 50 heads and 50 tails after 100 flips. In a short run of 10-20 flips, this average may be off a bit. But if 100 flips were done at random, with no focus on 'heads' or 'tails', it will come up 50-50 nearly every time with only tiny deviation. Therefore, any substantial deviation that you create by focusing on just tails is quite significant. By focusing only on the task at hand, stating your intention aloud or in your mind by saying 'tails', and seeing the picture of tails in your mind as you click the 'Flip Again' button, you will typically be able to make 60-70 out of 100 tails appear. This is actually quite an astounding feat! The best I have ever done is 79 out of 100.

How Is The Random Number Generator Affected?

How this is being accomplished, by what psychic ability or paranormal power, a Random Number Generator on a computer in some distant, unknown town can be affected, is a curious question.

The most likely source is the paranormal power of *telekinesis*, which allows you to physically control or move an object by the power of your mind and auric energy. Being able to influence a random number generator is often attributed to telekinetic power.

So the coin flip exercise helps you in two ways. It builds up your power of focus and concentration while simultaneously increasing your telekinetic powers.

Focus Exercise #2   Art Lover

1. Insure you are in a place in your home where you will not be disturbed by any person, animal, or any type of distraction. All phones are turned off.
2. Take a peaceful piece of art, a picture, a glass bowl, any intricate visual object. I use a large glass bowl I made some years ago with many colors and patterns. Set it alone on a wall or table near you without any other object to compete for attention.
3. Focus all of your attention on the piece of art. If any divergent thoughts enter your mind quickly sweep them away and refocus only on the art work.
4. Become one with the art work. Send your aura into it. Will it to be so. Feel your auric energy coursing through your body and going out and encompassing the art.
5. Run your eyes around the perimeter of the art, then spiral in toward the center noticing minute little details along the way that you can see.
6. Close your eyes and see the image you have been staring at in your mind. Notice all the details that you can.
7. Open your eyes and look again at the art. Stare at it. Become one with it.
8. Again close your eyes and see the art image in your mind. Notice all the details.
9. Open your eyes once more. Make a mental note or start a silent timer to see how long you can stay focused only on the art work. You can't think about the time either. When you find your mind wandering for even one stray thought, stop the timer and see how well you did.
10. Practice daily to increase your totally focused time.

Focus is Essential...Usually

When I see people who believe in psychic abilities and paranormal powers, but fail to manifest any, inevitably I also discover someone who lacks the ability to focus intensely for a sustained period of at least 5 minutes. Most people will tell you they have no problem focusing when they need to, but this is not the case if you watch them in action. Like my teenage daughter, they are easily distracted. The reality is it is an exceptionally rare person that can focus for more than just a minute or so, unless they have practiced concentration exercises like these on a regular basis until they have perfected the habit and ability.

The lack of success focusing and concentrating is probably not a short-coming of the individual as much as it is a problem created in everyone's lives by our hustle, bustle world that entices us with so many influences constantly seeking and even demanding our attention.

Just trying to find silence can be a challenge. Everywhere you go even in your own house, there are bells ringing from dishwashers and cooking timers, cell phones constantly chirping with news of new texts or calls, motors running from refrigerators to fans, outside noises from people and cars passing by, dogs barking, cats meowing and the list goes on.

Plus, add all the places you need to go: classes to attend, multiple stores to shop, medical and dental appointments, social activities and meetings with friends. Let's not forget school and work, or if you have kids, chauffeuring them to all the places ***they*** need to go.

On top of all those distractions, everywhere you are, from your car to your house, to your work, you are continually bombarded with advertisements, both visual and audio. The combined onslaught can be so distracting that they sometimes cause accidents.

It's really little wonder that people have such a challenge focusing on just one thing for even 5 minutes!

However, if you are a serious student of the paranormal, learning to tune out all these distractions and focus on a single action or thought for at least 5 minutes, is one of the great secrets to unleashing and expanding your psychic abilities and paranormal powers.

Focus Exercise #3   The Little Black Dot

1. Set aside a time when you can have 15-20 minutes of undisturbed time - no TV's phones, people, animals or other distractions.
2. Before beginning, sit in a comfortable, upright chair. Take a few deep breaths and exhale slowly and fully. Just relax. Put aside all thoughts of activities or relationships in your life. Let your mind relax and stop thinking about everything. You are entering a meditative state.
3. Look at the image below. If you are reading this as an eBook on your computer, you may want to print the image and look at it on paper. Your goal is to focus only on the black dot and not allow your eyes or focus to wander to any of the other images even for a microsecond.
4. When you are ready to begin, start a timer or note the time. Don't allow your mind to

think of the time again, until the moment you are first distracted from your focus on the black dot. Then note the time to monitor how long you were able to maintain your focus. You should be able to improve with each session.

As you continue to stare at the dot, it is a normal occurrence to begin to see an illusion of movement or an aura-like distorted space around the dot. Don't let either one distract you from maintaining your focus on the dot.

It is also alright to blink while maintaining your focus on the dot. But take extra care to keep your focus when you blink.

If any wayward thoughts other than the black dot try to enter your mind, just seal them out and re-energize your focus on the dot.

As you succeed in your focus you'll find time ceases to exist. It shows you have become one with the dot. When you finally break your concentration don't be surprised to see 10, 20 or even 30 minutes have passed even though it seemed but minutes to you.

Your first goal should be to maintain concentration and focus for at least 5 minutes with a final goal of at least 15 minutes after you have practiced a few to several times.

Focus Exercise #4   The Flower

Once you have been able to maintain your concentration and focus on the black dot for at least 5 minutes, you are prepared to move on to this next exercise, using a picture of a flower. Like the piece of art there is a lot of detail. But the flower is a picture of a living organism, so there is more to sense than just what you can visually see.

1. Again, insure you are in a quiet place of solitude, guaranteed to be undisturbed for 15-30 minutes.
2. Do a few calming, deep breathing exercises. Clear your mind of mundane thoughts

Focus is Essential...Usually

and enter a peaceful, meditative state.

3. Start the timer or look at the clock as you begin the exercise. You need to be able to maintain your undivided focus for at least 5 minutes; 15 minutes is better.

4. In this exercise, as you focus, you want to become one with the flower; to know it so completely that it seems as if it is a part of you. Enter deeply so that your perspective is inside the flower. Then zoom out and see it from an outside perspective. Then enter back into it like a bee standing on one of the petals. Though it's only a picture, you can transcend the picture with the power of your mind. As you look at the picture of the flower and see the drops of water on the petals, use your mind to remember what a droplet of water feels like. How cool is it to your touch? What does the wetness feel like? What if you touched it with the tip of your tongue? As you focus with no distraction on the flower, think about how it would feel to touch one of the water droplets with your tongue or finger tip.

5. With your eyes explore every part of the flower in detail. How many petals? How many pollen stems in the center? How many specks of pollen on the pollen stems? Let your eyes move around all parts of the flower, top, bottom, every petal, from the edge to deep inside the center. Notice the different textures. Are they smooth or rough? How are the leaves behind the flower different from the flower? If you touch the cluster of pollen stems in the middle what happens? You have pollen on your fingers. What does it feel like? Use your mind to remember how soft a flower petal feels. Reach out with your mind and feel the luxuriously soft petals of the flower in the picture.

6. Maintain your undivided focus as long as possible. When your first distracting thought or glance away from the picture occurs, stop the timer or note the time on a clock. 5 minutes of focus is barely a passing grade. Give yourself a B if you reached 15 minutes and an A for 20 or more.

After succeeding maintaining your focus and thoroughly exploring the flower, you will feel energized as you end the exercise. If you want to accomplish two things at once, do this exercise any time you are feeling tired or lethargic. In addition to continuing and improving your focus training, it should also perk you right up!

Focus Exercise #5   Ramping Up Your Sense of Smell

Here's an unusual focus exercise to break the mono focus of others.

This exercise will also accomplish two objectives. It will improve your ability to focus and increase your sense of smell. We are surrounded by odors and aromas everywhere we are in our everyday life, from home to work, to outdoor recreation. Unless a smell is particularly strong or unusual, most people don't even recognize or acknowledge them in their mind.

For this exercise you need to go for a walk in a park. The ideal park will have people, dogs, nearby shops and lots of blossoming flowers. If that's not available you can just go for a walk in

Unleash Your Psychic Powers

your own garden or yard. If it's winter a visit to the local florist would substitute.

In this exercise you want to recognize as many different smells that you can. It is not necessary to know what it is that is causing the smell. But if you can identify it from your memory of known smells, that helps keep you focused. Nor are you only looking for good smells. Bad odors will also do nicely.

1. Find a location you can sit or stand and close your eyes. Tune out any audio sounds you are hearing from people talking to dogs barking.
2. Inhale a deep breath and take notice of how many different aromas you sense. Do this several times, focusing only on the smells and not sounds or other sensory input.
3. After three or four breaths, open your eyes and move to another nearby location, far enough away to offer some new smells. While walking, limit your visual observation to the bare minimum necessary to safely move from one place to another and tune out any sounds. Just make them white noise background.
4. Once you have moved at least three times. Pick the favorite aroma you smelled. Walk around continuing to sniff the air until you identify the source and the item.

Focus Exercise #6   The Breath of Life

This is a great focus exercise. Because it involves continual action you're not likely to get bored. Plus it's good for your mental, emotional and physical health as well! Five minutes is all you need, but more is better if its comfortable for you. Be careful to not overdue it and to maintain very slow breaths, not rapid. If you get light-headed at any point, please stop immediately.

1. Sit in a comfortable straight-back chair with your feet on the ground. If you have a straight-back chair but it's not particularly comfortable, put a thin pillow on the seat.
2. Tune out all distractions and insure you will be undisturbed during your exercise.
3. Focus solely and completely on your breathing and the procedures of the exercise.
4. Lightly place your right index finger on the side of your right nostril with enough pressure to seal it.
5. Take a slow deep breath through your open left nostril. Fill your lungs as deeply as you can. Count to 10 and try to make your inhale last the entire 10 seconds. Comfort is more important than time. If you struggle to reach 10 seconds on your inhale, do it in a shorter time that is slow but completely comfortable.
6. Remove your finger from the side of your right nostril and press on your left nostril. Slowly exhale to the count of 10 out of your right nostril.
7. While maintaining your finger on the left nostril now breath in a slow, deep breath through your right nostril to the count of 10.

Focus is Essential...Usually

8. Switch nostrils being pressed back to the right from the left and slowly breath out the left nostril for the count of 10.
9. Repeat this procedure, switching form one nostril to the next for 5 minutes. You can go longer if it is comfortable.

Chapter 10
PSYCHIC SELF-DEFENSE

When you walk down the path of the psychic and paranormal, you are entering into a strange, wonderful new world where the limitations of the physical senses and the known laws of physics often do not apply. In this realm there are many unseen and unknown forces that can scare you at least, and hurt you at worst, if you are not prepared for them. Only the naive or inexperienced would doubt or deny this reality. However, there is nothing to worry or have anxiety about as long as you are aware of the challenges and prepared to counter them.

The practice of psychic self-defense is not something you should shrug off as "not necessary" or "no time for that." In addition to being a wise precaution, particularly when working with the energies of any other beings, be they ghosts, guides, or other off-world advisers, any time you practice any psychic ability, including self-defense, it improves all of your psychic abilities.

In everyday life precautions become habits in direct proportion to the perceived threat. You don't leave your purse or wallet unattended in your shopping cart when you are browsing in a store. You don't park your car in public places with the doors unlocked, the windows rolled down and the keys left in the ignition. Nor do you walk down the street with cash hanging out of your pockets, or leave the door to your house wide open when you go on vacation. You guard yourself in ways commensurate with the risk, because you know if you don't there is a chance that something bad might happen. It is very much the same when you are working with psychic and paranormal activities. You take simple, common sense precautions to insure there is no chance of anything unpleasant or harmful occurring.

I've seen practitioners throw caution to the winds and as a matter of personal principle completely disregard self-defense. They feel it is somehow giving into fear and calling in the very energy trying to be avoided. That is an empowered and noble attitude. In the more benign psychic endeavors this carefree attitude is harmless because low level psychic activities offer little to no threat. But if followed through into the more risky psychic endeavors it will eventually end badly in one way or another.

Like so many things in life, **balance** is the key operative word. It is equally as unhelpful to disregard the risks, as it is to be paranoid and overly consumed by them. Reasonable precautions, especially with any psychic activity where supernatural beings of any kind are involved, is just common sense. When you are aware of the risks and are prepared to counter them, there is little likelihood you will ever need them.

Truly, using supernatural abilities should be as pleasant as a walk in the park on a comfortably warm and serene summer's day. And it will be for you as long as you have your simple but effective psychic defenses prepared **before** you seek to explore your gifts too deeply. Too often people are so excited to learn and develop their psychic abilities and paranormal powers that they plunge into that aspect without caution or full awareness of dangers that may lie lurking. Learn and apply basic psychic defense procedures first and you will always have safe sailings on your supernatural journeys.

The threat level is not the same for every paranormal/psychic activity. If you are using Biblioelucidation for an answer to a simple question the danger level is basically nil. But if you are channeling in another being, allowing them to enter and control your body in a trance, the risks are much higher. The best path is to be neither overly cautious or overly dismissive of the dangers. Consider wisely what the possible dangers may be for any psychic endeavor and take appropriate measures equal to the possible risks.

Be Cautious & Aware, But Don't Give Energy To Fear

Belief is very powerful. It affects how well you can call upon and use your special abilities. It also can aid or hinder you in your self defense depending on whether you are defending yourself from a place of confidence and empowerment, or anxiety and fear. It is easy to give in to the latter. I assure you that you have **nothing** to fear from the unseen world as long as you take the proper precautions. I am happy to share with you potent defenses I have proven work 100% of the time.

<u>The First Defensive Step:</u>

Never proceed with anything of a psychic or paranormal nature if you are fearful.

Your emotions are like psychic magnets. They call to you that which you strongly feel. If you feel fear, those forces that feed on fear are drawn to you. If you feel confident and empowered, the forces that feed on fear are repelled. Fear is a darkness. When you have fear you call more darkness to you. Self-confidence and personal empowerment are light. Darkness cannot exist in the presence of light.

The Second Defensive Step:

***Do not associate with people who are fearful
when you are involved in psychic activities.***

Fear draws more fear. A fearful group of people draw an exponentially larger amount of fear and darkness. Both in the visible and unseen worlds, there are people, beings, forces and sundry energies that are empowered and drawn to people who are negative and fearful. The fears of those people and the darkness they draw to them can rub off on you when you are in their presence, especially when jointly involved in a psychic activity.

The First Psychic Shield:

Visualize and encircle yourself with a protective dome of sparkling golden white light.

Look at the cover of this book for a moment. Similar to the golden white light radiating from the hand of the lady, preface your psychic and paranormal activities by first creating a sphere of shimmering, golden white light surrounding and protecting you. You are the master. Set the parameters of your protective dome of light that no darkness, person, being or entity that would harm you can pass its protective walls.

Inside your golden sphere of protective light you are safe. It moves with you as you walk or travel from place to place. You can create it in the morning when you awaken and empower it with your belief throughout the day. You can create another or reinforce the one from the morning just before you sleep to protect you at night. If you are preparing to conduct a specific psychic task you can strengthen it again. To those who have never experienced the unseen world this may seem like a silly game. But to those who have, the golden white sphere of light has proven to be a very effective shield.

The Second Psychic Shield:

***In situations where the threat is greater,
empower your golden light sphere with auric energy.***

Your aura is an astoundingly powerful force. Not only does it well up from the very essence of your soul, you have the ability through it, to call in all kinds of wonderful reinforcing and supporting energies from near and far beyond. Your aura can repel physical people as well as disembodied spirits, otherworldly entities and all forms of dark or negative energy.

Its ability to repel people is easily seen with any person whether they are psychically attuned or oblivious. Whenever anyone stands face to face to speak with another person, they only stand as close to them as is comfortable for both people. This distance differs from person to person and it is not related to whether they know them or not.

If you randomly met 10 unknown people and engaged them in conversation, with most you would be comfortable speaking to them while standing about 2 feet away. Some you could stand closer to and it would feel fine. While standing that close to others among the 10 would make both you and them feel uncomfortable.

Why? Because you are pressing against the space where they have unconsciously set their auric shield, and though unseen, it is a very firm wall. If you try to approach them closer, they will actually take a step back to maintain the distance they have unconsciously set for their safety and comfort zone. If their back is to a wall and they cannot back up they will step to the side. If they are in a corner and can neither back up or step aside, they will get unexpectedly agitated if you approach too close, like a scared dog trapped in a corner. Try it out at the next group gathering you attend. The results are reliably predictable.

Easiest Way To Focus Auric Energy

The easiest way to focus your auric energy is between your hands. This is something you can physically feel within a few seconds. Close your eyes, rub your hands together vigorously for a few seconds, then clap them soundly once. Then hold your hands, palms facing each other about 1 foot apart. Now slowly bring them closer together. You will feel a thickening of the space between your hands. Some people feel a tingling or a hot or cold sensation. You may feel all of those! When your hands are almost touching, move them slowly apart. Repeat this opening and closing motion multiple times. You will become more sensitive to the thickening, tingling, hot/cold physical feeling of your auric energy between your hands with every in and out movement.

Create a Programmable Auric Sphere of Power (ASP)

The concentration of auric energy between your hands can be shaped, molded and programmed to do a variety of tasks. Usually practitioners of the psychic arts call this a 'psi ball.' When applied to psychic defense, I prefer 'Auric Sphere of Power.' This abbreviates as ASP, which is the name for a family of highly venomous snakes including the deadly Egyptian Cobra. I like to envision empowering my golden white sphere of light with focused, intentioned auric energy. The subsequent ASP that reinforces and strengthens my golden sphere protects me from all harm or negativity, like a circle of golden Egyptian Cobras.

Types of ASPs

Decide what type of ASP you are going to create. These fall into 3 categories:
  a. **Mirror ASP:** A mirror ASP simply reflects back whatever harmful energy is trying to pass through your golden sphere. For the intruder, this can be a fairly benign and painless defense. Or, it can be painful. It depends upon the type of intrusion.

Psychic Self-Defense

If your intention was to keep certain people away, such as those with negative attitudes, the result would be their negativity would bounce back at them. If they were intending to speak with criticism toward you, or about someone else, they would instead find they suddenly became mired in critical thoughts of themselves.

If someone were actually sending a psychic attack of any kind against you, a Mirror ASP would return the energy to the sender and hit them with whatever pain they were intending to cause you.

Mirror ASP's get stronger as needed when they are attacked. Because it is directly tied to your aura and energies beyond that it coalesced, the more it is attacked, the more energy it calls to the defense. As some of that energy is from universal sources, it is boundless and limitless. If you are protected by a Mirror ASP and someone is intentionally trying to hurt you with any type of psychic energy, they can become completely exhausted, even to the point of illness, by their fruitless efforts. Once the attack ceases, the Mirror ASP will soon return to a minimal, almost unnoticeable level of basic defense energy.

If you use a Mirror ASP, it is important when you construct and shape it between your hands that you command that any energies repelled are always returned to the sender. If you leave this crucial little bit out, the Mirror ASP will reflect the energy randomly. You will be protected, but other innocent people nearby may be hit and hurt by the reflection.

Mirror ASP's are my favorite. I have no desire to hurt another person or any other thing that might be trying to hurt me. But if they are injured by their own dark intent, simply because I chose to not be a victim and to protect myself...so be it.

b. Absorb ASP: If you really want to be nice to those dark forces that are not trying to be sweet to you, you can use an Absorb ASP. Negative psychic energies that hit the wall of your golden sphere are simply absorbed and neutralized. No harm to you, no harm to the attacking person or forces.

When you create your ASP between your hands, before you enlarge it into an protective sphere, remember to specify that it is an Absorb ASP if that is your intention.

I have found that using Absorb ASP's except for short durations when they are the best choice for specific challenges, can be stifling. When harmful energies hit the walls of an Absorb ASP, they are neutralized and absorbed into the shield. If you are being attacked over time by many dark energies, the weight of the energy being retained by the Absorb ASP can become heavy and burdensome, interfering with your thoughts and actions simply by it's 'too heavy to ignore' oppressive weight.

If you ever find this to be the case, reverse your construct. Using your hands, visualization and intent, pull in the Absorb ASP until it is once again contained within the space between your two hands. Vocally thank it for its good service, then release it and dissipate it.

If you are still in need, simply create another Absorb ASP that will not yet be oppressive because it holds excessive energy from attacks.

c. **Transmute ASP:** Energy cannot be destroyed, but it can be changed into another form that is unusable for its intended purpose. This is exactly what a Transmute ASP does. The results can be unexpected and quite consequential, which is why this type should only be attempted and utilized by experienced practitioners who are well versed in ASP control.

The construction of the ASP is similar to the Mirror and the Absorb, except your intention, which you vocalize, is to create a Transmute ASP. Harmful energy directed at you will not be reflected or absorbed, but instead changed into a form of energy that cannot negatively affect or harm you.

d. **Multilayered ASP:** I mention this type of ASP, even though constructing it will be beyond the abilities of all but those most experienced in use of their psychic and paranormal powers. This is really a type of punishment ASP. If someone or something has really been bothering you with ceaseless attacks of negative or dark energy and they haven't been deterred by their lack of success, it may be time to use a Multilayer ASP in your defense. It's like having a mosquito continuing to buzz and try to bite you despite all the benign defenses you have presented. When a mosquito seems to not care that you are sending it love, seems to be unaffected by all your golden light, and still lands on you and lowers it proboscis to suck your blood, it's time for a fatal swat! It is similar when you reach a point of frustration at continuing to be attacked despite your more benign efforts to protect yourself.

If you are tempted to use a Multilayer ASP, that means you have already tried Absorb and Mirror ASP's, and maybe a Transmute ASP. While they have protected you, they have failed to stop the attacks.

The most effective Multilayer ASP is to combine a Mirror with a Transmute. When dark psychic energy is hurled at you the Mirror will reflect it back to the sender. Remember however, that because it is couples with a Transmute, it will return in a different form, that may affect the sender in unknowable, uncontrollable, significant and consequential ways. Because of this, it is vitally important that you insure that the energy returns only to the sender and can in no way accidentally be off course and injure anyone else. State this clearly when you create the Multilayered ASP.

Though you can try to control and set the type of energy that the original energy will transmute into, there is no way to do this with a certain degree of success. There is so much even the most advanced practitioners do not know. When energies transmute from one form into another, they do it based upon their own natural laws, numerous. It's like planting what you think is an orange seed, only to see a grape tree appear. Or, even worse, a thorn bush.

When you are dealing with people, there are some who actually thrive on negativity. If they send you negative energy and it bothers and affects you, knowing that feeds them and they are happier. If you create a mirror shield that reflects the negative energy back to them, it just replenishes their supply and once again they are happy. However, if you use a Mirror and a Transmute to send altered energy back to them, it may affect them or change them in ways neither of you may want. They may go from an overbearing negative @&)*&% to a useless wimpy personality. The consequences of energy transformation can be that severe!

How to Create an ASP

1. Begin by forming the auric ball of power between your hands as previously described.

2. Sit in a chair with a small table between your legs, or the corner of a larger table that comes about to knee height or a bit taller. If you are creating a mirror ASP, place a hand mirror 6-12 inches in diameter on the table. If you are creating an Absorb ASP, place a large natural sponge on the table instead of the mirror. If you are creating a Transmute ASP, place two dissimilar objects on the table such as a coin and a flower. If you are creating a Multilayered ASP, place the corresponding items representing the ASP on the table.

3. Form your auric ball of power between your hands while looking down at the representative objects just below your hands. Whatever it is you need your ASP for, put that intention into the energy sphere between your hands.

4. State aloud, "I am forming a (type of ASP) to (fill in specifically the purpose of the ASP.)

5. Continue by saying, "I form this (type of ASP) with my own auric energy. I am connected to it and it to me."

6. Continue by saying, "I call upon all the energies of might and light to further empower this (type of ASP) to reflect away all (fill in specifically the purpose of the ASP.) As you say this look upward. See in your mind or with your psychic eyes a brilliant, golden white light beaming down upon you in a massive sparkling column of light from far in the heavens above. Allow the light to enter you and fill every cell of your body with its power. Visualize your body glowing and radiating the golden white light from every pore. Feel the energy of the light swirling inside of you. Concentrate it within your body. Then send it with your mental command and intent down your arms, shooting out the palms of your hands and immensely empowering your ASP.

7. Now pull your hands apart and see and feel the ASP retaining its shape, but getting larger and larger until it reaches the size you want it to be. Determine how big you want your ASP to be and visualize, manipulate and command it to be so. This may be as small as the personal space near your body that moves with you as you walk or travel, to as large as your home. Or perhaps you are in a room or even a home with other people working together on a psychic project and you need the entire space protected.

8. Pull your hands apart as you expand the size of the ASP. Once it is the size of your outstretched arms, begin a series of pushes with your palms facing out, until you have pushed your ASP outward far enough that it is encompassing the area of protection you desire. I also always envision the outer perimeter wall of the ASP to be full of ghostly, white or golden cobras reared up, with their hoods spread, ready to protect me as needed.

9. See the space between you and the wall of the ASP completely filled with light. Now draw your own aura back close to your body and see the space between you and the walls of the ASP become normal transparent space. Your aura is now back close to you, but the walls of the Auric Sphere of Protection are still visible, scintillating golden white light and alive with the energy in which you and the universe endowed it. Your ASP is now complete and on duty.

SPECIAL NOTES:

1. The larger the size of the ASP, the more diffused its energy. The smaller the size, the more concentrated and potent its energy. If you need to pump up the power of your ASP for a room or house, add quartz crystals as described further below in the section on Demons.

2. You should spend about 5 minutes each day repeating steps 7-9 to recharge and revitalize your auric energy shield, especially if you know it has taken some blows of negativity. ASP's work best when they are not used for too long of time. The power of the energy field you create does diminish as time passes unless it is regularly being restrengthened.

3. You can choose to restrengthen and renew your golden ASP sphere periodically through focused intention, visualization and vocalized commands. Or, you can simply deconstruct it by using intent and visualization, along with inward movements of your hands and arms, to pull the energy sphere back until it is once again contained within the space between your hands. Once there, simply thank it for its service and dissipate it with an opening movement of your hands and your intent.

Psychic Self-Defense

Wards

ASPs are effective, active shields against all forms of negative or dark energy and should be in your standard psychic tool kit. But what about when you need something extra potent, whose positive energy will dissipate more slowly than an ASP sphere? A Ward is the answer. Think of 'ward off' or 'keep away' when you think about Wards. Wards are a noxious energy to anyone or anything you have created them to repel.

Wards are constructed the same way ASPs are made: with your intention, vocalization and formed between your hands. Unlike the general defense of an ASP, with their large golden sphere of protection, Wards keep their energy concentrated in a small area, or in a larger area but with a single defined purpose. Existing for a focused, singular purpose, their energy lasts a long time; easily for days and often for weeks, or even months, before it weakens and dissipates.

You can also construct Wards for the benefit of other people as long as you place them in a location around the other person where they are needed. A good example is spiders. If you or someone you were creating a Ward for, cringed at the thought of the annual winter migration of spiders from outside to inside the house as the weather turns cold, an anti-spider Ward would solve the problem. Just use your visualization and movements of your hands and arms to create and place the Ward in a centrally located part of a room to protect, such as a bedroom, and you'll have no unwanted spider visitors in that room as long as the energy of the Ward remains.

What are the Threats?

This is a comprehensive but not exhaustive list of many of the threats and pitfalls that can be experienced by all who venture into the psychic and paranormal world. They are grouped as 'low risk', 'medium risk' and 'high risk.' Remember, this is a listing of risk or threat to your physical, mental, or emotional well-being. There are additional low risk items that are not listed, that may temporarily discombobulate you and make it difficult or impossible to use your psychic abilities, but they are not usually dangers to your safety.

LOW RISK

Inexperience:

The first obstacle is simply inexperience. Often an inexperienced practitioner will be frightened by something they see, hear, or intuit psychically, simply because it was completely unlike anything in their prior experience. Strange and unusual doesn't make it bad or dangerous. The unknown is frequently frightening or disquieting, even in everyday life. If you are walking on a dark night and see a shadow flit by, it can cause a lot of anxiety. But as soon as you observe that it was caused by a swaying branch or something else identifiable and non-threatening, your anxiety and fear vanish.

It is the same when developing your psychic and paranormal abilities. On your journey of psychic/paranormal exploration you will encounter far more that is new to your experience than you do in your everyday life. In this regard, knowledge is truly power. The more you learn about those psychic and paranormal powers that you are interested in and drawn to, the less unpleasant surprises you will have. The more you know, the less you will misinterpret benign manifestations as threatening. The more you know, the more you will grow.

Mental and Emotional Garbage

As we go through life we all experience unpleasant and sometimes traumatic experiences that negatively affect us throughout the rest of our lives until we purge them. Think about it as taking out the mental and emotional trash. The longer you wait to take out the trash, the more it builds up and stinks up your life. Many people just cover the refuse of life up with an out-of-sight, out-of-mind attitude. But no matter how much you bury the memories, they are still there putrefying inside of you until you cleanse yourself of them. You may think the refuse is gone, until something triggers the memory and all of the bad thoughts and painful emotions come rushing back. You have to literally take out and remove the trash if you want to insure it doesn't keep returning from time to time to sink you into a morass. You cannot allow mental and emotional garbage to remain active within the house that is your life and expect it not to affect the quality of your life; especially if you continue to just add more garbage to the pile and never act to remove it.

Every negative experience you have ever had was a life lesson. But once it has been experienced and the lesson learned, it becomes refuse to remove or energetically neutralize. A more agreeable way to think of the process is as emotional and mental cleansing. From the person you didn't even know that vented their anger on you, to the date that stood you up, to the grief you suffered at the loss of a loved one from separation or death, to the big regret that keeps causing you grief, to the over demanding boss or the demeaning spouse, from a dog bite to a really bad Monday morning, all of us have negative experiences on a regular basis. The negative mental memories and the emotional residue left behind by these experiences are the garbage that must be purged or neutralized on a regular basis, until doing so becomes an unconscious good habit of mental and emotional housecleaning.

This is not simply for your own mental and emotional well-being. Your ability to mount stout psychic defenses is weakened if you are in an upset state mentally or emotionally. This is true even for subconscious thoughts and emotions that you have buried inside and outwardly forgotten about. If they haven't been negated, then they are still percolating inside and insidiously hindering you. Any negative thoughts or feelings you are experiencing or have experienced and buried inside are your enemies. Hatred, jealousy, anger, frustration, regret, or any other emotional pain or mental stress, not only weakens your psychic defenses, it also inhibits all of your psychic abilities. Plus they are like an advertising sign, inviting negative energies and entities to come and bother you or worse. **Sound, clear psychic power requires a peaceful spirit, heart and mind.**

How To Purge Negativity

1. Take the stance that you will not allow negative energy to reside within your heart, mind or spirit. Be vigorous in not speaking negatively yourself and purging negativity when you realize it is festering inside of you.
2. If a negative thought or emotion wells up, allow yourself to vent it out. If you are mad at yourself, someone else, or a situation, don't just push it down and try to forget about it. Look at the wall and imagine you are speaking to the person or the situation, or yourself. Don't hold back your words or emotions and tell them why you are upset.
3. It is absolutely not necessary in most cases to confront the person or situation, unless there is an issue that can only be resolved by talking directly. In most cases, confrontation will only lead to additional anger and upset. Purging your anger, hurt, loss and upset to the impassive wall is very therapeutic and usually more than adequate.
4. After the wall purge go outside and find a rock that will fit inside your curled hand. Hold the rock in your hand and looking at it say, "Rock, into you I send all of my (anger, upset, hurt feelings, etc.)" Then throw it far from you and shout "Begone!" And so it shall be. If negativity return about something else, simply repeat the procedure until it is gone forever.

A Banishing Spell/Prayer

Some people are afraid to use any type of spell or incantation, but you shouldn't be as long as it is for a purpose of light. In fact, I find spells to be like focused prayers. To create a spell that rhymes and makes sense requires some thought and effort. Here's one you can use or modify that incorporates getting rid of your garbage utilizing a rock. *Concisely fill in the blank with as few words as possible describing the particular trash issue. Such as:*

"Dark energy of my work", or dark energy of my relationship with_____", or "dark energy of my memory of _____."

Dark energy of _____ lurking about like a disease

begone forever, bring no more unease.

The essence of feeling, which aches in my heart as if stabbed by a thorn,

(*or* The essence of thought, which aches in my head as if stabbed by a thorn,)

I forever cast away sealed within this rock, which none shall mourn.

This I command, this I decree,

Now and forever, so let it be.

Psychic Overload:

As you use your psychic abilities more and more, it is like finding yourself on a new planet where everything is different from what you have known and are accustomed to in your life. There are a great many fresh sensations and new situations that you must ponder to understand. Of course you're anxious and insatiable to learn and experience more and more. It's exciting, It's fulfilling. It's wonderful! But it can also knock you down suddenly and drain all of your energy if you take in and experience too much too fast. Just like any muscle, you need to strengthen your psychic abilities by regular and ever increasing use, while also being wise not to overdo it.

This is true not just for the novice, but even for very practiced and experienced individuals. All of us can experience a total fatigue of our physical body and mental and emotional well-being if we take on too much psychic exercise in too short of a time. The more psychically adept you become, the more psychic input you will begin to receive unbidden from many sources. Just like you have learned to tune out many of the sensory inputs received by your physical senses so you are not overwhelmed by everything you see, hear, and smell, you also have to acquire the ability to filter out psychic input that you have not sought. This is especially true while you are consciously aware and awake.

Think of yourself as a bottle. Every psychic input you receive pours psychic energy into your bottle. The more you get, the bigger your bottle becomes. That's great, it shows you are growing. But if too much psychic energy pours into you faster than your bottle can grow, the psychic energy spills out causing you to have psychic overload.

Psychic overload is easy to defend against. It's not like it's a poltergeist trying to harm you. At the beginning of your day, or during the day if you suddenly seem to be getting a lot of unsolicited psychic energy, simply create a Mirror ASP close to your body to reflect any undesired psychic energy back to where it came from.

Don't let the ease of dealing with this challenge lessen its importance. Insuring you are never psychically overloaded, keeps your physical body energetic, your emotional level grounded, your mental abilities clear and most importantly leaves you plenty of room in your psychic bottle to receive and work with the psychic energies that you choose.

Empathetic Overload

Some psychics cultivate the gift of psychic empathy. Through conscious or subconscious interaction of their auric field with other peoples, and a desire and focus to understand their emotions, Empaths are able to feel in their heart, exactly what is being felt in the heart of the person they are tuning into.

If the person is happy or euphoric, then it's a natural high for the Empath as well. But if the person is traumatized, fearful, despairing, or experiencing any negative emotion, their feeling will also weigh heavily on the Empath as it sinks into their own heart.

In this case, you cannot use a Mirror ASP, because that would be counterproductive to being open and receptive of another persons feelings. However, an Absorb ASP is very useful for Empaths. The Absorb ASP will take in the emotional energy radiating from the other person. Because the ASP is withing the space of the Empath's aura, they will be able to sense the emotions caught up in the shield, if they choose. They will still thoroughly know the feelings of the other person, while safely being shielded from having any negative energy entering into their own inner core.

Dismissive Opinions

Have you ever been feeling great, happy about what you are doing or is happening in your life, excited to share what's exciting you with friends and family, only to have them shoot down your high flying balloon with negative comments and derisive opinions? Thus is the life of the psychic and paranormal practitioner living in a world of mundane people who do not understand anything about you, and are usually afraid of what they don't understand. Classic Harry Potter and the Muggles, only this is real life.

Even well intentioned and loving family members can dampen your enthusiasm and make you question your actions. Because they are your family and you love them and they love you, any negative comments, or caustic or even mild unsolicited negative opinions they give about your psychic explorations, carry more weight than those of other people.

This type of negative energy can be quite disruptive and greatly inhibit your ability to utilize your psychic powers. At the least, they sour your mood and make you unable to connect to your psychic source. At worst, they can completely derail you and make you wonder if you just want to get off the psychic train at the next station for good.

Luckily this is another easy challenge to solve. You simply need to decide if a Mirror ASP or an Absorb ASP would be most appropriate. If you are dealing with family or close friends, an Absorb ASP would be most appropriate. Negative energy they willingly or unknowingly hurl at you will simply be absorbed by the shield. It will not affect you in any way. You'll be able to honor their opinion, without having your own mood or thoughts changed in the least. Nor will there be any consequences for them. You love them and don't want them to feel bad either. With an Absorb ASP, they will not. You two will simply be having a conversation with differing opinions without either swaying the others opinion, but also without either being hurt in any way.

If you are dealing with people who you feel are maliciously trying to hurt you by the negative comments they are making, especially if they are making their comments around other people trying to embarrass you, a Mirror ASP is more appropriate. It will bounce back the negative energy they were sending you right back upon them. The shoes they were hoping to make you wear they will find on their own feet instead. If you are in a group of people, the person making negative comments at you will instead find the others upset or making fun of them for their comments.

Negative Energy People

Occasionally you will run into nice people, who despite saying or doing nothing of a negative nature, still drain you of energy and affect your mood negatively. Often times they know they have that affect on people and they feel hopeless. They want friends, they want acceptance, they have no desire to hurt anyone, they want to be part of the group, but they realize something undefinable about them drives people away.

When you encounter people like this, in good conscience you should not abandon them and simply run away as everyone else has done. First protect yourself with an Absorb ASP, then, if they know they have a problem and are willing to accept help, offer to use your gifts to help them. It will be a great blessing and they will be forever grateful.

The root of problems like this, though they may stem from a variety of life incidents, ultimately are reflected in a very out-of-balance auric field. The first step will have a huge and immediate affect. Simply instruct the person how to ground and balance their 7 major energy centers. It works for you too!

To Ground:

1. Stand outside with your bare feet on green grass. If it is winter and the ground is too cold or covered with snow, stand indoors on a natural wood or stone floor, on the lowest level of a home or building.
2. Tilt your head back and raise your face to the sky. Lift your arms up high above your head with palms facing up.
3. Envision a beam of energy flowing from the universe through you, down into the ground.
4. Grab hold of the beam of energy and pull it slowly down through your body with your hands and bending over push it through your legs, out your feet and deep into the earth.
5. Visualize the energy beam now coming from the center of the earth running through your body from your feet, swirling all around inside of you, then looping back into the earth. You are now firmly grounded in an Earth Loop. You are also still connected to the universal energies in the heavens above, should you wish to call upon them.
6. Repeat 2-3 more times if needed. When you have succeeded you will feel calm, peaceful, grounded and not easily disturbed.

To Balance The Energy Centers:

In traditional eastern philosophy the energy centers are called 'Chakras.' I use the Celestine Light energy system fo greater accuracy. In Celestine Light the energy centers are called 'Root Ki.'

Psychic Self-Defense

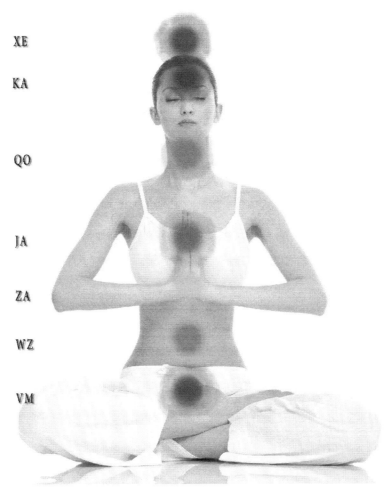

1. Take a look at the illustration to locate the energy centers.
2. In the following order visualize an omnidirectional, swirling sphere of energy at each location. Visualize one energy center at a time and go through this visualization for each one.

   a. See the energy sphere spinning omnidirectionally.

   b. Visualize it slowing down

   c. Visualize it speeding up

   d. Visualize it expanding beyond your body.

   e. Visualize it contracting down to a sphere the size of a tennis ball

   f. Visualize it returning to normal size, a little smaller than the width of the body at the spot it is located.

    g. Visualize it returning to a normal omnidirectional spin and speed.

    h. Proceed to the next energy center and repeat.

Energy Dampening Locations

Certain physical locations are full of negative energy. For reasons that may remain unknown to you, they will dampen your energy and mood very quickly when you are at one of these locations. Some of the sources of the problem include: electromagnetic radiation from overhead power lines, excessive gravitational fields from iron concentration in the earth, site of death, especially massive death such as battlefields and the location of a negative energy vortex.

In a home or building you can also experience Energy Dampening spots. The structure may have been built over a burial ground, battleground, or some other negative event that occurred in the past. Electromagnetic sources from computers to many modern appliances are also common sources of negative disruptions of your energy inside a building.

Certain locations, normally very specific spots, also can have high concentrations of naturally occurring psychic energy that a sensitive person will pick up on right away. But non-sensitive people will be affected as well. These locations are more often positive energy spots rather than negative. But the dampening effect might still be felt because the energy at these locations is so strong and concentrated, it simply overloads you. It can discombobulate your thoughts and emotions, as well as your physical balance for reasons that will seem perplexing unless you identify what is causing the psychic concentration.

If it is a positive energy it will usually be from a natural source source such as a concentration of quartz crystals or other energetic minerals, or from a Positive Energy Vortex. I have been to numerous positive vortexes, including the well known ones in Sedona, Arizona and the more numerous and powerful ones in Northern California and Southern Oregon. Some of the latter emit such intense energy fields that it is sometimes difficult to stand up without swaying with the movement of the energy and losing your balance.

At locations such as Stonehenge, and other unique or sacred sites created by man, you can also experience psychic energy concentrations of sufficient intensity to disrupt you. The geometric shape of structures is often a major contributor, if not sole reason, it is able to act as a psychic energy concentrator. Some locations have positive energy and others concentrate and emit negative energy.

If you are in a known area of concentrated psychic energy, you will know after your first visit whether you can handle it or not. If you do not have any discombobulation, loss of balance, queasy stomach, dry lips, sudden overly emotional reactions, or other typical manifestations, then you should just enjoy the extra energy and test some of your abilities, which should be enhanced at any of the positive localities.

If the location emits a strong negative energy, even if you feel you are not affected, it would be wise to protect yourself with either a Mirror or Absorb ASP, whichever you feel would be most effective. When you are surrounded by negative energy, regardless of its source, it does wear on you until it wears you down. It is always a good idea to protect yourself and neutralize the threat. Even a mighty, towering oak can be felled by nonstop chipping at its trunk.

MEDIUM RISK

Entities & Blobs

There's quite a numerous assortment of lower energy level entities that abound around us often referred to as 'entities' and 'blobs.' The terms are generally used synonymously, with entities sometimes given the nod as being as having a bit of consciousness, while the blobs just act instinctually without thought. Various religions have belief systems to account for them. They are not disembodied spirits. They have never had a body and do not have enough Soul Essence energy to exist in the body of even a primitive animal. Some are nothing more than vague, indistinct blobs of very faint negative energy. You can read a detailed description of these interesting energy creatures in the **Oracles of Celestine Light: Vivus**, chapters 94-98.

They cannot actively hurt you, but they are a drain on your energy and can end up causing you to hurt yourself or others. If you get enough of them attached to your auric field it can disrupt your energy sufficiently to have consequences. A little infestation will cause you to have a bad mood and be short tempered for no reason. A larger infestation may cause you to have a bout of depression and make bad choices regarding your own body, such as drug or alcohol use. A still larger infestation can cause your brain to disengage from rational thought and you can end up doing some really crazy things from having a sex orgy with strangers, to walking naked through town, to taking outrageous actions at work that get you fired.

A good deal of mental illness stems from an infestation of entities. Certainly removal of the entities by someone adept in that ability can be extremely helpful.

The best defense is simply to avoid situations and locations where entities and blobs are typically found as much as is possible. Entities like dark places, but not completely dark. Any places where people have woes, or are witnessing other people with woes is a likely hot spot. Mental hospitals, taverns, horror shows at movie theaters, regular hospitals, graveyards, anywhere human suffering is depicted or taking place, you'll find entities.

If you must visit or work in one of the places like these, a Mirror ASP is essential. If you are going to be watching a movie or even a TV show with a lot of violence or dark themes, protect yourself with a Mirror ASP and drink 1/2 cup of salt water prior to viewing the show. Avoidance is even better.

Salt Water

As explained further below in the description of Disembodied Spirits, salt is an anathema to them. It is like mosquito repellant for ghosts, entities and demons. Drinking a ½ cup of salt water is a quick way to rid your body of any other-wordly infestations, and to prevent any new

Unleash Your Psychic Powers

ones while you are watching a dark show or visiting a location where you might encounter the beasties. *However, do not drink more than ½ cup as you can get sick from drinking salt water. And the effects of ½ cup will usually only last for about 2 hours of protection.*

Scenes of Death & Destruction

If you have any type of psychic vision such as clairvoyance or precognition, you may sometimes see horrific scenes of misery, death and destruction. Once you are adept with these psychic gifts your visions will be exceptionally vivid. It will almost seem as if you are living within the scene. Obviously, living through hell on a regular basis can end up haunting your conscious thoughts. Both your everyday life and your psychic time can be seriously impeded if you cannot get horrible images and memories out of your mind.

I had this problem for years with one incident. Whenever something came up that reminded me of the serial killer Ted Bundy murdering my friend Georgeann, the scenes of her abduction that I had witnessed a couple of years before in a precognitive dream, would keep replaying over and over in my mind. My work days would become very unproductive and my sleep elusive as I couldn't get those awful images out of my mind. Mentally, I understood that it was ridiculous to still be enmeshed in emotional feelings about an event that happened in 1974, with the murderer executed for his crimes in 1989, and that I had no way of knowing would actually occur when I had the precognitive vision. There was never a problem 99.9% of the time when I didn't think about the events. But when something would come up to remind me...I would end up with a discombobulated day and night.

I tried numerous methods to avoid the haunting thoughts whenever they returned, but to no avail. Finally, after seeing it in a vision, I found something that worked wonderful for me. I had to search a bit to find the components, but the combination of a sizable piece of turquoise with a black tourmaline crystal was amazingly effective at negating any discombobulating thoughts or emotional connection to the events. The memories were still there, they just no longer affected me. I ended up calling the Black tourmaline/turquoise combination a *'Negative Energy Converter.'*

The black tourmaline absorbs the negative energy of the memory and the blue turquoise cultivates peaceful, calm feelings. This allows the memory to be recalled without inflicting mental or emotional

Negative Energy Converter

disruption. All that was necessary to invoke this power was to hold or have nearby, the tourmaline and turquoise Negative Energy Converter.

Another method I have not personally tried, but have had very good reports about from others is to use EFT Tapping to negate the bad memories. Here's a Youtube video specifically teaching how to use tapping for that purpose.

Energy Vampires, Regretful

A particularly unfortunate individual is a regretful Energy Vampire. They made a choice before they came into this life to increase their Soul Essence energy by stealing it from others rather than creating it by their own efforts toward personal growth and expansion. However, they do not remember this choice and are often depressed from not understanding why they are they way they are, and why they cannot change their nature, even though they sometimes try. Like their cousins the predator Energy Vampires, they are invigorated by personal confrontation and misery in others. But unlike the predator vampires, they often realize their behavior is wrong and wish it could be otherwise, not realizing this is their self-inflicted curse.

Where other people seek harmonious and peaceful relations, Energy Vampires need confrontation, turmoil and upset. The negative energy produced in upsetting situations is something they thrive on, to the point that it feeds them energetically by taking Soul Essence energy from the person they are in confrontation with. Because their precious Soul Energy essence is being forcefully sucked out them, of course the victim feels completely drained energetically and emotionally, while most often also ending up mentally discombobulated from the confrontation.

Most regretful Energy Vampires have a conscience and oftentimes feel a tiny bit of sorrow for their angry actions. They will often try to make amends by later being very nice and sweet. They know it is counterproductive to good relations to have verbally and emotionally violent confrontations. Yet, despite their attempts to maintain life and relationships on an even keel, things always turn sour. As much as they might desire it to be otherwise, they have a primal need for confrontation and the energy it brings them.

Energy vampires are always a challenge to deal with. Because you are struggling with their base energy makeup, one they made by choice before they came into this life, to be the template of their life, you will not change them; no more than you would be able to change the fundamental nature of a vampire that fed on human blood. A blood vampire might feel bad about drinking human blood, they might even rob a blood bank as an alternative to sucking it out of their victims; but their fundamental design would still require them to drink blood. It is the same for Energy Vampires, except through confrontation and discord they suck energy from the Soul Essence of their victims.

Please let me reiterate and make that perfectly clear. ***You cannot change the nature of an Energy Vampire***. It would be like trying to change the race of a person into a different one. Even if the Energy Vampire regrets the damage they may cause in confrontations, even if they swear they will never do it again, they sadly cannot help themselves. They will do it again. And like an addict, over time they will need to escalate the intensity of the confrontations, the mental, emotional and verbal abuse, in order to receive the needed level of energetic satisfaction.

Your best defense against any type of Energy Vampire is to cut them out of your life and avoid them entirely; no personal meetings, phone calls, texts or anything. Unfortunately, when you are dealing with family members, especially spouses or ex-spouses, total avoidance is not always possible.

If you must have meetings with an Energy Vampire, protect yourself with a powerful Mirror ASP. This will allow you to remain calm within the storm and not personally feed the confrontational fires. You still need to restrain yourself from responding. You can negate your own mirror shield if you choose to react and allow yourself to be drawn into a confrontation with the vampire. If you remain calm, the angry, negative energy hurled at you by the Energy Vampire will bounce back at them. A normal person would be stopped in their tracks by the bounce back; but the Energy Vampire will just feed on their own negative energy. It won't slow them down, but after a bit they usually become satiated, awash in their own energy and wind the confrontation down. If at any point in the confrontation you can physically get up and leave, you should do so; the earlier the better.

The only reason an regretful Energy Vampire is categorized as a medium risk rather than a high one, is that they do understand they are causing needless problems and with the best of intentions, they often make sincere efforts to limit or eliminate their confrontations. However, their confrontational nature will always return.

An Aura Note About Vampires
Energy Vampires are easy to identify before you have any need to interact with them once you are competent at viewing people's aura. The aura of a non-vampire will always flow with some harmony in its movement. Even if they are sick or upset, their aura will still move harmoniously, albeit with disruptions in the energy field over their areas of weakness. There will also be a distinct directional flow to the energy as it circulates through the the three pairs of Alpha-Omega Gateways in the body – the top of the head, soles of the feet, and palms of the hands. It is startling to look at an Energy Vampire's aura because their auric energy field jerks erratically, and the flow of their energy through the Alpha-Omega Gateways is exactly opposite of all other people!

HIGH RISK

Disembodied Spirits & Haunted Buildings and Localities
Ghosts, also known as disembodied spirits, are the coherent energy remnants of people that

have died. They have left behind a cognizant quantity of their Soul Essence energy instead of taking it all with them into the next life. Sometimes, all of their Soul Essence energy may remain behind as they never moved on to the next life at all! Over time the ghostly energy remnant will fade and eventually disappear completely. Without a physical body to contain it, the Soul Essence energy cannot remain forever on the physical plane; it is inexorably drawn to a realm beyond. But if it was a strong deposit of energy to begin with, the dissipation can take hundreds of years unless the ghost resolves their issues or realizes it is fruitless to cling to what they can never again have.

Most importantly as it relates to interactions with living people, is that disembodied spirits still have use of their mind and memory. The degree of mental clarity will vary depending upon the strength of their remnant energy that remained behind. This enables them to make conscious choices and actions, unlike mostly mindless entities and completely mindless blobs that are merely parasitically drawn to a person's energy.

Usually disembodied spirits are physically tied to a specific location by the energy of that spot that resonates enough with them to allow them to remain. If something tragic occurred to them and they haven't released the pain, they will still be able to maintain their energy at that location. If they had an obsessive fixation on a house or place, such as their own home, their energy can remain behind and manifest itself in various ways, until they no longer cling to that which is beyond their reach. If they had a very great love for someone, their energy can remain and they can manifest their energy in the rooms they most frequented together with their love.

With haunted houses or locations there may be an assortment of disembodied beings present from simple blobs, to slightly conscious entities, to fully aware spirits of the deceased, to sophisticated demons. If a location is hospitable to one type, it will usually be infested with others as well.

Most disembodied spirits do not have malevolent intent. Many may have positive purposes and actually be aids in keeping out negative spirits and influences and useful to you in multiple ways. How you feel about a spirit, welcoming and curious, or anxious and uncertain, are your auras way of telling you whether they are good spirits to keep around, or bad spirits to be rid of.

By definition, a disembodied spirit (ghost) has no physical substance. Nevertheless, they can affect physical objects in direct correlation to how strong their auric energy is that remains and how practiced they are in using it. These movements are caused by exerting telekinetic force, and obviously not by physically touching objects. This was depicted well in the movie 'Ghost.'

A weak effort would be to move an object a slight, but noticeable distance out of place, such as removing a book from a bookcase and letting it fall directly below on the floor. A greater effort would be aiming the book for a specific person or target as it is propelled out of the bookcase. A malevolent spirit may try to psychically harm someone by dropping objects on their head or putting them in spots where the living person might trip and take a dangerous fall.

In addition to possible physical threats, if you are in a building haunted by a spirit, especially one manifesting the movement of physical objects or creating spooky, inexplicable sounds, you can become mentally and emotionally distressed. This in turn is likely to affect your ability to call upon and use your psychic gifts.

An Absorb ASP coupled with a Transform ASP is quite effective for dealing with the malevolent actions of most spirits. Any negative energy sent your way is absorbed into the shield. As it is a shield of light attached to your aura, as long as your aura is strong, the darkness in the energy is changed to light. This can become quiet frustrating for disembodied spirits as you are able to simply ignore and be unflustered by anything they do.

Exorcising a building: Occasionally, if there is a really malevolent, powerful spirit involved, you may need to exorcise them from the building. This is not the same procedure as exorcising a person who is possessed by something evil. But the effect is the same - the spirit or spirits will be gone.

There are multiple methods, most based upon one religion or another, to exorcise spirits from homes and other buildings. If the spirit was a follower of a particular religion while they were alive, that religion's exorcism procedures will likely work to rid the building of the spirit. However, as it is unlikely that you will know which religion the spirit followed in life, religious based exorcisms only have sporadic success. The exception would be if you were in a country or neighborhood where nearly the entire population followed the same religion, such as all Jewish or all Catholic. Then it is far more likely the exorcism procedures of the religion matching the population would work.

A very ancient method that works 98% of the time and on spirits of all religious persuasions, including those with no religion, or those that worship evil, is to surround them with a barrier of natural salt leaving open one escape route. Threaten to forever close the escape route and you'll see a mad rush to get out of the house by every spirit in it; except for the 2% that are either too ornery, or too vacant in their mind to care.

Why salt works so well is open to debate. I believe that because pure salt is a natural substance of the Earth, it is very grounded to the planet. It exerts a powerful magnetic auric force upon spirits that are no longer of this world, binding them to the planet. Though they may have haunted a place for centuries, the thought of never being able to leave is incredibly frightening to them.

Salt also easily combines with other substances. It somehow interferes with the auric fields of all types of disembodied beings and energies from simple blobs, to entities, to ghosts to demons. Salt is a threat to their very existence. It is a powerful counter against them, and has been used for this purpose since the dawn of recorded history by many, many cultures.

The Procedure Is Thus

Obtain several pounds of natural sea salt or pink Himalayan salt. The Himalayan salt seems to be effective 98% of the time and sea salt about 95%. Determine the exact area within a building that the spirit moves about. Sometimes this will be a single room. Other times several locations may be involved. If you are unsure or if the entire building is haunted, treat the whole building.

Pour an uninterrupted line of salt completely around the perimeter of the building or whatever room or rooms you have deduced need exorcism. As you are pouring speak out loud to the spirit or spirits. Tell them you are encircling them with salt and that once the circle is completed they will be forever bound to that building or room. Tell them you are going further and that every room will also have a bowl of salt in it, creating a permeating energy that will forever be heavy and burdensome, perhaps even caustic to them.

Tell them you mean them no harm and invite them to leave several times while you are spreading the salt. When you have completely encircled the area you are exorcising except for a small strip the width of a doorway, tell them in a loud voice that this is their last chance. You are about to bind them forever to earth and forever to this exact spot on earth. They will never be free again.

Tell them they have 10 seconds to leave or condemn themselves to forever be bound. The choice is theirs. Immediately, begin a countdown 10, 9, 8, 7, … before you finish you will feel a rush of air as all the spirits in the exorcised location hastily flee before it is too late and they are forever bound in place. Even the blobs, which would have not understood a single word you spoke, will flee the aurically caustic encirclement of salt.

Technically, the salt perimeter will not work with every type of disembodied beastie, particularly demons. But most don't know whether it will or will not do what you are claiming - to bind them in place. The fact that salt is an irritant to them at least, and caustic at worst, lends credibility to your threat. It seems the fear of the possibility of being bound is enough to motivate virtually all of them to make a hasty and permanent exit.

If you are worried about future hauntings, leave the perimeter of salt in place with just the one open space the width of a door. Any spirits contemplating even visiting, will change their mind when they see it would only take a few seconds to bind them forever in place.

Though I gave this as a description for exorcising a room, house, or building of ghosts, it works equally well for all types of lower disembodied beasties such as blobs and entities. It will even work for some demons.

Alien Presence

I've never had a face-to-face alien encounter, but I know and have helped people that have. I have no doubt aliens from other worlds can and do visit our planet. On multiple occasions on trips far into the wilderness, away from all city lights and all trappings of man, I have seen the lights of UFO's close up, flying in places no flying ships or lights should or could be.

In 1999, observations with the Hubble Space Telescope led to a conservative estimate that there were at least 125 billion galaxies in the universe. Scientists further estimate that there are at least 10 trillion planets just in our own mid-size Milky Way galaxy. Multiplying it out, 10 trillion planets x 125 billion galaxies, is a very, very, very, big number of potential worlds full of life.

Just from a logical standpoint, it is the height of ego gone wild to assert that in a universe of billions of galaxies, each containing trillions of planets, that our Earth is the only one with intelligent life. Can anyone really make that assertion with a straight face? Just within our own galaxy the Earth is nothing more than a tiny spec of dust in relation to the size of the galaxy. Then our galaxy is nothing but a tiny spec of dust in relation to the size of the universe. Is there anyone that honestly believes that our tiny speck of dust residing within another tiny speck of dust, is the only place in the unlimited vastness of the universe with intelligent life?

Given that any reasonable person would agree that the universe is probably full of intelligent life, the next question is how do we stack up on the intelligence and civilization scale? Geologically, our planet Earth has been dated to have existed for about 4.5 billion years. Anthropologists have determined that modern humans have been running around on the planet for a mere 65,000 years. The universe itself is dated by astrophysicists to be about 14.5 billion years old. That means for 10 billion years before our planet earth was even born, other planets had the opportunity to form, be populated by intelligent life, and have billions of years of evolution to progress before modern humans were even waking up in caves. So yes, I believe in aliens from other planets and I'm sure there are many that are as far advanced beyond us as we are beyond chimpanzees.

I don't know what motivates aliens. By their very nature they are…alien, and at this point, unfathomable. But abductions, implants, and other intrusive actions blamed on alien visitors, have happened with sufficient detail, related by enough traumatized people, all who pass lie detector tests, to make me a believer.

I had one particular friend that was being terrorized at night by what she believed to be alien visitors. She would wake up startled in the middle of the night and see beings with alien faces and thin bodies standing next to her bed. Within a second or two of awakening they would vanish. Her great fear was what would happen, or already had, when she didn't awaken.

She asked me for help. After inquiring to a higher, more knowledgeable source, I was told about a combination of minerals that made an effective alien alarm. The basic mineral is raw carborundum (Silicon carbide).

It occurs very rarely in nature as the mineral moissanite. Usually it is a man-made substance, typically ground into fine pieces to make grinding wheels, ceramics and other uninteresting commercial uses. But in its raw state, it is a brilliantly hued, multi-faced crystalline substance. It has a harmonious interaction with your auric field and a strong reaction to non-human auras. When the carborundum is at your bedside within your auric sphere, if anything with a non-human aura, from an alien to a demon, passes thru the outside edge of your auric field, which is about 3 feet from you while you are sleeping, you will immediately be awakened from the energy disruption. If you lay a clear quartz sphere or pyramid on top of the piece of carborundum, it will extend its effective warning range about 3 times the usual distance from your body.

Psychic Self-Defense

Carborundum

Demons

Are demons real or just a fanciful construct of various religions? If they are real, where do they come from? These are questions I am asked from time to time, especially by people who profess no religion and consider demons, like gods, to just be religious myths.

Having come face to face with demons and fought them head on, I can assure you they are real and nothing to be trifled with. They may be big or small, but their capabilities are large compared to any other type of disembodied being. Most are not visible to your physical eyes. They often have powerful telekinetic abilities, but their specialty is tormenting or injuring you more subtly. They may have the ability to throw you off a bridge, but they derive much more pleasure from driving you to the point of despair where you commit suicide and throw yourself off the bridge.

As to where they come from - I have my own beliefs about that, but decline to impose them upon you. Various religions have differing ways to deal with demons and in my experience they are all effective if the person using them has courage, knowledge and confidence in prevailing. The foundation of any successful method to fight demons is to remember they come from a place of darkness and darkness cannot exist in the light. If you fight with light, with that which is good, noble and honorable, many means are effective in vanquishing demonic adversaries.

Please don't confuse the word 'light.' Though visible light is a potent power, you can't just shine a bright light on a demon and expect them to do anything but laugh. I use the words light and darkness both literally and metaphorically, with darkness representing reprehensible evil and light representing purity of heart and nobility of purpose. 'Light' in the context of fighting demons, means a purity of purpose and methods,coupled with an unselfish love in your heart to protect yourself or others from demonic attack.

The Movie 'Exorcist' Spawns A Demon

In my 20's, I was in the US Coast Guard stationed on Governors Island, New York. Our island was at an incredible location. The Statue of Liberty was just offshore and the tip of Manhattan and all the wonders of the big city, were just a short 10 minute ferry ride away.

One night after midnight, while I was alone in my room, I received a frantic, fearful call from my roommate Dan. I had never heard Dan be frantic or fearful about anything. He was 6'4" and a fit, muscular 240 pounds. Nobody in their right mind messed with Dan. But on this call his fear was palpable.

"Can you...come...and get me?" Dan stammered weakly.
"What's going on Dan? Where are you?" I asked.
"Hurry, before it's too late." He pleaded in a panic-stricken voice.
"Hurry where?" I spoke firmly, trying to get him to think and speak rationally.
"Ferry terminal...New York side...aahh...." These were his last words spoken in pain and then the line went dead.

I rushed down to the Governor's Island ferry and luckily caught the next ferry just as it was getting ready to pull away from shore. I was the only passenger. From the moment Dan had called in agony, terrible thoughts of what might have happened to him ran continuously through my mind. I was sure he must be injured, maybe shot or knifed in a mugging. He should have known better than to be out by himself so late at night in the city.

As soon as the ferry landed I hurried off and into the terminal. It was completely empty except for the lone figure of Dan sitting hunched over at the end of a bench in the corner. I went to him quickly, relieved to not see any blood pooling on the floor or on his clothes.

Dan was just starring down at the floor, not even looking up at me. "What's the matter buddy?" I asked.

He shook his head slowly in silence for at least a minute. Then with great effort he quietly muttered. "I went to see the Exorcist movie...something happenedto me...I think...I'm going to die."

I had not seen the movie and could not comprehend how a movie could have shaken him so thoroughly to his core. The ferry I arrived on returned to Governor's Island and Dan and I sat in the terminal talking for the next 20 minutes waiting for it to return. I reminded him it was just a movie, that nothing was real. By the time the ferry returned, friendship and consoling seemed to have restored the normal, stoic Dan I knew.

After boarding the small ferry, we went up to the open top deck to be in the fresh air and hopefully further clear Dan's head. Just as the ferry moved away from the dock it let out a blaring loud blast from its horn, which was mounted within 10 feet of where we were standing. We were both leaning against the rail looking at the Statue of Liberty in the distance. When the horn blasted Dan completely lost all control of sanity. Immediately he put his leg over the railing and attempted to leap over the side into the icy East River. Before I could react he already had both feet over the railing and was screaming like a madman as he balanced momentarily on the railing and made ready to jump.

 I knew I had to act immediately and forcefully if I was going to prevent his jump. I'm short compared to Dan, so I shot my left arm up and encircled his neck. It was the only part of his body I knew I would be able to get a firm enough grip and leverage to counter his weight. Pulling back with all my strength I flipped him back over the rail. He ended up on his back laying on the cold metal ferry deck. Luckily, we were the only ones on the boat at that late hour and our maniac actions were not visible to anyone in the Pilothouse.

 He reached up and held both of my arms with his hands and looked at me with a piercing gaze. "Help me," is all he said and then his eyes rolled up and he lay back on the deck breathing heavy.

 When he had first called, I worried he was injured from a mugging. After I saw him and verified he was physically uninjured, I thought perhaps he had food poisoning or some other sudden illness. But when he tried to leap over the side of the ferry, I knew something else had control of him. I was too inexperienced at that point in my life, to know what exactly the problem was; but I knew instinctively it was not of our physical world.

 As Dan lay on the deck, his breathing still coming in raspy gasps, I enveloped him deeply in my aura, connecting to every fiber of his being. I knew what his inner core aura normally felt like. I wanted to verify that it was still intact and normal. It wasn't! His inner core aura was in agony. It was twisting and convoluted as if it was fighting against itself. All of his energy centers were very diminished in size and erratic in their spin. I distinctly felt the aura of another being inside of him. A dark, foreboding, malevolent aura unlike any I had ever experienced.

 Prior to this, I'm not sure I even believed in 'possession.' But that was obviously what had somehow occurred and I became an instant firm believer. Deciding to act quickly and forcefully to counter the evil, I laid my right hand on Dan's chest as I knelt beside him. Holding my left hand up to the starry night sky I called out, "Come to me energy of might and light." Instantly, I felt a rush of amazing energy like adrenaline multiplied by ten. I could feel a whirlwind of incredible energy swirling inside of me, and could see my own aura suddenly luminescent with white light and tiny jewels of many colors. For just a few seconds I swirled my auric energy closer and tighter, concentrating it. Then with a mental command, I sent it shooting down my right arm, through my hand and into Dan's chest. There was a loud anguished scream, but it wasn't coming from Dan! He lay on the deck with his eyes closed and seemed calm and serene. Seconds later he opened his eyes and I could tell immediately by his weak smile and peaceful eyes, that my friend was back.

 As the ferry docked and we disembarked to walk back to our barracks we were both in our own thoughts and walked in silent contemplation. Climbing the steps to our building, Dan stopped and grabbed my arm. "Thank you. I think you saved my life." He said humbly.

"I think I just exorcised my first demon." I responded.

"Yeah, you did." He confirmed. "Yeah you did."

How To Cope With Demons

Unless you are a very advanced practitioner of the psychic and paranormal, I highly advise you to seek out someone that is an advanced practitioner if you feel you or someone you care about is being threatened by a demon. Like physical people, some demons are smart and others dimwits. But all can hurt you physically more than any other type of disembodied creature and they all have a passionate desire to do so. Worse, they can subtly convince you to injure yourself, especially with destructive habits such as drugs and alcohol. They are masters at influencing your emotions, making you feel depths of despair, agony, fear, worthlessness and loathing that you never imagined.

Why do they do these heinous actions? Unlike you and me and the billions of other people in the world, they will probably never have a physical body or an evolved spiritual body. They resent every person who does have the joy of a body and the many unique wonders it can experience. They will do everything in their power to get people in physical bodies to degrade and debase the great gift they are denied.

How To Tell If A Person Is Demon Possessed Or Just Mentally Ill

When you look at the dark lives of people like Hitler and other mass murders, or criminals that commit particularly gruesome and despicable crimes, you have to wonder if they did this on their own because they are fundamentally a heartless, evil person, or if they were completely mentally ill, or if they acted while under the influence of a demon. Certainly no well-adjusted person would ever commit many of the terrible crimes that seem all too frequent in today's world.

HERE'S HOW YOU TELL:

Mentally Ill: While there are a wide variety of symptoms for mental illness, depending upon the root problem, a mentally ill person will exhibit periodic to frequent bouts of aberrational behavior. Warning signs can include: big mood swings; irrational statements; problems with memory; inexplicable fatigue, difficulty expressing themselves logically; paranoid fears; sudden apathy; radical changes in sleep or eating patterns; new phobias; unexplainable increase or decrease in sexual desire; and any kind of uncharacteristic, peculiar behavior.

Possessed by a Demon: Balanced, positive people, who go through life with optimism rather than pessimism, and do not allow themselves to be put in an incapacitated state by alcohol or drugs, are rarely ever bothered or affected by demons. Demons are empowered by the fears and weaknesses of humans. They feed on human misery in every form. The more unbalanced and off track a person is in their life, the more susceptible they are to a demonic attack.

A person possessed by a demon may exhibit some of the symptoms of mental illness. But while a mentally ill person is usually disconnected from fully understanding they are mentally ill, a demon possessed person will be crying out for help, clearly knowing something is wrong with them beyond their control and desperately hoping someone can and will help them.

They often feel and express to others that they feel something unseen is attacking them or trying to influence them. The influences are often noticeable, particularly religious changes such as no longer wanting to go to church, temple or mosque, pray, or have any contact with crucifixes and any other religious objects. Demons hate anything associated with light, nobility, morality, or the divine, regardless of the religion.

Demonic influence is particularly noticeable when New Age people who often own many quartz crystals and other mineral power stones, are affected. If someone like this suddenly has an aversion to crystals and stones of power, especially to the point that they remove them from their house, it is a clear indication of demonic possession, especially if there are other signs present.

Another big sign is negative voices speaking in the mind. These can be both self-criticism and critical comments about others. Often the dark whispers will encourage breaking off relationships with good friends and encouragement to befriend new unsavory people.

Sudden desires to debase oneself in any way are another common indication of demonic influence or possession. These can include: sudden sexual promiscuity or infidelity, especially with a quick succession of multiple partners; an unexplained onset of aimlessness; increased alcohol or drug use; cruelty to animals or children; and disregard for rules and requirements, including the lack of desire to continue to do school or professional work competently.

Demons love to terrorize people in any way they can. Your fear is their food, your self-inflicted wounds their joy.

A truly bad person: When someone commits heinous acts without exhibiting the symptoms of mental illness or demonic possession or influence, they can be established as simply a depraved, twisted person. Perhaps they can blame it on their difficult childhood development. But the end result is often a monster who will appear as a perfectly normal person, one that you might even consider as a friend. A friend with an evil twin lurking inside. Many serial killers fall into this category.

An Effective Counterattack Against Demons

The best counterattack is the same as it is with all forms of self-defense from karate to jujitsu: avoid situations and places where you might be attacked, so you never need to use your self-defense abilities.

If you feel that you or someone you know is under attack, as I mentioned before, don't hesitate to call for assistance. Anyone from your local priest to a well-known psychic, to experts that specialize in ghost and demon hunting, can help.

Any item you have belief in can be a jewel of power for you to ward off demons. If you are a Wiccan and believe a pentagram has power over demons, so it shall be. If you are a Christian and believe a silver crucifix will drive demons away, so it shall be. If you are Jewish and believe a mezuzah on your door will thwart demons, so it shall be. If you are a New Ager and believe in the power of crystals to overcome demons, so it shall be. The stronger your faith and belief in the tools that you have a love and harmony for, the more powerful those tools will be. Faith is the real power. There is no mightier power in all the universe than faith.

Whatever defensive jewel you believe in, you can amplify its power by adding the energy of one or more fellow believers to it. For instance, if a Catholic priest blesses a Catholic crucifix, especially if it is specifically to ward off demons, his faith will be added to your own, making the power emanating from the crucifix that much more potent. If a Wiccan calls a coven and all within the group bless whatever object is chosen as the jewel of power, it will embody the faith and power of all those who blessed it.

Vocally imbue your jewel with the power of your faith, by holding it between your two hands and saying, "Within this jewel I call upon all the forces of good and light to reside. May it be empowered to thwart and repel demons by my faith and light and the faith and light of all who bless it."

Once you have your jewel of power, simply wearing it will repel most demons and keep them from possessing or influencing you. However, they can still be in your home or building and can cause mischief or injury by their actions. If this is the case use the salt perimeter described earlier. But before dispensing, have all the salt blessed by people of like faith, so the power of their faith is added to your own, dramatically increasing the potency and effectiveness of the salt.

These methods should rid most demons. Occasionally you may encounter an obstinate one. If your own training and understanding is not succeeding, don't be embarrassed or hesitant to call upon outside expert assistance.

Black Magic

There are two things you need to guard against with Black Magic: someone that is trying to use it to hurt you; or hurting yourself by dabbling in occult activities without knowledge of what you are doing.

What is Black Magic? If it is something you are doing, it can broadly be considered any occult activity that is not drawing you to righteous purposes that is of benefit to you or others, or one that intentionally injures or manipulates anyone. If what you are doing is causing you or anyone else to be fearful or hurt emotionally, spiritually, physically or mentally, it is not a worthy pursuit, be it magic or mundane.

Psychic Self-Defense

If it is something someone else is doing, it comes into the Black Magic realm when the actions involve using incantations, curses and tools such as voodoo dolls, to coalesce unseen energies to manipulate you and cause you to act in a way they desire, or attack and hurt you physically, mentally, emotionally or spiritually.

Magic itself is neither black or white. It is the intention in how it is used, either for good, uplifting and expanding purposes, or for evil, negative and dampening purposes, that earn it the moniker black or white. Unfortunately, there are both physical people and unseen beings that have devoted themselves to using paranormal energies for purposes that manipulate, hurt or injure others.

If you are learning about how to use spells, incantations and potions to harness energies to further your own desires, be careful not to slip off the higher path in your efforts to achieve your goals. Even something as innocuous as a love spell, depending upon how it is crafted and worded, can often be construed as black magic. If it is used to manipulate a person into having affections for someone they would not otherwise have amorous feelings for, then it is not of the light. If it is used to enhance your own beauty or improve your own personality that you might be more noticed and appreciated when you are talking with the one you have affections for, then it is non-manipulative of others, and of the light.

Your own choices and actions when dealing with the paranormal can expose you to the malevolent machinations of both people and unseen beings with dark intents. Dabbling in occult activities with little or no knowledge of the world you are calling upon, or the risks you are taking, lends itself to mischief from the unseen world. Sometimes the mischief can lead to serious physical and psychological harm.

Ouija Board horror stories, for example, from the experiences of countless innocent and paranormally ignorant inquirers, are legion. Do an Internet search for the subject. When I did, Google came up with 45,600 results. Typically a group of friends or family, all with little or no experience with the paranormal, gather around a Ouiji Board and just start playing around with silly questions. Sooner or later someone starts making paranormal type queries and then things can begin to get weird, soon progress from weird to scary, then from scary to dangerous.

Here's a typical result reported by Heather: "Then, they asked, 'Could you possess us?' and it pointed to 'yes.' They asked, 'could we help you?' and it pointed to 'yes' again. Then, being the idiot he was, my dad jokingly took a crucifix and touched it to the Ouija Board. The second it touched, Jesus fell off of the crucifix at hands & feet. My dad got royally freaked out and they decided to burn the board. A big mistake I swear to you. The next day, our house caught fire. My dad had to put it out with his hands seven times!!! Ever since then...strange things have been happening, and still do."

Contacting disembodied spirits, attempting magic spells, or trying to exert or call any paranormal power without clear knowledge of the subject, techniques and risks, is opening a door to some unpleasant experiences. It's like jumping into a complex lab experiment in the middle of a chemistry class, when you have never taken the class and have no idea what the chemicals are that are being used, or the dangers of mixing them incorrectly.

If an inexperienced person ever feels compelled by peer pressure or their own inner promptings to ignorantly dabble with the paranormal despite the potential risks, there is one simple thing that can be done to significantly lower the dangers. Before beginning, gather together with everyone else involved, hold hands in a circle and have one person speaking for all, say, "As we seek now to (whatever you are going to do), we call upon all the forces of good and light to be with us. We only allow higher beings who have our safety and well-being at heart or in mind, to be present. By the power of the light within us, we forbid any being that would harm us in any way from manifesting in any form or action." While not 100% foolproof protection, if said with power and forceful intent that procedure and incantation will keep most beasties at bay. If you are of a religious nature and you also call upon the Gods of your belief for protection, you will enhance your security still further. Your faith in the divine of your belief reinforces your own command that bars entry to beings of darkness.

How To Protect Against Personal Attacks

Two of the more common ways that someone may try to hurt you with black magic is through either voodoo or a magical curse. Many people are of the opinion that if they don't believe in Voodoo, black magic or curses, that they will have no affect on them, or that they will be automatically protected by their disbelief if evil energies are sent their way. I am not of that opinion. Your auric field can and is disturbed by a wide variety of energetic influences from things your five senses encounter, to things you eat, to exposure to harmful chemicals or electromagnetic energy, just to name a few of the common ones. Except in exceptionally rare circumstances, if you drink a glass of cyanide poison, you will be dead quite promptly regardless of your belief to the contrary. It is the same for negative and dark forces – they can hurt you, even if you naively believe they cannot.

This chapter has really been all about negative energies of wide variety that can dampen your personal auric field and ultimately physically, psychologically, spiritually or emotionally hurt you. Voodoo and magical curses can do so just as easily as any of the other psychic threats you may encounter, especially if you are being attacked by someone experienced in perverting paranormal energies for destructive purposes.

Once again, avoidance of situations that might end up being threatening should still be your first defense. Don't give anyone a reason to want to hurt you with voodoo or a black magic curse. Live your life as a good person, empathetic and caring of others, positive and hopeful in your outlook on life, and willing to lend a hand and be of service. Cultivate positive people as friends and limit or end your association with negative, critical people, especially those who have dark, fearful, spiteful, or self-destructive tendencies. Who you are and the way you think and act, choosing positive over negative and light over darkness, creates an auric field that repels negativity and a permeating energy that makes you invisible as a target of evil intentions.

I hope you don't think I'm preaching here. I am in no way trying to tell you how to live your life. I am simply giving you good advice based on a lot of experience as to a defense that is very effective.

Quartz Crystal Shield

While a positive approach to life and avoidance of negative energy people and places remains your best defense, it is not foolproof, and it is possible you could still come under intentional psychic attack by someone utilizing black magic. If you feel someone has cursed you, or that you are under any type of intentional psychic attack from living people or disembodied beings, you can create an impermeable barrier of energy to protect yourself with quartz crystals. This shield is very effective against virtually all types of negative energy.

You will need to purchase 4 fist size quartz crystals for use around your bed, another 4 for use in your bedroom, and 4 additional crystals for every room you wish to always be protected within. Smaller crystals can work as well, but with less of a power output to the shield. Both size and clarity are important when using quartz crystals for protective purposes. The less clarity it has, the larger size is needed. Conversely, the greater clarity it has, the smaller size is needed.

You can find a wonderful assortment of quartz crystals that you can order online by simply doing a search for "Arkansas Quartz Crystals." Buying direct from the quartz crystals mines with their small minimum order requirements, is always far less expensive than buying from any retail outlet. Two of the biggest in Arkansas are the Coleman Brothers in Jessieville. Jim and Ron own separate mines and run separate businesses right across the road from each other. Both have amazing quartz crystals in astounding quantity. But there are several other excellent mine outlets between Jessieville and Mt. Ida that have huge assortments of great crystals at very reasonable prices. If online buying isn't for you and you want to feel the energy of the crystals you buy, that area of Arkansas, centered around the picturesque town of Hot Springs, and the National Park of the same name, is quite beautiful and makes a very memorable road trip.

You will also need a single quartz crystal pendant of exceptional clarity to wear around your neck. The power of your overall crystal security system will be at least doubled if not more, by having the pendant around your neck in a setting of at least 14kt gold. 18kt. is superb. Gold is a fabulous conductor of positive energy. The crystals laid out in the four corners with a fifth personal crystal around your neck, create a laser-like lattice of white energy that any negative manifestation of darkness will not cross.

To Empower, Program, Sync And Activate Your Crystal Shield

1. Take all the crystals you will be using, including your quartz crystal pendant and gold chain and wash them thoroughly in a warm bath of salt water. Scrub off any dirt with a soft tooth brush and let them soak in a plastic tub of salt water for at least 24 hours. Metal tubs and bowls should be avoided as they may react with the salt water and alter

its composition.

2. After 24 hours discard the water, refill with fresh salt water and let set for another 24 hours.

3. If you do not have natural water from the ocean readily available you can make your own salt water. Add ½ cup of natural, uniodized sea salt to every gallon of reverse osmosis or distilled water.

4. The water should be preheated to approximately 80 degrees Fahrenheit (comfortably warm). To avoid internal fracturing, the crystal should also be within 10 degrees of the same temperature when it is placed in the water. If you have a small submersible water pump to maintain a flow of water movement within the tub that would be also be helpful; otherwise stir with a long-handled wooden spoon about once per hour while you are awake.

5. Let the water sit overnight, heat to 80 degrees again the next day, and stir the water vigorously.

6. After your crystals have soaked for 24 or more hours, remove them and let them air dry in a very sunny location where they are in direct contact with the bare ground. Leave them in the direct sun for as long as possible during the day. Bring them in once the sun is no longer on them. They are now ready to program for your protection.

7. Find any object that you can easily hold that represents divinity as you know and believe. This can be a crucifix for a Christian, a Star of David for those who are Jewish, the pentacle for Wiccans, the Tri-circle of Twelve Gems for practitioners of Celestine Light, or any symbol or emblem that draws you and calls you to the divine. If you have no belief in any divine or higher source, the crystal lattice shield will still work in most instances. But against a very strong psychic or demon attack it will crumble, unless you have imbued it with a very powerful, confident energy of your own. Imbuing it with a connection to the divine reinforces it with energy that is not only powerful, but also repugnant and repelling to demons and other creatures and people of darkness.

8. Cradle all of your crystals in your arms held against your chest, along with the symbol of divinity you have chosen.

9. Say the following prayer/incantation to program and encode the crystals for their purpose: "*Into these crystals birthed of Mother Earth, I call upon all energies of light to imbue with power to forever repel any and all energies or beings of darkness that would try to pass.*" The more passion and conviction you say this with, the more potent the energy shield becomes.

10. (Optional) If you are a believer in any form of the divine, you should also call upon the god or gods of your belief to charge the crystals with their power and light to "*forever repel any and all energies or beings of darkness that would try to pass.*"

11. Now set one crystal at each of the four corners of your bed and another four at each of the four corners of your bedroom. The placement can be on the floor at the base of the bed legs, or if your bed is on a raised platform you can set them on the platform by the corners of the bed. It you have an odd shaped room, set a crystal in every corner. Your bedroom is now super protected.

12. If there are any other rooms you wish to protect, place a crystal in each corner of the room. If you want to protect your entire house, you can place a crystal outside or inside at each corner of the house.

13. If there is more than 20 feet distance between crystals, you should place another in between to shorten the distance. This strengthens the protective shield.

14. Wear your crystal pendant on a necklace. This strongly connects your aura to the energy lattice field of the crystals.

Wolf in Sheep's Clothing, Off World

Channeling from the modern era, and spiritualism from earlier ones, have always been popular psychic endeavors. Whether it is contacting higher beings from worlds beyond Earth, or the spirits of deceased people, being able to make a connection and communicate with beings beyond our physical Earth is a powerful draw.

But great care needs to be taken when communicating in this manner. Whether you are just asking questions of a Ouija Board, or entering into a full-trance channel where a higher being takes over your body and speaks through your vocal cords, opening the door to other beings can be dangerous.

For full-body, full-trance Channelers, there is a physical danger if they have not taken actions to protect themselves. A being that can control your body, can cause it to eat or drink harmful substances, or act in ways you never would.

As full-body, full-trance Channelers are very rare, the hazard for most other channelers, both novice and experienced, is the possibility of receiving false information that was thought to be true. Acting on the false information can lead to ruin. For example, you may have been told to buy a certain stock as it was going to quickly double in value. After rushing to invest your savings, the stock instead collapses and you loose your financial stability. Or you might be told to take a marvelous health cure, only to discover that instead it further worsened your health.

Just because you think you are channeling a higher being doesn't mean that is actually the case. Certainly it is helpful before you begin to state aloud that *"I only call and allow higher beings, who have advice that will help me to grow and expand in the light, to come and speak to me or through me."* But on its own, those words only work in direct proportion to the power of your own aura and the strength of your own convictions. In some cases, with strong negative beings, those words alone will not work for anyone.

A good example of how people can be deceived, is channeling the archangel Michael. Michael is a popular higher being to channel, and there are many people who genuinely do, as the archangel is not committed to communicating only through one person. But how do you know that it is really the archangel Michael communicating? You are on Earth, the being communicating is somewhere else, and you have no way to verify with your physical senses who they are. Perhaps you feel a psychic resonance. While that is often a good confirming indicator, it is also not foolproof.

The Trojan Horse of Deceit

One of the sneakiest ways that disembodied beings, as well as living people that do not have your best interest at heart trick you, is to hide a damning falsehood among a bunch of truth. They will impart several gems of wisdom that reiterates and reinforces what you already know or believe to be true because it resonates with you. Because you accept these teachings as true you let down your mental and psychic defenses. Into that gap they slide a great falsehood. One that can cause you physical, mental and emotional pain or injury. They then quickly close the sandwich by spouting off again several things that are known and accepted as true. You may hear 95% truth that may seem at times to be uplifting and enlightening. But the 5% that is false can be so damaging that accepting any of the teachings becomes risky and a price likely to become painful to pay.

The Test of Truth

There is one foolproof test of any information purported to be coming from higher beings, or even from what you may think is your higher self. It works equally well testing any living teachers, gurus, prophets, etc. It doesn't matter whether you are the person channeling, or the person listening to a channeler or spiritualist and receiving the information they are dispensing. Apply this simple test and you will **always** know, if the wisdom imparted is true or false. To pass the test all three of these keys must be met:

Harmonious - Needful – Progressive

Harmonious: *Any information imparted must be harmonious with knowledge you already have that you know to be true.* If for instance, you had a friend that had shown you through many actions that they cared for you and had your best interests at heart, but then were told in a channeling that this friend was actually out to hurt you; that information would be contrary to all the evidence you had experienced; and if followed, could destroy a very supportive and beneficial relationship.

Needful: *You must have a need to hear this information at this time.* It must be useful information to help you in the present. True higher beings do not waste your time telling you something that has no application in your life today.

Progressive: *The information imparted must be new information, not just restating or* *emphasizing things you already knew.* For example, you might be told to 'eat more fruits and vegetables.' That would pass the first test, it would be harmonious with a lot of information available that lets us know that eating more fruits and vegetables should be an important part of everyone's diet. If you are lacking in your consumption of fruit and vegetables it might also pass the 'needful' test. But it wouldn't pass the 'progressive' test. Telling someone they should eat more fruits and vegetables on it's own is likely not progressive. Most people are already aware they should eat more fruits and vegetables. However, if you were told to eat more of a particular fruit or vegetable, because it had specific nutritional qualities you lacked and needed, then it would pass the 'progressive' test as well. Keying in on a specific beneficial food is probably not something you would have known on your own.

Wolf in Sheep's Clothing, On World

There are living people who have set themselves up as teachers and gurus, that can also give you false, misleading and hurtful advice; often designed to benefit them at your expense. Some of these are well known celebrities, psychics, healers, or movement leaders. The same test of truth works just as well for anything they tell you or advise.

Ask Yourself, Is What They Say:
Harmonious - Needful – Progressive

Energy Vampires, Predators

Please reread the section above on Energy Vampires, unintentional. Predatory Energy Vampires have all the same warped needs to suck Soul Essence energy from people during conflicts as the unintentional. The difference, is they are very aware it is a need, and they not only don't feel bad about preying energetically on others, they actually look forward to it, and strive to create situations of conflict where they can feed on the negative energy.

Serial killers become the worst manifestation of predator Energy Vampires. The fear that people experience as they are tormented, injured, then finally killed, is so craved by the worst of the Energy Vampires that one murder just leads to the next, as they develop an insatiable lust for the palpable fear and terror of their victims.

The same defenses outlined for the unintentional Energy Vampires apply to the predators. Even greater emphasis should be placed on complete and total avoidance, carried out as soon as possible, with no looking back. Even if this is a close family member or spouse, permanently leaving the relationship and the state or country if necessary, should be done without delay.

Psychic Defense Conclusion

I know this is a chapter that will make some people uncomfortable. It always seems easier to not have to look at the dark side of life. But it is there, especially so in the world of the paranormal. Ignoring the reality may give one a false sense of bliss and security, but it doesn't change the reality. Most people will never need much in the way of psychic self-defense. It is not like there are threats abounding. But should they show up, I hope you have learned a few of the lessons imparted herein and are prepared.

There is a great added benefit as well. As you study and practice your psychic self-defense skills, you will be strengthening and improving all of your psychic abilities and paranormal powers. Practicing anything of a psychic or paranormal nature works and builds all of your psychic and paranormal muscles. In the long run your psychic development will grow faster, and your everyday life will be safer and more rewarding at the same time.

Part II
PERSONAL EXPERIENCES AND TRAINING

UNLEASH YOUR PSYCHIC POWERS

Chapter 11
EMPATHY & INTUITION

Empathy and sympathy are frequently used interchangeably by many people. They are in fact very different aspects of understanding someone's feelings. Empathy means that you understand how someone feels even though you do not feel that way yourself. Sympathy means you understand how someone feels and you feel the same way yourself.

A perfect example is a grieving widow. If her husband was someone you did not know you would have empathy for her sorrow. You understand why she is grieving, but you have none yourself because you did not know the man. However, if her husband was also a close friend of yours, you'll likely feel a pain in your heart at his passing as well, so you sympathize with the widow. Though her grief is surely greater, you too will feel a sympathetic grief and sadness at the loss of your friend.

A fairly rapid way to increase your psychic abilities is to learn to tune into your power of empathy when you are around other people. Once perfected, you should be able to approach any person, from a friend to a stranger, in any situation, and confidently and quickly know the emotions they are feeling, even if you do not yet understand why they are feeling them.

But it would be a mistake to think that empathy is strictly a psychic ability, or to limit yourself to trying to perceive another person's feelings solely on your psychic perception. The comprehension of empathy, of understanding what a person is feeling, can be completely non-verbal, but it is also indicated by their body language, including their posture, the appearance of their eyes and mouth, and even the way they are breathing.

Many Empaths; psychics who specialize in tuning into peoples feelings; may think they are understanding someones feelings solely on their psychic perception, when in reality they are also unconsciously taking all of the body language indicators into account. The ability to tune into other peoples feelings, including consciously and subconsciously, noting the signs of their body language, is an ability born into every human being. Though you may be reading about it now, you already know how to do it. The fact that most people do not do it, is not evidence of a lack of ability, merely evidence of lack of attentive listening and observing of others, and being aware of their own feelings as they intuitively ponder what they are seeing and hearing.

Intuition plays a big part in becoming a successful Empath. You have to learn to listen to the still, small voice inside of you and be very sensitive to your own thoughts and feelings. Listening is such a tremendous key; one sadly lacking in most people. However, when it is lacking, it is not by some cosmic omission, but by their own conscience or sub-conscience choice. Each of us can choose, if we wish, to be better listeners, both of our own inner self and of others. Listening to yourself is as important of a skill as listening to others. Listening is not limited to hearing. It really means being aware of your own thoughts and feelings, and open to understanding the thoughts and feelings of others as they express them verbally or by other means.

In my earlier life I was in corporate positions where I had to hire people for various jobs. Sometimes I would need to interview dozens of people applying for the same job. Often times they had very similar work experience and education, so my decision would boil down to how diligent of a worker I concluded they would be, and how well I thought they would mesh working together on a team. Empathy and intuition are enormously helpful in these type of situations. In job interviews, sales pitches, and often in human romantic relations, people tell you what they think you want to hear to go along with their desires to get the job, buy the product, or agree to a date or a hop in the sack. Some people are making their case in sincerity and honesty. Others may be less truthful, more conniving and sometimes just outright dishonest. Being aware of your inner intuitive thoughts and feelings, while consciously or subconsciously tuning into the other person's feelings and noting their body language, can make the truth very evident and plain.

Of course knowing the truth and acting rightly upon it do not always go hand in hand, particularly in human romantic relationships. For instance, women by and large are more empathetic and sensitive to their intuition than men. They often know intuitively when a man is being untruthful or giving them a line, but sometimes ignore the promptings of their intuition and disregard their empathetic perception of a man's true motive; all because they have honest feelings for the man and do not want to face the reality that their emotional outreach is not truly reciprocated. So they will ignore the facts their intuition and empathy are conveying to them. They will move forward with a relationship that is doomed to fail once the man gets what he wants from it, which is often nothing more than a sexual conquest. Moral of the story? It is not enough to develop your intuition and empathetic skills. You must also be willing to act upon the truths they reveal.

The 50% Rule

Now there is a trap when you begin to rely more upon your intuition and empathetic abilities. Many people who tend to rely on their feelings end up doing so to an extreme that ignores their mental considerations. In an equation it would look like this: 100% feeling + 0% thinking = action. The other extreme is often seen with people who are very disconnected from their feelings: 0% feeling + 100% thinking = action. I've tried both ways and various shades in between over the last 50+ years. My conclusion is that the best choice of action, producing the most satisfying results, are from applying both your mind and your heart in equal measures when you are considering your choice. So your equation looks like this: 50% feeling + 50% thinking = action.

How To Increase Your Intuitive Abilities

Remembering that your mind will automatically and subconsciously take into account visual and audio cues that may be present from people or events, playing red light / green light is the easiest most effective method I have ever found to increase and learn to trust your intuition.

Picture a red traffic light in your mind. That means "no." Picture a green traffic light in your mind. That means "yes." Simply form a question in your mind that has either a 'yes' or 'no', or a 'true' or 'false' answer. Then let your intuition answer the question by displaying either a red light or a green light in your mind.

To get the red and green light images forming easily in your mind begin with things you know for certain to be either true or false. For instance in my case: "My name is Embrosewyn" - green light. "I am over 50 years old" - green light. "I have been married six times" - red light. "My daughter is a straight 'A' student" - green light. "I was a straight 'A' student in school" - red light. "I live on the ocean" - red light. "I want to live on the ocean" - green light.

Once you have established your mental imagery of red and green lights, start flexing and strengthening your intuition many times during the day with people and events. For instance: "Is this activity safe?" "Is this person safe?" "should I attend this event?" "Is this person telling me the truth?" "Will taking this action be for my highest good?" "Is buying this item a good decision?"

Dreams: The Secret Backdoor Passage To Intuition

I will delve more into dreams in Chapter 23 , but must include a bit about them here as they can be powerful backdoor connections to your intuitive insights. The meaning of dreams can be simple or quite complex. They also can have no purposeful meaning at all other than your sleeping body and resting minds way of relieving stress, or dramatizing the past or future days anxieties in a strange convoluted form. But sometimes dreams have very important messages.

When it comes to choices and decisions in life, dreams can often give you truthful, unvarnished images that you would never allow yourself to see or acknowledge in your conscious state, which give you the answers you seek. It is almost like being drunk, when your inhibitions fall by the wayside and you may say or do things that your cultural, religious or personal boundaries would normally never allow you to consider doing. Frequently, if you are looking for it, your dreams will show you answers to questions that are vexing you. The answers are revealed from the depths of your true desires and subconscious knowledge; not from the within the constraints you normally apply to your decision making process that limit the possible answers to your questions.

That doesn't mean you should just blindly follow where your dreams lead. For instance, just because you took part in an orgy with a bunch of strangers in your dream, does not in any way indicate it would be a good choice in your awake life. Be open to answers your dreams may be giving to you that are manifestations of all the aspects of your inner intuition. But when you are awake and clear thinking, put the answers you think you received in your dream through the filters of your conscious mind and heart. Ask your heart, "Heart how do you *feel* about this?" Ask your mind, "Mind what do you *think* about this?" And finally, red light/green light, "Is this for my highest good?" When all three filters agree, you have a very clear path in front of you.

If you want to use your dreams as a backdoor access to your intuition it is helpful to keep a Dream Journal. Whenever you wake up from a vivid dream or even one you only remember tendrils of, write it down in your dream journal and ponder it more deeply when you are fully awake.

Intuition May Have Saved My Life

I have been allowing myself to be sensitive and receptive to my intuition for so many years it is almost like breathing now. But when I was in high school, I was a science geek just learning to be open and trusting of my non-empirical intuition. Doing so may have saved my life.

In my sophomore year I tried out for the football team. There was a grueling month of practices with cuts made every week. After all of my hard work I was one of the ones cut in the end. During the month when I was still sweating and straining with all the other kids hopeful of making the team, there were not enough lockers for everyone, so newbies had to share lockers and I was assigned a fellow prospect named Jim as my locker mate. Other than football practice I had never met Jim, though I had seen him in the halls at school between classes.

Jim was a friendly guy. One day after practice, when we had been locker mates for about a week, I lamented the mile and a half walk I needed to take to get home with my sore, overworked body. In an effort to expand our friendship he asked me if I wanted a lift on his motorcycle. My mind wanted to say "yes" and was happy at the thought of not having to walk home. But a still small voice inside of me was shouting "no!" I didn't understand why, but I knew I needed to trust that inner prompting. I lied and told Jim thanks, but I still needed to do some work in the science lab. The next day before football practice the coach called me into his office. I thought I was being cut already after just one week. Instead he told me to go clean all of Jim's stuff out of his locker as he had been killed in an accident on his motorcycle after practice the day before.

Maybe if I had taken him up on his offer and had been with him, Jim wouldn't have been at the intersection he was, at the precise moment he was killed. Or maybe I would have been there

Empathy & Intuition

with him and not be here now to recount this event. I still empathize with his family that lost him to the tragic accident, but am ever so glad I had already decided at that early age to listen to my inner promptings.

How To Develop Your Empathetic Powers

Earlier I mentioned people who are disconnected from their emotions. If you ask them what they are feeling, more often than not they have to scratch their head and think about it awhile and still may not come up with an answer. It's not that they don't have feelings or are uncaring people. They do have feelings, but have likely spent a lifetime suppressing them, and not thinking about them or acknowledging them. Anyone who falls into this category has to first make the effort to open up to themselves, to let their feelings and emotions, good, bad, or ugly, out to run around a bit. It is certainly very difficult to have an empathy for another person's feelings if you don't even have an understanding or acknowledgment of your own.

Many people who suffer from suppression of their emotions do so because of personal beliefs that showing emotions is somehow bad. Some men in particular, feel being stoic and unemotional is a display of their manliness. On the other end of the spectrum, some women who are with a volatile male partner, may have developed a habit of suppressing their own emotions and feelings, fearing that to let them out would upset their man and cause problems. Regardless of the reason, the first step in becoming more empathetic is to become more aware of your own emotions and feelings and allow them some freedom.

Once you are in a well-balanced state of being aware and sensitive to how you are personally emotionally feeling, you are ready to start tuning in to how other people are feeling. Remember to use all of your senses! ***Your intuition is the sum of all of your senses, both physical and psychic, alerting you to what they are sensing, plus the innate understanding produced by the interaction of your auric field with another persons.***

When you are looking at a person, their face is a key. If I asked you now to make a sad face, I'm sure you could make an exaggerated expression that nearly 100% of observers would say was a "sad face." The same is true if I asked you to make a "happy face" or an "angry face." These are universal expressions in every culture on the planet.

The interesting thing is that these expressions are still present even when people are doing their best to hide how they are feeling. The expressions may be oh so micro and tiny; but most often, unless someone is a very practiced liar or a professional actor, they are still there.

Your conscious mind, even if it was looking for it, even if it knew what to look for, would probably not attribute any significance to the corner of a person's mouth subtly moving for only a flash, a mere millimeter downward, before they smiled when they first greeted you. But if you are purposefully open to empathetically feeling what the other person is feeling, that tiny, brief movement will be added to the other sensory input such as the inflection of their voice, the grip or lack of it in their handshake, and the feel of your aura interacting with theirs. In a moment, you will empathetically know they are sad for some reason, even before they have spoken a word.

Or, perhaps at a greeting with another person, there is an ever so slight tensing of the lips, before a big smile greets you. Consciously, you probably wouldn't even notice it. However, if you are desiring to feel what other people are feeling, if that is your intention, then that tiny, subtle tensing of the lips will be noted in your mind and correlated with all the other sensory inputs, including your auric interaction, to let you know that the person is not truly happy with your presence, even though they pretend that they are.

Emapthy Exercise #1
A big part of empathy is being able to put yourself in another person's emotional shoes even if they are not shoes you would normally be comfortable wearing. To help you develop empathy you can practice simply by writing yourself a little essay defending a hypothetical person's position that is the opposite of your own. For instance, maybe you are pro-choice, believing a woman should be allowed to decide if she wants an abortion, or as a good bumper sticker I recently saw succinctly summarized, "keep your laws off of my body." As you know there are pro-life people who are equally as passionate about limiting abortion.

If you want to learn to be able to understand and empathize with other people's emotions, do some research and find out why a person with an opposite position from your own *feels* the way they do. Forget the merits of your own position and see the situation through the other person's eyes, thoughts and feelings. Pretend you are them and write a short essay stating why you *feel* the way you do.

Remember you are writing as them. In this case, the pro-choice person would be writing an essay from the other person's perspective, stating why they *feel* abortion should be limited. If you are a pro-life person, you would write an essay stating the other persons point of view of why they *feel* abortion should be the woman's choice. Remember, these are essays **solely about feelings**. They are not about intellectual reasoning or medical facts. Write about how the other person feels. As you succeed in 'feeling' the other person's perspective, without interjecting your own contrary feelings, you will teaching yourself to become more empathetic. A big part of that is making no judgments about how another person feels, but simply and lovingly allowing yourself to feel what they feel. Remember, empathy means you understand how another person feels, even though you do not feel the same way yourself.

Chapter 12
SEEING, FEELING & READING THE AURA

Rather than rewriting that which I have already written, I am introducing this chapter by excerpting from my book, Auras: How to See, Feel & Know.

"It wasn't until the summer prior to the start of third grade that I thought to ask my mother what all the colored lights around people's heads meant. I was dumbfounded and uncomprehending when she told me to stop lying and that there were not lights around people's heads. When I insisted there were wonderful, beautiful lights around her head and everyone, she told me again to stop lying or she would wash my mouth out with soap. Not enjoying that particular punishment at all, I decided it would probably be wise to not mention auras to my mother again. But she took it a step further and specifically told me to not talk about such nonsense again to anyone, as she didn't want people thinking she had a crazy son. The first fleeting realization came into my mind that perhaps everyone else really didn't see auras after all.

My mother often accused me of having the things she told me "go in one ear and out the other," and so it was with her admonition to not talk about auras. Knowing I was not supposed to talk to anyone about auras made me anxious to ask all of my friends about them as soon as we gathered that afternoon to play. I had brought the subject up with most of them individually before without much reaction. This time I had six of them gathered together when I popped the big question, "What do you guys think of all those cool lights around people's heads?"

Strangest thing was they all gave me blank stares like they had no idea what I was talking about. At first I thought they were joking. Then I thought perhaps they had also been threatened with having their mouths washed out with soap by their moms. Then I realized they didn't have a clue what I was talking about. If I kept asking, they would begin thinking I had cooties or something, so I just laughed and told them I was kidding. And then, I never brought it up again.

Being slow to learn important life lessons in my early years, I also made the mistake when I was married at 22 years old, to a very religious woman, of sharing with her my amazing experiences seeing auras. I told her about the incredibly beautiful aura that surrounded her and how seeing it made me feel closer to her. She had a different opinion of what I "thought" I was seeing. It was like my mother part deux. Instead of smiling in happiness at the compliment and wanting to know more, she looked at me like I was a visitor from Mars.

During the preceding sixteen years, until that day with my wife, I had never spoken to another person about seeing human auras, but I seldom stopped thinking about them and looking at them. They fascinated me immensely and I had continued to be captivated by their mystery. I looked at kids in school, teachers, and just passer-bys on the street trying to correlate what I saw in their auras with the mood or actions they were demonstrating.

Auras came in so many colors, shades and shapes, and radiated in such an astounding explosion of tiny shards of light, it was hard to not look at them. I saw auras not just around people, but around every living thing from a dog, to a bug, to a plant. Even leaves that fell off the trees in the autumn still retained an aura for many hours, sometimes over a day, as they lay upon the ground. I even saw auras around inanimate objects though that was a little more of a challenge.

In middle school I became very interested in science and purposefully began to observe the auras around people and make written notes of how their exhibited behavior, mood or health, corresponded to what I saw in their auric field. By the end of middle school I could easily see full body auric fields extending about an arms-length from all parts of someone's body. I was becoming more confident from my scientific observations that I had a good idea what the various colors, intensities, opacities and other variations indicated. The field was always most intense around the head and that was generally the area of my observations.

Though I never spoke to anyone about auras during this time, I certainly kept my ears open to listen for anyone else that might bring up the subject. But it just seemed to be one giant void. Auras were never mentioned in school, on television, in movies I watched, or books I read. I began to think I was either hallucinating, missing a few marbles, or the only person that could see auras in the whole wide world.

Whenever I looked at my own aura by standing at a distance and looking in a mirror, it had a lot of purple and white in it. Though white was not uncommon, purple was a color I rarely saw even a little in other peoples auras. At that point, beginning to believe that I might be the only person in the world that could see them, I began thinking of myself as the only purple person in the world, as a way to be comfortable with my own strangeness. Thinking of myself in this way put me at ease and took away any anxiousness about being so different from other people. Of course I was different I told myself. I was purple and the others were not, so it only stood to reason that I might have different capabilities than the world of non-purples.

As I matured into my teenage years I became more self-conscious about looking at peoples auras, to the point that I would have bouts of guilt, as if I was seeing secrets not intended for me to see. After all, nobody had a clue that I saw their auras, and that by observing them I knew if they were sick, or mad at their boyfriend, or lying to me, despite what their outward appearance and words might indicate to the contrary. If they were choosing to present a false image of themselves to me or others, what right did I have to be secretly looking at the truth without their permission or knowledge?

After years of observation I thought I had come to a basic understanding of what many of the colors, opacities, strengths of the radiating flows and other indicators meant. I knew red about the head was a very angry person getting ready to explode probably in violence, while a mellower red about the heart area often indicated someone that had turned off their rational brain and were on emotional autopilot.

I had learned years ago that seeing auras was a function of how I looked at people. I could see them or not see them with an instant change in how I focused my eyes. Just like you break a board in karate by hitting "through the board" toward a point beyond it, seeing auras merely required a focus with the eyes beyond the object being observed. It was helpful to learn how to "turn off" the aura view because increasingly during my teenage years I felt like I was snooping into people's privacy uninvited.

And there were definite perks to being able to see auras. When I was still dating, I could always see which areas women were interested in me. This gave me somewhat of an unfair advantage in our relationships. By noticing which of their energy centers they were extending out to me, and which of mine they were connecting to, I knew if they were more interested in my body, my mind, my personality, or simply attracted by the general feeling of my auric field.

I will have to admit as well that despite perks like insight into opposite sex attraction, the more I observed auras the more confused I became about what they meant. I would gain a level of confidence about the meaning of certain indicators, such as the red around the head previously mentioned; only to be dismayed when I would see someone with the exact indicator I thought I absolutely understood the meaning of, not act in any way like the indicator said they should be acting. By the time I was a senior in high school, what I thought I was seeing in an individual's aura was evidenced by their actions to be incorrect at least 30% of the time. Without reliability, I began to wonder if there was actually any useful purpose in being able to see auras.

I had never given much attention to the interaction of two or more people's auras, but in my senior year of high school with serious romances going on among many of my friends, this became a new area of interest. If you hold your arms out from your sides, perpendicular from your body, the distance from the hand on one side to the hand on the other is the approximate size of the aura that surrounds a healthy body under normal conditions. But I noticed three things when a boyfriend and girlfriend approached each other. First, as they neared one another both of their auras would expand in size larger than the norm. Sometimes this expansion would grow to two to three times normal size so their auras extended a good six to ten feet from their bodies, which made their auras touch while their bodies were still twelve to twenty feet away.

Second, the closer they got to each other the more intense the light radiating from their auras would become. This was often two to three times the normal intensity of light and in some instances even more.

Third, as they embraced there would often be a rapid and dramatic change in one or more parts of their aura. Light might dim in some parts such as around their heads, and intensify around their hearts and groin areas. The colors would also change and there would be a merger of colors between the two. They each would still retain their individual colors, but they would diffuse as if they were being blended in part with the color of their partner. Areas of strong attraction such as the heart and sexual areas would begin to radiate many thin, diffused beams of white light shooting through the overall predominant color of the area, connecting one heart to another, one sexual spot to another. Once they embraced, their auras that had been expanded beyond the normal boundaries as they approached one another, now contracted to a bubble surrounding them both that was contracted tightly around them, as if they were closing out auric interaction with any other people.

I had a new fascination and spent much of my time quietly but intently observing multiples of people interacting. Not just couples, but my teachers when they taught their class, and my friends when we were standing in a circle talking. Even the crowd in the stands at a basketball game or the athletes out on the floor with teammates and opponents.

It was very interesting to see how much auras actually fluctuated in size. Observing an increase in size became a reliable indicator for how sincerely a teacher really cared about teaching their students. If they could care less, their aura stayed the normal size around their body and their teaching presentation was boring. If they cared some, their aura would expand outward and touch the auras of students in the nearest rows. If they had a passion for what they were teaching their aura expanded outward to include everyone in the class. And it wasn't a one-way street. If the teacher's aura was expanding outward, every student whose aura was touched paid rapt attention and obviously benefited far more.

Observing the auras of crowds at sporting events also became an avid interest. While each person still retained their individual auric characteristics, a group auric field developed that expanded, contracted, and changed colors in unison. The group aura would expand to include large sections in the stands. Sometimes, such as when a winning shot was made, the entire spectator section for the scoring side would be enveloped in a singular group aura.

Most interesting was seeing two auras interact and react while the people themselves might not be having any visible notice of one another. For instance, a basketball player shooting a foul shot might be having a strong auric interaction with an opponent standing some distance away along the foul perimeter line waiting for the rebound after the shot. The two players may not even be looking at each other or noticeably communicating in any way, while their auras were having fits with each other. Even more interesting, there were often other players in between the two, and the auras of these were completely uninvolved and not having any interaction with either of the two players that were having auric confrontations.

A lot happened to me in my life between age 15 and 17. Events that ran the gamut from traumatizing to energizing and inspiring. Many events that changed my life dramatically, and

Seeing, Feeling & Reading the Aura

even now, over 40 years later, still motivate some of my actions. One of those events was getting my first pair of prescription eyeglasses when I was in 9th grade. I got aviator style because I thought I looked cool. For a couple of days I had an extra strut to my step in school thinking I was impressing the girls by looking both scholarly and cool with my glasses. My feelings of happiness with my new glasses came to a sudden, screeching halt, when I tried to see someone's aura for the first time since I had been wearing my glasses. There was nothing! Not even the slightest hint of an aura.

At first I was sure there must be something radically wrong with that person that they had no aura at all, until I tried seeing another person's aura and they didn't have one either! I hurriedly took off my glasses like they were a caustic chemical on my face and with a deep sigh of relief to be rid of the impediment, looked confidently at another person to see their aura. Yikes! Still nothing! Seriously beginning to worry that my one claim to fame, to be the only person in the world that could see auras, was suddenly gone, I looked at person, after person, after person, trying to discern even the faintest hint of an aura. It was all for naught. I simply could no longer see auras at all.

I was beyond devastation. As much as I sometimes felt guilty about looking at people's auras and learning some of their secrets, when I could see them no more I realized I missed the ability as much I would miss my Mom or Dad if they suddenly died.

At this point, though I understood that focusing beyond the person was the secret to seeing auras, I had no understanding about rods and cones in the eyes and why the distant focusing actually worked. Nevertheless, I was sure my glasses were the source of the problem and never wore them or any other type of corrective lens again after that day. I consoled myself that my ability would return shortly. After all, I had only worn my glasses for a couple of weeks. At the longest, I should have my ability back after a few weeks to recuperate. But a week passed, then a month, then months, and my ability to see auras did not return.

For the first few weeks I was angry and in a real funk, completely frustrated by what seemed to be a devastating loss that was beyond my ability to correct. Like an alcoholic craving a drink, I desperately wanted to once again be sensitive to auras.

Bereft of sight, but intent on having something in the aura realm to cling to, I began to take more notice of feeling people's auras. It was something I had always been able to do from my earliest memories, but had neglected early in life in favor of the far more interesting Technicolor show of seeing auras.

To my surprise, I soon found feeling auras actually had its own reward when I took the time to appreciate it. There were strange and fascinating sensations as I walked by people; tinglings, heat, cold, pressure. But there was more. I could in no manner read people's thoughts, but I became very aware of somehow perceiving, through at that point means unknown, their emotional state and their feelings. Correlated with what they were speaking, and the physical sensations I felt when near them, I found to my surprise that I was able to ascertain many things about them that would be completely oblivious if I was just listening to what they were saying. It didn't take too long for me to realize I was feeling auras. I had lost my ability to see them, only to have it replaced by a wonderful new field of study.

After about six months my ability to see auras returned suddenly and completely. But during the intervening time I had been applying myself with great enthusiasm and focus to learning everything I could about feeling auras, through observation and experimentation. And the things I learned shocked me to my core.

Seeing auras had always been my comfort zone. The ability was like my best and most trusted friend. But as I stated earlier, I found my interpretations of what I was witnessing to only prove by subsequent events, to be about 70% accurate. To my utter and complete surprise I soon realized that feeling auras was actually far more accurate than seeing them on some levels. The human aura is multi-layered. Each layer reveals distinct characteristics of a person. Feeling was at least 90% accurate and probably more with most aspects of the aura, with the significant exception of being unable to zero in on health problems as is possible when looking at auras visually.

At first this would seem to be ludicrous, that what you felt was more accurate than what you saw. But aiding the overall insight, there are several other indicators that combine with the transmitted feelings to create a very accurate understanding of many aspects of a person. A very helpful visual component that was previously completely ignored when I was just observing the vivid, dancing colored lights of a visual aura, was body language, which quickly became a fascinating field of study all its own. Body language, plus the feelings in your body of physical sensations of heat, cold, pressure and tingling as you enter another person's auric field, along with the intuitive empathy with another person's true feelings, proved to be astoundingly accurate in understanding them.

Note Though in my case it caused a problem, wearing eyeglasses or contact lens has never impeded anyone else I know from seeing auras."

Being able to see, feel and understand auras has proven to be the single most useful psychic ability I possess and one that has been with me since my earliest childhood. There are others that are more powerful. Some that are more dramatic or spectacular. But auric interaction occurs everyday, with every person, making it the most useful and helpful ability in everyday life.

Though for many years of my youth I thought I was special, even the only person that could see auras, as my knowledge and experiences expanded I came to realize just the opposite; everyone that has vision out of both eyes can see auras! I know in some circles it is counted as a spiritual ability. Among some other aura viewers it is considered a psychic gift. But as I have proven in over 15 years of giving "How to See" aura classes, everyone and anyone that has vision out of both eyes can see auras. And there's a very simple technique to learn that will allow you to begin seeing the first opaque, translucent field and the first white field within just 5 minutes of practice.

I discovered that seeing auras was not a psychic ability or a spiritual ability, but simply a new way of focusing your eyes. I learned that the eyes have components that are called "rods" and "cones" that change shape depending upon whether you are focusing near or far, or at the big picture or the small detail. By looking at something close, but focusing on something further away, your rods and cones create am eye shape that results in the aura popping into view. The

Seeing, Feeling & Reading the Aura

more you practice seeing auras, the easier it becomes for you to lock into this sp and the more colors you will begin to see.

Although I provide many eye exercises in my book Auras: How to See, Feel & Know to help you train your eyes to easily be able to see auras, the very best and easiest to access is the Magic-Eye 3D pictures. Here's an excerpt from Chapter 11 of my book that explains it. You can actually view these pictures for free on the Internet and it works just as good as having a printed picture in front of you.

"The invention of MagicEye 3D pictures created the single most effective tool for learning to see auras. When your eyes refocus in the manner necessary to see the 3D image you have just used your rods and cones in the exact manner necessary to begin seeing auras. When you see a 3D picture you are looking at something that is close, but your eyes are focusing on something that is farther away, beyond the object you are actually looking at. That is the exact technique for seeing auras. Although there are many other eye exercises you can do to help retrain the rods and cones in your eyes, including some in this book, all of them pale compared to MagicEye 3D pictures. I cannot emphasize enough that doing your eye exercises with the MagicEye 3D pictures will help you not only see auras quickly, it will help you see them in vivid colors and far greater detail than any other method you employ in your training. If you do no other eye exercise except learn to see MagicEye 3D pictures within an instant of looking at them, you will be well on your way to becoming very proficient at seeing auras in full, vibrant color.

Time after time in "How to See Aura" classes I have taught, there would always be students who struggled to see more than the thin opaque white auric outline after concluding the basic eye exercises. But once they successfully could zoom in to the MagicEye 3D pictures, they immediately began to see auras in wispy, pale colors and the world of seeing auras truly began to open for them.

An Internet search for MagicEye 3D pictures will find several sites where you can view a wide variety of MagicEye 3D pictures. Here are links to a few good ones:

http://www.magiceye3ds.com/pictures.aspx?page=1   http://www.magiceye.com
http://www.vision3d.com/sghidden.html

If you truly want to see auras in fullness and in vivid color, please visit these sites and incorporate viewing and seeing MagicEye 3D pictures for at least 15 minutes each day. This is the fastest method to retrain the rods and cones in your eyes to see auras. With some people, one 15 minute session is all they need. Other people may need several sessions before auras are seen in color and fullness. Persist until you succeed. As long as you have vision in both eyes, even if it's terrible vision, you will succeed if you persist. The longest I've known someone to persist until they achieved success is 16 fifteen minute sessions. So even if it's challenging for you it should not take that long before you are having great success seeing auras.

You should know that your eyes will not be damaged by viewing Magic 3D pictures. In fact, just the opposite, as eye specialists use Magic Eye 3D pictures for vision therapy. Think of viewing

MagicEye 3D pictures as Zumba for the eyes.

If you are viewing the MagicEye 3D pictures on your computer, to insure eye safety, maintain a normal distance from your monitor screen and remember to blink normally.

In addition to helping you be able to see auras, according to the Magic Eye websites, MagicEye 3D pictures are also useful for "improving vision, relaxing the body and calming the mind."

To have the MagicEye 3D picture "pop" into view simply focus through the picture. You can do this most easily by picking a single, tiny spot near the center of the image and from a distance of a foot to two feet, focus solely on that spot. Fairly quickly the 3D picture should pop out. Once the 3D picture becomes visible the longer you look at it the sharper the image will become. Once it is in focus you'll be able to move about in the picture, viewing different aspects and locations."

Angel's Baptism

One of the more amazing manifestations of the human aura I have ever witnessed was the baptism of my daughter Angel when she reached the age of accountability at 8 years old. As practitioners of Celestine Light, we believe that ultimate authority for important life events rests within us, not governments or religions or their leaders. It is based upon that precept that my wife Sumara and I officiated at our own wedding, and by that same precept that I had the honor to baptize my daughter Angel. But something very special happened on that day far more than just a baptism...

We were living in the NW corner of Washington State at the time, in a town called Sequim. It is nestled in a broad scenic valley between the towering Olympic Mountains and a large inland sea called the Puget Sound. During the middle of summer we decided to have Angel's baptism in the salt ocean water. The only problem being that the water in Puget Sound, even on the hottest days of summer is very cold, barely reaching 50 degrees Fahrenheit. However, we had a plan to overcome the cold! Following is an account I wrote in 2006, shortly after the event.

There was a tidal estuary near our home that was very shallow. We thought perhaps it might heat up enough during the long summer days to be tolerable for the few minutes of a baptism by immersion. With that thought in mind we made the 1½ mile hike down the beach two weekends before the scheduled baptism to check out our theory. It was a hot, lazy summer day, and to our joy we found the shallow water in a small section of the estuary right at the end of a long sand spit to be comfortably tepid.

Now that we knew our spot definitively, we sent out invitations to family and friends and timed our 1 ½ mile hike down the beach to arrive at the sand spit at high tide.

But we were in for a rude awakening. Unlike the day we scouted the area, the day of the baptism was partly cloudy and there had not been enough solar exposure to heat up the estuary. The water was ice, and I mean ICE cold! I could barely stick my toe in it without having to pull it back in pain. I'm a wimp when it comes to cold water.

Several people had brought their cameras to record the special event and everyone was still finding a place to sit on the sand dunes when I called Angel to come stand by the water's edge with me. "What do you think?" I asked sticking my toe in the water.

She stuck hers in next to mine and instantly had a shocked look on her face. It was really cold! Without speaking to anyone else we decided to be quick and waded out up to my knees, which was as deep as I could tolerate. I held Angel's right wrist in my left hand so she could bring her right hand up to hold her nose as she went under the water and she rested her left hand on my forearm. I held my right hand to the square and after saying her full name, I spoke nearly the same words Yeshua did 2,000 years ago when he baptized his wife Miriam, the same words I had said when I had baptized my wife, and the same words she had said when she baptized me, "With the purity of your heart as the witness of your soul, I immerse you in water that you will come forth with a greater love of God, to ever guide you upon the path of light. In the name of Elohim, so be it."

It was a perfect baptism; Angel's face just glowed with joy. Her aura was unearthly and astounding. But it was also very quick because of the cold water. Angel and I were back on shore before most people had even realized what had just happened. In fact, more than one family member was a little miffed at having walked 1½ miles on the beach and looking at another 1½ miles to get back, without even having seen the baptism because we did it so fast, before everyone had been situated and prepared.

The bigger concern soon became apparent: in our haste, though there were at least a half dozen cameras present, as far as we knew, only Kristelle, one of our other daughters, was the only one that had managed to snap any pictures of the actual baptism. Our main concern at that point was that we wouldn't have many pictures for Angel to remember her Baptism by, but it grew into a disaster when a day later Kristelle accidentally erased all the pictures on her camera!

A couple of weeks later we got an email from Shaina, another daughter, who lived in Seattle. Unbeknownst to us, she had also taken pictures of our adventures that day. Unaware that there was not a single picture of the baptism taken by anyone, when she had time about a week later, she emailed us copies of the pictures she had taken that day. As Sumara and I scrolled through the email looking at the photos of people walking down the beach, picking flowers, playing with seaweed, and posing for pictures, we were overjoyed to discover a single shot of the Baptism. But we quickly noticed there was something odd about it, different than all the other pictures taken that day; and it was something wonderfully odd!

Looking at the picture, our eyes popped open a little wider and we looked at each other amazed. Were we really seeing what we thought we were seeing? Angel's amazing aura showed up in the photo! It radiated from her, almost blindingly intense right over her body. It was easy to imagine that we were looking at the image of a true angel. I was holding her, but none of the effect was showing on me even though we could see a faint rainbow arc three feet away from Angel's body. In our minds that ruled out a problem with the camera. Plus all of the other pictures Shaina had taken that day were perfectly normal. The fact that it was a digital image also ruled out a problem with film, such as exposure to light.

Another very unusual effect you can see is that the shadow of Shaina taking the picture was interrupted by the intense glow of Angel's aura in the apex of her heart area. You can see a bit of Shaina's shadow on Angels face, but it is completely absent over Angel's body and not visible in the water behind her aura, even though her aura is translucent!

Noting all these unique things, we knew we were looking at the recording of a very miraculous

moment of divine energy, on a very special day, in the life of a young lady who is truly an angel walking among us, and one that surely brings an amazing light to the world.

We were reminded of the account in the Oracles of Celestine Light of the baptism of the Apostle Cephas, "And Cephas came up out of the water all aglow even as Miriam had been when Yeshua baptized her." Vivus 18:12. That is a certain and perfect description of our daughter Angel on the day of her baptism, and we hope she will carry that heavenly glow all of her life."

UNLEASH YOUR PSYCHIC POWERS

Chapter 13

ANIMAL WHISPERER

"Lots of people talk to animals.... Not very many listen, though.... That's the problem."
~Benjamin Hoff, The Tao of Pooh

That's an incredibly accurate quote by Benjamin Hoff. Humans communicate directly with one another mainly by speaking. Animals speak too, but in a foreign language that very few people take the time to try to understand. It's funny if you think about it. Our pets, which we think of as lower life forms compared to humans, actually are all bilingual, even though most humans are not. Dogs for instance, speak their own language with one another. Barks, whimpers, growls, yips, howls and many more sounds and inflections, all have distinct meanings to other dogs. But all pet dogs in daily association with humans also understand the pertinent parts of their human's native language as well, even if they cannot speak it to us. They are in affect bilingual. I've even known dogs that were trilingual! They were the pets of people from other countries living in the USA. At home the owners spoke their native language and that is what the dog learned for commands. But their pets were equally comprehended the same command when it was given in English.

Plus, all mammals and birds are absolute masters of body language, which I certainly count as a stand-alone language. That makes most dogs at least trilingual, and many quad-lingual! We can even add a fifth language for many, which is sign language. I have both parrots and a dog and all have been taught both verbal and several silent hand motion commands. If for instance, I wave my hand in a downward then upward half circle motion parallel to my body, my little toy poodle knows that she is to trot off in the direction my hand last pointed. If I raise my hand up in the air and look at my parrots, they know they are supposed to fly to my hand.

Animals are very smart and if you spend time with them they can really begin to communicate with .you. Not just understand when you tell them something, but also tell you something that you comprehend. When your dog goes and lightly scratches at the door most people

Unleash Your Psychic Powers

Cat Body Language

understand they want to go outside. When they carry their food dish over to you and drop it at your feet you understand they want something to eat. Both of those examples are typically not taught behavior, but self-created by the dogs own initiative and innate intelligence to non-verbally communicate with you.

Amongst their own kind, animals communicate primarily by body language and a wide variety of sounds. Scent can also play an important role, especially during mating season and with males marking their territory.

Each species of animal has its own distinct non-verbal body language and verbal means of communication. Whatever animal you have in your life, your relationship with it will be so much more fulfilling if you learn to understand their body language and as much of their verbal language as possible. Combine that knowledge with your intuition and empathy and you'll become a regular Dr. Doolittle.

Animal Whisperer

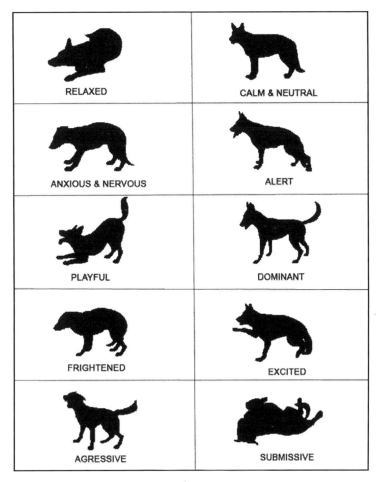

Dog Body Language

    With people, a good beginning to understanding what they are trying to convey is to simply be a good listener. With animals the secret is to be a good observer of their behavior and body language. Remember, they are trying very hard to communicate with you. Increase your level of observation and you'll increase your level of understanding.

    Here are some of the more common body language indicators from the three of the most popular pets: dogs, cats and horses.

UNLEASH YOUR PSYCHIC POWERS

Chapter 14
LUCID DREAMING

I'll always remember the dream series in which I first became aware that I could alter what was happening in my dream with a conscious thought while still continuing to dream. I was about 17 years old and living in Spain at the time. In my dream I was in an old European style city with a large fountain in the center of a circular roundabout, paved in cobblestones and surrounded on the perimeter with old, mostly two-story white-washed buildings.

I was nonchalantly strolling across the circle, almost to the large fountain, when two men in dark suits on the far side of the circle started shooting at me with pistols. I quickly ducked behind the thick walls of the stone fountain for shelter. Bullets were zipping and splattering into the water right in front of where my head and body were hunkered down below the low, two foot wall of the fountain. I could tell by the zinging sound of the bullets coming in from different trajectories that the men had split up and were trying to flank me on either side. It was only going to be a matter of seconds before I was helplessly shot to ribbons.

So, like I did whenever I had a scary dream, I woke up. The dream had been so real that the first thing I did after startling awake was to gingerly feel my naked body for bullet holes and oozing blood. It was only after I reassured myself that there were no holes in my body or dripping blood that I was certain it had all just been a dream. An incredibly vivid life-like dream!

The next night unfortunately, I had the same dream. It played out exactly the same way up to the moment that the gunmen began to flank me. The dream altered at that point as I found myself wishing I had a pistol so I could shoot back. Instantly there was a pistol in my hand! It took me a second to overcome my shock at a pistol magically appearing and then I was shooting back with a vengeance. But it only delayed the inevitable as I was a terrible shot and the two men continued to inch closer to me around the flanks. At the very moment they both had clear shots at me from each side I woke up again!

The third night I had the same dream once more. Like the night before, as soon as I thought to have a pistol in my hand one appeared while I was pre-emptively running to hide behind the fountain, even before the gunmen started shooting at me. But while still completely within my dream, I remembered I had this dream the previous two nights, and that it ended the last night just as I was about to get shot by a flanking gunman on either side. It occurred to me that if I could make a pistol appear out of nowhere in my hand I could make a bigger gun appear. Before I could even think of what type of gun I should conjure, I was suddenly holding a gigantic machine gun! Quickly blasting away at my two assailants left them full of holes and stone dead on the ground.

At that point I woke up, not from fear but with a euphoric excitement. I realized I had been able to control my dream while in the dream! I had totally been able to change a dreadful outcome where I would have been shot full of holes, into a far better one where I lived and the bad guys died. Incredibly, these conscious thoughts had all occurred while I was completely in the dream state! Plus, this was not just a lucid dream, it was a vivid dream. Amazingly detailed and seared into my conscious mind in a way that even after over 40 years I can still remember it clearly as if it had been a real event in my life.

Prior to this spontaneous dream experience I had never had a lucid dream that I was aware of. In fact, I'm not even sure I knew what lucid dreaming was other than a vague understanding that it was somehow a more vivid dream.

I thought a fabulous new world of nighttime adventure had opened up to me only to be disappointed when I went the entire next month without a single lucid dream. I had dreams every night, some of them quite wonderful, but none that I was able to consciously create any change in what was occurring.

Determined to experience the fantastic world of lucid dreaming again, I tried various techniques to stimulate the proper biological alchemy to allow lucid dreaming. Though my original series of lucid dreams seemed to have no connection to my techniques, I tried them anyway. These included, eating really bad combinations of food just before going to sleep, such as mixing ketchup, hot chocolate with milk, and orange juice. I was quite successful in producing an upset stomach and a tortured sleep, but no lucid dreams. I also tried taking a really hot shower in one bathroom then hurrying over to the other where I had prepared a cold bath with a bag full of ice cubes poured into the water. Again, though my teeth chattered and my testicles disappeared, no lucid dreams occurred that night while I slept.

Then I tried setting my alarm clock to go off every hour. The theory being that needing to wake up every hour and set the alarm for the next hour, I would never get into a sound sleep and hopefully find a dreamy state in between sleep and awake where I could dream and still have conscious control. But this experiment was also a complete failure.

Yet having once tasted such a vivid state of being an all-powerful, in control of my life super dude, able to face deadly threats with no fear of consequences, I was not willing to quietly forget about lucid dreaming and chalk it up to a freak one dream series experience. I was determined to lucid dream again.

Lucid Dreaming

I next considered a modification of my alarm clock plan. Realizing that the dreams I most remembered every day were those right before I awoke in the morning, I decided to have my alarm clock ring just once about 2 hours before I would normally awake from my normal 8 hours sleep. My hope being I would be able to go quickly back to sleep and back into whatever dream I had been dreaming, but with lucid control. I tried this every night for a week, experimenting with varying alarm times from 5 hours after retiring to 7, and still not one lucid dream.

At the end of the week I was venting my frustrations with my friend Karen and she suggested instead of going right back to sleep after awaking to the early alarm, that I instead got up out of bed and played a game of solitaire. She suspected I was on the right path trying to wake early during the time I most remembered my dreams. But she speculated that if I awoke and focused on a meaningless mental task that forced me to stay present in the moment, that awareness might carry over into my dreams when I returned to sleep.

The first two nights I tried her suggestion I couldn't get back to sleep and was groggy and zombie-like all the rest of the day on both occasions. I couldn't bear the thought of a third day of being almost asleep while I was awake, so I abandoned Karen's experiment. I learned years later that she was actually on to something. Dream researchers using EEG machines to monitor the sleepers, discovered that a similar technique was the most successful at inducing lucid dreaming.

Then one day while I was not thinking about lucid dreaming, a realization suddenly popped into my head that I had been lucid dreaming for many years and just never realized it before. For as long as I could remember back into my earliest childhood I had dreams of flying; but they did not start out with the ability to fly. It was an evolving process and one that I had been consciously developing while in my dream state for many years.

The first flying dream I remember from when I was very young, was nothing more than running and taking extra big skipping jumps as I ran. But that consciously evolved while I was dreaming, into making great bounding leaps of several feet every time a foot touched the ground. Finally the day came when I was able to leap off the ground and actually fly some distance, albeit still quite close to the ground and only from a hilltop down the slope. I spent many dreams after that trying to fly further and eventually higher.

After several years I was able to fly low over valleys, mostly in a horizontal line from one hilltop to another. Eventually, I was able to soar up high into the air like Superman and it created an amazing euphoric feeling that would stay with me the entire next day while I was awake. I understood now that these were lucid dreams because while I was dreaming I was aware of my previous flying ability and was consciously striving to improve it in each subsequent dream. The most fascinating part for me was to realize that I learned to fly in my dreams over a period of years of practice and experience, just like I would learn a skill during my awake times during the day.

Though I was able to lucidly improve my flying ability with each dream I had no ability to consciously create a flying dream on any given night. I loved them so much and the happiness rush they gave me that I yearned for them every night I closed my eyes to sleep. Sometimes I would have two or three in a week. But other times I would go months in between flying dreams. That created some frustration as flying dreams were something I really wanted, but had no ability to consciously manifest. They just happened when they happened. When I was lucky enough to have one I always had lucid control in the dream.

A Lucid Dreaming Method That Works

Finally, I found a way to instigate lucid dreams. It works for me and I hope it will work for you as well. I reasoned that the entire lucid dreaming experience was taking place in my mind, but was probably also connected to the depth and quality of sleep my body was experiencing. Waking up every couple of hours to an alarm or eating food that gave me an upset stomach were not conducive to a quality night's sleep. With these understandings I set two parameters.

Lucid dreams were occurring in my mind. I was the master of my mind, therefore, I commanded my mind to lucid dream that night. As I lay my head upon my pillow and closed my eyes to nod off, one of my last conscious actions was to command myself to lucid dream and to remember my dreams. I actually whispered out loud, "You will lucid dream tonight Embrosewyn and you will remember your dreams." I repeated that command at least three times before I drifted into sleep.

Having determined that a long, quality sleep was vital to success, I decided to not even try to lucid dream if I had any problems that had been vexing me during the day that I was still thinking about anytime in the evening. Relationships, school, health, anything that might be causing any kind of anxiety that might give me a fitful night's sleep, eliminated that night as a potential for lucid dreaming. In this same vein, I also negated trying to lucid dream on any night where I went to bed late or ate or drank anything, even a snack, within 4 hours of bedtime. I didn't want to have to get up to pee or have devils dancing in my belly from food digestion wars. When none of those stoppers were in the way I was cleared for takeoff to dreamland and a night of lucid dreams.

The first night I tried this I had a marvelous lucid dream. The next two times I determined to lucid dream, I failed. The fourth time I succeeded, then had three more misses before another success. Over time my success rate improved and after about a year of practice, only making attempts one or two nights a week, I reached about a 70% success rate of having lucid dreams when I commanded them to occur.

This has proven to be a very good technique for me. If you desire to lucid dream I highly recommend you give this method a try. And don't be discouraged if you have never had a lucid dream. In the seventies, Stephen La Berge, Ph.D, a Lucid Dream Researcher at Stanford University, concluded that though only about 20% of the population naturally experienced lucid dreaming, every person could lucid dream if they invested serious, sustained effort and focused mental discipline.

Lucid Dreaming

For many years I was sure lucid dreaming must be occurring in the Theta state as that is where most regular dreams reside. But I wasn't surprised when the Neurological Laboratory in Frankfurt, Germany concluded studies of lucid dreamers in 2009 that showed the participants were in a Gamma state at 40 Hz while they were lucid dreaming. That is a brain level activity far higher than normal dreaming and even higher than normal awake consciousness! Many great psychic abilities and paranormal powers are generated in the Gamma state, so it seems obvious now in retrospect that of course lucid dreaming would also be occurring in Gamma.

Another technique I have used and many other lucid dreamers have found successful, is to take a daytime nap of at least one hour. Two hours is even more effective. It's useful to have some familiar sounds going on in the distance, such as a TV on, a family member working in the house, or activity on the other side of your closed office door, if you are at work. It helps to be very drowsy. Working at a computer or reading a book is often helpful to induce a state of drowsiness. I'm not sure why this method works, but if you get to sleep you have a good chance of entering into a lucid dream, especially if you have commanded yourself to lucid dream before you nod off.

Sleeping patterns and dreams have been a subject of continual interest to scientific researchers. Using EEG machines (electroencephalogram) the electrical bursts of neuron activity in the brain can be monitored while sleeping and correlated with eye movement and other physiological muscle movements.

Sleep researchers have categorized five distinct periods that occur during sleep. Usually a person getting a sound sleep will go through the complete five step cycle four to five times during the night, with each cycle typically lasting about ninety minutes. The most vivid and detailed dreams occur in the fifth stage known as REM (rapid eye movement). As each sleep cycle gives way to the next, the length of time in REM increases while time in the third and fourth stages decrease, so that the complete cycle still lasts about 90 minutes. If you are having a night full of intricate, vivid dreams you may entirely omit stages three and four and just skip from stage two to REM.

- Stage One is a light sleep state that usually lasts less than ten minutes and will often contain disconnected images or short dream flashes of people you encountered or were thinking about in your day.
- Stage Two is typically another ten minute period. During Stage Two the brain waves slow down and drop into Theta in a light sleep. Dreams will still have short disconnected threads and will morph from one disconnected thing to another.
- Stage Three is a transition from Theta brain waves into Delta and is characterized by a deeper level of sleep and longer more detailed dreams, although dreamers report to researchers that dreams in Stage Three tend to be more rational and mundane and less full of fantasy and dream-like imagination.
- Stage Four is mostly in the very slow Delta brain waves and a very deep sleep. A

person roused from their sleep while in Stage Four will likely be somewhat disoriented. There may be some drifting back into Theta with vivid and detailed dreams, but not lucid.

- Stage Five is REM, also known as "paradoxical sleep." This is where fully formed dreams occur. This is the storybook that comes to life and typically you are the star of the show! If you happen to awaken in the morning after just finishing the Stage Five REM in your sleep cycle, you will vividly remember your last dream.

The reason Stage Five is called paradoxical is because brain activity often shoots up from Theta into the Beta range and in the case of lucid dreaming, into the Gamma brain wave level. These are levels normally associated with awake consciousness, yet the body remains so relaxed the muscles are virtually paralyzed. Many dream researchers believe that the body's muscle paralysis occurs in the vivid, detailed dreams of Stage Five REM, as a safety mechanism to protect dreamers from hurting themselves or others by getting up and acting out their dreams, perhaps even with fatal results.

It should be noted that sleepwalking and night terrors have been observed to be sleep arousal conditions, which occur in stages three and four and are not related to Stage Five REM sleep.

Humans are not unique to the world of dreaming and the same brain wave activity stages appear in other mammals during sleep as they do in humans. The source of the Theta brain waves generated frequently during REM originate in the hippocampus deep in the inner brain. Theta brain waves seem to occur with all mammals during REM sleep. Unfortunately there is currently no way to know if animals have lucid dreams because they cannot report back to the researchers on what they were dreaming like human test subjects. But it is certainly interesting to wonder about. I know there is far more to animals emotionally, psychically and with innate intelligence than most people credit them.

Another interesting observation of REM sleep is that newborns and very young children spend most of their dream time in REM. Young children are like sponges absorbing tremendous amounts of new information each day. The fact that they spend so much of their sleeping time in REM would seem to indicate that dreaming while in Stage Five REM is critical to the learning process and retention of information gathered during the conscious awake periods. There is no reason to doubt that this built-in mental facility continues into adulthood, albeit with less frequent periods of REM dreams.

There is another form of sleep called narcoleptic sleep paralysis that is noteworthy. It is a state between deep REM sleep and wakefulness where the sleeper seems to be caught in both worlds. It usually occurs just as someone is falling asleep or just as they are awakening. They often experience terrible, very vividly real nightmares, made all the more frightening because their body is in a state of complete paralysis and they cannot move. They are most often aware enough to know that they cannot escape by fully waking or moving. This exact state is frequently cited by people claiming alien abduction, as the condition they were in during their abduction.

Lucid Dreaming

Everyone enters Stage Five REM sleep and dreams long, detailed dreams. But according to Stanford researchers only 20% of the population naturally have lucid dreams during their REM sleep. It is interesting to note the significant differences between normal REM sleep and dreams and REM sleep with lucid dreams. In normal REM sleep, the aminergic neurons in the brain stem are at their lowest level in the 24 hour day. With lucid dreamers that is not the case and their REM sleep and dreams are noted for high central nervous system activity.

In normal REM sleep brain neurotransmitter activity is switched off sufficiently that bizarre dreams are just blindly accepted, watched almost like a fantasy movie, with no inclination to influence or change anything that is occurring, any more than you would think to change a movie you were watching at the cinema.

During lucid dreaming, the aminergic neurons and the associated critical thinking ability are mysteriously switched on into active mode, while the body remains in sleep paralysis. Stanford researcher Dr. Stephen La Berge surmised that lucid dreamers are freed from the compulsion of habit because they can act reflectively in their dreams. Could it be that lucid dreaming is not some quirky abnormality, but in fact, an advancement in human evolution, allowing us greater abilities to absorb knowledge and adaptively mold our lives and create our future? Lucid dreamers expound with every dream, "I am the master of my life and I can create what I dream."

Unleash Your Psychic Powers

Chapter 15
DISRUPTING ELECTRICAL DEVICES

Disrupting, negating and even permanently killing electrical devices is one of my foibles and from what I've read, it's not uncommon and is often shared by others with psychic abilities and paranormal powers.

From my earliest memories in childhood I've had a strange effect on streetlights. Even as a youngster I couldn't help notice how streetlights that were on would go dark just as I passed by. The opposite was true as well. If one of the lights on a street happened to be off while the others were on, it would likely flash on as I walked by.

My Mom used to joke I should be on the *Outer Limits* TV show because often when she turned on a hand held transistor radio tuned to a local radio station and brought it within a few feet of my body, it would start emitting a bunch of static. The closer she brought it to me the more static erupted. When she finally touched my body with it, the static would overwhelm the radio broadcast. There was no rhyme or reason as to how well this would occur. Sometimes it worked spectacularly and other times hardly at all. Whenever my mother tried to demonstrate the transformation to visitors, the affect was often only slight. She would always feign anger with me then, telling me I was doing it (or in this case, not doing it) on purpose.

I had a much more reliable affect on television broadcasts. This was back in the days before cable and satellite TV. We had a multi-armed antenna up on the roof that would need to be rotated and pointed in different directions depending upon which channel you wanted to pick up. As a standing rule in my house I was not allowed to go near the TV when other people were watching it because almost always my presence disrupted the TV signal, making good signals bad.

The only exception to this rule was when after all the fiddling with the antenna direction the channel picture still would not come in clearly. Then it was my job to go stand next to the TV and put my hand on it, which always would clear up the picture. But I had to continue standing next to the TV with my hand resting on top of it for the picture to remain clear. This got rather old after just a few minutes. Besides being tiring, I also had to stand to the side so everyone else in the family could clearly see the picture screen. At such a severe angle, I really couldn't see anything!

Lest you think that the effects with the TV were nothing more than my body acting as an antenna, this was disproved when anyone else would try to influence the TV signal for better or worse and would have entirely no effect on it. While I could immediately follow them and create either a bad signal if the current one was good, or create a strong, clear signal if the current one was weak.

I never seemed to have any affect on electrical motors, but only on electrical devices that did not have motors. As a kid I didn't encounter many non-motorized electrical devices. But through the years technology has advanced in leaps and bounds and today there is a plethora of electrical devices everywhere you look, from cell phones, to computers, to iPads, to a kitchen full of appliances. So I have had an increased awareness over the years of my abilities to affect electrical devices.

One of my biggest bugaboos is with computers. As I am a writer I spend several hours a day working with my computer. Though fighting with my computer would often be a more apt description! I have good technical knowledge of both the hardware and software, but it avails me little when the computer goes wacko on me. When my wife has technical issues with her computer she hesitantly asks my help. She knows I will be able to resolve the technical problem, *if* I do not make matters worse by my physical proximity discombobulating the electrical components in the computer.

Both incandescent and CFL light bulbs are also frequently problems. Whatever their stated lifespan by the manufacturer, their actual life will be about $1/3^{rd}$ if they are near me. This is especially frustrating with CFL's which cost a lot more money to buy, with the promise that they will last much longer than incandescent bulbs. Not the case. With incandescent bulbs under normal circumstances, after they have reached the end of their life, they will burn out at the moment they are turned on and have a surge of current through the thin tungsten wire filament. But with me, fairly new lights that are already on, sometimes pop out just as I walk by.

Clocks are another big challenge. I have seldom been able to buy a digital clock that will keep accurate time for any significant period. Sometimes they lose two to three minutes a week and sometimes they gain two or three minutes a week; but they never, ever keep accurate time. Often they just stop working, even though they have fresh batteries or even if they are plugged into a wall socket. Interestingly, I seem to have the same effect on some mechanical clocks, even after I make adjustments on the clock to account for it running too fast or slow. As a result I have given up on clocks. I don't wear a wrist watch and don't use personal clocks to keep track of time during the day. I should note that the clock in the lower right corner of my computer never seems to have been affected by this time warping energy. Though I do not own a cell phone, I also seem to have no effect on the cell phone clocks of my wife and my friends.

I have at various times affected security alarms and airport scanners, in both cases making

Disrupting Electrical Devices

them go off without justification. Car alarms are quite sensitive and I have frequent problems setting those off just walking by. The list goes on and on. All of my family is so accustomed to strange electrical occurrences in my presence that they automatically assume I caused it whenever anything electrical malfunctions, and I'm sure at least some of them are normal malfunctions.

I have often wondered why and how it is that I affect electrical devices. My conclusion after many years of observation of the events and my own aura, is the electrical disruptions occur for one of three reasons.

- When my auric field is stronger and larger than normal it can create electrical disruptions with many types of electrical devices that are encompassed within my field as I pass by. Other than streetlamps, I have never intentionally disrupted an electrical device, so this usually will occur from a spontaneous auric expansion that occurs when I am in an upset emotional state or intense focus on a particular subject or project.
- Just like the sun has periodic solar flares, so do auras. It seems to be both cyclic and also random and unpredictable. I have never been able to figure out when one is going to spontaneously occur. However, there is no doubt when it happens, as light bulbs pop and multiple pieces of electrical equipment in the vicinity will fail or malfunction within minutes of each other. The stronger a person's aura, the more powerful their auric flares will be when they occur.
- Consciously projecting and focusing an auric flare such as turning off distant street lamps is another possible source, but it works best over distance when multiple people focus in unison.

Learning to Do It

So how do you develop your ability to blow up light bulbs and disrupt electrical devices? You'll probably have to start by being a little quirky to be interested in wanting to do it in the first place. Once you succeed, its not the best idea in the world to let people know you have that particular ability. If you break someone's expensive electronic toy or screw up their computer or video game, you could have some very irate friends, family and co-workers on your hands. And as I mentioned previously, once people know you have that ability they tend to blame you for every electrical malfunction, even when you had nothing to do with it!

This ability is completely rooted in your auric field, as are many other supernatural gifts. Learning to sense your aura and control its various aspects is a HUGE step in unleashing your psychic abilities and paranormal powers. If affecting electrical devices is something you seriously aspire to do, I highly recommend getting my book, Auras: How to See, Feel & Know , as it is filled with great exercises to help you master your auric field.

1. The very first step is to be able to physically *feel* your auric energy emanating from ***within*** your body. Seeing your own auric field is easier. Mentally imagining it and manipulating it is easier still. But to have useful control you need to be able to physically *feel* your inner auric energy.

Think about times when you have physically felt sensations inside your body. (Not including upset stomachs, heartburn, or sore muscles). The heart area is the most common location to sense physical sensations caused by dramatic changes in your aura. A "heart*ache*" over a lost loved one or lost love is a tangible, physical sensation inside your heart energy center. On the other end of the heart spectrum, deep love for another person, especially when the relationship is very new, can create a powerful, physical sensation in the heart area.

If you have ever been suddenly frightened, you probably physically felt like your stomach just dropped. You'll also typically feel a sensation like an electrical charge shooting through many of your nerve channels as adrenaline is instantly pumped into your bloodstream by your adrenal gland.

These are the types of the internal physical feelings I am talking about. When you physically *feel* your inner aura it will be a unique sensation, but it will also be a tangible physical sensation, just like the three examples above.

1a. A good way to become more aware of physical sensations deep within your body is to lay flat on your back comfortably on a bed with no noise or distractions in your vicinity. Close your eyes. Now tune into your heartbeat. You should be able to feel your heart beating in the center of your chest. Some people feel the beat just above their stomach area instead. If you are not sensing anything, really focus your thoughts on sensing the heart / abdomen area. Tune out any other sensory inputs you might be hearing or feeling and focus all of your attention on the heart / abdomen area. Most people will be able to feel their heart beating within a minute or two. If you are not sensing the beat, just keep focusing and tuning out other sensory inputs and you will succeed.

1b. Now feel your incoming breath. Still lying flat on your back on the bed with your eyes closed, take a deep breath through your nose, as deep as you can inhale. Be aware and focused on the feeling of the incoming air passing through your air passages, filling and expanding your lungs. Don't focus on the feelings in your nose as the air passes by. That's too shallow and easy. You want to be aware of the sensations deeper inside your body as the incoming air travels through your inner passageways and fills and expands your lungs.

You'll likely be able to feel the rushing air and expanding lungs on your very first breath. If not, simply exhale slowly and when you are ready, perhaps after a few normal breaths, once again take a very deep breath, as deep as you can, and be acutely aware and focused on what it feels like inside of you as the air rushes in and fills your lungs. If necessary, repeat this for a third breath after you have exhaled and breathed normal breaths for a couple of minutes. Most people discover that with each successive deep breath they can breathe a little more deeply, filling and expanding their lungs a bit fuller, with greater awareness of the feeling of the moving air and organs inside of them.

Now that you are familiar with how it physically feels to consciously and with intention, sense movement inside your body, you are ready to begin feeling the energy of your aura swirling inside of you.

Feel Your Internal Aura

You can most easily feel your inner auric energy at the very end of an exhaled breath, before you inhale the next breath. You can let your breath out via either your mouth or your nose depending upon your preference. Exhaling through your nose is helpful for some people to be able to let their breath out slower, which seems to help swirl and feel their inner aura at the bottom of the breath.

You should be able to do this equally as well from either a standing or sitting position, whichever you prefer. It is not as easy to manifest laying down, as that's a little too comfortable, which causes loss of focus. It works most easily if your upper body is in a vertical position, as this aids your inward focus at the end of your exhaled breath.

With your eyes closed and your hands loosely held at your side, palms facing forward, mentally envision your whirlwind aura swirling in a vertical column through the length of your body. Focus now on envisioning the swirling just in your abdomen. Take a deep breath through your nose. Maintaining the visual image of the swirling aura in your abdomen, exhale deeply. As you near the end of your exhale, focus on what you are feeling physically inside your abdomen.

You should feel a very unique sensation. It may be a warm and fuzzy feeling, or like a slight electrical tingle, or even like how your heart felt when you first met the love of your life. It will be subtle at first, so practice multiple times until you distinctly feel it. The feeling can be through your entire abdomen from your shoulders down to your waist. Or it may be more localized, such as just in your heart area or near your stomach.

Sending an Auric Flare

Once you have successfully, intentionally swirled your inner aura and physically felt it, you are ready to move on to the next step of sending out an auric flare. Just like the sun, you have an electromagnetic field about your body, which is part of your aura. And just like the sun, you can shoot off powerful flares of energy. Your auric flares can do wondrous things from miraculous healing of disease and illness, to more mundane games like turning street lamps on and off!

Your mind is the master controller and you are the master of your mind. Nothing energetically occurs in your body without either your conscience mental direction or passive sub-conscience consent. To send out an auric flare, simply do the same exercise as just mentioned, to feel your aura spinning internally in your abdomen.

Now do it two more times, where you consciously spin your aura at the bottom of a deep breath, before you inhale again. You'll feel the sensation most strongly at the bottom of your exhale and your feeling may diminish as you take in another breath.

After the third exhale and auric spin, take a fourth deep breath through your nose filling your lungs. This time when you are nearing the end of your exhale and are physically feeling your aura spinning inside of you, raise your right arm perpendicular in front of your body with your palm upturned facing forward. Mentally command and envision the auric power surging up your abdomen and shooting out of your raised right arm and palm facing forward. When you are succeeding you will physically feel the rush of auric energy spiraling through your raised right arm and blasting out of your upturned palm. After your success, take a moment to breathe normally and realize the momentous thing you have just accomplished. You have now learned a great secret and with that knowledge many wonders can be manifested.

Returning to the street lamps. If they are within 100 feet of you, they can be turned on and off with the power of your own aura, or if necessary an auric flare. The older the bulb in the street lamp, the more of its life that has passed, the easier it will be to manipulate it energetically. If the street lamps are further away, it is best to combine your auric flare with those of one or two additional people. When three stand together in unison, the power expelled is far greater than the sum of three.

Chapter 16
EARTH ENERGY SENSITIVE

I had to create a new category for this psychic ability of sensitivity to energies emanating from the earth, as I could find no pre-existing pigeon hole to put it in. The closest appellation would be Geomancer, but that is really just a distant cousin.

My first memory of becoming acutely aware of unusual energies emanating at certain locations on the Earth was in 1969 when my family moved across the country from Connecticut to Washington State, camping along the way on a six week trip. I was heading into 9th grade that fall and I loved science, especially geology. I had been president of the Rock & Mineral club in my Junior High School and already had a big collection. By matching nearby tourist attractions of interest to my parents and sister, that were also on the route of family we wanted to visit, I convinced my Dad to stop at several locations around the country so I could look for mineral specimens during our summer cross country camping trip.

One of those much anticipated mineral collecting localities was Crater of Diamonds State Park near Murfreesboro, Arkansas. I was extremely excited to have the opportunity to go to this location, the only spot in the United States that had ever had a commercial diamond mine. The state of Arkansas had recently purchased the property and turned it into a state park that anyone could come to and look for diamonds. Several big, valuable diamonds had already been found there. Natural diamond crystals are very rare. Of one thousand diamonds found maybe one is a well-shaped crystal. Perfect ones look like two pyramids joined base to base. Though clear internally, they have a cloudy surface appearance and are quite slippery! I had daydreams about finding one of these rare beauties and adding it to my collection.

We arrived at Crater of Diamonds State Park in the late morning, found a nice camp spot at the park campground, and after a short lunch walked over to the entrance of the diamond mine. We had to enter through a park visitors building and pay a $1.25 per person entrance fee. There were some exhibits and historical displays in the building, but with great enthusiasm to find my quarry, I ignored them all and dashed through the building and out the door following the sign pointing to the diamond mine.

What a letdown! It had just rained hard the evening before and early that morning. As I exited the building and squinted into the late morning sun, all I could see was a giant field of clumpy gumbo mud! Undaunted and still sure I was going to find a diamond, I raced ahead of my family and waded into the field of thick mud. With each step I took more mud stuck to my sneakers. Within minutes my shoes were so heavy with caked mud that I could hardly lift my feet to walk.

Though progress was slow I gravitated toward a small spot of the gumbo mud about the breadth of my arms spread, that was a slightly different color. Standing on top of it and squinting down I saw nothing but boring mud. But I still felt inexplicably drawn to the location. I looked closely at the ground again with greater scrutiny, but was once more left frustrated and empty-handed.

My father came up and asked how things were going and if I had found anything yet. I had explained to him on our journey to the park that over 30 different types of collectible minerals could be found at the Crater of Diamonds, including beautiful amethyst quartz. He was sure I must have found something by now as I always quickly did at other mineral collecting sites we had visited on the trip. I shook my head negatively and complained that so far all I had found were just useless little slivers of white quartz. I told him I had felt drawn to this little strangely colored patch in a very odd kind of way that was almost physical, but it hadn't turned up a diamond or anything else interesting, even after very close scrutiny. His only comment was that the mud looked the same color as all the other mud to him.

In the distance I spied a small, old mine building of some sort and told my Dad I was going to head over there to check it out. Laboriously trudging through the heavy, sticky mud I spent about 15 minutes circling the little shack and painstakingly looking at the ground for the cloudy sheen of a natural diamond, but all to no avail.

I headed back toward my Dad who had walked over toward the edge of the plowed field.

"Any luck?" I asked, not really expecting my Dad, who had zero knowledge of collectable minerals, to have had any luck.

"I think I did find something." he replied nonchalantly. Reaching in his pocket he pulled out his prize. I was expecting a small piece of amethyst or agate. Opening his closed fist he revealed a perfect, BIG bi-pyramidal diamond crystal sitting on the palm of his hand! He could see I was about to whoop for joy and he held his finger to his lips and shushed me. "Be quiet," he cautioned. "I don't want anybody here to know about it."

"Why?" I asked confused.

"Well it's big," he pointed out. "And if it really is a diamond, you said crystals like this are very rare. They might not let me keep it."

I was still sky high with excitement, but I whispered it. "I am soooo happy you found this Dad, I've been wanting one in my collection forever!" Thinking to go and look for some of its brothers I added, "where did you find it?"

My father was a naval officer and he had a somewhat gruff and stern disposition. He put the diamond back in his pocket and held up his index finger staring at me with his piercing, ice blue eyes. "First, this it is not for your collection if it's a diamond. If it is, I'll have it made into a ring for your mother. Arkansas is the state I was born and raised in. It would be very special for her to get a ring with a diamond I found in my home state. If it's not a diamond, you can have it." I was shocked and horrified at the thought of wasting a perfect diamond crystal to cut up to put in a ring, where it would look indistinguishable from the billions of other cut diamonds in rings.

He pointed back into the field of mud. "I found it over where you and I first talked before you went off to look at that shack. I had a heavy clump of that mud clinging to my shoe and when I lifted my foot to reach down and knock the mud off, there was this strange rock right in front of my hand. I remembered you talking about diamond crystals looking like two pyramids stuck together, so I thought I better hold onto it and have it checked out."

I understood my father's romantic reasoning for wanting to cut the diamond crystal int a faceted gemstone to put in a ring for my mother; but understanding did not lessen my own sense of loss. Not only was my Dad not going to give me a perfect bi-pyramidal diamond crystal for my collection, but that particular gemstone had been calling to me! He found it on my spot, the very spot to which I had been inexplicably drawn. I pleaded with my Dad, pointing out that my mother already had a nice diamond wedding ring and after all, he had found the diamond standing on my "holy" location and it would be almost criminal to cut up a natural diamond crystal. But he just gave me one of his stern looks that told me the subject was closed and to stop talking about it.

We didn't hang around long after that as my father was anxious to leave the park and go to one of the nearby rock shops to see if the crystal he had found was really a diamond. I told him it was, but he didn't put a lot of faith in my teenage geologic expertise. Driving about ten minutes out of the park, we came to a roadside rock shop. We all went in and my Dad showed the proprietor the crystal he had found. The man immediately verified it was a rare bi-pyramidal crystal of very nice size and commented that it appeared to be quite clear inside. A "real find" he congratulated my father. My Dad confided that he hadn't told the park people about his discovery and wanted to know what the policy in the park was about finding such a stone. The proprietor assured him it was "finders keepers" regardless of how valuable a diamond you found and that there were no immediate taxes or fees required to be paid on gemstones found. He encouraged my father to go back to the park and show them the stone so they could register the find. So we returned to the park and they measured and weighed the diamond. It weighed 1.75 carats and was noted as being exceptionally clear inside.

Some weeks later, after we had settled into our new home in Washington State, my father gave the diamond crystal to a local jeweler, who sent it back to New York to be cut. It could have made an impressive faceted diamond of over 1 carat if my Dad had directed it to be cut for the largest size possible. But it was more important to him to have it as perfect as it could be. There was a single teensy, tiny, internal inclusion deep inside the gemstone that could only be seen under a microscope. But my Dad wanted that cut out so the diamond he gave my mother would be flawless. Following his instructions, the final diamond was flawless, but it ended up only being .75 carats as a cut stone, having lost an entire carat in the cutting process! As a sidenote, if you want to gauge how much inflation we've had over the years, he paid $45 to have the diamond cut and $49 for the 14 Karat gold ring he had the faceted stone set into, in 1969.

My mother passed away in 2000, and the only thing I wanted from her estate, after waiting decades, was that diamond that had called to me so many years ago. But it was not to be. Though I asked for it, reminding him of the circumstances of its finding in 1969, my father gave it, along with all my mother's other jewelry, to my sister. He told me that jewelry was for girls and so it should all go to the only girl in the family.

During the years in between 1969 and 2000, I returned to the Crater of Diamonds on two other occasions. But I was never called to another gemstone there, let alone a bi-pyramidal diamond crystal. At the time of my two other visits, I did not feel drawn to any particular area. I remembered the exact spot where the off-colored mud had been where my father had found the diamond, but the dry dirt there on my subsequent visits was all the same color and there was no force of any kind drawing me to the location.

Over the years as my psychic and paranormal abilities have manifested and grown, I have reflected back to that day in July, in 1969, when I felt so inexorably drawn to that odd colored patch of gumbo mud at the Crater of Diamonds. And equally curious, why I did not feel a similar draw on two subsequent visits to the park. Nor could I find any spots in the diamond field with the strange colored mud, even though I was sure I was standing very near the spot, by triangulating my position from the park building to the old mine shack that was still standing.

I remembered my father's comment that the mud at that special location of the diamond find had looked the same color to him as all the other mud in the field. And of course it was. I had not been seeing the true physical color of the mud, but an auric color that was being projected by the diamond laying just beneath the surface. I had dearly desired to find a diamond exactly like that bi-pyramidal crystal. One just happened to be there close to the surface on that day and everything came together to manifest it to me. I felt it with my aura and had been drawn to the exact location by physical feelings and psychic energy, compounded by a strange auric color of the mud that apparently only I could see. It took me years to understand the full ramifications of that day. To realize that though I never got to possess the physical diamond I sought and located, I had discovered gifts of power that I had never imagined before. And they have proven to be far more precious than the bi-pyramidal diamond crystal I never got to possess!

Earth Energy Sensitive

Meeting a Dinosaur

During that same cross country camping trip in 1969, I had one other occasion to experience my new found sensitivity to energies of the Earth. We were driving through "Big Sky" Montana on a two lane hi-way, way out in the country somewhere. I had been sleeping in the car when I was suddenly roused by a burst of energy radiating through my nerve endings like a sudden rush of adrenaline. I immediately thought of the sensations I had felt with the diamond in Arkansas. "Dad, pull over." I implored.

"It's the middle of the nowhere, I can't pull over." He replied matter-of-factly.

"I really need you to pull over right away," I urged.

"You can hold it and wait till the next town to go to the bathroom." He advised.

I actually didn't need to relieve myself, but I told my father, "I can't hold it Dad, please pull off the road the very next little spot you can."

Within a minute a spot came up and my father pulled off the road into a fairly substantial dirt pull off area. I noticed a dry wash leading away from the edge of the pull-off. I got out of the car and headed down it like I was looking for a likely spot to do my business. But my true agenda was to discover the source of the energy pulling me up the wash. Even though we must have traveled a mile from the time I first asked my father to pull over until he actually did, I was physically feeling an attraction to the dry wash I was heading further into.

I heard my Dad yell out behind me, "You don't need to go that far to pee!" Continuing to look forward as I walked, I looked back and yelled that I was also looking for rocks. My Mom then shouted she was going to make lunch at the pull-off so go ahead and look. She knew I loved my rocks. With permission to now take my time, I stopped, closed my eyes and tuned into what I was feeling. It felt like there was a slight pressure pushing on me from my left, so opening my eyes I scrutinized the hillside in that direction more closely. About 30 feet ahead and 8 feet up the hill I could see what appeared to be a board sticking out of the hill. But this was a rock hillside and there shouldn't be a board embedded in it, so I went over to investigate further.

Coming up to the "board," which was jutting out a couple of inches from the soft sandstone rock hill, I quickly noticed the center area was lighter in color than the outer and had a notable porosity. I went back to the car to grab my pointed rock pick and returned to chisel what I was sure was a dinosaur bone out of the crumbly rock. It only took about ten minutes of not very careful chipping with the rock hammer before I had my prize. To this day I have no idea what dinosaur it belongs to, but I treasure it nonetheless, mostly because of the way I discovered it.

It is so easy to be caught up in the mundane world. Seeing that old fossilized bone from a stop in the middle of nowhere, Montana in 1969, reminds me not to get so caught up in living in the everyday world that I forget I am more than a mundane man. I believe this is true of each and every person on this Earth. We all just need to discover the uniqueness that is too often dormant inside of us. As David McKay once said, "I believe there is something great within every person, calling for something greater."

High School Rock Seer

Through my High School years I continued to self-study my sensitivity to energies of the Earth, particularly when I ardently wanted to find special crystals and minerals. While living in Washington state, I was president of my school Rock & Mineral club for two years in a row, mainly because I was very adept at locating the best places for the club members to dig on field trips to find the most fantastic specimens. Some of that ability certainly came from my geologic knowledge and pre-trip research. But once I was in the field, just like in Arkansas I would be called to the exact spot we should dig or crack open bedrock to discover treasures within. I have used this ability for decades to discover a wide variety of museum quality crystals from many previously undiscovered collecting localities.

Ancient Sharks in Spain

By the time I was a senior in High School, I had fully accepted that I had some sort of psychic gift for finding treasures of the Earth and was continually trying to find new ways to test it and expand it. In the summer before my last year of High School, my family moved to Rota, Spain, where my father took command of a Navy ship home-ported there. Our house was on a cliff on the naval base, overlooking a long, uninhabited beach. Because we lived on a military installation, the beach was off-limits to civilians and patrolled by the Spanish Guardia Civil; but families living on the base were free to use it.

As far as my less than thorough research revealed, there were no interesting minerals anywhere nearby. But I learned that Spanish treasure galleons, returning laden with gold, silver and gems from the New World, made landfall and ported in the ancient city of Cadiz, just across the large bay from Rota. I had a psychic insight that some of the galleons, having been ravaged by storms crossing the Atlantic, had limped into port and dropped some pieces of treasure in the bay right at the end of their long, perilous journey. Plus the fact that the area had been inhabited for so many centuries and by so many cultures, made it a ripe location to find relics and ancient man-made treasures.

We had purchased a metal detector before we moved to Spain and just two days after we moved into our new house, I was down on the beach testing it out. I found no metallic treasures, but I did find a well-worn petrified sharks tooth which I was thrilled about. The next day I brought my mother down to the beach with me and we looked for petrified shark's teeth together on the small gravel bars that formed on the sandy beach by the wave action. I found two more and she found three! She was hooked after that and came down to the beach three to four days a week to look for petrified shark's teeth. By the time our family moved back to the states two years later, she had a collection of over two thousand teeth, including a couple of enormous teeth from the prehistoric Megalodon shark, which looked like a Great White but grew to sixty-five feet in length!

Because they were abraded each day by the waves and coarse grains of sand, the teeth from the beach, though beautiful, were dulled and had rounded edges. Above the beach were some imposing compacted sand and clay cliffs that towered anywhere from fifty to one hundred fifty feet above the beach below, depending upon the location. Scanning the cliff faces while standing on the beach, I could see some thin strata layers exposed through the length of the over 1 mile long cliff. I suspected the teeth we found on the beach were eroding from the cliff face and if I could find any there, they would be in pristine condition. However, in most locations the cliff face was vertical and inaccessible.

Nevertheless, I took a morning one day to walk slowly along the base of the cliff as best I could for its entire length. I verified my theory was correct by finding four sharks teeth just lying on the ground that were in perfect condition. They had razor sharp edges and deadly points. Plus, having never been worn by sand and wave action, they still had the same brilliant enamel sheen they had when they were in a living shark's mouth. Because the enamel was already a calcium mineral, it never changed. The petrification process millions of years ago, occurred inside the tooth with the soft tissues and with the part where it had been attached to the shark's jaw. This had all turned to stone.

For a couple of weeks I hunted along the cliff base for petrified teeth and found about 30 total during that time. They were just laying on the ground having eroded out of the strata layers on the cliff above. Though beautiful, most of the prehistoric shark's teeth were small, about one inch in length and almost all were a plain, uninteresting gray color. If there was anything better in the vicinity I knew it was unlikely I would just stumble upon it walking along the cliff base. This seemed like a great test of my Earth energy sensitivity.

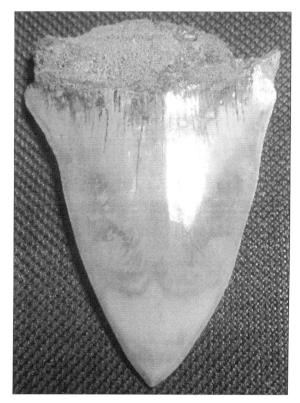

My Favorite Petrified Shark's Tooth From Spain

The next day, I traveled down the beach until I came to the location that was approximately at the center of the cliff. By looking right and left, I could see the entire length of the cliff. Intently focusing on my quarry - to discover an outstanding, amazing, petrified shark's tooth; I tuned into what my aura was feeling. I soon felt a pressure pushing on my auric field from high on my right side. Looking up at the cliff in that area I saw a strata layer running horizontally about thirty feet below the nearly flat top of the cliff. That looked like a place I might be able to pound in a metal anchor stake at the cliff top and go down on a rope to investigate the strata.

I decided to check out the top area for anchoring a rope and after about another half hour of walking and climbing I reached the spot. When I got there I was surprised to see two 8th grade boys that I saw from time to time also collecting shark's teeth on the beach below. I had showed them how to look near the cliff to find shiny, sharp-edged teeth. One of the kids, Jeff H., took a tooth out of his right jeans pocket that he said he had just found the minute before I arrived, in a tiny gully near the top of the cliff. It was big and filled up the palm of his hand. Looking at it, I was astounded. That was the tooth I was being led to discover! It was the most beautiful tooth I could imagine. Larger than any I had collected it had a burst of colors that seemed to erupt out of it from near the tip. For some reason, Jeff didn't seem as enamored of it as I was, so I offered to trade him the 6 teeth I had in my pocket for that one. He thought about it for a moment and then we made the trade. Thank goodness most kids are more

1603 Treasure in Spain

It wasn't just natural treasures I was drawn to. As I mentioned earlier, I lived on the Bay of Cadiz, the very location treasure laden galleons ended their journey from the Americas. After a little digging I discovered the beach below the shark's tooth cliff was exceptionally unique and conducive to finding old Spanish treasure. It was a mostly sandy beach with narrow gravel bars where we would find the sharks teeth. Scattered randomly through the beach were small boulders about the size of a washing machine or a bit smaller. One day I was psychically inspired with visions of treasure, to dig through the sand beside a boulder. I was rewarded beyond my greatest expectations. Beneath one to three feet of sand there was an impermeable layer of gray clay. As I reached the base of the boulder where it sat on the dense clay layer below, I was delighted to find a little trove of treasure. Every heavy artifact for hundreds of years had quickly disappeared down into the lighter sand. They traveled through the sand until they hit the impenetrable layer of slippery clay. Once on the slippery clay layer, they would slide down the slope back toward the ocean until they ran into the base of one of the boulders sitting on the clay. From there the artifacts could go no further, as they could neither pass by the mass of the boulder or sink into the clay.

Soon I was coming down to the beach every day to dig up another boulder. Every single one had a pocket of treasure at its base. My finds included many handmade bronze and copper nails, bullets of every era from musketballs to modern projectiles. Copper and silver coins from the 1600's up until the early twentieth century, silver and brass buttons from the uniforms of soldiers of many eras, silver crucifixes, jewelry and much more. All in all, a wide variety of great relics and coins. Who knew finding treasure could be so easy? I didn't even need my metal detector!

However, some boulders yielded greater amounts of treasure than others, so I decided to try zeroing in on the best ones with my psychic ability. Like with the shark's teeth on the cliff,

Earth Energy Sensitive

I merely stood on the beach, set my intention to find the most treasure under a boulder, closed my eyes and then tuned into where on my auric field I was feeling the greatest pressure. I was led to a substantial boulder in an area where the sand layer was the thickest on the beach, so I knew I was going to have to expend a lot of energy diging the sand away.

I came back early the next day and began my excavation. Around noon my mother came to the beach to look for shark's teeth and had been kind enough to bring me a sandwich and some water for lunch. I had been so excited to get to my dig in the morning that I had completely forgotten about food and drink. By noon I had dug completely around the base of the boulder and found a lot of handmade nails, bullets, old well-worn Arabic and Spanish coins, jewelry and other trinkets, but absolutely nothing spectacular. Honestly, I was certain with my psychic guidance I was going to find something made of gold.

Sure that there was something special in that location, I spent the afternoon expanding my excavation. By 4:00 I had completely removed the sand down to the impenetrable clay layer in a six by six foot area. That was a LOT of sand! But it was all for nothing. Other than the treasures I had found beneath the boulder, I didn't find a single item in the other areas of the excavation. But I wasn't going to give up. I went home and returned with my metal detector. I knew there was something there and I was going to find it! I had complete trust in my auric sensitivity.

Very carefully I searched the entire excavation area sweeping the coil of the metal detector over it. I could not believe that I still was not finding anything! My mother came over to show me the sharks teeth she had found while I had been digging my way through tons of sand down to the clay. I needed a break so I asked my Mom if she would stay at my excavation and keep an eye on the metal detector while I went out for a short swim.

I returned about 10 minutes later and my mother had the biggest grin on her face I had ever seen her have. "Look what I found!" She announced with dramatic flair. She was holding up a large copper coin. I had found many copper coins beneath the boulders but they were worn quite a bit from their journey through the abrasive sand. This coin was very different. The impressions were exceptionally sharp. Though it was corroded copper green, the details were so clear I would have been sure it was a modern coin, except for the crack. Ancient coins were made by putting a coin blank against a die and then using a hammer to strike the blank on the other side with another die. This crude die sandwich process imprinted the coin images onto the blank through the heavy pressure of the strike. In early coins this often resulted in a pressure crack beginning on the outside edge and radiating inward. Looking closely at the coin I spied the date - 1603! This was a fantastic specimen of a 1603 8-piece Maravedis! It was the first truly beautiful and intricate design the old Spanish empire made into coinage. 1603 was the first year they experimented with this radical new design. This was a historic coin in beautiful condition.

I was perplexed not only on how my mother had possibly found this coin, as her expertise was finding shark's teeth on the beach. I was also curious as to how it had avoided the abrasive wear of the sand like every other coin I had found on that beach. My mother answered both

My 1603 8 Maravedis. Notice the vertically aligned date on the right center of the coin

questions. She told me while I had been out swimming she decided to run the metal detector again over my excavation to see if I had missed anything. She was detecting right along the edge of my excavation when she came upon a fist size rock partially embedded in the clay. She kicked it out of the clay with her foot then passed the metal detector over the hole. A loud beep from the detector revealed the 1603 Marvedis down in the hole in the clay. The fact that it was completely unworn and beneath a rock in the clay, made me suspicion that someone almost 400 years ago must have buried it in the clay. That action had preserved it in pristine condition for nearly four centuries.

Then I had two big disappointments. First, my mother said I could get the coin when she passed away, but she was going to keep it until then, even though she had found it inside my all-day labored excavation. Even worse, later that day, while I was elsewhere, she took the coin home to clean. After sticking it in some vinegar to loosen the corrosion, she took a wire brush to its surface to further clean the corrosion off the coin. In her anxiousness to see the coin more clearly she actually severally marred the surface and even took out some chunks of what had been a coin so perfect that it looked like it had just been minted the day before, not nearly 400 years earlier.

As I mentioned, when my mother passed, my father gave my sister the ring he had made for my mother from the diamond he found on my spot at the Crater of Diamonds in Arkansas. But true to my mother's wishes he did give me the 8-piece Maravedis. Though it is not as perfect as it once was, it is still a great treasure to me because it is one more memento of what became a very important psychic ability in my life.

The Crystal Tower

The most astounding crystal specimen I ever found, was discovered using my auric Earth sensitive ability. It was in the valley of the mid-fork of the Snoqualmie River, in King County, Washington State, back in the early 80's. The mineral bearing areas of the narrow mid-fork valley are found in pockets up to one hundred feet in diameter, on the very steep, high mountainsides of the last six miles, before the valley ends abruptly in a rugged mountain face. The famous Spruce Quartz Crystal Mine is located on the mid-fork. Outstanding specimens of quartz and pyrite crystals from this mine have been sold to museums all over the world, including the Smithsonian, in Washington, DC.

On a warm day in late July, my favorite hiking, exploring and collecting buddy, Chris D. and I were bushwhacking up a steep, heavily vegetated mountainside. We were trying to reach a geologic formation called a breccia pipe which we had located in an old mining report. Breccia pipes were the very best places to find quartz crystals. The slope we were ascending was so steep we had to hold on to vine maple branches dangling from low growing trees above us to both keep from slipping and rolling back down the mountain, and simply to make any forward progress. But just clamoring through the maze of branches from a single stand of vine maple on a steep mountain can wear you out! It's nature's obstacle course.

We were about a quarter a mile away from our destination, a vertical granite mountain face, which we figured would be so daunting to ascend that it was possible that no one else had ever been there. Suddenly I got an auric tingle. An amazing, euphoric feeling swept through my body. I rarely felt the sensation, but through the years, by then, I knew what that special feeling was telling me. Though we were simply trudging up an unknown mountainside I knew we were very close to a treasure.

I told Chris to start looking through the dense foliage for a vug opening. Quartz crystals from the mid-fork are found in vugs, which are naturally formed crystal caves. Typically about four to six feet in diameter, they are lined on their entire inner surface: floor, ceiling and walls, with quartz crystals projecting inward toward the center. A single small vug can yield hundreds of pounds of shiny crystals. The biggest vug I ever saw on the mid-fork, one discovered and worked by some other crystal miners, was about five feet in diameter and thirty feet long. At the end of the vug it was all amethyst crystals!

Being especially alert, Chris and I ascended further up the mountainside parallel to one another about twenty feet apart. Suddenly Chris was yelling out, but it was in pain, not the joy of discovery. I looked over to my left to see what all the commotion was about and Chris was tumbling down the mountain, yelling, "yellow-jackets!" He grabbed a hold of a vine maple, swatted away a few of the stinging insects that followed him down the mountain, and warned me not to venture any further to the left as he had stepped on an underground yellow-jackets nest. I was standing very still because I could see the furious activity of the flying stinging machines swirling around the place he had been standing. I was close enough that I didn't want them to notice me as an additional target of their wrath.

After a few minutes they settled down and Chris worked his way back up the mountainside until he was standing just below me. For all the hullabaloo he only had a couple of stings. "I think your crystal compass is off course." he stated good-humoredly. "We found something underground, but it wasn't a vug and it dealt pain not reward", he continued dryly.

"There's something here Chris." I promised. "I can feel it. I know it."

I looked back uphill to reconnoiter the ground that lay ahead of us, and just a few feet ahead of me I saw a small opening in the leaf and vegetation covered soil. It was barely big enough for me to stick my hand into the dark opening. After Chris's encounter with the yellow-jackets I should have been hesitant to stick my hand in that obscure, dark cavity in the mountain. But I reached in with utter confidence and no fear, feeling very certain that there was a treasure inside.

The chamber enlarged inside. Reaching up toward the roof I felt innumerable crystal points. "It's a vug!" I exclaimed. Suddenly as I was still feeling the points projecting down from the ceiling a heavy mass of crystals just dropped down onto my open palm. It was too big to fit out of the small opening my hand was thrust through. Chris came up and using a rock hammer chipped at the opening until it was enlarged enough for me to extract the specimen. Gently holding it in both hands we were both in awe as we looked at it. It had a narrow triangular piece of rock matrix about one foot tall. Attached to this were hundreds of slender, three to four inch-long quartz crystals radiating out in every direction from the central matrix. It was one of the most spectacular specimens I had ever seen!

I moved several times in the following years to different homes. Each time I carefully packed my crystal treasure in layers of bubble wrap. But it was so fragile with those slender crystal wands sticking out in every direction that I worried with each move about breaking some off. Eventually I moved onto a cruising sailboat. With the tossing and impacts of crashing into waves while under sail, I became certain my special specimen would eventually get damaged. My sailing partner Skye and I were getting low on money so it seemed like the right time to part with my crystal pillar.

Putting into port at Ft. Lauderdale, Florida, we located the first store selling quartz crystals we could find. I didn't really want to part with it. So when I offered to sell it to the owner I told her the price would be $700.00, which I thought would be more than she would want to pay. Back in the early 90's that was a lot of money, at least to me. I was therefore very surprised when she immediately said, "I'll get the money," turned on her heel, quickly went into her back room and returned with seven one hundred dollar bills, which she counted into my hand. I passed the crystal tower to her with some sadness to see it go; but she was beaming with joy and frisky with excitement. As Skye and I walked away from the store my outlook changed to happiness as I realized that my special crystal tower would obviously be very appreciated and safe. I knew if it had stayed on the boat it would eventually have been damaged, perhaps even destroyed, and that would have been a real tragedy. My only regret was that I never took a picture of it.

Vortexes of Dark & Light

Going into 9th grade my family moved to Lakewood, Washington, a suburb of the larger city of Tacoma, after our summer cross-country camping trip. Every Sunday during the late summer and early fall, we would drive on short trips to become familiar with the area around our new home. During one of these trips I experienced a profound expansion of my Earth Sensitive ability that had nothing to do with treasure.

Earth Energy Sensitive

One of the locations we visited one Sunday was nearby Ft. Steilacoom State Park, which was only about a 5 minute drive from our house. I was really looking forward to visiting the park as it still had historic buildings from the 1800's, plus a sandy, salt water beach on Puget Sound. As we approached the entrance however, I couldn't believe what I was seeing. I'm sure my eyes bugged out of my head as I strained with incredulity and wiped them with my fingers to try and make what seemed to be a dark mirage disappear.

Despite the fact that it was a beautiful, sunny day, the entire park within my sight seemed to be shrouded in a dark, slowly revolving mist. As shocked as I was to see it, years of scoffing disbelief by my family at my psychic sights, ensured I didn't let a word out about the darkness we were driving into to anyone else in the car. It was foreboding and fascinating at the same time. I had never seen or even imagined anything like it before. Once we were inside the park, inside the black mist, I could see we were actually inside the maul of a gigantic, slow moving vortex of dark energy of some type. I could feel the hairs on the back of my neck standing up and I felt queasy in the pit of my stomach.

I told my Dad I felt really sick to my stomach and after just a quick drive through the park he reluctantly drove us back home. He wanted to go again the following weekend, but I deferred with some lame excuse.

The following year, when I was in 10th grade, Washington State history was a required subject at school. Everyone had to do a report on some aspect of the state's history and I chose Ft. Steilacoom. I had never visited that almost scary place again, even though it was the most popular hangout for many of my friends and kids from school. I hoped in research for the report to find an explanation for the black mist vortex and an understanding for my continuing aversion to the place. I soon found what I was sure were the answers. Some terrible, terrible deeds had surely taken place at Ft. Steilacoom.

First, I discovered that once the fort had been deactivated in 1868, many of its building were converted and used by Fort Steilacoom Asylum for the mentally insane in 1871, which later became Western State Hospital for the Insane, the 2nd largest mental hospital west of the Mississippi River. It doesn't take much imagination to visualize the many horrors that must have taken place upon the unwilling residents within the secret walls of the asylum. The strongest evidence that once a person was committed to the asylum they were no longer even considered human, and therefore all manner of atrocities could be performed on them, was the graveyard.

Not far from a parking lot in the modern park, is a graveyard of over 3,200 people who died while committed as mental patients at the asylum. Their final resting spot is marked by 3,200 small, numbered stones. No names, no identifying information of any kind. To this day nobody knows who those 3,200 people were. Once they were committed to the asylum, they were no longer considered human enough to bother with records. Think about it; 3,200 is a large number of graves, bigger than the entire population of many small towns. Many of the graves are reputed to also be mass graves. What unknown horrors did the many who died take

Unleash Your Psychic Powers

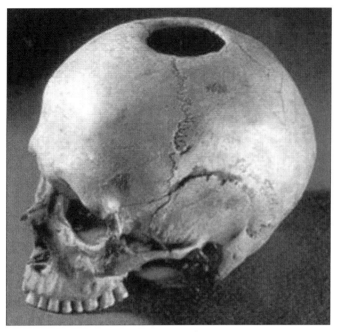
Skull showing trepandation surgery

to their anonymous, secret graves?

Many psychiatric treatments that were considered normal and mainstream even into the 20th century, and some even into current times, are right out of Dr. Frankenstein's manual for maim. Consider the psychiatric treatment called **trepanation**. Widely used by many cultures in ancient and medieval times, it continued to be used right up into the early 20th century. It was based on the psychiatric theory that demons lurked in a person's brain causing them to be insane.

The solution was thought to be cutting a hole in the afflicted persons skull. Hopefully, if the person survived the operation, which they occasionally did, the demon would have a way to escape and the patient could be restored to sanity. If they didn't survive, which was the more likely outcome, death was still considered to be a better choice than being possessed by a demon.

Frontal lobotomies, where an ice pick-like probe called a leucotome is inserted under the patient's eyelid and into the brain and then swirled around to destroy brain connections and nerves, was reported to have been a frequent procedure at the mental hospital into the mid twentieth century. Electroshock treatments and Insulin Shock treatments were also common procedures used to first electrically and then chemically shock the insanity right out of a person. The fact that quite a few patients the procedures were performed on died or became vegetables, was considered an acceptable risk.

I understood very clearly now what could be causing the black vortex of negative energy. Just thinking about all the inhuman, torturous, atrocities that must have happened to thousands of people on the grounds of that park gave me a headache. But as I did additional research I found that further back in its history, while it was still a US Army fort, there was another unrighteous act whose latent negative energy could very well be contributing to the black, negative vortex in modern times.

In the mid 1850's there were some skirmishes with the Native Americans of Washington Territory who felt cheated by the most recent treaties. Civilians, army soldiers and Indians all lost their lives in skirmishes across the state. Territorial Militia Colonel, Abraham Benton Moses, was killed in a small battle. After over a year eluding capture, Chief Leschi of the local

Nisqually tribe was arrested for his murder.

The army and civilian sheriffs had both been unsuccessful locating Leschi, as many of the local white settlers knew him as a trusted and helpful friend. The settlers didn't believe for a minute the chief had anything to do with the death of Colonel Moses and they helped hide Leschi. It was his own nephew Sluggia who surreptitiously captured Chief Leschi and turned him over to the army for a reward.

Leschi's first trial ended with a hung jury. Those who wanted him killed were frustrated by the many white friends he had who refused to cooperate, and by the additional non-cooperation of many of the army officers who felt that even if Leschi had killed Colonel Moses, it was during a war in which there were casualties on both sides and therefore could not be classified as murder.

A second trial was ordered and the judge refused to inform the new jurors that someone killed during a battle in war could not be considered for murder. The chief was convicted and sentenced to be executed. His conviction was appealed to the territorial Supreme Court. They refused to hear new evidence that proved Leschi was nowhere near the battle when Colonel Moses was killed.

Though the US Army was slated to hold the execution, they declined to do it on the grounds that no murder had been committed, as the death occurred during a battle and the rules of war should have applied. They were so incensed with the verdict that they would not even permit the gallows to be erected on army property.

Local county officials took charge of the hanging, which took place on Februaray 19, 1858. Even Leschi›s hangman, Charles Grainger, later admitted, "I felt then I was hanging an innocent man, and I believe it yet."

During his appeal to the Supreme Court, Leschi made a recorded statement through an interpreter.

"I do not know anything about your laws. I have supposed that the killing of armed men in wartime was not murder; if it was, the soldiers who killed Indians are guilty of murder too. ...

I went to war because I believed that the Indian had been wronged by the white men, and I did everything in my power to beat the Boston soldiers, but, for lack of

Chief Leschi of the Nisqually tribe

numbers, supplies and ammunition, I have failed.

I deny that I had any part in the killing.... As God sees me, this is the truth." (Wilkinson).

With the atrocities of the asylum and the injustice of the hanging of Chief Leschi, I knew without doubt the cause of the large negative vortex slowly circling Ft. Steilacoom Park. It wasn't until many years later that I learned how to dissipate those fields of negative energy; but I have never been back to Ft. Stielacoom park, so it is quite possible the negative energy vortex is still present. In the case of Chief Leschi, much of the negative energy lingering by the injustice of his hanging was likely dispelled in 2004, when he was exonerated by a historical court.

The unanimous verdict issued by a panel of seven judges, did not legally change the verdict of the territorial Supreme Court, but it did set the record straight.

John Ladenburg, a former prosecutor who helped Leschi's descendants present evidence to the historical court, summed up the case well, saying, "We cannot bring Leschi back to life, and we cannot restore Leschi to his land. We can, we must, restore his good name."

Enter the Light

Within hours after leaving behind the ominous, dark vortex at Ft. Steilacoom Park, I started seeing many other energy vortexes around everything from a tree to a pointy rock. These were colorless and more ethereal, almost mirage-like in nature. They looked like the translucent heat waves dancing on a hot asphalt road except they swirled in a slow moving vortex that seemed to keep the same diameter from the ground up until beyond sight in the sky. One might envelope an entire tall fir tree towering over 100 feet. Another might just be exiting the tip of a house sized pointed rock or hill with a diameter as small as my arms breadth. Some had innumerable, tiny, multicolored sparkles of energy that would burst into view and then be gone in the blink of an eye, only to be replaced by many more. I was flabbergasted that I had never noticed these energy vortexes before as they seemed quite common and abundant.

During my 9th and 10th grade years in High School I spent many hours and days, walking alone through the forests, the mountains, and the salt water beaches, specifically looking for energy vortexes, observing them, noting how I felt around them, how my aura reacted and felt when I was inside of them, and trying to determine what they were indicating.

I found some as tiny as the width of my palm radiating up through a single small plant. Others were as large in diameter as an entire hill or mountain peak. Occasionally I would find one that had a darker energy. Not nearly as large and ominous as the one at Ft. Steilacoom, but with the same black misty quality. These were always out in the middle of nowhere. Without doing more historical research than I was willing to do, I had no idea why they were there.

I discovered many, but not all pointy mountain peaks had positive vortexes and that the size of the peak did not necessarily correlate to the size of the vortex. But I found vortexes at other interesting locations as well, including every single water fall I ever visited, big or small.

Interestingly, some waterfalls had both a positive and a negative energy vortex within close proximity. When there were two nearby shoots from the same river, creating two nearby waterfalls, I was most intrigued to discover that sometimes one was a dark energy vortex and it's nearby neighbor was a light energy vortex. It made little sense to me at the time.

Walking through old homesteads I sometimes came upon old stone encircled wells. Most had been filled in and all had dark, negative energy vortexes. I assume that was from all of the junk and debris that was thrown in or fell down the wells over the years, but I can't say for certain why all the wells had dark energy.

The Disappearing / Reappearing Tunnel of Light

One day my Dad and I decided to hike to the Paradise Ice Caves on Mt. Rainier. The caves form during the hot summer months from melting ice at the bottom of an enormous glacier hundreds of feet thick that rests on the mountain. They are a beautiful blue color inside as sunlight filters in from the entrance and through the ice.

As we walked through the caves, we parted ways a bit, each exploring short side channels. There was a spot where some small angular boulders were exposed along a vertical ice wall at the base of the melting glacier. But there was something very strange about these dull, dark brown rocks. I could see what appeared to be an opening right in the center of the rocks about the size of an orange. It not only appeared lighter in color, it seemed to actually have an electric white/blue light shining through it.

I walked over for a closer inspection and squatted down to peer through the opening. I was amazed to see an illuminated tunnel of opaque white/blue light, maintaining the small diameter of an orange and extending as far as I could discern into the distance. A curious feature that definitely should not be on a rocky mountainside under 300 feet of glacial ice pack!

I yelled for my Dad to come to me. Not hearing a response I got up to go find him and he was just 50 feet away down an adjacent side corridor. "You won't believe what I just found Dad. Come over and take a look!" I exclaimed excitedly as I tugged on his parka to pull him along faster.

Quickly coming up to the rock formation I was confused and dismayed to not see the slightest evidence of the tunnel of light I had just been gazing down. I felt the rock and it was solid at every point with not the tiniest hint of light emanating from even a single grain. "Never mind Dad. I guess I was seeing things." I admitted sheepishly.

"It's OK. Let's head on out." My Dad turned on his heel and began walking toward the entrance to the ice caves. I got up to follow him but not without taking one last look back toward the rock exposure as I exited the side channel. "*Dang! There it was again!*" While my Dad continued walking back toward the ice cave entrance, I hurried back to the exposed rocks to view again what was now a tunnel of light as wide as a small watermelon.

I knelt down low to look inside. Because the opening was larger than the previous occurrence, I was able to see much further down the tunnel, but could still not make out anything discernible

other than a tunnel of opaque white/blue light. I felt a strong tingling in my auric field as I knelt next to the inexplicable opening. Cautiously I reached out my hand and it easily passed the edge of the rock and into the tunnel up to my wrist, confirming that it was a tangible, physical opening. But it was also unearthly, the auric energy felt very alien, and I quickly pulled my hand out, motivated somewhat by a fear of the unknown.

My Dad was yelling for me to "come on," so I reluctantly left the unearthly tunnel of light behind. Despite the physical reality confirmed by my hand entering the tunnel space, when I saw the size had changed I knew it could not be a natural phenomenon. It had to be something to do with an energy; probably one I could see, but not my father. So as excited as I was and as much as I wanted to talk about it, with some difficulty I kept quiet and just continued nonchalantly hiking with my Dad that day.

The following week I returned to the exact spot in the ice cave with my friend Patrick and hung around inside the natural icebox for over an hour, but once again didn't see the slightest evidence of anything abnormal. After that, I was too busy with other summer activities and did not return again that year. I did go back a couple of times the following year, but each summer season the ice cave forms differently as it melts and I never again was able to find that exposed rock outcrop at the bottom of the glacier or see a remanifestation of that particular tunnel of supernatural light.

Over the following years and decades I found the energy remnants, a distortion of space that is left behind from similar light tunnels that had been recently present, but were not at that moment. In years past I would only encounter a remnant every 3-5 years in my wanderings. But in recent years I have been looking for them more diligently and finding many more. I never unearthed any information about them in my research and never heard of another person seeing something similar until the very detailed account revealed in the ***Oracles of Celestine Light***: Vivus, Chapter 97 in 2007.

As strange as it may sound I agree with the explanation in the Oracles that these tunnels are gateways to other dimensions of space and perhaps even of time. Much more study needs to be done to draw firm conclusions. However, that has been a challenge as they appear so infrequently and in the strangest most unpredictable locations.

How You Can Become an Earth Energy Sensitive

Becoming sensitive to the myriad of energies that emanate from the Earth and coalesce in certain locations should be an extremely rewarding and personally expansive endeavor for anyone who desires to pursue it. I believe everyone has the ability to become sensitive to the unique energies of simple positive and negative energy vortexes, as their personal auric field comes in contact with them.

Both positive and negative energy vortexes are quite common. Many steep hills or pointy peaks have positive vortexes. Waterfalls, even small ones, are another easy place to find them. Negative vortexes are most often found in depressions in the ground or in caves. You'll tend to feel really good and invigorated when you are near or in a positive energy vortex and apprehensive, anxious and uncomfortable when you are in or near a negative energy vortex. Headaches are also common near negative vortexes. People unfortunate enough to live near negative vortexes likely have an abnormally large number of physical ailments.

Though vortexes can be frequently found, most are small and affect an area not larger than a few meters in diameter. You need to be right inside one of the small ones, right on top of the peak, or right in the waterfall, to feel the full rush of exuberant positive energy. With small negative vortexes you would need to be right in the cave or depression to feel the full dampening effect.

However, there are some vortexes that are quite large and their affect on your mood, emotions, thoughts, physical feelings and conditions, can actually be felt for better or worse, up to 100 meters or so away from the center of the vortex, sometimes even further.

Sedona, Arizona is one location that is world famous for the energetic effects of the large vortexes found near the town. There are other locations far less known that have even more magnificent vortexes such as the Southern Oregon/Northern California area. But they are in isolated locations, or in the case of Southern Oregon/Northern California, the vortexes are spread out over a 100 mile area, so are not as conducive to quick, easy visits.

The power of a vortex is not simply a factor of its size. Some very large ones have a subtle affect on you, while some of the smaller ones can be so activating or discombobulating to your energy that you may feel like you just drank five cups of coffee! Many people lose their sense of balance near powerful positive vortexes, so make sure you are on level ground with good footing. The constant difference between a large or small vortex is simply in how large an area the affect can be felt, not in its power.

There is no special training needed to feel simple positive or negative vortexes. I have taken complete disbelievers to vortexes and asked them to simply close their eyes and become aware of any physical sensations they are feeling. Within 5 minutes, even the most insensitive know they are feeling something very different than they have ever felt before!

Familiarity is the best teacher. Wherever you live, locate and visit the nearest waterfalls and the highest peaks. There will likely be positive vortexes at every one. Even small pointy hills have potential. Visit these type of locations often and stand as close to the center of the waterfall or the tip of the peak as you can. Close your eyes and tune into any physical sensations you are feeling on your skin, or inside your body.

It is important to also seek out negative energy vortexes so you have a reference to understand how different their energy feels from a positive vortex. Locate caves and low ground depressions in your area. The cave does not have to be large. It may only be an indention in a rock face a few meters in size. Every cave or depression will not have a negative vortex. Probably only about 10% of the locations do, so you'll need to look a bit more to find the negative locations. But even when you find nothing you will be finding something. Comparing the feelings when a negative vortex is present verses when one is not, helps you to clearly understand the difference between presence and absence, as well as positive and negative.

Abnormally formed trees are another location to find both positive and negative vortexes. Determine which it is by how you feel next to the tree. Every species of tree has a normal way for it to grow- straight trunk, branched trunk, etc. When you spot a tree that is not growing normally for its species, and it is surrounded by similar trees that are growing fine, you should suspect a vortex and investigate further.

For instance, my wife and I were married outdoors next to a positive energy vortex running up through a nearby Douglas Fir tree. Normally a Douglas Fir trunk grows quite straight up to over 100 feet. This tree was over 100 feet, but its trunk was spiral shaped! Because vortexes are a swirling energy, trees that usually grow straight but instead have grown in a spiral shape, are highly likely to harbor a vortex. Especially when there is with no other noticeable force nearby that could have conceivably influenced the tree to grow into such a peculiar shape.

Finding Gold

Recently, I have raised my treasure sights and have been using my Earth Energy Sensitive ability to find gold in Northern California. It is still very physical work to get the gold, which may be beneath a couple of feet of gravel or under a big boulder. But at least I'm confident in expending

Earth Energy Sensitive

the energy to dig, feeling certain my prize sits on the bedrock below waiting for me to lift it up to gleam in the light of day, perhaps for the first time in millions of years.

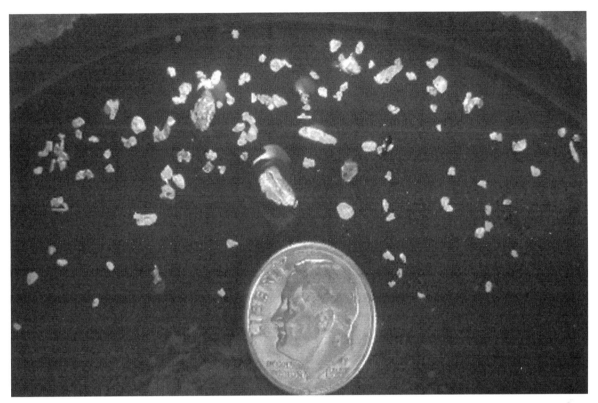

Some of my recent gold

UNLEASH YOUR PSYCHIC POWERS

Chapter 17
PRECOGNITION

Precognition is a firm knowing of a future that has not yet occurred. It is not thinking or feeling, or maybe it might happen. It is the classic psychic ability of ***knowing*** the future. Thinking something will happen, or getting a strong feeling something may occur, is more correctly put in the intuition or premonition category, even though it is very often mislabeled precognition.

It is also frequently confused with Clairvoyance. The subtle but important difference is Clairvoyance refers to knowing about people, objects or events in current time or very close to it, by a psychic sense, while Precognition sees further into the future. Knowing which cup the hidden ball was under at a carnival while you were standing in front of it would be Clairvoyance. Knowing which cup the hidden ball ***would be*** under when you visited the carnival on its next visit to town in 3 months, would be precognition.

True precognition is knowing the future regardless of how far away it might be, without a doubt. It can occur in nighttime dreams or daytime visions that vividly depict what shall be. These are especially portending if they are repeated on subsequent days. It can also be as simple as an unwavering knowing of something beyond your five traditional senses, that suddenly comes over you.

The most memorable time this occurred in my life was meeting and marrying Sumara. At age 16, both Sumara and I had clear visions of each other as the Soulmate of our destiny. But our powerful visions of one another from our teenage years had diminished by our early 20's when we still had not met, and we both ended up marrying other people. When we finally did discover each other in our late 30's, memories of the precognitive visions of our teenage years rushed back and helped propel us together despite significant obstacles.

Back in the mid 90's I was involved in a fairly new network marketing company called Emprise. I attended one of their motivational/educational meetings one night and was sitting near the back row of the room waiting for the meeting to get started. Just as the opening speaker strode up to the podium I noticed two ladies that had entered the room and were walking up the aisle to my right. By the time I observed them they were already far enough ahead that I could only see them from their backs. The lady on the right was an elderly woman I recognized, named Julia. The other woman with long, straight auburn hair wasn't anyone I had met before. I certainly would have remembered her beautiful long hair!

However, seeing was not necessary; I was overpowered almost to tears by the auric connection I with the mysterious lady. Even over the 30 or so feet that separated us, I was profoundly and powerfully connecting with her on every one of our energy centers. I had never felt anything like it. It was more potent by far than the auric connection I had many years earlier with my first wife's younger sister, and I had thought I would never find a connection greater than that one. My connection to the mystery lady was an unmistakable Soul Mate connection!

When the meeting adjourned I made a point of going over to meet Julia and asked her to introduce me to the enchanting younger lady beside her. Julia happily obliged and introduced me to her friend, Sumara. My very first impression as I looked somewhat in awe upon her ever so lovely face was, *"This is the girl from my vision!"* As we shook hands and our auras closely interacted on every single energy center, I immediately knew that this alluring woman, whom I had just met seconds before, was going to become my wife. As the days from that first meeting came and went through a great deal of turmoil and momentous events that followed, I never doubted for a moment that I was going to marry Sumara; the beautiful woman with the glorious long hair. This was precognition of a high level. It wasn't about a disastrous event, but a blessed and wonderful one.

When I went home after the meeting I told Skye about my meeting with Sumara. Even before I described all the details, Skye reacted with astonishment just hearing her name. As her eyes looked upward I could tell her mind was whirling with thoughts as she quietly said, *"She's the one."* One year later Sumara and I held hands and looked into each other's eyes as we exchanged vows that we had written ourselves. We were in God's temple high up in the mountains of Southern Oregon, next to a sparkling creek, on a perfect fall day, with most of our children, both sets of parents, and many friends in attendance. Sumara and Skye became the very best of friends; long lost soul sisters. Skye acted as our wedding planner, insuring everything went off without a hitch and was a memorable event for everyone in attendance.

Today, over eighteen years later, the three of us are still best friends, who work and play together and share many of lives joys and challenges. It is because of our psychic gifts that we came together, have been immensely fulfilled, and continue to look forward to even grander adventures in the future.

Consider These Psychic Connections:
- Sumara and I both had visions when we were 16, clearly showing each of us who the other was, with the understanding that this was our Soul Mate.

- Skye had a communication with one of her Guides about Sumara coming into our lives about 1 year before she did.
- When Sumara and I met, physically she was the girl I had 'seen,' and I was the man she had 'seen' when we were teenagers.
- When I first saw Sumara, though it was only from the back and at a distance, I immediately knew she was the one as we were aurically connecting on every energy center; a rare Soul Mate connection.
- Skye relates that she "powerfully knew" Sumara was the special woman we looked to be coming into our lives with momentous impact, just by hearing her name.
- Skye and I had just recently moved all the way across country from Florida to Ashland, Oregon, a place neither of us had ever been, because our psychic sense told us that was the place we needed to be. We arrived with almost no money remaining after the cross-country trip and relocation expenses, and neither of us had income or a job. But we knew, that no matter what, we needed to settle in Ashland, Oregon.
- Sumara had lived in Nevada for the previous 16 years. She too was prompted by her psychic sense to uproot her life and move to Ashland, Oregon 1 year after Skye and I did. She too came without employment or connections to the town.
- Despite financial and other obstacles, we were all inexorably drawn to the specific location we needed to be to meet, when the time was right in our lives.

The Soulmate Visions

Embrosewyn: Forgive me, but the hopeless romantic in me has to share some more of the details of the precognitive visions Sumara and I both had when we were 16 years old. They are happy memories for both of us, but also startling examples of how clear and important precognitive dreams and visions can be.

In 1971, when I was 16, my friend Patrick and I had gone on a bicycle camping trip to Mt. Rainier National Park. The night before we had camped at the nearest campground to the park village of Paradise and had decided that day to climb to Camp Muir, the 10,000 foot base camp for the summit climb of Mt. Rainier. About halfway up the trail around the 8,000 foot level, Patrick started feeling queasy. The first signs of altitude sickness were not surprising as we lived down near the town of Tacoma, at sea level. I was still feeling fine and wanted to continue the climb up to Camp Muir. Patrick demurred and said he was heading back down and would meet me later that night at our camp.

I watched Patrick descend for a bit then continued back up the mountain. As much as possible I stayed off the glaciers and scampered over the many rocky outcrops that had been exposed in the summer sunshine. There came a point where I had wandered off the beaten trail to Camp Muir as I followed the available rocky ridges. Climbing a rock exposure upward,

I came to a sharp promontory that dropped off several hundred feet. I was a bit disappointed realizing I would need to backtrack to find a new way up, as the pinnacle I found myself on was an upward dead end.

The view from the pinnacle was sweeping and grand, looking thousands of feet down the high mountain valley. I decided to rest there for a moment and enjoy the scenery, drinking in big gulps of the bracing mountain air. Startled by a voice behind me, I turned quickly to see who had snuck up so quietly and where they were managing to find a spot to stand on the sharp little peak I rested on. But there was no one there! My first thought was I must also have altitude sickness and was hallucinating. Then the voice came again, addressing me in a strange name I had never heard before - "Embrosewyn."

I saw a vague outline of a person standing in the air in front of me. I knew I had to be hallucinating. He was bearded with dark auburn hair and piercing gray eyes. He had on a white robe with intricate patterns of golden and colored threads woven into the hems. "I am Yeshua", he said. (I had no idea at the time who that was).

He raised his left arm perpendicular to his body toward the vast valley below me. "Look and see what shall be."

I saw two distinct scenes, one after the other. The first showed a most beautiful woman with flowing long hair and lithe and athletic in appearance. She had a dazzling smile and totally amazing blue eyes. "This is your soulmate." Yeshua said simply.

Next he showed me in a winter scene. I was sitting alone in the woods holding a shotgun. A squirrel scampered onto a tree branch across the clearing from where I was sitting and started scolding me in squirrel talk. For some reason, I could never imagine myself doing, I shot and killed the squirrel with my shotgun. "All life is precious." Yeshua said. Do not take that which you do not need." Then the man and the vision were gone.

I thought about my vision for along time afterward. Nothing like that had ever happened to me before. I thought it might have been some type of psychic insight, but as time went on I leaned more to it being a hallucination brought on by the thin air and lack of oxygen at the high altitude.

However, the vision came rushing back to me that winter when I was deer hunting with my father on Green Mountain. I had sat down on a log in a clearing to rest after trudging up and down the mountain for hours looking unsuccessfully for deer. A Douglas Squrrel on a tree across the clearing started chattering at me and for some reason I just raised my gun up and shot him. Tears came to my eyes as the memory of my vision on the mountain during the summer came flooding back to me. I realized I had killed what I didn't need to kill, exactly like I had seen in my dream. I walked out of the clearing vowing to never hunt again or kill an animal again unless it was life or death survival. Over the last four decades, I have never had to break that vow, though it did take me a little longer past that day to become a vegetarian.

I now knew my vision wasn't a hallucination but a true precognitive experience. I looked for the mystical girl who seemed too beautiful to be anything but a dream for some years, but I didn't find her. Eventually, I lost my way and married another. Eighteen years came and went, until one day, at a business meeting in Ashland, Oregon a mysterious lady with long, flowing hair walked past me and sat down at the front of the room. My heart skipped many beats and my aura became all aglow... But you know the rest of the story.

Sumara: Growing up in a small town in Michigan, I always found the wooded area ("the woods") behind our house to be one of my favorite spots to explore, and to just commune with nature. I never got tired of it, even though it was not a very big area – probably not more than 40 acres. I have many fond memories of the woods. I can still recall the pungent smell of the Earth that changed from season to season, each with their own appeal. The trail that led through the woods went from our property to the High School so by the summer of my 16th year I knew it so well that I'm sure I could have walked it blind-folded.

It was in the woods on a warm sunny day in the summer of 1973 that I had a most extraordinary experience. As I was rounding the pond like I'd done a zillion times before, I heard a voice call out my name, followed by a strange name that I did not recognize, which I later learned was my Soul Name. This voice was very unusual because it sounded as though it was coming from everywhere all at once – like it was piped into a surround sound system right in the middle of the woods (I don't even think they had surround sound systems back then so that was out of the question). I did not feel alarmed though. I heard my name again, followed once again by that strange name, but this time, along with the compelling voice, came the image of a very handsome man and an exquisitely beautiful woman, appearing before me, reflecting in the pond that I was by now standing in front of. I don't know if they said it, or if I just knew that their names were Philos and Saneen.

"We are Angels, sent by God to tell you about your special calling in life," spoke the compelling, yet vaguely familiar voice. "We have come to help you achieve your destiny by sharing with you some very important things that you must do, beginning today."

As he/they spoke, images appeared before me, reflecting in the pond. I saw myself with a man, whom I was told was my "eternal mate" and would be my husband in this life. We also shared the same destiny. I saw us speaking before very large groups of people. I had long flowing hair and even though I did not appear old, I did not resemble at all my appearance at 16 years of age, as all of my current facial features and short hair were quite different from the image before me.

I was shown a chronology of pictures of "my husband" from a young age to current time, continuing into the future. I also saw the most incredible, dazzling city upon the sea that looked like it could be God's own Kingdom. "This city would embody a lifestyle that would bring all who resided in the community closer to God," I was told, and that we would be instrumental in creating this most magnificently beautiful city. There would come to be many of these ocean cities around the world, along with many land-based communities that held the same standards and ideals. They would be linked together by common goals, peace and prosperity.

I was told that it was very important for me to keep my body pure for I had a special gift that depended upon my body being kept in pristine condition. I was never to drink alcoholic beverages, smoke cigarettes or take recreational drugs. And I should not take the life of any living creature for sustenance when there were other alternatives. If I did these things, I would be blessed beyond measure.

This may have all happened in just a moment, like an instant download, I really can not say, for I was transported to another reality where time was irrelevant.

How did I feel when this "vision" was complete and I was once again standing before the pond that just moments before was a superlative picture show? Instead of feeling excited and totally awe-struck after having such an incredible experience, I felt completely overwhelmed, panic-stricken and nauseous. I thought there was no way in the world that I could ever be the person that I was being shown and do the things that were being asked of me. I felt like I had been shown someone else's destiny, not mine. Surely there had been a mistake! I just wanted to be like everyone else my age, living for the moment with little care for the morrow; in other words, p-a-r-t-y! Furthermore, I wanted to be in charge of picking out my own husband and not be told, this is your "mate." I simply didn't know how to cope with this information. It was too much for me at the time so the only thing I could do was to forget that it ever happened, which I managed to do for over 20 years…until the man of my precognitive vision walked out of my dream and into my life.

Precognition Comes With All Types Of Events

Precognition is not exclusive to momentous events. You can have precognition over simple and mundane activities as well. Sumara told me of one time in her life when she had precognition of winning a raffle. She had entered a fund raising raffle sponsored by the High School, for a season pass to the local ski resort after she received a strong psychic knowing she would win. She had never won anything in her life and would normally have no expectations of winning the raffle. When the winner was announced two weeks later, of course it was Sumara. Less than a momentous moment it is true, but one still special because it was a verification of Sumara's psychic ability of precognition.

A Psychic Experience Full of Regret

When I was in 10th and 11th grade, in the early 70's, I attended Lakes High School in Tacoma, Washington. In a couple of classes I had the good fortune to occasionally sit next to a vivacious girl, with an engaging personality named Georgeann in a couple of my classes. She was one of the most personable and popular girls in school. But unlike most of the 'popular kids' Georgeann wasn't stuck up or snooty in any way; just the opposite. She was friendly to me and every other person. She spoke with interest and sincerity to everyone she ran into from the nerds, to the jocks, to the outcasts. It's no mystery why she was voted homecoming queen; she liked everybody and everyone liked her in return.

Precognition

Whenever we sat in adjacent desks, Georgeann and I would always have a short conversation while waiting for class to start. She was the only popular kid I knew who expressed a sincere interest in what was going on in other people's lives, rather than just wanting to tell you about their latest escapades. I think everyone in school counted her as a friend. Even if she didn't know a person's name, she would smile and say "hi" to them as she caught their eyes passing in the halls.

One day she was sitting at the desk in front of me as we were waiting for class to begin. I told her I had a vivid dream about her the previous night. She laughed, "You can't do that, you know I already have a boyfriend."

I looked at her very seriously. "I wish it had been something like that." I smiled feebly. "I don't know if I should even tell you because it wasn't a pleasant dream." I stammered.

Her smile changed to a stoic look at my words and demeanor. "Go ahead, tell me," she encouraged.

I began hesitantly. "I saw you helping a guy in a small car. I don't think you knew him. It was dark. You were carrying something and he was thanking you. He was injured or couldn't walk normal. Then something terrible happened to you in the car. I don't know exactly what. It was not so much what I saw, as what I felt. It was so awful I woke up suddenly. My heart was pounding and I was really, really frightened."

Georgann's eyes were wide in surprise. She obviously wasn't expecting a dream description like that. I quickly tried to undo the damage and spoke dismissively of my own words. "I didn't mean to scare you. Don't make too much of it, it was just a crazy nightmare." The I added one light-hearted caveat. "But just to be safe, don't get into any cars with strangers in the middle of the night, OK?"

She looked at me quizzically for a moment, then her radiant smile shinned again and she said "OK", then turned around as the teacher began the class. I never thought about the incident again while we attended school together and actually felt kind of stupid for talking to her about it.

I spent my senior year in Spain, but after graduation from High School, I returned to Washington and Georgeann and I went to universities at opposite ends of the state. One day I was talking with some of the guys I had gone to High School with when Max, another one of our High School mates came rushing into the room with news that sent us all into disbelieving shock. It was being reported on the news that our friend Georgeann Hawkins had vanished after a short walk late at night from her boyfriends house to her sorority house. It was being speculated by the news media that she was another victim of an unknown serial killer that had been killing young women in the Seattle area at a horrific pace.

Immediately I remembered the horrible dream that I had dismissed and forgotten, including details I hadn't shared with Georgann. An awful pit of disbelief grew in my stomach and I felt faint. I had to sit down. Everyone was talking with upset and anxiety around me, but I faded into my own little dark world and their concerned conversation just seemed like aimless noise in the background.

So many of my psychic gifts were still very new to me. I didn't know what to make of a lot of the strangeness I had experienced. Were my experiences real or did I just have a good imagination? All the guys were saying they were sure Georgeann was still alive and I wanted to believe it too. Even if she had been taken by a killer, she was so level headed and personable that we were all sure she would talk him out of killing her. I held onto that belief and kept hoping Georgeann would someday walk back into the world and joyously surprise everyone. But it was not to be. In 1989, shortly before he was executed, serial killer Ted Bundy admitted that he had captured and murdered Georgeann the night she disappeared.

For years afterward, until I learned the psychic defense to vanquish sorrowful thoughts and feelings (see **Chapter 10**) , I put some blame on myself. For a time, I held a great sadness inside because of it. I saw the dreadful events clear enough to give Georgann better warning. Precognition is an ability of your brain to receive information from psychic energy sources regarding events that have not yet occurred and are not obvious to your five traditional senses. I received it, clearly; but I didn't know until years later what I had received. And by then, it was far too late.

After Bundy confessed to all of his killings just before he was executed in 1989, I wondered if I could have prevented Georgeann's murder if I had gone to the police in the mid 70's with the full details of my precognitive dream. Maybe with that information they could have captured Bundy before he committed more atrocities. More likely I would have been dismissed as a kook. But at least I would have tried to make a difference.

I don't believe precognition shows an unchangeable future set in stone. But for better or worse, it reveals a very likely outcome given the current circumstances and flow of energies. One of the benefits of precognition in personal circumstances, and with people that you know, is the precognitive has the opportunity to alter the future to a more beneficial outcome. Perhaps, if I had been more aware and accepting of my gifts, there was more I could have done to help that heart-rending tragedy to have never occurred.

Precognition and Intuition are Universal Gifts

I also believe that precognition and it's preceding little cousin intuition, are abilities that lay latent inside every person. You should not wonder if you have the gift of precognition, but rather accept the reality that you do have, it and seek to understand how you can unleash its power within you.

Sometimes precognitive signs come in the form of symbols or significant sightings of unusual animals or phenomena. The challenge in these cases is you need to use your mind, with all of its biases and preconceived beliefs, to interpret the symbols and signs, and you very well could interpret incorrectly.

Precognition

How to Cultivate Your Precognitive Abilities

1. Consciously be aware of your dreams, particularly vivid, detailed dreams or repetitive dreams that are about events that have not occurred ,or have people in them you do not know. If you have one and wake up in the middle of the night, roust yourself enough to write down the details.

2. Take note of any sudden ***thoughts*** that pop into your mind while you are awake that have nothing to do with the subjects your mind was working on or thinking about, especially if it has to do with people or events. Did you suddenly think of a person, perhaps one you do not even know? Did you flash on an event that has not yet occurred? Sometimes, you may get a sudden hit on an idea. This is different than a thought. With precognition you are looking for thoughts.

3. Become aware of when you have an unreasonable aversion to anything or anyone. This can drift down into the intuition/premonition/clairvoyance categories, but is worth noting as a precognitive sense if it leads you to specific emotions or thoughts. For example maybe you are out with some friends and get a strong feeling to not get in the car with them again. By itself this is just intuition or premonition and can have several possible meanings. If along with that sense you get a foreboding feeling of doom, it is likely the car will soon be in an accident. But you are still in the clairvoyance/premonition area. However, if you see a vision flash of the car in an accident or even greater details, that's certainly clairvoyance or precognition and should be acted upon.

    Remember, if you do see such a disaster, that the future is not set in stone. Warn your friends not to leave right then, or even better, to take alternative transportation. If they think you're a bit daft if you say something like that, simply think of a reason to postpone leaving until a later time. It may not make any difference in the outcome you were forewarned about, but it might.

1. Be alert for, and aware of psychic knowings you experience. With intuition, you will think or feel something, but will be cloudy on the details. You can likely be persuaded that it's all in your imagination. With a precognitive knowing, you may not understand it, but you will be firmly rooted in the reality of the future you saw, and will not be easily swayed from what you know.

2. Make awareness of precognitive dreams, visions, knowings, symbols and phenomena a habit. The more often you do something, the more proficient you become.

3. Limit or eliminate situations and states of being that inhibit precognition and every other psychic ability. These include alcohol consumption or use of mind or mood altering drugs, including caffeine from coffee and tea. Stress is a hindrance to all your abilities - psychic, physical, mental and emotional. Physical fatigue similarly inhibits your psychic abilities as well your mental and emotional capabilities. Psychic abilities

are also usually dampened if you are being dominated or disrespected. This can occur in every type of relationship including parent-child, romantic, and work related.
4. Meditation, yoga, relaxing music, and any other situation that puts you in a calm, but still alert state, is very conducive to receiving precognitive visions.

Historical Examples of Precognition

Some people believe that the future seen in precognitive dreams cannot be changed. I believe it can. In at least the instance of Abraham Lincoln, we have to wonder how different the world might have been.

Two weeks prior to his assassination, Lincoln told his wife Mary, that he had a dream of a funeral at the White House. He saw himself standing in the dream with the onlookers and asked one of them who was in the casket they were all standing around mourning. The person in his dream told him the man in the casket was the President of the United States.

He related the same dream in detail to Ward Hill Lamon, his friend and biographer, just three days before his assassination. Lincoln told his friend:

> *"About ten days ago, I retired very late. I had been up waiting for important dispatches from the front. I could not have been long in bed when I fell into a slumber, for I was weary. I soon began to dream. There seemed to be a death-like stillness about me. Then I heard subdued sobs, as if a number of people were weeping. I thought I left my bed and wandered downstairs. There the silence was broken by the same pitiful sobbing, but the mourners were invisible. I went from room to room; no living person was in sight, but the same mournful sounds of distress met me as I passed along. I saw light in all the rooms; every object was familiar to me; but where were all the people who were grieving as if their hearts would break? I was puzzled and alarmed. What could be the meaning of all this? Determined to find the cause of a state of things so mysterious and so shocking, I kept on until I arrived at the East Room, which I entered. There I met with a sickening surprise. Before me was a catafalque, on which rested a corpse wrapped in funeral vestments. Around it were stationed soldiers who were acting as guards; and there was a throng of people, gazing mournfully upon the corpse, whose face was covered, others weeping pitifully. 'Who is dead in the White House?' I demanded of one of the soldiers, 'The President,' was his answer; 'he was killed by an assassin.' Then came a loud burst of grief from the crowd, which woke me from my dream. I slept no more that night; and although it was only a dream, I have been strangely annoyed by it ever since."*

Despite the exceptionally clear warning of this dream, on the night he was assassinated by John Wilkes Booth, President Lincoln went to the play at Ford's Theatre and was cavalierly careless about his safety. Policeman John Frederick Parker, his assigned bodyguard stood guarding the entrance to the booth during the first act of the play. But during intermission Lincoln told him he could skip his duties for the second act and return at the end of the play.

Precognition

That single choice, heedless of his ominously portending dream, likely changed the history of the United States.

Mark Twain's Precognitive Ability

Samuel Langhorne Clemens, known to this day by his pen name of Mark Twain, had two very clear precognitive dreams of death, including his own. He was born in 1835, a year that Haley's Comet passed through the skies of Earth. On numerous occasions Twain told people that he had "come in with Haley and would go out with Haley." True to his vision, he died in 1910, the day after Haley's Comet returned.

In his younger years when he worked on riverboats, as did his younger brother Henry. Twain had a strong precognitive dream of his brother's death, which he related to his sister. He saw Henry in a metal coffin supported by two chairs, at his sister's house in the sitting room. A bouquet of white roses with a single red rose in the center lay on his brothers chest. Just a few weeks later his brother was killed in an enormous boiler explosion on a river boat that also killed 150 other people. Twain attended the funeral at his sister's house and saw everything exactly like his dream except there was no bouquet of roses. No sooner did he make that observation than a nurse came into the room and placed a bouquet of white roses with a single red one in the center, on his brother's chest.

Scottish Earthquake

On December 6, 1978, the Scottish newspaper, Dundee Courier & Advertiser, headlined a story 'Prophet didn't have a ticket.' It recounted how an unemployed, self-professed prophet was kicked off the train en route to London because he didn't have a ticket. It reported that Edward Pearson, 43 years of age, was on his way to warn the Prime Minister of an impending earthquake in Scotland. The readers probably got a good laugh out of the article as earthquakes are very rare in the United Kingdom. But just three weeks later an earthquake struck Scotland shaking people awake in their beds and causing structural damage to buildings in Glasgow and other towns in Scotland.

Sinking of the Titanic

There are many stories, some 19 of them collaborated before the fact, of people who had tickets aboard the Titanic on her maiden voyage, but declined to go aboard after having visions and dreams of the ship sinking.

Perhaps the greatest precognitive display was a novel written in 1898, by struggling writer Morgan Robertson, entitled 'Futility.' It told the tale of the sinking of the 'unsinkable liner' the 'Titan' after she hit an iceberg in the Atlantic on her maiden voyage. Most of her passengers perished because the Titan, like the Titanic, had too few lifeboats.

For those who think it might have just been a coincidence that the writer chose that story line,

	Titan	**Titanic**
Nationality	British	British
Length	800ft	882.5ft
Metal	Steel	Steel
Weight	45,000	66,000
Horse Power	40,000	46,000
Propellers	3	3
Masts	2	2
Watertight compartments	19	16
Number of Lifeboats	24	20
Passenger Capacity	3,000	3,000
Passengers on board	3,000	2,228
Speed at Impact	25 knots	22.5 knots
Time of Impact	near midnight	11.40pm
Point of Impact	Starboard	Starboard
Month	April	April
Number of Survivors	13	705

as travel by ocean liner was common in the day, consider the eerie exactness of the similarities between the fictional novel ship the Titan, and the real life ocean liner the Titanic.

My Precognitive Great Grandfather

A chapter on precognition wouldn't be complete without sharing a couple of memorable events from among the many in the life of my great grandfather Charlie Love. Great Granddaddy was quite a character. His family had been among the first European inhabitants in what became the state of Maryland. His ancestor arrived in Virginia in 1660 and received large grants of land on both sides of the Patapsco River in an area that now includes the Baltimore city limits. Only the family name wasn't Love then, it was Bond. His progenitor was Peter Bond Sr. One of my great grandfather's great uncles, Shadrach Bond, became the first governor of the state of Illinois. My great grandfather's birth name was John Thomas Bond, Jr. Why he changed his name is an interesting story.

Having lied about his age, he served in the Union Army during the Civil War when he was only 16. Returning home after the war with a good friend of his and army buddy, Tolbert Gorsuch, they were informed that while they were away the local school master had whipped his friend's sister as punishment for some infraction. Great Grandpa and Tolbert decided they needed to mete out some punishment of their own to the school master in return. They tracked him down and beat him within an inch of his life. When they left they thought they might have killed him.

Precognition

Worried about being arrested for murder, they told no one about their assault on the school teacher. That night Great Grandpa had a precognitive dream that his own father turned him over to the authorities for his crime. Not wanting to have that occur, he slipped away from home before sunrise and never looked back. After wandering up to Pennsylvania and then down the Ohio and Mississippi rivers, a year after he left Maryland he ended up at Alabama Landing, in Union Parish, Louisiana, which was then only a scarcely populated frontier. He put down roots on both sides of the Louisiana-Arkansas border area.

Before arriving he changed his name to Charlie Love just in case anyone came looking for John Thomas Bond Jr. Great Grandpa went on to become a self-taught lawyer who built a large practice along in both Union Parish, Louisiana and adjoining Union County, Arkansas. He was well known for helping couples who came to him to get divorced to reconcile their marriage, and then charge them the same fee he would have to divorce them. At times he also served as the Justice of the Peace and at other times Mayor. He fulfilled a popular saying at the time that he 'well played the hand he was dealt.' When he died it was noted in his obituary that though he had been a Union soldier, he was invited each year to meet with the local Confederate veterans during their reunions and he was warmly welcomed and held in high esteem.

Interestingly, many of the recorded precognitive experiences of people have to do with death. Great Grandpa had his last and most famous precognitive vision about his own impending death. In his 93rd year, he was sitting on his front porch, slowly rocking in his rocking chair, staring off into space, very likely having a vision, when he suddenly got up and told his wife, "I'm going to die." He wasn't ill in any way and quite healthy and active for his advanced years, so she didn't take him seriously. She was 20 years his junior but could hardly keep pace with his daily activities. He asked her to let everyone know it was his last day and to say goodbye for him if he didn't get to see them first.

He went and laid down on his bed, for what Great Grandma thought was just a nap. But he never woke up. According to his death certificate he died of 'old age.' Those who knew him felt he had done everything he had wanted to in life and having seen his death while rocking in his chair on the porch, he had calmly accepted it knowing it was a door to an eternity of further adventures.

Unleash Your Psychic Powers

Chapter 18
DIVINE INTERVENTION

There are two types of Divine Intervention. The first comes in the form of spontaneous visions or ideas popping into your head while you are awake, completely unrelated to what you were thinking about. Or, if they are related to your current thoughts it will present an angle you had not previously conceived or considered. Often they are the first thought you think of when you awaken in the morning. I've had more of these type of light bulb ideas suddenly popping into my head than I can count. Almost all of the inventions I've imagined or created came to me spontaneously while I was thinking of something else or as my first thought in the morning. Many of the ideas for books yet to be written I had either as a spontaneous thought or a vivid, detailed story played out in a dream while I slept.

My challenge comes when I have an innovative idea pop into my head, but do not have the technical expertise to create it and bring it to fruition. Then it just becomes another one of the many pages in my 3 ring binder labeled, "Ideas for Future Development."

The more dramatic form of Divine Intervention is when lives are saved in miraculous ways that have no logical explanation other than that God or your Guardian Angel was watching out and protecting you.

These experiences have happened on more than one occasion in my life and I certainly am grateful and humbled that I am still here. I know I would not be if it were not for the intervention of a force greater than me.

The Flying Sled

The first time I recollect having my life saved was in 4th grade when I was living in Connecticut. We just had a big snowfall and I was sledding with some friends on a hill across the street from my house. We would race down the compact, snowy slope, then at the base zip across the compact ice on the road and end up in my yard.

It never occurred to us that cars might try to traverse the steep, slippery, ice covered road.

But on one of my fastest runs of the day, as I came screaming down the sledding run, to my right I spied a car coming around the curve and slipping and sliding down the hill. I instantly knew I was on a collision course and that within seconds the car and I were going to meet. I exerted all of my strength to turn my sled. I was so close to the oncoming car that I knew even if I fell off, my forward momentum on the slippery, snowy slope would still crash me into it.

My feeble efforts were futile. I was laying low on my sled and closing my eyes I knew there was nothing I could do to prevent sliding under the car tires. Just when I expected to be being crushed by the heavy car I felt my sled hit a bump, lift up into the air and plop back completely stopped on the ground. As I slowly opened my eyes, I was amazed both to still be alive and also to not be underneath the car. It was stopped right next to me. I was literally right up against the outside of its back tire; but I was parallel to the car. Somehow when I hit the bump, while my eyes were closed and my sled in the air, it turned ninety degrees and came to a complete stop right next to the automobile. I knew, I really KNEW, at that moment, how very close I had come to death and how miraculous it was to still be alive.

Sumara's Miraculous Car Crash

In my wife's Senior year of High School she had two incidents of what could be Divine Intervention within a two month period. I'll relate both, as having been saved from death twice in two months had an effect on her entire outlook on life. She knew after these incidents that there had to be more to life than just living, and powers divine or within her, far beyond the abilities of her five senses to know or consciously manifest.

Sumara was driving in her car with her friend Beth to attend a High School basketball game at a school in a neighboring town. She glanced at her speedometer and realized that 52 mph was too fast to be driving on a bumpy, dirt road at night, but she didn't slow down as the only important thing in her mind was hurrying to get to the game. Moments after looking at the speedometer, on a straight stretch of road her tires lost traction on the loose dirt and tiny gravel of the road's surface. Suddenly the car was fish tailing uncontrollably. To their right was a deep, 15-foot wide ditch. As the car lurched that direction, even though the edge of the ditch was flat, it felt like the car literally flew up into the air, with all four tires off the ground. It catapulted completely over the wide ditch, landing on the far side as it ripped the bottom from the car. However, it still managed to remain upright on all four tires. Both girls were completely unhurt.

Later, when the police arrived at the scene they were scratching their heads in disbelief. Besides the fact that both girls were unhurt, they told Sumara there was no physical way her car traveling 53 mph could have flown so far through the air to have completely cleared the ditch. According to their calculations, the car should have hit the far side and flipped. It seemed impossible, but there was no other explanation as to how the car got there.

Divine Intervention

Sumara's Rescue at Zurmatt

Sumara's second miracle, another escape from death's clutches, came just two months later when she was skiing in Zurmatt, Switzerland, near the famous Matterhorn mountain. I'll let her tell the story.

"My family had gone to Zurmatt, Switzerland for a two week ski vacation when I was in my senior year of High School. My Dad let me bring my friend Pam along as she was my good ski buddy. On one particular day we had been having a great time exploring the different ski trails when we came to the top of a wide, steep, icy slope high up on the mountain where there was a big warning sign that said the run was closed due to icy conditions. However, we could see other skiers heading down the trail, and as teenagers always up for a challenge, and as usual, not using our brains, we followed along.

Pam & Sumara at Zermatt

When we skied around the corner and saw that the few other stupid people who had chosen to go down that run, despite the warning sign, were having to carefully side-step down the very steep slope because it was much too dangerous to ski, we thought, 'hmmm, maybe this wasn't such a good idea after all,' but it was too late, we were already committed and there was no other way down. The slope was like a 45 degree ice-rink with a hairpin turn; and if you didn't make that turn, it was thousands of feet straight down, and there was no railing or protection to prevent someone from falling off the cliff if they didn't make the turn.

We proceeded to carefully side-step down the slope, but then my skis slipped out from under me. In a second I was on my side sliding rapidly and uncontrollably down the icy slope toward the cliff below. About halfway down the slope I came near a lady skier standing with her ski edges embedded in the ice. I frantically reached out for her legs to stop my free fall and breathed a single breath of relief when I caught the bottom of her pants with one hand.

One breath was all I got because immediately she began hitting my hand and arms with her ski poles, forcing me to let go in pain. I knew she was just protecting herself and didn't want to be pulled over the edge with me. But I didn't think about it for more than a second because I was now wide-eyed in terror as I raced for the edge of the precipice and could do absolutely nothing to slow or stop myself. I was numbed to silence by what was happening. Everything seemed to be in slow motion. I caught my breath as I felt a powerful push that shoved me *vertically and* I was almost instantly airborne as I flew off the edge of the mountainside. I heard my friend Pam scream a bloodcurdling scream somewhere on the mountain above, but just as I had almost resigned myself to death, *I came to rest on a tiny snow covered ledge that my body barely fit upon.* I breathed slowly and cautiously, afraid if I took too big of a breath it would be just enough to push me off the narrow ledge.

The ski patrol were amazed that I had fallen where I had fallen because the trajectory of my slide indicated that I should have fallen off at the hairpin turn, not where I had. And had I fallen off at the hairpin turn, there would not have been a little ledge for me to fall onto.

It wasn't until many years later that I really began to understand the mysterious force that pushed me onto the one tiny ledge of safety on an immense cliff.

Can You Call Divine Intervention?

I'm not sure true Divine Intervention can be categorized as a psychic ability or paranormal power. If it is actually a manifestation of a higher power completely separate from us. The miracles that ensue are not projections of our power, but beings of higher realms.

Surely there are many incidents of Divine Intervention that have come as a result of prayer and in that context it is properly labeled 'divine.' There is great power in prayer that flows both from the innate power of the group energy and desire, and from the external power of the divine called in. But there are many other incidents that simply happen, such as some of the examples I gave above, and not necessarily to people who are devoutly religious. Neither my wife nor I were, at the time of some of our miracles.

Because the life-saving incidents seems so improbable, so miraculous, it is easy to attribute them to a divine energy or the benevolence of higher beings far greater than ourselves. But is it possible that the force that lifted my sled and turned it ninety degrees and then held it completely stopped, and the force that countered the trajectory of Sumara's plummet off the cliff and physically pushed her back onto a ledge, as well as the force that lifted Sumara's car over the ditch, were all manifestations of unknown powers of our own, that lay dormant inside of us until such instantaneous life and death situations called them forth to rescue and protect us? I believe it is not just likely, but certain. It seems to me just as probable and possible that these are powerful, paranormal energies of our own, as they are forces of higher beings protecting us.

But I do not in any way negate the outside influence of divine forces completely beyond us. It would also seem possible that both options are true at different times. There might be some instances where true Divine Intervention of higher beings or forces beyond ourselves, deliver us from death. Other incidents may call forth unknown force-field like physical powers within us to protect and preserve us when we would otherwise perish.

How Can You Call Divine Intervention or Manifest Your Own Force Field?

Depending upon which your heart and mind believe and have affinity for, your steps to have Divine Intervention on your side, or to be able to manifest your own personal force field when you need it, would be quite different.

One would have to assume that to call upon the love and grace of a higher being, from your concept of God to an angel, would necessitate some degree of harmony with the divine. If you're making an honest and sincere effort to live the dictates of your religion and have a personal connection to the energy of the God of your conscience, certainly it would be assumed that you have the best hope of having a Divine Intervention should you ever need one.

If you have more harmony with the concept that many incidents of Divine Intervention are really manifestations of your own hidden power coming to the fore when you need it most desperately, then your approach to insure it is there when you need it would be to regularly do everything you can to discover, unleash and expand the supernatural powers that are within you.

What is this power? From my myriad and widely varied experiences with the auric field I believe the force that physically pushes us, when it is not divine, is an aspect of our own aura.

Do you know how an airplane flies? It all has to do with the shape of the wing. Once the airplane has sufficient forward speed the airflow over the wings creates dramatically different pressure between the top and the bottom of the wings. The air pressure difference creates the physical lift that keeps the plane aloft as it is propelled through the sky.

Your auric field can work in exactly the same way to lift and move you. It is possible to increase the density, pressure and extent of your auric field at any point within the energy sphere of auric power that surrounds you. This can be done consciously or can occur spontaneously and unconsciously in any emergency that triggers an adrenaline surge. Just as the airplane gets its lift from dramatically different air pressure between the upper and lower surfaces of the wing, you can be physically moved by great differences in the density and size of your auric field.

In my book, *Auras: How to See, Feel & Know,* there are many exercises to help you develop and expand your auric powers. Beyond the exercises, how you chose to live your life does make a difference in all aspects of unleashing your own psychic abilities and paranormal powers.

Though it is not a message some will want to hear because it runs counter to their lifestyle, refraining from alcohol and mind and mood altering drugs, plus eating a healthy diet and keeping your body in a balanced, energetic state, does help your supernatural abilities, just as it enhances your mental and physical capabilities. Treating your body right and regularly practicing to discover and expand your supernatural abilities are simple but effective keys to success.

Chapter 19
KI FORCE

Unless you have been involved in high level martial arts, you have probably never heard of the Ki Force, also known as the Chi Force. 'Ki' is Japanese for 'Life Force Energy.' It is surely one of the most powerful paranormal powers that can be manifested. In a nutshell the Ki Force gives you superhuman strength, speed, and mental capacity, but only for less than a minute and usually less than 30 seconds. But you can accomplish a great deal in those few ticks of time!

Of the multiple powers of the Ki, superhuman strength in times of emergency, such as accounts of a mother lifting a car off a trapped loved one, are the most known and recorded. Where does this astounding strength come from? Skeptics claim incidents like this must have had other factors such as a car laying on a slope so not much weight was actually lifted. Many doctors and physiologists will tell you that other than a professional weightlifter, the human muscle and skeletal structure of a normal person simply cannot lift much more than their own weight without injury. But Michael Regnier, a professor and vice-chair of the bioengineering department at the University of Washington disagrees. He has studied both weightlifters and regular people, including in emergency situations. He says that normal people in abnormal situations, "can lift six to seven times their body weight."

The common explanation given by physicians and first responders in the past, whenever a situation was encountered where someone seemed to have superhuman strength, was to explain it away as an "adrenaline surge," flooding the body and giving an extra burst of power to the muscles. That's partially accurate, but it is only part of the real story, especially if the full powers of the Ki Force come out.

Adrenaline plays an important role in preparing the body for action in emergency situations and even greater abilities when the Ki Force kicks in. As adrenaline floods the body systems, it causes the lungs to breath faster and deeper, enriching the blood with more oxygen. The heart immediately increases the power and number of beats, pumping up muscles and invigorating all organs with increased oxygen. Wave after wave of special enzymes and proteins rapidly release, helping people sustain their superhuman efforts long enough to succeed. Endorphins flow out of the pituitary and hypothalamus glands bringing a surge of self-confidence, dampening any pain that might be experienced and giving an extra boost of power. The extra oxygen rushing into the cells also enables the neural connections in the brain to connect faster and in greater number. This is the main reason everything often seems to move in slow motion when the Ki Force is activated. It's not that events are suddenly occurring in slow motion. Instead, your brain begins operating at a greatly enhanced level that is so fast and comprehensive that events being observed seem slow.

When I was in my teens and early twenties, I studied and practiced both judo and karate, As I advanced to the higher levels one of the abilities both disciplines encouraged us to cultivate, was a special force inside us that would allow competitions to seem to slow down and our opponents actions to seem obvious before they were able to do damage. Very similar to Spiderman's 'spidey sense' or the Matrix movies bullet-time scenes. This martial arts ability is called by various names including, "Judo Sense" and "Body Sense."

The highest level practiced among martial arts masters is called the "Ki Force." The Ki Force not only makes everything happening around you slow down, but also gives you amazing strength and speed for a very short span of a minute or less. Preceded by the preparatory flood of adrenaline, when the Ki Force kicks in, your breathing passages relax allowing you to suck in more oxygenated air. Your muscles enter an energy rich, sugar charged state of glycolysis, allowing them to perform usually impossible muscular feats. Blood flow to vulnerable extremities decreases, limiting bleeding if you are cut or injured. Dopamine is produced in the endocrine glands in the brain to further act as a pain killer if needed. Peripheral vision becomes acute if it's needed, but otherwise is ignored so complete focus can be on the danger or task immediately in front of you. Your reflexes and reaction times become laser fast.

But the most amazing change is the ability of your brain to think. Not only does everything around you seem to be occurring in slow motion, but your brain is suddenly able to think at a speed far more rapid than normal. It has been said that in the moments before imminent death a person's whole life can flash before them. If they had the Ki Force right at that moment I'm sure its true.

I had multiple experiences with the "Ki Force" during the time I was involved in Martial Arts, although most of the experiences were not in martial art competitions. It came easily to me when I needed it or commanded it to come. I was far too inexperienced in Martial Arts for that to be the case, but nevertheless, there it was when I needed it. On more than one occasion it saved my life.

I started learning both karate and judo when I was in 8th grade to help save me from weekly beatings from classmates. I was the smallest kid in school my age and was incessantly beat up by bullies just because they could. Though my house was only four houses away from the bus stop, I dreaded getting off the bus every day, because on at least one occasion each week, one bully or another would beat me up before I got home. I'm not talking just being pushed or shoved, but bloody noses, black eyes and bruises. They didn't want anything from me. They weren't trying to steal my lunch money or get me to do something for them. They just took macabre pleasure in beating up the little kid.

Just a few months of intensive study and practice in the martial arts, aided by my first experience with the Ki Force, solved my problem with bullies. I clearly remember the shock of the first bully, Timothy G., who tried to beat me up after I knew how to defend myself. He was accustomed to getting his weekly jollies by socking me in the gut or giving me a bloody nose. Getting off the bus on this fateful day, he came up behind me and grabbed me by the shoulder to spin me around so he could give me a punch. The moment he touched me I felt an adrenaline rush. As I came around to face him I experienced something far greater -- *the Ki Force*! I subdued him with ease because it seemed as if he was moving in slow motion while all my actions were just a blur! I grabbed his ridiculously slow swinging right arm at his inside wrist, right behind his clenched fist, with my left hand. In one fluid motion I then put him in a headlock with my right arm wrapped around his neck, immobilizing his right arm by gripping him under his armpit with my right hand coming around his neck. I took him to the ground with me on top and him not able to move at all, and used my legs to grip his tightly so they couldn't move. I then took my free left hand and made a fist right in front of his face. I pointed out that because he could not move, if I wanted to I could just pound his face into a bloody pulp.

He was so amazed by what I had just done I think he was more curious than scared. He had been in motion to punch me and then the next thing he knew there was a whirlwind and he was tied up like a pretzel on the ground and I was threatening to hit him! He wanted to know how I did it. I told him I knew martial arts now and I wasn't going to hit him this time; but if he ever bothered me again, he would really, really regret it. He readily agreed to never bother me again and he passed on what had transpired to all his bully friends. I never had to hit any of the bullies to enforce my threat, and I never had a problem with any of them ever again. More importantly for my future, though I actually had never heard of the Ki Force yet, I had my first taste of it's astounding power and I knew I had experienced something wonderful.

Cliff Fall in Spain

When I explained to my Karate and Judo Sensei's (master instructors) what had happened to me in the confrontation with Timothy G. they were both skeptical at first and just assumed I had an adrenaline surge. But during the next months, as they observed my progress in their Martial Art disciplines and in competition tournaments, they decided I must have somehow had the Ki Force come to me spontaneously.

They explained how the Ki Force was something Martial Arts masters seek to be able to call to them on command, but it usually takes decades of practice before this is possible. But as it seemed that it might have come to me spontaneously, they felt I might have a natural affinity for it and they began to teach me how to call it. This was a great honor and I was very humbled as the secrets of calling the Ki would normally not have even begun to be revealed until someone was in an advanced black belt level, which I was far from.

In learning to call the Ki Force, I also discovered a personal shortcut. I don't know if it would work for anyone else. It might sound ridiculous, but I found if I hit myself in my ears, it hurt like hell and triggered something inside that facilitated the Ki Force coming easily if I called it immediately after hitting my ears.

My Senseis forbid me to ever call the Ki Force in a Martial Arts competition and cautioned it was only to be used in dire emergency situations. They warned it was unpredictable and should never be used against another person unless my life or the lives of my loved ones were in danger. So though I practiced calling it on command when I was alone so I could understand how it felt, I never allowed it to come fully in and never had the opportunity to use it again for an emergency until my Senior year in High School.

This was when were living in Spain. Our house was near some cliffs overlooking the ocean that varied in height from fifty to one hundred fifty or so feet. The cliffs were made of highly compacted clay and were really not safe to climb. Clay outcrops that seemed firm when first grabbed could easily crumble away under the pressure of your weight. Foolishly I climbed them anyway. When I was young I had frequent urges to free climb cliffs, and I gave into my urges often. To climb a cliff unassisted by ropes, or carabineers, or rock anchors, was exhilarating. Safely reaching the summits and looking out over the vast expanse below was always euphoric. But on this fateful day I chose the wrong cliff to climb.

The portion of the cliff I chose to ascend was nearly vertical, but only about fifty feet in height so I didn't see it as much of a challenge, just a bit of exercise. The top of the cliff was almost flat and the base abutted the ocean beach, which was mostly sand with a few small boulders scattered about. Climbing the face I was very aware of the crumbly nature of the compacted clay and was extra cautious to make sure my hand and foot holds were firm before I put any weight on them. I also strictly followed the 'Three Point Rule,' which gave some measure of safety by requiring me to have two feet and a hand, or two hands and a foot always firmly planted. That way if the free hand or foot seeking a holding point slipped or the hold broke, the other three points still holding firm should keep me from falling.

Using these standard free climbing techniques I quickly and safely ascended the cliff. However, as I reached the flat top and lifted my body up on two hands and swung my leg up to roll onto the flat top, disaster struck. With all of my weight on the outside edge of the friable cliff supported solely on my two hands, the clay edge broke away, immediately throwing me backwards into space. Instantly, without a conscious thought I was filled with the Ki Force. Though the entire event took no more than three seconds, everything seemed to be in slow motion because my thoughts were speeding so rapidly through my brain. I flipped over in the air with my feet pointing toward the onrushing beach below. I was headed right for one of the boulders projecting up about a foot above the beach and could see no way to avoid it. I thought to perhaps hit it and bounce into a judo roll, but realized I would be impacting too hard and would probably still break a leg or ankle. My only recourse would be to straddle it and land with my feet in the soft sand.

With utter and pure confidence of the Ki Force coursing through every cell of my body, I had no doubt I would land safely. I impacted astride the rock, with my feet lightly grazing each side of its smooth surface. My legs absorbed the impact like steel springs. My bottom hit the rounded rock, but not sharply, and I ended up in a sitting position on the boulder, once again thanking God that I was, not only alive, but unscathed and blessed with the Ki Force.

Assburn Hill

I called the full Ki Force one other time prior to my fall off the cliff. It was on a different portion of the same cliff, but this section was about two hundred feet tall, and it was not in an emergency. Though my Senseis had warned me to only call in the full power of the Ki Force in life threatening situations, in this one incident I did not obey their admonition. I had been practicing calling in the Ki Force, by first hitting my ears, then pounding my fist into the palm of my hand and commanding the Ki Force to come to me in the secret way that had been taught by my Senseis. As soon as I felt the adrenaline rush and the first hint of supreme Ki Force confidence I turned it off by thinking about algebra. I really hated algebra in school and thinking about an algebra problem immediately dampened the physical aspects of the oncoming Ki. I had done this several times and rationalized I needed to find an opportunity to fully let the Ki Force out so I would have a greater understanding of what to expect.

There was an informal cliff jumping competition coming up the following week, called the "Assburn Hill Jump." There was a portion of the cliff that was well-suited for jumping and sliding a great distance down a long talus slope of dried clay balls after you landed. The friction of rapidly sliding down the steep slope generated a lot of heat on your bottom, hence the name.

This was a very dangerous competition, which usually had no more than six participants, mostly young, local Spaniards who came to the neighborhood during the day to work as gardeners. Few Americans knew about the low-key event, which had to be conducted somewhat in secret as it took place adjacent to the residential section of a joint Spanish/American naval base. Antonio, the gardener that worked at our house, told me about the crazy people that jumped off the nearby cliff. I guess he ranked me up with the crazies because he took me over to the edge of the two hundred foot cliff, the highest part of the 1 ½ mile long cliff, to see if it was something I might want to participate in. It wasn't! A person would have to be insane to jump off that cliff! There was a large section of completely hard clay about half way down the cliff at slightly less than a vertical incline. Below it was the large clay ball talus slope. Above it was the standard landing area where people would jump, fly about forty feet through the air, then slide across the hard clay section and down the long talus slope below it.

According to Antonio, many people had broken legs and hurt their backs jumping off the cliff. The reason was the landing. If you didn't make a perfect five point landing on the steep slope above the hard patch; both hands, both feet and your butt, all at the same time, you would end up tumbling across the hard clay patch and down the abrasive talus slope instead of sliding safely on your bottom. My first impression was this was definitely something I would never do. By the next day however, I was reconsidering.

I went back to revisit the cliff. Looking down the steep slope I realized if I could run fast enough on the top and take off right at the extreme lip of the cliff I might be able to sail far enough horizontally that in the downward arc I could skip over the hard patch of clay and land directly on the talus slope below. That would make a jump twice as far horizontally and at least three times further vertically than anyone had ever done. This intrigued me. I wondered if it could be done with the aid of the Ki Force. The downside was if I fell short I would impact the hard clay patch, which was as solid and hard as concrete. I'd probably be killed. After some vacillation back and forth I decided a couple of days later to do it. I wasn't going to make the attempt. I was going to do it and succeed. I trusted my abilities with the Ki Force.

The next day I asked Antonio to let whoever needed to know, that I was going to jump. The following day he told me to be at the cliff at 2:00 in the afternoon. When I arrived, Antonio was there along with Juan and Eduardo. "This is it?" I asked. "Just two guys?" "We are not here to jump." Eduardo explained. "Antonio said you are going to try to jump over the hard patch. That is not possible. You would probably be killed' if not killed, hurt very badly in ways that could not be explained. But if you want to do a normal jump to the soft place above the hard patch, we will witness and measure your jump from the top of the cliff to the place that you land. That is how we do this competition - one person on any day, so we don't draw attention to what we are doing."

I could tell I wasn't going to get anywhere trying to explain about the Ki Force to people who would have no conception of what I was talking about, so I fibbed and agreed to just do the best jump I could to the top soft landing area above the hard patch. Eduardo explained they would grade me on both how far I jumped and how I looked taking off and flying through the air. They added that no American had ever won this competition.

"If this is a Spanish thing, why is it called Assburn Hill?" I wondered.

"Because the idea for jumping came from an American service man who fell off this cliff some years ago and burned his butt sliding down the slope. He named it. Americans have never done it much, but some of the local Spanish workers that come each day to the base, have turned it into a sport."

With the preliminaries concluded, Eduardo carefully worked his way down the steep slope until he was standing near the soft spot above the hard patch so he could observe my landing. Juan positioned himself off to the side near the edge of the cliff so he could witness my takeoff. Antonio stood off to the other side just so he could watch and be entertained.

I stood back about thirty feet from the edge of the cliff. I hit my ears hard to get my adrenaline pumping. Using the techniques I had been taught, I called in the Ki Force and immediately felt like the Incredible Hulk. Forget jumping, I felt like I could fly! In a heartbeat I was racing for the edge. My arms pumping strongly, my legs a blur. I hit the lip of the cliff perfectly and pushed myself off with far more power than I had ever experienced from my legs. At the same time I thrust my arms forward and upward to help lift me up and carry me further out into the empty space in front of me. What an incredible, exhilarating, euphoric feeling it was to by flying free through the sky! The vast expanse of ocean stretching out below me was breathtakingly beautiful.

I saw the look of horror on Eduardo's face as I passed above him high over his head. I'm sure he thought I was going to land on the hard patch. But no worries. I sailed far beyond that and actually landed midway down the lower talus slope. I had so little distance to slide that my butt hardly even got warm.

Flying through the air like a bird was the most incredible, amazing feeling I have ever felt. I hurried back up the hill because I just had to do it again. Everyone's eyes were as big as saucers when they met me on top. Nobody could believe I had just jumped *over* the hard patch. They were even more dumbfounded when I told them I was going to do it again. Eduardo and Juan shook their heads in disapproval and soon departed. They felt I was very lucky the first time and didn't want to be present when I would surely crash on another attempt. Antonio felt obligated to stay because he had told me about Assburn Hill and was employed by my parents. He was obviously relieved when I told him he could also leave.

Left alone, I called the Ki Force two more times that day and made two more jumps, both times landing below the hard patch. I knew this was an experience I didn't ever want to forget.

Unleash Your Psychic Powers

The next day I asked an acquaintance from school if he would come and take some pictures of me making the jump. He worked his way down the steep hill so he could take the pictures looking up at me as I launched. In the first picture I have just taken off from the top of the cliff. You can see my arms lifting up to help me rise into the sky and the little puff of dust from my launching foot as it pushed off the dry cliff top. In the second picture I have already begun my descent and my arms are outstretched with the pure joy of flying free without a parachute. An astounding, unforgettable experience. Thank you Ki Force!

The Ki Force and My Mission for the Church

When I was nineteen I was baptized in the Mormon church as a convert. I was very excited about it when I first joined and went on a mission for the church less than a year after my baptism. I remained active just a short time after I returned home and eventually left the church and asked to have my name removed from the records. My disillusionment began with a watershed event that occurred on my mission.

After I had been on a mission about five months, I was transferred to a new area and given the responsibility of a brand new "green" missionary to train. We got along great and did well in our area. But my lifetime strong constitution record of almost never getting sick took a big hit. For some reason just a couple of weeks after I was transferred, I stopped being able to keep any food down. I didn't feel sick or have an upset stomach, but whenever and whatever I ate, never seemed to stay in my stomach but came right back up.

This went on for over two weeks and I lost some noticeable weight. My District Leader and

Ki Force

his companion came over and gave me a laying on of hands blessing to be healed, but there was no improvement. Becoming quite concerned, I went to a doctor and he couldn't figure out what was wrong with me. Then things got worse. I became unable to hold down liquid, even water. It wouldn't even make it to my stomach before it would come back up. The doctor had given me some pills to take and they would get down into my throat and then come back up along with the water I was using to try to swallow them.

After two days of not being able to keep liquid down, I was getting a little scared. The District Leader and his companion came over and gave me a second blessing. But once again, I did not improve. I became bedridden and weak. I wanted to go to the hospital but my missionary companion and the District Leader didn't seem to think that I was as bad off as I thought I was. They told me to give some more time for the Lord to heal me.

When I awoke on the morning of my fourth day without appreciable water, I knew there was no help for me within the church. I felt if I didn't do something I was going to die. I reflected back upon my life and the one force that had literally saved my life on multiple occasions: the Ki Force. After praying about it, I concluded that the Ki Force was a true gift of God and that it was only by that gift that I would be restored to health.

I asked my companion to call the District Leader. When he and his companion arrived, I asked if they would take me to the tallest hill in the area and help me get to the top. They asked why, and explaining as little as possible, I told them I just felt being in a high place would help me. In reality, I knew from seeing energy fields that the tops of hills and mountains were apexes of focused energy traveling between the earth and the cosmos. In my mind, calling upon the Ki Force at a location such as a hilltop, was my best hope to be cured of my mysterious malady.

In accordance with my wishes they brought me to the top of a large hill. I laid down upon the ground and asked them in a feeble voice to please go to the bottom of the hill and wait for me. The District Leader said they would stay, so I was forced to explain why I wanted them to leave. I told them, I felt if I did not do something I was going to die and explained about my experience with the Ki Force. I told them for less than a minute it would give me great speed and strength, but also no control over my actions and I feared for their safety if they were too close.

Saying that only made matters worse. The District Leader said, he felt Satan present very strong, and they would not leave. At that point I didn't care if they stayed or left. They had been warned, and now it was time to do what I knew I had to do. I called the Ki Force. It took about five seconds and suddenly I was filled with the power! It seemed to me as if I was propelled high into the air from my prone position. I landed firmly on my feet and I felt an incredible electric sensation emanating from my core, traveling through my body, then my arms and legs, and exiting in an explosion through my fingers, toes and head.

I felt great! Unbelievably, my lost weight seemed to be restored in that instant. I don't know what the three missionaries saw, but they were all standing there speechless with their mouths gaped wide open. Finally, the District Leader asked, "What was that!" I calmly told him, "That was the Ki Force, a power God puts inside everyone, but few can ever find."

I fairly skipped down the hill whistling while my three companions followed behind, speaking in amazement about what they had seen. I felt incredibly exhilarated and alive!

That night I received a call from my Mission President. The District Leader had called and told him everything that had transpired from my sickness and previously emaciated state, to the trip to the hilltop and everything they had witnessed there. I thought the president would be calling to commend a miracle, but instead he was calling to condemn what had occurred! He told me that the Ki Force was not a teaching of the church and was of Satan. He told me never to call upon it again.

I protested that calling upon the Ki Force had saved my life while two blessings from the missionaries had done nothing. He was unmoved and adamant that I should never call upon the Ki Force again.

I admired my mission president but could not understand his reaction to my restoration of health and vigor. I sought an answer from God by praying and seeking enlightenment by opening the Mormon scriptures at random to let my finger fall upon the verse that would open my eyes to the truth. My finger rested upon the 6th chapter of Moroni in the Book of Mormon. As I read through the chapter there could be no doubt that the Ki Force was of God, not Satan. Some excerpts: v11, *"For behold, a bitter fountain cannot bring forth good water; neither can a good fountain bring forth bitter water..."*, v12, *"Wherefore all things which are good cometh of God;"* v13, *...behold, that which is of God inviteth and enticeth to do good continually...*".

I reflected upon all of my own experiences with the Ki Force: I had never been compelled to sin or do evil because of it, and it had only served me for good, even a great good whenever it had been called upon. I thought about the stories told by my Martial Arts Senseis and the reverence in which they held the Ki Force as an energy of good that could only be called upon by the humble and pure in heart. I knew with these reflections that my mission president was wrong and that I could not stay another day on a mission in Pennsylvania. That was not where I was supposed to be.

In the early morning while my companion slept, I called a cab to take me to the airport. While I waited for my plane, my mission president showed up at the airport and tried to talk me into staying. I explained that he was wrong about the Ki Force; it was of God not Satan, and hearing him denounce such a good and wonderful energy was my final confirmation that I could not stay on a mission in Pennsylvania. I headed home on the next plane.

Denny Canyon

There have been multiple times when I should have died, but instead, not only did I live, but I was uninjured. This gave me a sure knowing inside that God had a purpose for me and whenever my time came to meet my maker it would not be before I had fulfilled that which I was called to do on Earth.

Ki Force

In addition to the example I gave of my fall from the cliff in Spain, I had another fall that was a lot scarier. I had hiked up the dangerous Denny Canyon near Snoqualmie Pass, in the mountains east of Seattle with Skye in search of amethyst scepters, a rare type of quartz crystals. At that time, there had already been several people who had been killed over the years within 50 feet of the spot we were looking for crystals. The canyon rises very steeply as you ascend it and there is one spot where there are vertical walls rising 200-300 feet on either side that are only 50 feet apart, and the vertical wall of a dry waterfall rising directly in front of you about 60 feet in height. After ascending that wall, the canyon forks and quickly ends at a small box canyon with both forks within 300 feet of the top of the dry waterfall.

The dangers arose with even a small rock fall from above. There was literally no place to hide and with the tall, narrow canyon walls, any falling rock acted like a pinball, bouncing off of the walls and taking out any people below. The dry waterfall area had also accounted for many of the deaths, as it was tricky to negotiate with few handholds. It had unforgiving boulders projecting from the bottom, and was a common place for deadly falls.

In this area the crystals grow in little caves called 'vugs.' After successfully ascending the dry waterfall, we initially started looking through the talus for single crystal points, as many fine ones had been found there over the years as they weathered from the cliffs above. As I looked up one of the tall vertical walls, I saw what appeared to be a small vug about 100 feet up, directly above the right side of the dry waterfall. Even though I had not brought any climbing equipment, I decided to free climb up to a spot that might be a virgin vug. Because it was so inaccessible I figured there was a good chance no one had ever been to it.

With happy thoughts of a virgin vug full of crystals, I carefully worked my way up the cliff face which rose at about a 70-80 degree angle. It was a very treacherous climb, as it was virtually a smooth rock face with only the tiniest of toe and finger holds spread out very sparsely that were never projections, just little cracks you could stick your fingers or toes into. I was about 10 feet below the vug when suddenly my foot that was carrying most of my weight slipped out of the little hole it had been jammed into and I began to rapidly slide down the cliff face.

In a flash I flipped over onto my back and spread out my arms and feet so I could slow myself a little bit and see what was coming. The Ki Force rushed into my body unbidden. Even though I was plummeting towards my death on the jagged rocks below the dry waterfall, everything went into slow motion.

I looked for any little ledge sticking out that I could stop my fall, but the only thing I saw was a tiny projection about the size of a bent thumb, about 20 feet below me to the right, but out of the reach of my outstretched foot by almost two feet! There was nothing else visible, and 10 feet below that point the cliff became entirely vertical and dropped to the death rocks at the base of the dry waterfall. I knew I had to reach that little protrusion. Stretching as far as I could stretch to the right, I could see I was still going to miss it. Just at the last possible second some unseen force gave me a little nudge from the other side of my body, and the heel of my right boot caught on that tiny projection of rock, and stopped me in what would have been my last breath.

I looked over at Skye and she had the most horror-stricken look I have ever seen on anyone's face. She had been sure she was watching my death and was relieved and dumbfounded to see me still alive. She climbed up the canyon a bit, tied off a rope and threw it down to me, which allowed me to swing over to safety.

The Denny Canyon fall was a special instance where I can say with certainty that multiple paranormal powers came into play. The Ki Force was powerfully present allowing my mind to think far more rapidly than it normally could, which seemed to greatly slow down an event that actually occurred in just a few seconds and allowed me to understand what I needed to do to survive. Once I reached the tiny nub of a projection that my heel caught on to stop my fall, I also had the Ki Force to thank for the strength in my single leg to stop my momentum. But getting my right foot over to that nub, that was something even more special. Either God or angels directly intervened and pushed my over to the nub, or my own aura drastically increased its density on the opposite side of my body to push me toward the projecting nub. Either way, I thanked God for either saving me or blessing me with the paranormal powers to save myself.

How To Call the Ki Force

Everyone, absolutely everyone, has the paranormal power of the Ki Force lying dormant inside them. For 99.9% of the people it will never come out on its own. Tens of thousands of people the world over are caught up in emergency situations each day, many of them life or death, but the Ki Force does not come out to help them. Why does it come out to give one mother among a thousand superhuman strength to save her child pinned beneath a car, while the other 99.9% gain no special powers to help their children in emergencies? Desire and attitude make the difference.

You must have an intense desire to achieve the outcome you want. Seeing someone you love in peril often will usher in that intense desire. Certainly, any parent who loves their child will have a deep desire to help them if they are physically threatened, especially in a life or death situation. However, though it is a prerequisite to calling the Ki Force, alone, desire is not enough. It must be combined with an irresistible will that doesn't hope or pray for success, but commands it to be so! An almost angry determination, so overpoweringly certain that the outcome will be exactly as you want it to be, that there is not the slightest sliver of a thought in your mind that there is any other possibility.

When desire is intense and doubt non-existent, the Ki Force is prepared to come out and make you superhuman for a fleeting minute, if the situation is extreme enough to warrant its manifestation. One last little boost to ensure you will have the Ki when you need it most, a Martial Arts secret I shouldn't reveal, but it is so critical that I cannot leave it out. Unless it comes spontaneously, you must call the Ki, in a loud voice. It can be as simple as "Ki come to me!" If your purpose is noble and

Ki Force

righteous; if there is no other way to save yourself or one that you love; if you have a burning desire and a will that cannot be swayed by doubt; call the Ki and it will be there when you need it.

UNLEASH YOUR PSYCHIC POWERS

Chapter 20
ASTRAL PROJECTION

Out-of-body experiences (OBE's), Astral Projection, and Remote Viewing are all related. Each, in different levels of complexity, projects your consciousness out of your body. Some people claim it is your soul that is separating from your body. Others simply call it your ill-defined 'astral body.' In my experiences, my consciousness is certainly separated from my body, which I can look down and see. And I sense that my consciousness is still in some form of a spiritual body. However, while I can look down and see my physical body that I have separated from, I cannot see any part of the separated ethereal body that is retaining my consciousness.

Despite my many psychic and paranormal experiences growing up, astral projection in any form was not among them until my senior year in High School, while living in Spain. In fact, as I was not well-read in the psychic genre, I'm not sure I even knew what Astral Projection was until one night when I spontaneously experienced it.

During the summer of 1973, when I was eighteen, I was studying the Latter-day Saint religion (Mormons) and contemplating joining the church. Spirituality and religion had always been very important to me. But to officially join a church, especially one so out of the main stream of Christianity, was an enormous step and I was giving the matter a great deal of prayer, study and contemplation. It was such a big step I needed to have firm knowledge that it was the right thing for me to do at that time before I could proceed.

To reach that firm knowledge I read the scriptures for one to two hours a night, usually late. After reading, I took a short walk from my house to the cliffs overlooking the ocean and knelt down to pray aloud. I would normally remain praying for fifteen to twenty minutes. I did this reading/praying ritual every night for two weeks. I asked specific questions about beliefs of the Latter-day Saints and most earnestly inquired, in many different ways, if joining their church would be helpful for my own spiritual growth and expansion at that time.

I got many warm, fuzzy feelings inside. However, I knew that anyone would get similar feelings if they spent two hours reading scriptures and followed it with praying aloud, alone on a cliff, with bright stars overhead and the moonlight glistening off the wave caps on the ocean below. It was a scenario that lent itself to warm, fuzzy feelings. But in those two weeks, I never received something more, something undeniable that joining the Latter-day Saints was a path I should take at that time; until the night that I did. Then my whole world changed forever.

The fateful night began like any other, reading the scriptures alone and undisturbed in my small bedroom. But it began to be different the moment I started walking toward the cliffs. I was struck by the beauty of the full moon and enraptured by how gloriously and radiantly it lit up the landscape. Upon reaching the cliffs and venturing near the edge, looking down on the moving waves brightly reflecting the moonlight was magical. I felt different before I ever knelt down to pray.

A twenty minute prayer was not necessary this night. As I began my prayer: "My Heavenly Father...," my consciousness and my spirit immediately but serenely left my body and remained hovering about thirty feet above my physical body which was still kneeling in the prayer position. My conscious spiritual body took a moment to look around in wonder at the world suddenly more glorious than ever before, from the twinkling stars in the sky, to the vast moonlit ocean expanding beyond sight in the distance, then back to my physical body. But now it was my conscious, spiritual body, hovering in the air above, that continued the prayer, not vocally, but in clear, audible words in my mind. With every question I asked, I received a powerful affirmation that it would be most expanding for me to join the Latter-day Saints at that time. When my answer was sure, without doubt, my ethereal body and consciousness slipped calmly back down into my physical body. The moment they reunited, full consciousness was back in my body. I leaped up in euphoria and raising my eyes to the heavens let out a big 'thank you.'

Though I only remained active in the Latter-day Saint church for another ten years, and subsequently asked to have my name removed from the records, I met many wonderful Mormons, learned a great deal, and became a far more spiritual person during my sojourn among them. Joining that church at that time was certainly the correct choice for my personal growth and expansion and a momentous enough turning point in my life, to be worthy of my first out-of-body experience.

I firmly believe that every single person has the capacity to have vivid out-of-body experiences. In fact, I believe that most nights while we sleep, we take out-of-body excursions and Astral Travel to places far and wide, even beyond the bounds of our planet. But as these adventures are initiated by our Night-Self, our Day-Self is usually mostly oblivious to the travels. Obviously these two parts of ourselves do not communicate very well. I'll speak of this dichotomy and the solutions to its puzzle in greater detail in **Chapter 23:** *Dreams & Dream Interpretation*.

Returning to the differences between the types of OBE's it works best to begin with the simplest and progress onward upon the foundations of that which came before.

Lucid Dreaming: Chapter 14 was on Lucid Dreaming and many if not most proponents of OBE's propose to have them while in a sleep paralysis, dreamlike state. Because of this, most

Astral Projection

teachers of OBE techniques ask their students to first begin having Lucid Dreams, where they are consciously able to control their dreams. Successful Lucid Dreaming then becomes the foundation for Out-of-Body experiences.

While it is certainly possible to have OBE's while in some sort of sleep/awake, many skeptics look at the scenario and write it off as simply a form of dreaming. And how can you prove, even to yourself, that it is not?

I have had OBE's while in that half awake-half asleep, sleep paralysis state, and as offshoots of a lucid dream, and have found such experiences while interesting, tend to be unsatisfying, pale, weak shadows of the vivid OBE's and Astral Projections experienced when you are fully awake and aware, such as my experience on the cliffs in Spain. Just like dreams, OBE's experienced from any type of sleep are difficult to remember in fullness and clarity when you are awake. And from reports I have heard from others, just like dreams, OBE's begun in a sleep state can often be like nightmares. The opposite is true for OBE's and Astral Projections begun from a fully conscious state. In my experience, they are without exception, euphoric, inspiring and uplifting.

Out of Body Experience: (**OBE**) The next level above a Lucid Dream is an Out-of-Body Experience. This can be as simple as a sensation of floating out of your body. It can also be more complex to the point of being able to look down and see your physical body. If there are other people present you'll see them too. Near-Death-Experiences are a type of OBE. Morphing from a Lucid Dream into an OBE is perhaps the most common way people have Out-of-body experiences. OBE's tend to be simple observation phenomena. Even in the most cognizant OBE's you tend to be limited to a specific location and scene, with little ability to do anything other than observe what is happening in the scene you are looking upon.

Astral Projection: Once you are no longer confined to a room-sized location and a single scene, and can consciously exert your will to move to another place of your choice, you have progressed out of a simple OBE and into Astral Projection. This is a very fun new world! Many people writing about Astral Projection speak of it in out-of-worldly terms, literally. It is described as a very lucid form of Lucid Dreaming or the movements of a "mystic body double" in a "parallel world or astral plane." Some writers claim when you Astral Project, "you ascend to a spiritual realm where the earthly definitions of time and space don't work."

While I do not discount their explanations, my experience is more down to Earth, or at least in this universe, in this plane of existence. However, I do find that I have no conscious thought or awareness of time other than knowing if it is day or night. I do have a definite awareness of space when I astral travel. It's no different in that regard than flying in a plane. If you look down and notice the landscape below, you have an awareness of the space you are traversing. If you don't look down, you may simply have an awareness of traveling through space, then suddenly arriving at your destination.

Astral traveling used to be more exciting before the Internet, where every bit of information on virtually any place or anything is immediately available. If I wanted to see the Taj Mahal, taking an astral travel trip there was as stimulating as preparing for, and experiencing a real vacation, which I couldn't afford. Today, I still cannot afford the real vacation, and it is much quicker to just read about the Taj Mahal and watch other people's videos on the Internet. But of course reading and watching videos on the Internet does very little for my personal growth and expansion, yet it is so much easier and less time consuming! There is certainly a degree of will power needed to continue taking the time and making the effort to astral travel, but it is truly more fulfilling than surfing the Internet and without a doubt worthy of the extra time and preparation required, because we are exercising and expanding a supernatural ability!

The method that has worked best for me to Astral Travel with the most satisfying results, is to be fully conscious and wide awake, but in a deep state of prayer or meditation, reaching out to God or a higher source beyond this world. This needs to follow a period of at least 40 minutes to 1 hour of undisturbed, very focused meditation or study about the subject I would be praying about or seeking to know from a higher source.

It can be challenging in our busy lives to completely tune out the world and be solely focused on a single subject in your mind and actions for that long. Any disruption that diverts your focus also seems to derail your astral traveling adventure for that day. The great benefit of this method is you are fully conscious during your astral travel and have complete and detailed recall of everything you see while traveling. As an added bonus, all your astral traveling experiences are positive. At least all of mine for the last forty years using this method have been.

The one drawback I had for many years with the meditation-prayer method, is I seemed to be limited to remaining within sight of my physical body while astral traveling. I could consciously decide to move about and observe anything in the vicinity I desired, yet there seemed to be an invisible barrier that prevented my astral body from traveling beyond sight of my physical body. That barrier was broken when I consciously astral traveled while asleep. But the results while sleeping had their own unique drawbacks.

After years of experimenting I discovered the secret to astral traveling while awake and being fully conscious was to succeed at tuning out the world. Easier said than done. For me, laying in a lusciously warm bath, or sitting on a stool or in a chair under a perfectly hot shower does the trick as long as I have done the other necessary prior meditation. It's also important that the water of the bath or shower is the perfect temperature to enjoy, but not notice; neither too hot or too cold.

The bathroom, even in a small house or apartment, seems to be the one room where you can 'get away from it all.' It's best to do plan your astral travel adventure for a time when no one else is home; the phones, music and TV are turned off; and any other potential interruptions or distractions are negated. Once in that relaxing, quiet setting it's just a matter of getting out of your head. Stop thinking about anything, including astral traveling! If you have a particular place you want to visit, study up on it during your one to two hour pre-astral traveling meditation. Once you are immersed in the water just let all thoughts go from your mind. Don't be distracted by a fly on the wall or an ant moving across the floor or anything happening in or

Astral Projection

out of the house. Just relax. Completely relax.

I have found with so many psychic abilities or paranormal powers that audible vocalization is helpful. If you want to astral travel to the Taj Mahal for example, once you are in the shower or bath say a deep, continuous, sincere prayer to the God of your choice. Or simply speak to the universe at large stating your intense desire to visit the Taj Mahal right now. You want to go now. You want to see the magnificent structure for yourself right now.

I am only successful astral traveling about 1 in 16 attempts using this method and it usually takes a good 30 minutes to an hour of deep, focused study and meditation before I begin the astral travel attempt. If I am going to succeed, it will usually happen within the first minute of making the attempt after the meditation.

The most successful way I have found to astral travel is the same way I had my first out-of-body experience on the cliffs of Spain. After studying/meditating for one to two hours with complete focus and no disturbances, go out to a place where you have an expansive view, overlooking the ocean, or a wide inland valley, or the top of a high hill; but do it on a comfortably warm night, under the light of a full moon high in the sky. This is already almost another worldly setting. My success having fully cognizant astral travels using this method, are about 1 out of 5 attempts.

It took several astral travels that were limited to remaining in sight of my physical body before I learned how to overcome this limitation. With your physical body you simply need to hold something in your hand that is intimately tied to you and very easy to remember. I didn't discover this technique until after I was married, so I always use my wedding ring. I take it off my finger and clasp it tightly in my closed hand.

Many teachers of astral travel speak about the silver cord that connects your physical body to your astral body as the connector that brings you back from your travels. In truth, I have never seen a silver cord connecting my astral and physical body. Perhaps it exists, but I have looked for it and never seen it. But then again, I have never seen my astral body either, so perhaps the silver cord is likewise something I just can't see.

My grounding connection is my wedding ring held tightly in my hand. I can astral travel anywhere, including off-planet to other worlds, and the very moment I think of my wedding ring, my astral body is reunited with my physical body in the blink of an eye.

I believe most of us astral travel every night while we sleep. We simply do not remember our journeys because there is such a disconnect between our awake Day-Self, which deals within the structure of the familiar everyday world, and our Night-Self, which is unhindered by the physical limitations of the body while we sleep, and has a propensity to travel to weird and quirky places. Our Night-Self can travel each night to worlds so strange that our Day-Self can't even comprehend what the Night-Self is viewing. Some freaky, convoluted dreams may simply be the sleeping Day-Self part of the brain trying to make sense of images coming in from the eyes of the Night-Self during its astral travels that the Day-Self simply has no point of reference to process or understand.

The easiest way to Astral Travel, and certainly the quickest way for newbies to first experience it, is at night while you are sleeping. You are likely doing this every night already and simply not remembering your journeys. So the trick isn't to astral travel while you sleep, but to have some conscious control of where you go, and adequate memory of where you have been that it is a fulfilling and expansive experience.

The best way to enhance your experience is to begin by lucid dreaming, then remember and record your experiences when you first awake and they are fresh in your mind, as explained in detail in **Chapter: 14** *Lucid Dreaming* and **Chapter 23:** *Dreams & Dream Interpretation*. Consciously astral traveling while sleeping is really a form of advanced lucid dreaming. In normal lucid dreaming you find yourself in a dream and then exert control over your dream body and the dream itself. To astral travel, you take it a step further and decide, you don't actually want to be in the particular dream you found yourself in at all. You would prefer for example, to visit the Taj Mahal! So goodbye to the old lucid dream and hello to a trip to the Taj Mahal. And so it will be if all goes according to plan, which is a big 'if' when using the sleep method. The other downside of this method verses the fully conscious meditation-study-prayer method of astral traveling, is the difficulty of clearly remembering everything you see.

The meditation-study-prayer method is done thru your fully conscious and aware Day-Self, while the sleep method is accomplished thru your foggy, enigmatic Night-Self.

The common limitations are: Day-Self astral travel is usually restricted to remaining within sight of your physical body unless you are an advanced practitioner, while Night-Self astral travel has a hazy memory and understanding of what is viewed and experienced, plus, an exact control over where you go and what you see, until you are well practiced.

Remote Viewing: The traditional explanation for Remote Viewing labels it as an advanced form of Clairvoyance, of being able to see things in your mind that are not present. In my experience, Remote Viewing can be much more. It can be based upon conscious, wide awake, Astral Traveling and has nothing to do with clairvoyance, but you will not likely see that explanation anywhere. The thought of someone being able to consciously Astral Travel and spy upon whatever or whomever they desire in great detail and total recall, is too scary for most people to handle. So a lighter, gentler, fuzzier form based upon clairvoyance is promulgated.

Traditional Remote Viewing evolved from programs created by researching parapsychologists at the Stanford Research Institute. They developed procedures and techniques to instigate Remote Viewing Clairvoyance, the projection of the Remote Viewers consciousness to a distant location under controlled conditions. Unlike Astral Projection, which gives the sense of your entire astral body traveling, Remote Viewing through clairvoyance merely expands the consciousness to become aware of things in distant places.

Though I've only experimented a little with Astral Traveling Remote Viewing, I am very excited about the prospects for the future. I am currently practicing observing greater detail in my travels. If I see a book on a desk for example, then I want to be able to move in closer and read the title of the book. Even better, if I am watching someone read the book, I want to be able to look over their shoulder and read along with them. The ramifications of repeatable, dependable success are huge as it would satisfy my long lost scientific training, by allowing very exact testing with indisputable verifiable results.

The Remote Viewing program conducted by the military, which many people are familiar with from books and popular shows, began in 1972 and was eventually shut down in 1995. After extensive review of the results it was determined that none of information provided in the 20+ years had been specific enough to actually be of any use for military intelligence. If that's the case, I would suspect it was because they practiced Remote Viewing Clairvoyance, which by its root nature is hazy and open to interpretation, rather than Remote Viewing Astral Traveling, which can be extremely specific and detailed.

How You Can Have an OBE, Astral Project or Remote View
Prayer Method

My favorite method, which I explained previously, is simply to have a completely undisturbed one to two hour period of study, contemplation and prayer on a single subject you wish to know more about. Follow this with a visit nearby to a place where you can have an expansive view, overlooking a valley or ocean, under the light of a full moon. After taking a moment to take in the breath-taking view, kneel and bow your head and ask whatever God, higher being or source you seek wisdom from, to help you see or know that which you seek. Keep praying out loud, tune out the world, and reach out from the depths of your heart to the higher source you seek. At some point, when you are successful, you will feel the separation from your body and be able to look down and see your physical body below you.

Beanstalk Method

Another method I have successfully used, which can be done both when you are awake and conscious, or while you are asleep in a lucid dream, is, after 30 minutes to 2 hours of contemplation, study and meditation, imagine Jack's big beanstalk going up through and beyond the clouds. Just like Jack, you need to climb the beanstalk. An amazing new world awaits above the clouds. Regardless of whether you are asleep or awake, do not move any part of your body. Use your imagination to climb the beanstalk. Visualize reaching up to grab the stems of the giant leaves sticking out from the stalk. Feel the coarseness of the plant fibers as you squeeze the stems tightly to insure you don't fall. Stay perfectly relaxed. Begin to climb the beanstalk faster as you are excited to pass through the clouds and see the new world. As you near the bottom of the cloud you should begin to sense your astral body quivering to be set free. As you pass through the cloud into the brilliant sunshine and blue sky above, look down and see your physical body still holding onto the beanstalk, or lying on a bed, or kneeling on the ground, or wherever you left it.

Superman Method

Here's another method I have used both while awake and conscious and while asleep in a lucid dream. After 30 minutes to 2 hours of contemplation, study and meditation, imagine a long tunnel with a bright light at the end. See yourself flying like superman through the tunnel, faster and faster as you near the light. As you burst out of the tunnel and into the spacious light, your astral body separates and you can now look down and see your physical body where ever you left it.

Tarzan Method

After 30 minutes to 2 hours of contemplation, study and meditation, either while awake and conscious or asleep in a lucid dream, see yourself as Tarzan standing and swinging on a very long vine, on a very long swing. Feel the wind rushing through your hair and the feeling in your stomach as you take off on a long downward swing, then you reach the lowest point and begin to swing upward in the pendulum arc of the swing. As you reach the pinnacle, the highest point of the arc, let go and fly out free into the empty space beyond. You will experience immediate separation at that point and be able to look down on your physical body where ever you left it.

Levitation Method

This technique is best used when you first awaken from sleep, especially if you prefaced your sleep with 30 minutes to 2 hours of contemplation, study and meditation. This can be in the morning or anytime at night that you happen to awaken from a dream. It works really well if you use it in conjunction with the OBE software mentioned below. After you awaken, don't move a muscle. Immediately imagine yourself levitating off the bed. Be aware of the sensations inside your body and feel yourself getting lighter and lighter as your body lifts off the bed. You may quickly have astral separation and with your astral eyes soon be looking down at your physical body lying on the bed.

OBE Software

There is also a free website you can visit (*http://astralforum.org/oobe_inducer.php*) that will stimulate you to astral travel by using your computer to awaken you 4.5 hours after you have gone to sleep. A recorded message will remind you to not move any part of your body, and to keep your eyes closed and to go back to sleep. Later, you will be awakened again by the recorded voice, which will once again remind you to remain still and go back to sleep. After a series of these awakenings you reach a state of conscious sleep paralysis where your mind is awake and your body cannot move. In this state it is easy to astral project using any of the above methods.

Chapter 21

BIBLIOELUCIDATION
(Be-Lucid)

This is one of the easiest methods you will ever find to receiving psychic and intuitive insight and answers. It's also an excellent, quickly learned method of divination. Traditionally you simply ask a question aloud, then with your eyes closed, open up a book of your choice and shuffle through the pages at random until you reach a page you *'feel'* has the answer. With your eyes remaining closed, scroll down the page with your index finger until you reach the location you 'feel' has the solution or insight you seek. Open your eyes and read it. Occasionally it may need to be interpreted, but more often than not, it will give you a very exact answer to your question.

Originally a Bible or spiritual book was used for this purpose. However, any book can be used. 'Biblio' is from the Greek word for 'book' and does not imply use of a Bible. 'Elucidation' is from the Latin 'elucidaus', which means to enlighten or clarify. So Biblioelucidation (or Be-Lucid as I like to shorten it) means to use your psychic abilities and a book to explain or enlighten.

Stichomancy is another archaic name for Biblioelucidation.

Rhaspsodomancy, also known as 'Prophetic Rhapsody,' uses the same technique, but with a book of poetry instead of a spiritual or other type of book.

The Be-Lucid technique is commonly used with the I Ching, the 'Book of Changes,' which is likely the oldest book of divination in existence, dating back to at least the end of the 2nd millennium BCE.

In modern times 'Angel Cards,' 'Oracle Cards,' and other type of insightful card decks are popular forms of Be-Lucid.

I've used Be-Lucid frequently and received some important answers to life questions through this technique. In the previous chapter I related the account of my out-of-body experience when seeking to know whether it would be expansive for me to join the Mormon church at that time. It was not long after I joined that I found a need for Be-Lucid as well.

For the first several months after I joined the Mormon church, I shared my experience on the cliff with many Latter-day Saint members, including recounting it at on more than one occasion at the once-a-month Fast & Testimony meetings. It had been profoundly exciting for me and I wanted to share it. I naively assumed that such things were common occurrences with other members of the church, at least during very special moments in their lives. But I soon came to realize that no other Mormons in my association, had ever experienced an OBE. With a smile of tolerance for the enthusiasm of a new member, many people thought I was a little daft. So, as I learned to do in my youth with my ability to see auras, I just stopped sharing my experience with anyone.

After I had been in the LDS church for about two years, I continued to be surprised to have never heard of, or read of, another Mormon having a similar OBE experience, where their spirit separated and lifted above their body. As real as the moment had been to me at the time, I began to wonder if perhaps in my great desire to KNOW the path I should take, I had just imagined my OBE. To gain some insight into whether my experience had been real or imagined I inquired of God.

One of my favorite ways to get answers to questions for years before I had ever joined the church, was to use Biblioelucidation and ask to be guided to a scripture that would give me an answer. I had a book of scriptures called a "Quad" in LDS circles. One thick book contained the Bible, Book of Mormon, Doctrine & Covenants and Pearl of Great Price, which are the four books of 'scripture' used by the Latter-day Saints. Having all four books in one made it very convenient to seek Biblioelucidation answers by asking to be led to a scripture.

Following my usual method, after a prayer asking for an answer, I closed my eyes and opened the quad to whatever page tended to want to open. With my eyes still closed I put my finger on the page at a particular spot I felt guided to. Opening my eyes, I looked at the verse my finger rested on knowing here was the answer to my question.

My finger fell upon Alma 29:16 in the Book of Mormon, which records the Prophet Alma saying, *"Now, when I think of the success of these my brethren my soul is carried away, even to the separation of it from my body, as it were, so great is my joy."*

Reading this was extremely satisfying. Though no modern Mormons seemed to have had similar experiences or even understood what I was talking about, their own scriptures recorded an ancient prophet having an identical experience and that was good enough for me! It gave me unequivocal confirmation of the reality of my OBE despite how strange it seemed to the Latter-day Saints of my association.

Biblioelucidation is also popular as a form of divination, of seeing into the future. A great example, Shelia H., shared with me is how she used Biblioelucidation to find the man she married. She said she had already used the same technique twice previously during the last couple of years to eliminate prospective husbands.

Like me, Shelia loved books by Edgar Rice Burroughs. In fact, I met her in a used book store while we were both looking for Edgar Rice Burroughs books. As we talked about Burroughs

Biblioelucidation

writings, she told me the story of how she came to know her fiancee would become her husband long before he ever proposed.

She owned at least two dozen Burroughs novels in paperback. To determine whether her current boyfriend Robert G. would end up being her husband, Shelia put all her Burroughs books in a paper bag, then shook the bag vigorously, including turning it upside down a few times to thoroughly mix up the books. Without looking, she then reached into the bag and pulled out the first book her fingers touched. Again without looking, she thumbed through the pages until she stopped on a page. She let her finger stop near the middle of the page because that was where she felt moved to find her answer.

This is what she read from page 147 of **A Princess of Mars**: *"I have done many strange things in my life, many things that wiser men would not have dared, but never in my wildest fancies have I dreamed of winning a Dejah Thoris for myself---for never have I dreamed that in all the universe dwelt such a woman as the Princess of Helium. That you are a princess does not abash me, but that you are is enough to make me doubt my sanity as I ask you, my princess, to be mine."*

Burroughs books are great action adventure novels, but they are very, very sparse on romance. Despite this, Shelia was led to the one book in the entire bag where the hero proposes to the heroine. That's Be-Lucid at its best!

How You Can Find Answers with Biblioelucidation

Whether you are seeking answers to current day vexing challenges, seeking to know the path you should take, or desiring to divine a glimpse of the future, Biblioelucidation may be the easiest, quickest and surest method to help you find the answers.

-Choose one of your favorite books. Or, if you don't have a favorite, use Shelia's method and just put a couple dozen of your favorite books in a bag and mix them up.

-Biblioelucidation works best if you spend at least one hour beforehand contemplating the subject you are going to be asking about.

-Just before grabbing hold of your book, say a prayer out loud, or speak out loud exactly what you wish to discover in the book.

-With your eyes closed, open the book to a random page. You can just let the book fall open, or if you prefer, you can thumb through the pages until you come to the one you feel has your answer.

-Place you finger at the place on the open page you feel has your answer.

-Open your eyes and read beginning at the place your finger is pointing to. Your answer may be in the first sentence. If not there, then in the first paragraph. Sometimes you may need to read the entire page and maybe even more than one, but read closely, your answer will be there.

One of the great advantages of Be-Lucid over almost all other forms of intuitive insight or divination, is the answers tend to be very clear with little, if any interpretation needed. You have no need to pay money to a professional card reader or psychic to give insight into your questions. The answers are right at your fingertips with your favorite book and the amazing powers you have within you!

Chapter 22
FAITH, SPIRITUAL & AURIC HEALING

Faith, Spiritual and Auric healing occur when the healer or healers are transmitters or conduits of the Ki life-force energy or a greater vitality energy from beyond themselves, that miraculously and quickly heals a sick or diseased person of their infirmity. The sickness can be as common as a cold, or as life threatening as cancer. The healers can come from a religious community, a secular group, or even just a single non-affiliated person with deep love and compassion for the less fortunate. The life-force energy can come from within the healer or healers themselves, or they may be mere conduits for a vitality energy from higher realms beyond our world.

Faith healing has been practiced since time immemorial in many forms from simple prayers to laying on of hands upon the head of the infirmed. Sadly, it has received a bad reputation among many because of prominent fraudsters, particularly preachers of various religious denominations who purport to heal people by the power of faith, only to be later be discovered to be nothing more than shysters out to separate humble people, desperate for hope and a cure from their money.

Personally, I believe true healing from one person to another, be it faith, spiritual or auric, is an act of love. And love originating in a pure heart would never be sullied by asking someone to pay for gifts of life. I understand that someone who is spending a great deal of their time to help others may need some financial backing and energy reciprocation to continue their ministry, but let it come in the form of voluntary, unsolicited donations of gratitude afterward; not set-fees or coerced 'set price donations' requested beforehand.

In its simplest form faith healing is a prayer of one or more people for the God of their belief to intervene and heal a person in their congregation from sickness. Certainly faith in itself is a great power and it is not married to any particular religion or even any religion at all. The faith and prayers of multiple people united for a common cause can have an affect far greater than just the addition of their numbers.

Some religions teach the 'laying on of hands' in addition to a prayer said at the same time. In this, one or more members will lay their hands on a sick person's head and pray for their healing. Most do not realize or understand the significance of the 'laying on of hands. If they think of it at all, most simply consider it as part of the ritual. In fact, by laying their hands upon the head of the sick, they are not only calling in energy from a higher power through their prayer, but they are also focusing and sending their own Ki Force/Life Force energy through their hands to replenish that which has diminished in the sick and revitalize their health.

The basic premise of faith healing, regardless of the simplicity or complexity of the techniques employed, is simple faith. It may rely on the faith of the sick in their God. Or, perhaps simply in their faith to be healed. It may also require that those praying or laying on hands also have great faith in their religion's tenets and God. If a healing is successful it is deemed so because the faith was sufficient. If it fails to heal, it is blamed on faith that was lacking.

Spiritual healing is also birthed in love for the less fortunate. It espouses a connection to God or a higher power or source, but leaves out the religious fervency of faith healing, and does not depend upon the intervention of God to affect a cure. It is seen in modern forms such as Reiki, that though thought of as secular in the Western world, is firmly based in spirituality. In fact Reiki is a blending of two Japanese words. 'Rei' means, 'God's wisdom or Higher Power,' and ''Ki' means 'life force energy.' The combination means 'spiritually guided life force energy.'

Spiritual healing can have many components and be accomplished by a wide range of procedures and techniques from Native American shamanism to New Age crystal healing. Some such as Celestine Vibronics, utilize the best techniques from several other methods, plus many original treatments activating all the senses, to affect a quick and full recovery.

Auric healing is most prominently seen in China in Qigong, a rapidly growing philosophical and physical way of life, that also practices auric healing arts that call in the life force energy with frequent miraculous results. In fact, there was a large Qigong medicineless hospital in Fergrun, where more than four thousand people lived, including doctors, patients, teachers, supporting personnel and trainees. It was closed in 2001 by the government for political reasons. The simple formula for the remarkable success they had was: exercise, love and life force energy. Over the years since the first Qigong clinic opened in 1988, they treated over one hundred and eighty diseases with greater than a 95% success rate of cures. Even more amazing when you consider that many people came there only after they had been told they were terminally ill or incurable by mainstream medicine practitioners. Cancer, diabetes, tuberculosis, arthritis, heart disease, malaria, severe depression, respiratory infections, paralysis, dengue fever and systemic lupus are just a few of the many diseases and illnesses they successfully cured.

The hospital practiced a hybrid form of Qigong called 'ChiLel' that blended in modern medicine with the life force techniques of Qigong. It was pioneered by the founder Dr. Pang Ming, a Qigong master as well as a physician trained in both western and traditional Chinese medicine.

Luke Chan lived for a month at the hospital to observe all the different aspects and to interview the patients and doctors. He recounted how many times he was moved to tears by their humbling stories of struggle and recovery. " One mother told me she was so weak that she couldn't even pick up a kitchen knife to kill herself and so attempted to end her life by not eating. But when her six year old son tried to spoon feed her a bowl of milk while her eleven year old held a towel to wipe away any spills, she decided to live at any cost. Since doctors couldn't help her she turned to ChiLel and, against all odds, she recovered."

My Most Memorable Healing Experience

I have had multiple experiences both being healed, and being blessed to be the healing conduit for others. These are events that are life-changing and unforgettable. My most memorable and miraculous occurred shortly after I went on a mission for the Mormon church when I was nineteen years old. I had only been on my mission for about two weeks when my companion and I were called by a hospital to come and give a blessing for the sick, to a lady who was receiving care.

This was new territory for me. Not only had I never participated in a blessing, but as I was a freshly minted member, I had never even seen one! My more senior companion quickly explained that there were two parts to the blessing, which was normally just a prayer for the sick, accompanied by the laying on of hands, to give them peace and call upon God to heal them quickly. One Elder (Mormon title for missionary) anointed the person with a drop of olive oil; then both Elders laid their hands upon the head of the person to be given a blessing. The Elder that did not do the anointing, would say the blessing. There were no set words to say, just whatever you were led by the spirit to speak. Just the thought of having to bear that kind of responsibility shook me up. But my companion assured me I could do the anointing and just watch and learn while he gave the blessing.

When we arrived at the hospital we were met by a doctor at the entrance to the woman's room. He drew us aside and explained that she had terminal cancer and only had about a week to live. He said she was not LDS, but had a son in England who was. Her son was on his way to the states to be with his mother for her last days. He had told her if she was ever in dire need to call the Mormon Elders. The doctor told us he knew we were there to give his patient a blessing, but cautioned us not to say anything to upset her or give her false hope. If I was trepidatious before about the blessing ordinance, I was triply so after hearing that the lady was not even a member of the church, and was terminally ill. I felt sorry for my companion who was going to have to give her a blessing. I couldn't even imagine what could comfort or appropriately be told to a person that you had never met that was going to die within a week.

As we introduced ourselves and spoke to her she didn't outwardly seem terminal. Though she was obviously weak, she had a sweet smile and spoke with joy at seeing us. But when I looked at her aura, I could see it was very dim and knew she did only have a short time left.

We talked with her about her son and how she had come to call us, and it was a very touching story. Then my companion explained how a blessing worked. He told her about the two parts, then asked her who she would like to do the anointing, and who she would like to give the blessing. Though outwardly I appeared calm, inwardly I panicked! He hadn't told me anything about giving her a choice! He told me he was going to give the blessing. I couldn't even imagine what I could say to a person who was about to die. I said a non-stop prayer in my mind that she would pick him to give the blessing, and then held a deep breath for a moment when she said she wanted him to anoint and me to give her the blessing.

She had only days left to live. I was completely unprepared by my very young life experience and zero training in the church procedures to say anything to her. I was literally shaking with fear and trepidation after my companion reverently anointed her and I approached to lay my hands upon her head to give her a blessing. It was an ordinance I had never performed or even seen, Nor had anyone even had explained it to me in detail.

I came up to the side of the hospital bed, which was angled so she was in a reclining sitting position. I took a deep breathe and laid my hands upon her head to give her a blessing. At the very moment my hands touched her head a great calm and peace came over me. It flooded into my body, filled my spirit with wonder, and expanded my aura big and bright.

I began to speak, but it was not me speaking. It was my voice, but not my words. I had no control over the words that I spoke; they just flowed out unbidden and unknown before they were uttered. And this sweet old lady was told, not to fear, that the sickness inside her was gone even from that moment. The voice speaking through me told her she would be back in her own home before a week passed.

When I took my hands off her head I looked at her in loving amazement. We both had tears in our eyes and I told her, "That was not me speaking. That was the Holy Spirit of God."

"I know", she said through her tears, "I know."

I looked again at her aura; it glowed in brightness and health. I knew she would be fine.

Despite the fact that blessings for the sick are common in the LDS church, this type of experience was not. Just a couple of days afterward I was transferred to a new area. I never saw or spoke to that precious lady again. But while attending an Area Missionary Conference about a month later, where missionaries from several areas gathered, I had the opportunity to speak with the missionaries that had taken my place. They told me that she returned home at the end of the week, without a trace of her terminal illness, and to the great amazement of the doctors and the joy of her visiting son.

I would like to say that such miracles of healing were common with me after that, but the reality is I have never again been in a similar situation. I have been blessed to be a part of healing many less consequential illnesses, but I have never again experienced the humbling healing power of the intervention of a God energy far beyond me, to the point that my words were no longer mine, but Gods.

Faith, Spiritual & Auric Healing

Your Path To Energy Healing

I have witnessed or participated in many forms of faith, spiritual and auric healing. I firmly believe this is a power that is within every person that will come out when applied with good techniques and empowered by both love and faith with the amazing energies that lie dormant inside of us, plus those greater and beyond us.

If you are a religious person, and faith healing is the most appealing to you, please consider investigating some of the active faith healing religions such as the Latter-day Saints, Christian Scientists, or Presbyterian Church, to name a few. Give prospective churches a call and ask what they do to heal the sick. Every church prays to the God of their belief to intervene and heal the sick. But active healing churches do something more such as the laying on of hands.

If you consider yourself spiritual, but not religious, you should look into Reiki, Qigong, or Celestine Vibronics.

Most New Age people do consider themselves 'spiritual,' but neither religion or spirituality are required in many of the New Age healing practices, which focus on the use of a wide range of tools such as crystals and drums to call in and concentrate healing energies from various sources. If this resonates with you, then you should learn more about the myriad of New Age alternative healing modalities to see which really interest you. Just type 'new age healing' in the search box on Amazon and you'll see many choices to learn about and explore.

Unleash Your Psychic Powers

Chapter 23

DREAMS & DREAM INTERPRETATION

What would your life be like if you completely forgot what you did during two hours in the day when you were involved in some of your most important tasks? And that this critical memory loss occurred each day of your life and could never be recalled? Thus it is every night for almost every person with their dreams. Most people have 4 to 7 dreams a night. If they live an average of 72 years they will have between 100,000 to 200,000 dreams in their lifetime. That is a very large number of events in your life to not remember. Especially when some of your dreams might have been trying to tell you something very significant.

How Many Hours Each Night Do You Dream?

According to sleep researchers the average person dreams about 2 hours each night. The dreams become progressively longer as you remain sleeping. The first one will typically only be about 5 minutes long, while the last one is often 45 minutes to 1 hour. Typically your body will go through a series of short preparatory cycles before each dream begins. Your Dreams occur during periods of REM (rapid eye movement), which typically is about 20-25% of the time you are sleeping. While in REM your mind is as active as it is during times when you are awake, but only certain portions of your brain are active.

How Long Are Dreams?

While some dreams can seem quite long, the reality is they are fairly short. After you have gone to sleep, gone through the dream prep cycles, and begun your first dream, it will usually be the shortest dream of the night, averaging only 5 to 10 minutes. This will be followed by another series of dream prep cycles, then a new period of REM and another dream. Your final REM and dream of the night will likely last about 30 to 35 minutes and is the one most likely to be remembered, both because of its length and that you are waking up from the dream, so it immediately becomes a part of your conscious memory.

Why You Can't Remember Your Dreams

Unless they wake up in the middle of a dream most people will not remember any part of a dream other than vague and quickly vanishing images and events that occurred in their very last dream. Even if you wake up in the middle of the night with a very vivid dream, thinking you'll clearly remember the details, when you awake again in the morning, chances are you probably will not remember much. Consider that in a week you will have 28 to 49 dreams, all while your conscious mind was turned off! It's little wonder that most people can only remember fleeting images and emotions from their last dreams of the night.

Even the Blind Dream

Demonstrating how integral, perhaps even vital, dreaming is to human well-being, even people without sight dream. If they became blind sometime after age 5 they will have visual dreams plus dreams involving their other senses. If they were born blind, or became blind very young before their mind recorded enough visual images, they will still have complex and sensory full dreams each night. But they will mirror their abilities when awake with all of the dream being composed of sounds, smells, tastes and sensations of touch.

You Are Completely Paralyzed During Your Rem Dreams

When you are having detailed dreams during the REM cycle, your body is completely paralyzed. This is referred to as 'REM atonia.' If you can become conscious during this time it is an ideal period to easily astral travel and is referred to as 'sleep paralysis.' It is not uncommon for sleep paralysis to occur when you first awaken in the morning, or if you awaken from a dream in the middle of the night. Have you ever suddenly awakened in the middle of a frightening dream only to find you can't move? That's sleep paralysis. If you are fortunate enough to have this occur, be prepared to astral travel.

I can remember when I was still a kid and would awaken from scary, vivid dreams where I had fallen off a cliff, or been shot, or attacked by a mountain lion, or something equally horrible. My eyes would flutter open and my consciousness would click on, but my body wouldn't move. After several dozen seconds or a couple of minutes, I would slowly be able to lift one arm and would gingerly feel my body to see if my leg was really broken, or my body full of gunshot wounds dripping blood, which had been my last dream images before I awoke. It was always such a relief to realize it had all been just a dream!

During REM atonia the neurons in your brain responsible for physical movement are inactive, which is why your body can barely twitch a finger if you're lucky. Sleep researchers feel the main purpose of REM atonia is to prevent you from getting up and reacting to events occurring in your dream, which could cause you to accidentally injure yourself physically.

Universal Dreams

Many of your dreams revolve around personal themes unique to your life. But several themes commonly found in dreams such as being chased, falling, feeling frozen in place, naked in public, flying like Superman, late for events, or attacked, are common among all people of the world regardless of their religion, culture, education, sex, race, or background.

Calvin S. Hall of Western Reserve University collected over 50,000 reports of dreams from the 1940's up until 1985. After categorizing the many variety of dreams they concluded that people from every culture and country in the world dream the same dream themes, simply flavored by their own culture and experiences.

Sex Dreams (*Warning: PG-13 rated comments follow*)

Another type of dream that seems to be common across cultures and with both men and women, are sex dreams. In erotic dreams it is not unusual to act out kinky scenarios that would probably be quite repugnant to you when you are awake; everything from infidelity, a very common dream, to bizarre fetishes that you wouldn't even consider when you are conscious.

In fact, you can have a sex dream, even when you're not dreaming about sex! According to Barbara Bartlik, MD, a New York based sex therapist and psychiatrist, "Women have orgasms during their sleep just as men do. These orgasms often accompany erotic dreams, but they also may occur during dreams of a non-erotic nature. When women dream, it's not uncommon for their genitals to become engorged and lubricated. This occurs during REM sleep, which happens several times during the night." She says men experience the same type of arousal while they sleep regardless of the content of their dream. "Men get erections during REM sleep, whether or not the man is having an erotic dream."

The Hall data previously mentioned, found that sexual dreams only occur about 10% of the time, with greater frequency in teenagers and less in the elderly. A related study by Zadra concluded that both men and women dream sexual dreams about 8% of the time.

Are Your Dreams In Color or Black & White?

People who grew up only watching television in black & white were found to dream in black and white about 25% of the time, according to a study done at the University of Dundee.

Dream Incorporation

If your sleeping body hears, smells, feels, or tastes something while you are dreaming, such as a telephone ringing, it may often be incorporated into your dream. But likely in a strange way completely unrelated to the stimuli being experienced by your sleeping body.

I've experienced this a lot. One time I dreamed I was drowning in a swimming pool and when startled awake from my dream my pillow was covering my face, from my tossing and turning while asleep! I was so glad I had that dream and woke up.

Many people that have incontinence report dreaming of urinating whenever their sleeping body involuntarily does it.

Learn While Your Sleep

In college I did some interesting experiments that proved you can learn real world information while you sleep. For awhile in my Freshman year I struggled to get good grades. The wide variety of extra curricula activities available were too much fun, and studying was not one of my strong points, as I was easily led away to the fun. The night before a test, I would usually go over my class notes and the text book, speaking aloud the key points to hopefully help me remember them the next day. Then I got the brilliant idea to record my spoken words while I was studying and play them back while I was asleep. Wow, did that ever help! I went from a 'C' average on tests to an 'A', immediately. I would get a 2 hour cassette tape, record silence on it for the first 60 minutes, then record my spoken study words for the last hour of the tape. I put the tape player close to my head as I lay down, with a mid-level adjustment for the sound. The last thing I did before closing my eyes was to turn on the tape player. One hour of silence would ensue before my recorded voice came on and I would be sound asleep long before then. For the next hour my subconscious heard all of the key words, phrases and observations for my upcoming test. The next day the answers just seemed to leap out of my mind.

This is not as unusual as it sounds. According to researchers at Harvard Medical School dreams can be a way your brain processes, integrates and understands new things you learn. Their research indicates that when you dream parts of your brain are activated that help you to solve problems.

Various Theories About Dreams

As dreams can often be very disturbing or poignant, as well as a very confusing part of our life, one that occurs every single night, as would be expected that many 'experts' have weighed in with their opinions as to just what dreams mean. In addition to the hundreds of books available for dream interpretation, here are the conclusions of several prominent researchers concerning the meaning of dreams:

Sigmund Freud. the late 19th century psychotherapist, believed that dreams were a manifestation of "wish fulfillment." Freud felt the content of a dream was shaped by the desires of the unconscious mind, and that these often stemmed from childhood memories and experiences. He felt dreams had both key parts that related to wish fulfillment and other superficial parts that were just meaningless filler. But he also believed that the important parts, which he called "latent," were often hidden within the meaningless parts, which he called "manifest." Freud believed that nightmares and bad dreams were the brains way to learn how to exert control over real life distressing experiences. He also proposed that most meaningful wish fulfillment was sexual in nature.

Dreams & Dream Interpretation

Carl Jung was a contemporary of Freud's during Freud's later years. He disagreed with many of Freud's premises and theories. Jung believed that dreams were messages from the dreamers subconscious to their conscious mind that could help reveal and resolve emotional or religious challenges and fears. For their own good he felt it was important for dreamers to pay attention to their dreams.

Jung felt reoccurring dreams were especially important and demanded attention. He explained a reoccurring dream was an indication that the dreamer was neglecting something important in their life. He also felt that daily memories, which he termed *'day residue,'* were interposed into dreams and the unconscious played with the memories while the ego was at rest.

Interestingly, Jung also felt that dreams could not just be looked at as stand-alone individual events, but that all dreams were connected in some way in "one great web of psychological factors."

Fritz Perl theorized that dreams were manifestations of various aspects of self that were being ignored, rejected or suppressed while awake. He felt that even inanimate objects in a dream represented some aspect of the dreamer.

Jie Zhang proposed that dreams were a manifestation of brain activation and synthesis, and that the main purpose of sleep was to record and transfer short-term memory to long-term memory as needed. He also postulated that dreaming and REM were actually not controlled by the same brain mechanisms.

Ioannis Tsoukalas theorized that REM sleep, when the most vivid dreams are experienced, is an evolutionary progression of the primitive *tonic immobility reflex*. This ancient instinctual reflex causes some animals to become immobilized and feign death to make attackers no longer interested in them. Humans also become paralyzed during REM sleep.

Eugen Tarnow proffered that dreams are stimulation of long-term memory, and the convoluted strangeness is due to extracting bits of information from the structure of the long-term memory.

W. Robert, a physician from Hamburg, Germany, and another Freud contemporary, postulated that dreams are an essential need. He proposed that they take the sensory impressions, emotions and knowledge learned during the day, and either erase or suppress them as useless, or clarify and record into the short and/or long-term memory.

Crick and Mitchison expanded upon Roberts work in 1983, by creating the 'reverse learning' theory.' They compared dreams to the cleanup maintenance of a computer, theorizing that dreams removed or suppressed useless junk information and other types of parasitic nodes.

Hennevin and Leconte took an opposite view in 1971, stating that dreams had a memory consolidation function that occurred during spontaneous firings of neural patterns.

Richard Coutts explains that dreams play a key role in a two-step sleep process, which improves the brains ability to function optimally when awake.

Alfred Adler theorized that most dreams are emotional foundations for solving problems.

Flanagan has a unique take on dreams, feeling they actually serve no function and merely "...came along as a free ride on a system designed to think and to sleep."

Hobson also feels that dreams are merely by-products of the sleeping process and have no meaningful effect on waking life. He states that people go about their daily activities without any memory or effect from their dreams. He feels the odd content of dreams can be attributed to certain parts of the brain trying to create a coherent story out the bizarre information that flashes into it.

Deirdre Barrett looks at dreaming as "thinking in a different biochemical state." She theorizes that people work on the same problems while they dream as they did when they were awake. Her research shows that any human problem from relationship or business challenges, to math, science, musical composition, or any other endeavor, may be scrutinized in a dream and solutions revealed that *escaped* a person when they were awake.

Mark Blechner has a similar theory he calls "Oneiric Darwinism." He believes dreams create new innovations and ideas by generating random thought mutations. Many may be rejected by the mind as not viable, while others will be retained and encoded in memory as valuable.

Sandor Ferenczi encouraged dreams to be told. He felt doing so could communicate points of importance that were not being expressed clearly when awake.

In the *Oracles of Celestine Light: Vivus*, Yeshua of Nazareth gives a unique description of certain aspects of dreams in Chapter 74, *The Importance of Dreams*. After listening to a diverse recounting of the previous night's dreams from all 12 of his Apostles, Yeshua told them, "...none of you have fully understood the essential nature and opportunity that dreams present to you each night, nor the potential for harm..."

Yeshua's explanation touches on aspects others overlook, so I quote it at length below:

23 Dreams serve many purposes, but there are only a few that I wish to emphasize today.

24 The world in which man dwells and the world in which the Elohim dwell are like the land and the sea from the perspective of a tortoise.

25 The tortoise is a creature of the land. He can look upon the sea, but he cannot go there lest he would perish, even as man can look to our Father and Mother in the heavens but cannot go there to be with them while they are still in the flesh.

26 But it is possible for the tortoise to go to the edge of the sea and walk into it for just a bit so that its feet still firmly touch the land beneath, while its body is immersed in the waters of the sea. Thus it is at one moment, both on the land and in the sea.

27 So it is with your dreams. It is a hallowed time when you remain still in the flesh, but can also touch a part of Heaven and commune directly with our Father and Mother and the angels of Heaven.

28 For those like each of you, who seek the purity of the Celestine Light, this is something you

Dreams & Dream Interpretation

are already doing each and every time you sleep, even though you may remember it not.

29 Dream time is a time when a part of your spirit is freed from the bonds of your body and this world and can visit and commune with all other worlds, and other spirits wherever they may be, as well as travel and explore the world in which you live in ways your physical body never can.

30 But this is also a time of great vulnerability for the unprepared. For even as a part of your spirit can commune directly with the Celestine Realm while you sleep, so too can your spirit visit other worlds while you dream and interact with the spirits of those dwelling there.

31 But even as your spirit of the night can travel far and wide to places beyond the understanding of your day spirit, so too can spirits of those from other worlds and from living people in this world also come to you in your dreams while you sleep and interact with and influence the part of your spirit that remains grounded in this world, even those that would lead you to darkness and away from the Celestine Light.

31 Therefore, it is greatly important that you set your intentions before you pass into sleep and not just thoughtlessly fall into your dreams.

32 In your nightly prayer with our Father and Mother in Heaven, ask to be shielded from all evil while you sleep and be led only upon dream paths that will uplift and inspire you and reveal greater light and understanding. Ask no less for the night than you do for the hours when you are awake.

33 Thus, you will be protected from that which would do you harm and open to receive a fullness of Celestine Light from Heaven, both that which you ask for and that which is brought to you as a gift.

34 When you seek an answer to a question, small or great, concerning matters either temporal or spiritual, ask in your nightly prayers to be shown the solution in your dreams, and so it shall be given unto you.

35 Even if you do not recall your dreams, a part of your spirit of the day will remember the essence of what your spirit of the night learned and will be pulled into a resonance with it while you are awake.

36 But for the Children of Light, it is very beneficial if their spirit of the day remembers the travels of their spirit of the night.

37 This is even more important for you, my Apostles, as your dreams are the time when you can touch the realms of Celestine Light and receive pure answers for your questions, learn more of your gifts and powers, and gain divine inspiration for your family and your personal growth.

38 Most importantly, it is a time to receive heavenly messengers, to hear the guidance of Elohim and see great visions of things that are to come that you might be prepared to prosper and not perish.

39 Your dream time, when your spirit of the night visits the Celestine Realms, is also your divine school of knowledge where you may learn and practice the mysteries of all things.

40 Each day, I teach you how to use your gifts and develop them into powers that can benefit the Children of Light and the world. But your learning needs not end with our times together, for each moment that you sleep, you can receive further instruction from the angels on high in your dreams.

41 In your travels of the night, you can observe others using their gifts that you might be more prepared to use yours. And you can practice using your powers in places where a mistake causes no pain or damage, but merely becomes an opportunity to learn how to become successful.

42 All of this and much more is available to you as you remember more and more of your dreams.

47 Now if your spirit of the day were always in total recall of the adventures of your spirit of the night, you would become very haggard in appearance, because the time you most easily remember dreams is the time when you are not yet into a deep sleep or are just awakening out of one.

48 Therefore, it would only be by failing to have a sound sleep that you would be able to remember everything you dreamed in the night. While remembering essential parts of your dreams is important, so is a long and sound sleep that your body will wake refreshed and with renewed vigor for the day that dawns.

49 For this cause, when you seek something of great importance, a prophecy or clear guidance, do not seek it in the night, but...sleep for two hours during the day while the Sun is still in the sky. By resting in this manner at a time you are normally active, you will usually not fall into as deep of a sleep as you do in the long and accustomed hours of the night.

50 By sleeping lightly at this time, you will remember much more, even all of your dreams, especially if you set that as your intention before you nap."

In **Chapter 70 of the Oracles of Celestine Light: Vivus**, Conversion of Adronicus and Yunia, Yeshua gave detailed enlightenment concerning 5 main types of dreams.

41 "What about dreams?" interjected another. "Can you interpret dreams? Because I had quite a nightmare last night." And at his words, there was much laughter.

42 Yeshua rose again after his question and said unto him, "I will speak to you about dreams, not for you alone, but for the edification of my Apostles.

43 Describe if you will what you remember of your dream."

44 The man did as Yeshua bade and related the details of his dream. "I saw a great army invading; I know not where. But I found myself completely naked, holding only a knife, as a horde of soldiers descended upon me. I awoke just as they were all attacking me so I know not how the dream ends, but I fear the worst, for what can one naked man with a knife do against many soldiers with swords and javelins?"

45 This statement was again greeted with much laughter, but Yeshua answered serenely, saying, "To interpret a dream, you must decide what type of dream it is, and there are five possibilities:

46 Your most common dreams are simply your spirit of the night, taking events of your last days and recreating the themes with real or fictional characters in scenes that may or may not exist in reality. And you may or may not be one of the characters in the dream.

47 These dreams may be a continuation of thoughts you were pondering just before passing into sleep or completely unrelated to your thoughts during the day. Either way, they are often useful

Dreams & Dream Interpretation

to help you understand problems that may be vexing you from perspectives you may not have considered during the times you were awake.

48 Therefore, do not dismiss these dreams as mere fanciful wanderings of your night spirit, but seek to remember them and consider how their lessons can apply to your current life challenges.

49 If your dream is of this type, you will seldom awaken from it at the end of the dream.

50 The other four types of dreams are dreams of fear, dreams of hope, dreams of lust, and visions of prophecy or revelation.

51 The dream of being naked and almost defenseless while being attacked by overwhelming numbers is a dream of fear."

52 Yeshua looked at the man that had spoken of his dream, and he said unto him, "In your daily life, you may be fearful of being exposed for something you have hidden from others and, once exposed, attacked and perhaps even killed because of what was revealed, with little to save you from your fate.

53 Even if such a thing is unlikely to happen, your guilt from your transgression causes you to fear just retribution, and this can be manifested in dreams such as you have described."

54 The other men at the table looked at their friend now with suspicion, and he leaped up proclaiming wildly, "It was just a silly dream! Why are you all looking at me like that?" Then grabbing his wife by the hand, he pulled her to her feet, snapping angrily, "Come we are leaving, this is nonsense!" Quickly, they strode across the room and departed from the house.

55 Yeshua continued to speak, saying, "Then there are dreams of hope. They often relate to your daily life. For instance, if you are a fisherman, you may see yourself catching a net full of fish, more than it can hold.

56 If you are a bachelor seeking a wife, you may see several beautiful women desiring your favor. If that scene becomes sexual, it transitions into a dream of lust.

57 Dreams of hope can also be fanciful. You may see yourself flying in the air like a bird or discovering a treasure chest of gold.

58 Dreams of fear and hope do often have a common ending. When they are powerful, they will cause you to awaken from your sleep.

59 If you have had a dream of fear, you will awaken with a dread in the pit of your stomach and a heart that is beating rapidly.

60 If it is a dream of hope, you will awaken with a feeling of euphoria in your heart and a joy that fills every part of you.

61 Like the dreams of fear, dreams of hope often relate to your daily life, but more often in a less-direct way than dreams of fear.

62 If you have just asked the woman of your heart's desire to marry you, and all is well, you may dream that night of flying like a bird, for in truth, your spirit is soaring with happiness.

63 On the other hand, you may dream of women without love, but only with lust, or women may have lustful dreams of men or even of another woman or a man of another man. Lustful dreams imagine acts that your awake-self likely would find repugnant and would never contemplate, much less consummate.

65 "But at night, while you sleep, or in the morning when you are half awake and half asleep, or in the night as you drift into slumber, lustful dreams are not a sin if they are of imaginary people, but a benign means Elohim has given you to harmlessly expunge the natural urges that build up during the day, that they will not prompt you while awake to commit acts which you and others would forever regret.

66 Visions of prophecy are rare and do not come to ordinary men or women, for they are sent by Elohim to warn those who walk the pleasing paths of Elohim of things to come. But they can come to Children of Light wherever they are found without regard for race, sex, religious beliefs, or social standing.

67 If you live your life with honesty and honor, show kindness and respect to others, and treat your body like a temple of God, you can receive dreams of prophecy and revelation concerning that over which you have been given responsibility.

68 A true vision of prophecy will come more than one night while you sleep. They will be very memorable, vivid, and detailed, and you will almost always awaken directly after the vision.

69 Unlike dreams of hope and fear, you will feel neither dreadful nor euphoric, but will simply understand in calmness.

70 Most importantly, a true vision of prophecy will repeat more than once and sometimes often, even nightly, if it is showing you an event that is to occur very soon.

71 Successive visions of the prophecy will always show again that which you have already seen, but they may also add additional details with each reoccurrence.

72 Understanding your visions of prophecy correctly is of great importance, and it is sometimes prudent to seek out the advice of a knowledgeable Child of Light to correctly interpret that which you have seen, for sometimes the vision shows an actual event as it shall occur and other times, it shows representations of reality, such as a lion representing a king, or a soaring eagle representing victory.

73 Understand foremost that your prophetic visions will only involve your sphere of responsibility. If you receive a vision of something beyond your responsibility, it only pertains to how that vision will affect your sphere of responsibility.

74 Even as Noah saw great destruction coming upon the world, but did not try to save it, but only used his vision to prepare to save the worthy Children of Light he could reach and the animals that came to him, as he was commanded by Elohim.

75 Therefore, if you are a parent, you may receive a vision of prophecy or dream of revelation regarding your children.

76 If you are the owner of a trading caravan, you may receive a vision of prophecy or dream of revelation about your business.

77 If you are the leader of a community, you may receive a prophecy or revelation concerning the community.

78 If you are the leader of a congregation of worshipers, you may receive a prophecy or revelation concerning your flock.

79 If you are an Apostle, you will receive prophecies and revelations about the specific responsibilities of your calling, but never for all of the Communities of Light unless all the other Apostles received the same vision of prophecy or revelation.

80 If you are the prophet of Elohim, you will receive visions of prophecy and revelation concerning not only all of the Children of Light, but all the world as well.

81 Beyond this, there is no constant meaning in the images you see in dreams, but each must be understood and interpreted according to the life and challenges of each person and the type of dream or vision that was seen."

The Nine Types of Dreams

Now it's my turn. I have studied and pondered my dreams all of my life, as well as always having been fascinated by the dreams of others and what they could possibly mean. Many significant actions in my life were initiated because the content of my dreams motivated and inspired me to act. I have invented several devices that aid me in various ways in my non-writing work. Without exception these all first came to me in dreams, or immediately when I awoke in the morning as my first conscious thought after a night of dreaming, or as a daydream vision popping into my mind out of the blue in the middle of the day.

Once I was able to segregate my dreams by themes it became much easier to clearly understand what, if anything, the dream was trying to tell me. As you review the type of dreams below, keep in mind that it is not uncommon for a single dream to have elements of two themes blended together.

Irrelevant

Not every dream has a message or a motivating purpose. In classifying them as irrelevant I don't imply that they don't still serve a purpose, only that their function is transitory. Some dreams, particularly those you have when you are not in REM sleep, are not meant to be interpreted or searched for greater meaning. You'll be hard pressed to remember even a fleeting glimpse of these short snippet dreams anyway. The non-REM dreams do serve a useful 'flushing out' function; be it a bad dream or a good dream, unresolved emotional baggage accrued during the past day from anxieties, anger, joy, frustrations, sexual desires, etc., can be purged and the mind balanced to begin the new day when you awaken. If your dream is not a vivid story occurring during REM sleep, it is most likely to be an irrelevant dream. This is why you don't remember it in the morning. It served its function while you were sleeping and has no further purpose once you awaken.

Hope

Many vivid dreams revolve around some aspect of 'hope.' There are a wide variety of subjects within the hope theme. In a sub category of 'wish fulfillment', you'll find everything from hoping to excel in school or work, to desiring to have the perfect man or woman for a mate or liaison. Other type of hope dreams instill a sense of inspiration, self-assuredness and confidence that carry over into the next day while you are awake. This usually comes about from overcoming obstacles in the dream, such as scaling a mountain and reaching the peak. Inspiration/self-confidence type of hope dreams most often involve exciting dream adventures.

Fear

Dreams that involve any type of failure or inadequacy at work, in love, at school, etc., are fear dreams. These dreams are frequently filled with emotions of anxiety and often revolve around real-life people such as the infidelity of a spouse. Anything or anyone you are fearful of when you are awake, may be expressed with great fear and even terror in a dream. However, you do not have to feel fear in the dream for it to qualify for this category. The apprehension of a spouse having an affair is reported by dream researchers to be the number one fear dream. But it usually occurs with the dreamer as an unseen fairly emotionless observer. The anxiety and greater fear comes when you wake up and wonder if the dream was warning you that you have something to worry about.

Primal

When put in the perspective of the 50,000 year existence of modern Homo Sapiens, modern man has not been modern for very long. There are numerous instinctual memories encoded in the brain of every human from birth that have nothing to do with our modern world but are often still expressed vividly in dreams. Have you ever had a dream of being chased by some kind of animal from a large snake to a tiger? Chances are you will never need to be worried about such an attack in your life, so why dream about it? Though a tremendous amount of dream interpretation symbolism is frequently put on the elements of these dreams, a simpler explanation is that our ancestors for tens of thousands of years **did** have to worry about being chased and eaten by large wild animals And a host of other life and death situations every day of their existence.

Our progenitors were lucky to live to be 35 years old. To continue their genetic line and even the survival of the human species, their lives were a constant, competitive battle for survival. They had to compete for food resources with ferocious animals, as well as other humans. Shelters, mates, children, all had to be fought for and protected once won, against both human and animal predators.

Dreaming about such encounters replicated dangerous situations experienced regularly and helped our ancestors to act out their flight or fight responses while they slept, continually reinforcing their primal instincts for survival. These instinctual dreams honed ancient survival skills. They are still an integral part of modern human dreams because they are encoded in our

DNA.

Instincts are amazing abilities. They are traits and skills you have from birth passed along in your DNA that never need to be taught to you by a parent or anyone else; though they can emphasize and reinforce what your instinct already tells you.

For example, I am blessed to have parrots for friends. I have one mated pair of Sun Conures, that never knew their parents. The human breeder took them as eggs from their nest on the day they were laid and hatched them in an incubator, then hand fed them until he sold them to me. These two birds came from separate parents and later after interacting and squabbling with each other for two years, bonded and mated. The male prepared their nest. He took about a week to do it, working some hours every day. He had never seen another bird make a nest and was never in a nest himself as an egg or a baby, yet he knew how to do it. The instinct and knowledge was encoded in his DNA.

When the female laid her eggs, she knew she needed to sit on them practically 24 hours a day for at least 3 weeks to hatch them, even though her mother never had the opportunity to sit on her egg. Nor did she experience hatching or being cared for as a newborn. Yet instinct motivated her to do it, and she knew how to do it because the knowledge was encoded in her DNA.

Human mothers have similar natural instincts toward their young. Can there be any doubt that if a woman had matured devoid of any knowledge of maternal responsibilities, she would still instinctively know to offer her milk swollen breasts to her newborn? And that her newborn would instinctively know to look for the mothers breasts and suck with gusto once contact was made?

Humans have other inborn, genetically encoded instincts related to our ancient ancestors needs for survival. Though some are overlooked by modern man, they are still present. Simple ones are instincts such as knowing to eat when you are hungry. But there are more complex ones as well, such as the ability to distinguish people who are genetically different than us based just on smell. Another primal instinct is to seek out a mate that is genetically different enough to have children born from a union to have a stronger immune system than either of the parents.

One of the strongest primal instincts that still remains close to the surface of modern human reactions is fright and survival. Both instincts are heavily played upon in action/suspense movies. Regardless of who you are, if someone or something scary enough confronts you in a threatening manner, you don't just stand there and wave hello to them. You jump up and immediately begin unconsciously weighing whether to fight or run. Your heart starts beating much faster, adrenaline pours into your system, making all your muscles stronger with quicker reactions. And then you act! You either run faster than you have ever run, or you grab the nearest item than can be used as a weapon and you fight.

Survival, to live at all costs, is perhaps the strongest of all primal human instincts. Actions in which you can react completely without thinking and your unthought-of actions will save you. Drowning is a perfect example. If you are suddenly thrown into deep water, even if you do not know how to swim, your primal instinct will immediately have you frantically flailing your arms, kicking your feet and doing everything in your power to reach the surface of the water. You don't just plop in the water and calmly sink to the bottom.

Not all primal dreams are about threats. Some are about opportunities. Besides being adept at avoiding being eaten by predators, our ancient ancestors were also very opportunistic, especially sexually as an instinctive way to ensure genetic diversity. It is not unlikely that infidelity was common, and that both men and women took every opportunity to have sex with partners other than the one they kept back in the home cave. To this day, this theme of sex with strangers continues to be a common dream subject.

A great confusion and frustration, often accompanied by a lot of guilt, is expressed by otherwise prim and proper men and women to dream researchers, about sexual dreams they have involving people other than their spouses, and often complete strangers. They really shouldn't feel guilt. These are merely primal dreams that their ancient ancestors passed on to them in their DNA. They may never think an adulterous thought while they are awake, but when they sleep they are under the influence of their primal DNA code.

Learning

If you go to sleep after you have been intensely pondering a problem during the day, especially if you do so immediately before sleeping, it is common to dream about that problem, directly or indirectly, and often come up with the solution that escaped you while you were awake. The challenge vexing you while you were awake can run the gamut from a math problem from school, to a work issue, to a relationship challenge. Once you are dreaming, knowledge you have forgotten, as well as knowledge you never knew that is encoded in your DNA come into play. Plus, alternative neural paths in your brain are activated when you dream that will often present a solution by looking at the problem from a completely different perspective than the neural paths used when you are awake.

Prophetic

From time immemorial mortal men and women have received direct communication from higher beings, from 'God,' through vivid, detailed dreams. Prophetic dreams are powerful. They are remembered in exact detail, both in what you see and what you hear. I have been blessed to have experienced many of these dreams that foresee future events. In fact, I used to publish an annual newsletter on the first day of every year, 'The Prophet's Voice,' that I provided to the Children of Light to forewarn them of upcoming dangers, as well as opportunities because of world events. Here are a few tiny excerpts:

"As long as the USA is acting like the empire builders of old, the world, and especially the USA, will see an ever increasing rise in Islamic fundamentalism and terrorism, and pay an increasingly

painful price, both in blood and money, inflicted by an enemy that cannot be defeated by military means, and is only strengthened by every military action taken against it." Jan. 2006 Prophet's Voice

"The sub-prime mortgage problems that have recently been reported by the news media are just the tip of the iceberg of coming economic woes that will likely touch the lives of most people in the US and around the world. 2008 has the potential to be the worst economic times anyone alive has ever seen, and like the terrorist attacks on the World Trade Center, Americans and the people of the world will not see it coming until the house is falling down. ...you will see failing banks, bankrupt insurance companies, falling corporate giants, bankrupt cities, defaulting states, and foreign creditors cashing in their US securities." Jan. 2008 Prophet's Voice

"Drug related crime in Mexico will escalate in 2009, including killings, beheadings, kidnappings and executions of police and government officials." Jan 2009 Prophet's Voice

"Look for the Chinese and their proxies to go on a buying spree in the USA for real estate and companies." Jan 2009 Prophet's Voice

"The results of all the various economic stimulus will not improve the economies of the world. But it will enrich the most powerful banks, financial institutions and families, while giving the governments of the world far greater power over the lives of their citizens than they ever had before." Jan. 2009 Prophet's Voice

Lucid

Lucid dreams are most often combined with one of the other categories of dreams. In simplest form a lucid dream is one in which you are aware that you are dreaming. The more control you can exert over your dream to affect the action, the more deeply you are lucid dreaming.

Astral

Astral traveling while you are sleeping is the most common method of astral travel. But the astral travels of our Night-Self tend to be unknown or at the least, quite murky to our Day-Self. To bridge this gap, a Dream Journal is exceptionally helpful. Often when you have a Lucid Dream you will also be astral traveling. If you are not, as you are already lucid dreaming, it is a great moment to decide that you will also astral travel and make it so by your command.

As you are consciously aware that you are dreaming, when the dreaming is winding down or just completed, wake yourself up and have handy at your bedside a journal that you can quickly write down the details of your dream before they vanish into a fog. Or, alternatively, if you don't wish to turn on a light, you can keep a small micro recorder at your bedside and just orally record the details of your dream.

You will know you are astral traveling in your dream when you are in a vivid, lucid dream and can choose to change the venue and location of your dream to anywhere; from places you have been, to places you have only read about, to locations beyond the Earth that you have only imagined.

Innovative

Dream time is a wonderful opportunity to come up with brilliant new ideas. Most of my concepts for books first came to me as dreams telling the story. All of the inventions I have conceived from Wave Breakers to Elemental Separators, first appeared to me in a dream or flashed into my mind out of the blue while I was daydreaming. And yes, daydreaming counts. If you are zoned out far enough, without using drugs or alcohol, to be oblivious to the sounds and activities around you, you are in a perfect place inside yourself for astounding wakeful dreams.

There are multiple reasons both sleeping dreams and wakeful dreams work so well to come up with new, innovative ideas. All the information you have ever heard, read or taken in by sight, was recorded in some part of your brain. Most is forgotten as not being significant or useful in your everyday life. But the knowledge is still there, shuttled to some dead end street in your neural pathways, unlikely to ever be consciously accessed. But when you dream, random neural points are activated and the information stored in the mental dead end streets suddenly comes roaring out onto your main neural highways. There it meets many other random bits of long forgotten, but still stored information. Alone, the information from one dead end may be useless and meaningless. But when suddenly combined in your dreams with many other lost tidbits of information, plus the active knowledge of your everyday life and intellect, all the parts can suddenly coalesce into something meaningful and even spectacular.

How To Interpret Your Dreams

Although there are professional dream interpreters and a myriad of books on interpreting your dreams, there is no one better suited to the task than yourself. You are the only person that has all of your knowledge, experiences, emotions, dramas and traumas to fully put your dreams into an applicable context.

Most people like things categorized and put in nice little mental boxes. With dreams they want to be able to know unequivocally what they mean. The reality is the meaning of the same type of dream, for instance a forest fire, could have radically different meanings depending upon what is happening in your life at the time and the type of dream you feel it is. The forest fire could be a symbol of something good, such as your current entrepreneurial effort taking off like a wildfire, or something bad like a sign of catastrophe or illness, or something neutral, for instance, you may be sleeping in a cold room and are dreaming of a fire to keep warm.

Best Free Online Dream Dictionary

If you would like to know what the majority of dream researchers think the symbolism in your dreams mean, you can find an excellent online dream dictionary with 5,600+ descriptions at: http://www.dreammoods.com/

Even Bizarre Dreams Can Be Important

Quite often you will get seriously mish-mashed dreams that would seem impossible to have meaning. Something like you were fishing with your Dad and caught a junk car, which you never should have been able to pull out of the water without breaking your fishing line, but you did. When you and your Dad pried open the rusted shut, water weed encrusted door, you found a turtle reading a book inside. When you looked at him he became a cobra and spit at you. When your Dad wiped the cobra spit out of your eyes he started laughing. Then a small airplane flew out of the car and you both grabbed onto its wheels as it passed overheard.

Though many dream analysts would have a field day telling you what all the symbolism meant in this dream, the reality is that though it could have meaning, it may have none at all. However, it could still be an important dream sending you a message, particularly if you woke up from the dream. The message may not be in the symbolism, but in how you felt after the dream: happy, sad, euphoric, upset?

Often times when mish-mashed dreams involve people we know, they allow us to feel deeply embedded emotions about them that our conscious mind never allows us to feel. Releasing these pent up feelings in a dream can be a wonderful cathartic cleansing of the heart that leads to a better relationship when you are awake with the person in the dream. Another result may be having created the feeling in the dream, you may now have the courage to express your deep emotions in-person that you had previously been reticent to speak openly about.

One Dream To Never Overlook

Some dreams reoccur. Small details may be different, but the overall story of the dream remains the same. These are very important dreams to not ignore. The dreams can fall into any of the 9 categories listed above. The more frequently a dream returns, the closer the events or action it portends, are likely to be. Or, the more vital the message is that the dream is trying to convey to you.

When you have reoccurring dreams, it is important not to forget them. Wake up and write down or audio record the details. In the morning, analyze the message of the dream by looking at both the story and the symbolism in the context of your life and relationships. What are you not doing in life that you should be? Or, what are you doing that you should not be? If the action in the dream doesn't make a coherent story and message on its own, then the meaning is in the symbolism. Are you exerting yourself physically in the dream? Perhaps it is telling you to get in better shape. Do you keep falling down and splitting your lip? Dreams involving the mouth needs to be looked at as probably conveying a communication problem. If anything good or bad happens to any part of your body in a dream, focus on what that could be telling you about your own life. Though the same symbolism can have many meanings, it becomes easier to narrow down and define when looked at in the context of your life, your challenges, hopes, dreams, fears, lusts and desires.

Reoccurring dreams are also prime candidates to turn into Lucid dreams. When you've had a dream at least twice, you can have an expectation that you are going to have it again. Decide before you go to sleep that if your previous dream reoccurs you are going to become aware that you are dreaming and take control of the dream. Once you are in control, explore your dream, the setting, the people and events more deeply. In this way you will gain greater insight and understanding of the message that the dream is conveying.

Chapter 24
DOWSING & PENDULUMS

Dowsing is the most ancient psychic practice for which we have evidence of use. It is also known as divining, water witching and doodlebugging. Cave drawings found in Spain dated 40,000 – 50,000 years ago, depict dowsing. Detailed prehistoric murals estimated to be around 8,000 years old, painted on the walls of Tassili Caves in the Sahara Desert, show a tribesman using a forked stick to search for water while other tribesmen stand around and watch; comparable to what happens when a modern dowser is at work. Similar dowsing drawings were found in archaeological excavations in Iraq, dating back 8,000 years. Dowsing tools were even found in King Tut's tomb.

Artwork from both Egypt and ancient China, including a famous woodcut from 2000 BC, depict people using forked sticks in the same posture as a dowser. Old Testament scriptures describe Moses and his brother Aaron using a "rod" to find water. During the 1500's, Queen Elizabeth 1st invited German miners to come to England to teach English miners how to locate valuable ore deposits using dowsing. It was specifically mentioned in Middle Age texts as the reliable method used to locate coal deposits in Europe.

There was also noted opposition from Middle Age religious leaders. The term "water witching" was coined by the priest Martin Luther in the 16th century, who along with many other religious leaders, felt the uncanny ability of dowsers to find water, could only be attributed to witchcraft.

Archaeological and historical evidence have revealed the ubiquitous use of forked sticks for discovering water and objects hidden beneath the ground throughout history in cultures across the globe. When the same, exact technique has been developed independently and used for thousands of years by cultures around the world, even skeptics take notice and wonder if there just might be something to it.

Although skeptics remain, Albert Einstein was convinced of its authenticity. He defended it saying, "I know very well that many scientists consider dowsing as they do astrology, as a type of ancient superstition. According to my conviction, this is, however, unjustified. The dowsing rod is a simple instrument which shows the reaction of the human nervous system to certain factors which are unknown to us at this time."

Dowsing has been practiced by other well-known people from history including Leonardo De Vinci, the father of modern chemistry Robert Boyle, and Nobel Laureate Charles Richet. During WWII both General Rommel of the German Army, and General George S. Patton of the US Army, utilized dowsing to find water in the North African deserts. Don Nolan in his article, *A Brief History of Dowsing*, detailed that Patton, "had a complete willow tree flown to Morocco so that a dowser could use branches from it to find water to replace the wells the German Army had blown up." He also noted that in modern times, in 1982, "The British army used dowsers on the Falkland Islands to remove mines."

There has also been credible scientific testing of dowsing. One of the most startling results came when Professor Hans Dieter Betz, a physics professor from the University of Munich, coordinated a team of scientists to determine if professional dowsers had an ability that utilized some unknown laws of physics that could quantitatively be measured.

To make the challenge as great as possible the took a group of dowsers to 10 different countries that had scant water supplies or difficulty in locating underground water. The most challenging country was Sri Lanka, which is notorious for its scant, elusive underground water, found in disjointed locations due to the arid climate and convoluted geology of the region. On the advice of the dowsers, 681 wells were drilled. Ninety-six percent came up with a useable flow of water.

Subsequently a team of geohydrologists were given the same task. They took 2 months to complete the survey, while the dowsers had finished in a couple of weeks. After drilling all the wells at the locations indicated by the geohydrologists only 21% produced a usable flow of water. Based on the results of this head to head comparison, the German government paid for 100 dowsers to travel to the arid regions of southern India to pinpoint locations to sink wells for drinkable water.

More recently dowsing has been called Radiesthesia in some circles, which is based loosely on a blending of Latin and Greek terms for radiation and perception. But I still prefer the term dowsing. Though most commonly associated with a forked stick looking for water, dowsing can also use alternative tools such as pendulums and L-shaped metal rods. It has also been used to find many things buried underground besides water including mineral veins, oil, treasure, archeological artifacts, miscellaneous lost objects, and even the bodies of missing people.

How exactly dowsing works is still a mystery. Even among professional dowsers there is a difference of opinion and the reality is nobody really knows. The most common theory is that the dowser is somehow tuning into the slight variance in the electromagnetic field over bodies of water, moving streams and hidden objects, somewhat like a human metal detector. This theory stems from the fact that many animals, such as pigeons and dolphins, are known to be able to travel vast distances unerringly guided by their sensitivity to the electromagnetic field of

Dowsing & Pendulums

the Earth and the far more miniscule fields of local areas.

Other than fortune telling, which is infamous for frauds, dowsing is one of the few psychic abilities that can be used as a basis for a profitable business. Most phone books in rural areas in countries all around the world will have listings for professional dowsers. Their services are still in great demand anywhere there is a need to sink a water well because they get cost effective results.

First Test Of Dowsing

My first experience with dowsing came in 1980 when I owned a window company. Accompanied by a new salesman I was training named Roger, I went to a home of a late middle-aged gentleman named Burgess that wanted an estimate for converting his single pane windows into insulated double panes. While in his home I noticed several forked sticks and asked him if he was a dowser. He said he was, and enthusiastically began describing his dowsing exploits.

He invited us to test him. He handed a dime to me that he took out of his pants pocket and told me to hide it anywhere I liked on his property. After I returned, he said he could locate it within 10 minutes by dowsing. That seemed unbelievable to me at the time. But just to make sure I decided to hide it really well. While I went outside to hide the coin, Roger stayed and spoke with Mr. Burgess to insure he didn't get up and walk around to observe where I was hiding the dime.

The Burgess house was on a lake and had a dock extending about 30 feet out from the shore. Walking onto the dock I decided to hide the dime underwater. I laid down on my stomach on the wooden deck next to the second piling back from the lake end of the dock. Reaching down below the water I inserted the dime firmly into a crack in the piling on the right side of the dock. Smirking all the way back to the house I knew there was no way he was going to find that dime.

When I came back into the house Roger and the customer were still sitting exactly as I left them and Roger assured me that neither one of them had gotten out of their seat. For this test the man chose to use two L-shaped metal rods rather than a forked stick. He took another dime and held it in his right hand while simultaneously holding onto one of the L-shaped rods in that hand, with his left hand holding the other.

We went outside to the front yard. Mr. Burgess held the two rods parallel to each other extending out from his body and asked us to note the time. Moving slowly while standing in place, he completed a 360 degree circle. His rods crossed completely backwards when he was facing the frontage street. To be sure of his direction he repeated another slow 360 degree turn and once again the L rods turned all the way back when he was facing away from the lake. "When the rods act like this," he explained, "it indicates the coin is in the opposite direction. So you must have hidden it somewhere out back." I didn't respond and tried to hold a poker face in reply.

He didn't even hold the rods up as we walked around the house. Only after we were in the middle of the spacious back yard did he hold them up into the parallel position again. Once again he did the 360 degree maneuver and once again the rods turned back on themselves when he was facing away from the lake toward the house. "This is telling me the coin is behind me toward the lake." He explained. I was beginning to become impressed.

Turning to face the lake he made movements back and forth, right and left as he walked slowly toward the lake. The movement of the rods seemed to be indicating exact directions to him, as he soon was walking unerringly toward the dock. Moments later he was on the dock. In seconds he turned to the right, standing exactly over the post where I had hidden the dime. "You must have thrown it in the lake right here," he stated. I started to reply, to tell him that was a pretty amazing demonstration, but he shushed me and focused again on his rods. He changed the height he was holding them up and down, while maintaining them level. The rods made back and forth movements as he moved them up and down. After about 10 seconds he said, "That's odd; I thought you must have thrown the coin in the lake below the dock here, but the rods say the coin is only about 4 feet away."

I was flabbergasted and immediately laid down and reached underwater to pull the dime out of the crack in the piling where I had wedged it. I heartily congratulated him and realized this was a potent paranormal ability I was absolutely going to need to learn.

My Early Dowsing Experiments

After asking many questions of Mr. Burgess before we left his home, I excitedly began my own experiments with dowsing the very next day. I cut a forked willow branch and also made two L-shaped rods and experimented with both. Both had amazing results!

I used both dowsing devices to locate quarters I had my wife hide and also did experiments passing over a bucket of water and a hose with water moving through it. What surprised me most was the force exerted by the willow branch when it passed over the bucket of water or the hose. While holding the branch when it is not passing over water, it has a dynamic tension, like it is on a spring. As it is held in your hands with this tension, it can move easily up or down and is just as easily held in one position parallel to the ground. I was quite astounded when I first passed over the water as the willow branch pulled down strongly. It was unmistakable, as if an invisible person had grasped the branch and was pulling it toward the ground. On the second pass it did it again. By the third and fourth passes I was experimenting to see if I could prevent its movement, but to no avail. By the fifth pass I was determined to hold onto the branch so tightly that it could not possibly move downward. But it was a hopeless attempt. I simply could not hold it tight enough to prevent its very forceful downward movement when I passed over the bucket of water. That was unbelievable! Needless to say, I was hooked on dowsing.

The Pendulum Knows...

In the mid 90's two of my teenage children that had been living in France with their mother

Dowsing & Pendulums

for the previous 6 years, decided to come and live with me in the states. Skye and I were living at the time on a cruising sailboat. Though it was spacious for the two of us, it quickly became cramped when 2 teenagers were added. Shortly after the kids decided to stay we moved to shore and rented a place on a large exotic parrot farm.

Not long after we moved in, there was a news cast that spoke about a criminal that had passed through our county a couple of nights before. When he was captured he confessed to a murder and said he dumped the body somewhere along his travel route through our county.

Neither of my children had much of a belief in psychic abilities, so they were mostly amused when Skye took out her pendulum and started concentrating in response to the news cast.

"What are you doing?" My son Tai wondered.

"Well, the news said someone dumped a body in our county." Skye answered. "I'm just using my pendulum to see if the body is anywhere around here."

"That's not going to work." Tai scoffed.

"You might be surprised." Skye replied. "The pendulum is saying that the body is nearby."

Suddenly Tai and my daughter Lyndi were interested.

"Let's go look for it." Tai proposed excitedly.

Skye agreed and all three of them went outside to the front yard. Skye just started walking down our driveway. When she came to the intersection with the road, she held the pendulum facing each possible direction of travel. The pendulum indicated they should veer to the right, so off they went. At every driveway or intersection Skye stopped and used the pendulum to determine the direction they should go, and to continue to affirm that they were getting closer to the body.

Ultimately she was led to a driveway of a house. The pendulum indicated they needed to proceed down the driveway. They didn't know if the house was occupied, but there didn't seem to be anyone around, so they continued walking down the drive. With every step down the drive Skye got a stronger feeling of foreboding. Before they got to the end where they could peer around to the back yard, she stopped and told the kids they all were going back home. Tai and Lyndi wanted to keep going but Skye was insistent. She told Tai she was sure the body was back there and it was nothing they needed to see.

Back home we thought of calling the police, but vacillated on whether it would be worth calling and if they would give any credence to locating the body with a pendulum, especially as no one had actually seen the body. We decided to sleep on it overnight.

When Skye and I came back from work the following day we found the place had been swarming with police and news vans. The murderer had been able to lead the police back to the spot he had dumped the body, right behind the house that Skye had located with the pendulum!

Tai, said he had excitedly tried to tell the news people that Skye had located the body the previous day with a pendulum, but apparently they were not interested in a fanciful story from a 13 year old boy. But from that day forward Tai and Lyndi, from first-hand experience, were believers in the psychic and paranormal.

Tools of Dowsing
There are 3 primary tools used for dowsing:

Forked stick: Most often this is a forked willow branch with the widest part of the fork where it is held in the hands about 10-12 inches apart. The stem of the fork extends anywhere from 6-18 inches past its joint with the Y, depending upon the preference of the person dowsing. Other types of wood beside willow can also be used. The ends of the Y are held in each hand and curled at about a 90 degree angle in the hands. This creates a dynamic spring-like tension that makes the branch stable but still very responsive to energy fluctuations. When it passes over water the branch will pull strongly downward. The stronger the downward pull the closer the water.

The exact dimensions of the water source can also be scoped out by using the willow fork to

The correct way to hold a forked dowsing branch is by gripping the ends with palms up, arms close to body and bent 90 degrees at the elbow. The branch should easily be able to be held parallel to the ground, but also easily move up or down if it reacts to energy fields.

Dowsing & Pendulums

define the boundaries. For instance, if it is an underground reservoir, walking the 4 points of the compass, the willow branch will pop back up into the parallel to the ground position once it passes beyond the outer perimeter of the underwater source.

The correct way to hold a forked dowsing branch is by gripping the ends with palms up, arms close to body and bent 90 degrees at the elbow. The branch should easily be able to be held parallel to the ground, but also easily move up or down if it reacts to energy fields.

L-shaped rods: The L-shaped rods are also commonly used for dowsing. They can be made of any straight, smooth metal from welding rods to brass rods. Even metal coat hangers will work. One is held in each hand parallel to the ground and parallel to each other. They are often

L-shaped dowsing rods should be held parallel to each other and the ground, in a pistol-grip in your hands, with your arms bent at 90 degree angles at the elbow.

used when searching for items other than water, but they can also be used to discover water. When passing above the object desired the rods will cross. They will often flip backwards if you walk over the object and it is then behind you.

L-shaped dowsing rods should be held parallel to each other and the ground, in a pistol-grip in your hands, with your arms bent at 90 degree angles at the elbow.

You can also use a single rod to locate water or pinpoint the direction of its flow. When just one rod is used it will align itself with the direction of the water flow, if it is an underground stream. It will continue to try to hold that alignment as you move back and forth over the water source.

Pendulum: Another common dowsing method is to use a pendulum. A small, pointed, weighted object is suspended from a string or chain 6-12 inches in length. Quartz crystals or other minerals shaped into cones are popular as the pendulum pointer, but any small, heavy object with a point seems effective. It is best to experiment with several types of weights until you find the one that most resonates with your energy to facilitate the highest accuracy results.

The optimum way to hold a pendulum is with the cord or chain held between the thumb and the index finger. Some people have equal success adding their middle finger.

1. Begin by holding the pendulum cord or chain with your

hand and stabilizing the weight so it is perfectly still.
2. State aloud whatever the parameters for your pendulum are, such as: "Yes -- spin clockwise. No -- spin counterclockwise."
3. Begin searching for your object remembering to walk slowly, and steadily so your own movement does not affect the pendulum. Each time you come to a spot that a choice of direction needs to be made, stop and ask aloud, "is this the right direction?" If there is more than one choice at that location, ask the question at each possible alternative.

If you are searching for water with a pendulum, before you begin walking, simply state aloud the direction the pendulum will rotate when it is over water.

Pendulums are also useful for map dowsing, where hidden objects are located from remote distances. You can use the spin technique with maps or tell the pendulum to forcefully be drawn to the spot on the map that is the correct location when you set the parameters before you begin.

With map dowsing using a pendulum, it is helpful to have a series of successively more detailed maps. You first pinpoint an area on a broad overview map, then get closer and closer to the exact location with maps that blow up small sections of the bigger map so you can zoom right to the exact spot.

With dowsing it really is helpful to do your own experiments. How the tools of dowsing work for you may be different than how they work for another dowser. The way the energy flows from below the surface of the ground, into and through the dowsing tool and into you, then returns back creating the energy circuit will be different for different people because of many factors, including experience, natural affinity and conductivity and the size, shape and quality of the tools you are using.

How To Practice

Using the dowsing tool of your choice:
1. Ask someone else to hide or bury an object somewhere on your property. Bigger is better when you are first learning. Make sure to advise them to insure there is no physical trace remaining of where the object was hidden.
2. Decide what the parameters will be for your chosen tool to indicate when it has found the object.
3. Make sure you are holding your chosen dowsing tool in the correct and optimum manner.
4. Begin walking using your dowsing tool as you feel best. This might be by checking direction periodically as Skye did when looking for the body, or Mr. Burgess did when looking for the dime. Or, it could just be walking without asking for periodic directions and just ask the dowsing tool to indicate when you have located the object.

You can choose to walk at random and trust your inner insight to lead you in the right direction. Or, you can choose to walk a grid pattern to insure all ground is covered.

5. Walk slowly and stay focused in your mind on the object you are trying to locate. Keep a picture in your mind. If it is a small object like a coin, you can even hold a similar coin clasped in your right hand.

6. When you get a positive location reading with your dowsing tool, stop and check if that is the spot. If not, continue on and keep looking.

Water test

When testing for water it is impractical to hide the water source, unless there is a buried water pipe that a friend or family member knows about that you do not. But just walking over a hose with moving water, or passing over a bucket of water, even if you know it is there, will give such a noticeable reaction that it is still a great way for you to learn what a reaction feels like, so you'll know it when you are out in the field looking for an unknown source.

Special Tip:

If you have been at your search for a while unsuccessfully, take a break and try again later. A different time of day, or searching before or right after a meal or a nap, can be among the many variables that can make a difference in whether or not you have success. Even the weather can be an influence, particularly when you are first learning to dowse.

Chapter 25
CLAIRVOYANCE

Clairvoyance is the ability to obtain knowledge and information about a person, object, or event, over any distance and in any location, without use of the normal senses. A psychic 'knowing' about the recent, but still unrevealed death of a loved one is a commonly depicted example of clairvoyance. Similarly, many people have been saved from death when rescued by a loved one that saw a clairvoyant vision of their peril.

Clairvoyance is easily confused with Precognition, which is similar, and the two terms are sometimes erroneously used interchangeably. The subtle but distinct difference is *precognition sees events in the future that have not yet occurred and may not yet occur for some time, while clairvoyance sees people, objects and events at, or very near to the current moment in time.*

A person with very advanced clairvoyant abilities can also see into a specific time and place in the past or future, to witness a person, object, or event in 'real time' during that time period.

The word ***clairvoyance*** has roots in the French words *clair* meaning 'clear,' and *voyance* meaning 'vision.' It is the preeminent of the many psychic varieties of 'Clair,' including ***Clairaudience*** (clear hearing), ***Clairsentience*** (clear sensation or feeling), ***Clairscent*** (clear smelling), ***Clairtangency*** (clear touching), ***Clairgustance*** (clear tasting), ***Clairempathy*** (clear emotion) and ***Claircognizance*** (clear knowing).

Most of the 'Clairs' are higher psychic senses correlating to lower physical senses and abilities, such as taste, touch, smell, hearing, inner sensations and mental understanding. Of the 'Clairs,' clairvoyance is least encountered, and those that correlate more directly to the 5 physical senses are the more commonly experienced.

You can find a quick online test to possibly have some insight into what 'Clair' abilities you have, by visiting http://quizfarm.com/quizzes/quiz/EmberDust/ and choosing the test for the 'Clairs.'

I've had so many 'Clair' experiences of all types I could write a book just on that subject. However, I had one particular experience that had big ramifications in my life, values and thought processes that I'll share. It was a pretty funny incident.

I grew up in a Southern American family that had a tradition of hunting and fishing to put food on the table most days of the year. I was hunting with my own shotgun from the age of 8 and brought many a meal of squirrels, rabbits, and a big assortment of game birds, home for dinner even from those young years. That all ended in my 16th year. I never hunted or killed an animal again and later became a vegetarian. The events of this day contributed to that decision.

My father and I used to go duck hunting on the east shore of Puget Sound in Washington State, about 1-2 miles south of the coastal town of Steilacoom. We had a 12 foot aluminum boat with a 10HP outboard motor, which we launched at Steilacoom and motored down to the location where we would set up our very realistic duck decoys floating out in the water off shore.

Occasionally, my Dad would bring one of his Navy buddies along. On this particular day he invited a long-time friend named Stan. Stan was anxious to accompany us because we always got our bag limit. However, when my father called to invite him, he wanted to know if he could bring along his two house guests. They had just graduated as officers from the US Naval Academy. My father said, "fine," but told Stan his friends would have to walk to our duck blind as there was not enough room in our small boat to carry everyone.

We arrived at Steilacoom about 6:00 in morning. It was early winter and still dark outside. Stan and his Navy officer friends met us at the boat launch and he introduced them to us as Jim and John. There was a double set of parallel railroad tracks that ran up and down the coast, elevated a bit on rip rap along the water's edge. My Dad decided he and Stan would take the boat down to the blind and set up the decoys, while I walked down the railroad tracks with the two young Navy officers to the guide them to the location.

After we had been walking for a while, trudging along the tracks carefully in the dark, we passed a large, steep, rounded hillside that the railroad tracks had to take a wide curve to get around. Jim and I were walking together and chatting, but for some reason, John kept lagging further and further behind. I remember thinking he must be pretty out of shape that he was struggling to keep up on such an easy walk. By the time Jim and I were about 100 yards past the big hill, John was lagging far back.

Suddenly, I got a clairvoyant shock! I saw a train with its large front light beaming brightly into the darkness coming around the blind curve on the outside track. I stopped and hurriedly looked back at the hill. I saw John lagging about 75 yards behind us in the early light of the dawning day, but no train. Jim saw the concern on my face. "What's the matter" He asked. "I think there's a train coming." I replied calmly. "It's on this track. We need to get off right now."

"I don't see or hear a train." Jim stated a bit perplexed. "Why do you think one is coming?"

"I sense it." I answered simply and truthfully. Jim smiled a bit and chuckled. "Well I think we would see or hear it if it was close," he assured me.

I pointed back at the large hill behind us. "That hill completely blocks all sound. With your eyes and ears alone, you'll not know the train is coming until it surprises you and pops out around the bend." No sooner had I finished speaking, still pointing in the direction of the hill,

Clairvoyance

which we were both turned and looking at, than out of nowhere a train came barreling around the blind curve on the outside track.

Jim nodded his head in appreciation. "Well I guess you were right," he said, as we both casually stepped off the outside track and onto the inside track to give the train plenty of room to pass us safely.

We looked back down the track at John, expecting him to have already stepped off the track as the train was only about 25 yards away from him. But he was still walking along oblivious to the metal monster bearing down upon him. Both Jim and I yelled at him and waved our arms to let him know there was a train coming and to get off the track. He stopped for a moment and looked at us like he was trying to understand what we were saying. The engineer driving the train saw John walking between the rails of the track as soon as the train swung sufficiently around the bend for its big front beam to shine on him. An incredibly loud horn blared, warning Jim to get off the track. A simple action to take, but not the one he took. Abruptly a light seemed to dawn in his dimwit mind as he looked back and saw the locomotive illuminating him in its bright head light as it bore down on him.

Then one of the funniest, most unbelievable sequence of events I have ever seen occurred. Rather than simply, safely step off the track to either side, John took off running like a madman straight down the track, trying to outrun the massive locomotive and train. In short, he panicked, big time.

Jim and I looked at each other in momentary disbelief. Surely nobody could be so stupid to just run down a track with a train rapidly gaining on him from behind. But John just kept on running as fast as he could churn his legs.

Jim and I were both yelling continually for him to just step off the track. We were using exaggerated arm movements to visually encourage him to simply step off to his left. Nothing had an effect. If he wasn't a newly minted Naval Officer fresh out of the academy, I would have thought he was stoned out of his mind.

John was getting closer and closer to us and the train was bearing down closer and closer to him. When John and the train were only separated by about 50 feet he suddenly must have realized that he had to do something other than just run down the track to escape his impending doom. But his brilliant epiphany wasn't to step off the track and get out of the way of the million pound roaring monster. Instead he took his shotgun, which he had been carrying over his shoulder in a case, and violently ripped it off his shoulder and threw it away. It landed on the track behind him. The train was now so close that it ran over the gun in the case almost the moment it hit the track.

In those few intervening seconds John was up almost abreast of us. The train was only a couple of feet away from running him over. At that last possible second, with us yelling at him to get off the track and encouraging him with big movements of our arms to do the same, he finally took a giant step off the track toward us and the safety of the inside track. But it was too late, the train hit him a glancing blow just as he was reaching with his outstretched left leg and arm to vacate the track.

To this day I can't explain any of what happened next. John was basically in a stretched out, spreadeagle position when the train hit him. The next thing Jim and I knew, John was flying over our heads spinning like a top with both his arms and hands widely outstretched. He passed over our heads, flew over the inside track and the wide drainage ditch beside it. He landed in what seemed to be a lifeless clump in a bush of thorny blackberries on the hillside.

The train engineer knew he had hit somebody and the train immediately applied emergency brakes and quickly came to a complete stop, with the engine about a dozen cars up from where we were. Jim and I rushed over to see how badly mangled John was, or if he was even still alive. We were relived and a little surprised to see he was still breathing. As we pulled him gingerly from the thorny blackberry bushes we were even more amazed to discover that he had no broken bones or even a sprain; just a bunch of scratches, mostly from the blackberries!

I was disgusted that an Ensign, a US naval officer, had panicked so completely and utterly over a situation that wasn't even threatening. It would have been a simple matter with many seconds to spare for John to have simply stepped off the track out of harm's way. This was a man that might someday be the captain of a nuclear submarine armed with nuclear missiles that could destroy a good portion of the world. And this is how he acted under a little stress? This is the type of man I might be trusting my future, my unborn children's future, and the future of world peace to? UGH!

Then my disgust and disillusionment with the quality of newly minted US naval officers was doubled. Now both John and Jim panicked! They were like frightened kids that were worried about getting caught for some mischief. They both looked at me, the 16 year old teenager, with an almost frenzied look. "You have to hide us." Jim stammered. "They can't discover two navy officers in this situation." My eyes widened in incredulity at his statement.

"They know they hit me," John added still shaking from his near miss with death. "The train is stopped. They're going to come looking for me. Please find a place to hide us."

I had to laugh a bit as I swept my arm around panoramically. "Hide you where?" I wondered. "On the other side of this train there's nothing but water," I said pointing to my right. "Over here on this side," I pointed to my left, "the hillside is too steep to climb and covered with impenetrable blackberry bushes."

It became a moot point as while they were nervously mulling over where they could hide, the train lurched forward and began moving again after just a few minutes of being stopped.

A few minutes later Stan came walking alone down the tracks. He was surprised to see the three of us standing around as the train engineer had told him and my Dad that they hit someone on the tracks. Both men assumed that it was the 16 year old boy that had been hit, not one of the naval officers. My Dad apparently was sure I was dead and was too shaken to come, which is why Stan was there.

A few minutes later we had all walked down to the duck blind, where I never saw my father so happy to see me. On the other hand he was so angry with the two young Ensigns that he told them to keep walking down the tracks until they were at least a mile away as he didn't want to have to see them the rest of the day. Stan went with them. But that still wasn't the end of the story.

A few hours later two men came walking down the tracks and stopped at our duck blind, which was just below the raised railroad bed. They were dressed in regular clothes and in every way were just like two normal guys, until they asked the question. "Have you guys seen anything on the tracks?"

"Anything like what?" My Dad asked.

"Like a dead body," one of the men replied. It seemed like these fellows were from the railroad company. The engineer had reported that he had hit somebody. Apparently the idea that someone had survived such a collision didn't seem probable, so these two guys had been sent to find the body. My Dad told them to keep walking about a mile down the track and they could talk to the corpse in person.

I hope the recounting of this event wasn't too long for you. It was a momentous moment in my journey, one of several events that occurred when I was 16 that dramatically altered the course of my life. At the time it was the most powerful instance of clairvoyance I had experienced; one that was almost immediately confirmed as authenticated. This realization continued to nag at me through many of the next years as I became more immersed in science. Though it was unexplainable by any scientific method, I could not deny it or explain it for anything other than what it was - clairvoyance.

The experience also deepened my belief in God, in a higher power than us mere mortals. In no other way than Divine Intervention, could I imagine John escaping that catastrophe, basically unscathed. Though why God would want to intervene for this fellow remains a mystery.

How You Can Manifest and Expand Your Clairvoyant Abilities

You probably have experienced clairvoyant abilities many times in your life and just did not realize that's what had occurred. If you have ever, out of the blue, thought of something just before it happened, with no stimulus or reason why the thought suddenly popped into your head, you likely just experienced clairvoyance. Here are some examples of common manifestations of clairvoyance that many people experience.

- Have you ever suddenly thought of a person you have not had contact with for a while, only to have them show up or call the same day, or even in the next few minutes?
- Have you ever been driving along thinking of something else, when suddenly the thought pops into your head that the car in front of you was about to turn or brake, even though they had no turn signals or brake lights on, but quickly thereafter they did?
- Have you ever unknowingly misplaced your keys, wallet, purse or cell phone, unsuccessfully started looking for them, when suddenly an exact mental image of their location popped into your mind?

- Have you ever had an odd pain in a specific part of your body, only to find out later that someone close to you, but distant geographically at the moment, had an injury to that part of the body at or near the same time?

The Secret is Imagination

If you have a good imagination, if you can easily visualize scenes in your mind, you are more likely to be able to manifest clairvoyant abilities. The same part of your brain that can see the mental images of your imagination, sees the psychic images of clairvoyance.

How then do you know which images are simply your imagination and which are true images of clairvoyance? If you thought of it, if you instigated and made efforts to imagine it, then it is simply your wonderfully creative imagination. Bravo! Having a great imagination is a powerful step toward becoming a potent clairvoyant. On the other hand, if a vivid image or scene suddenly flashes into your mind unbidden, or expands in clarity and detail after merely setting your intention, without any effort to imagine the result, you are experiencing clairvoyance; especially if the images are showing a person, object or event in current time, or the future just minutes away.

You just need to let yourself relax, release any fears you may have about learning of things you would otherwise not know. I find laying in a deliciously hot bath or standing in a quiet hot shower, really helps me to just tune out the world, blank my mind of any thoughts, and be very receptive to receiving visions.

Release Your Fears – Whatever They Are

Many people have fears that they might see something with clairvoyant sight that they really do not want to know, such as a spouse cheating on them; so they never make a serious attempt to bring out their clairvoyant abilities.

Other people may say they are afraid of what they might see and use that to justify why they do not make attempts. But if they are honest with themselves, they are really afraid of trying and failing. Rather than risk discovering that they are not clairvoyant, they will say they are afraid of what they will see. As long as they never make a sincere attempt, they can never fail, right? They may not be successes, but neither are they failures. For some people that seems to be an important distinction. Personally I have failed more than I have succeeded as I practiced bringing out my gifts over the years. However, I see each failure in a positive light, as giving me valuable knowledge about what doesn't work, and bringing me that much closer to success.

In my experience, most people can choose to bring out a great number of psychic abilities and paranormal powers if they have enough perseverance and are willing to see failure as a stepping stone to success. We all have these hidden special abilities as much as we have our 5 physical senses. You have to believe in yourself and your ability to manifest these empowering gifts. It will happen as long as you persist until you succeed and are using good methods of

Clairvoyance

discovery and activation.

Manifesting your clairvoyant gift is really no different than being able to see with your eyes. If your eyes had been covered since birth and you had never been able to see, but were told you could, it would do you little good unless you were instructed correctly in how to achieve it. If someone told you "lift your right arm and you'll be able to see," it would not work. If another person told you to meditate about seeing for a week, then lift up your head to the sun and chant, it still would not avail you because those were the wrong techniques. Finally, when a person came along and told you to remove the blindfold and open your eyes -- marvel of marvels, what you would see! It is the same with your psychic abilities and paranormal powers. They are there, but to reveal and activate them, you need to apply proven techniques that have worked in the past for many other people on their journey of discovery.

Try This Test For Mental Visualization

In the imagination of your mind picture the evolving scene described below in the greatest detail. Don't just read the words. Create a movie in your mind of the action *as* you read the words. See the scene unfolding in vivid color and action in your imagination. Feel free to expand and elaborate on the movie in your mind as the story unfolds. The more detailed and creative your imagination, the easier it will be for you to unlock the part of your brain necessary for clairvoyance.

Notice a man rowing a small, wooden boat across a lake. It's a large lake, but you can still see the far shore in the distance. He pulls on the two oars in unison as they swivel and squeak in the metal oar locks.

Look up into the blue sky. See the scattered, small, puffy white clouds? There is something strange about those clouds. Red spheres about the size of beach balls, seem to be extruding out from beneath the clouds. The man in the boat is looking up and notices the red orbs just as they begin falling in great number from the clouds and are splashing heavily with big explosions of water all around his little boat. He rows frantically now to escape the downpour of unknown red spheres crashing down into the lake all around him. Once the spheres hit the lake they bob buoyantly in the water and become obstacles to his fevered rowing.

Then, my goodness, his oars turn into hissing serpents! Startled and confused he lets go of their wiggling tails that a moment before were his oars, and they slither into the water and swim away. Now his boat is dead in the water, he has no means to propel it, the red spheres are still splashing down all around him. Could it get any worse?

The poor man is distraught, sitting in his little boat, holding his head between his hands, knowing not what to do. Suddenly an enormous fish the size of a small whale, leaps out of the water and swallows the man and his boat in one gulp! Moments later the fish raises his massive head out of the water next to the near shore. He spits a geyser of water out of his mouth and out flies the man and his boat, landing with a thud on shore. The boat splinters into so many pieces that not one board remains affixed to another. The man slowly stands up feeling his body all around, amazed and befuddled how it could be that he is all in one piece, safe and sound.

Additional Imagination Strengthening

Any thoughts you can think and expand upon in your imagination are helpful exercises. It is in this same center in your brain that clairvoyant images arrive from whatever source they originated. By strengthening your imagination muscles, you improve your ability and facility with clairvoyance. Here are just a few examples to get you started.

- Imagine being taken out to your favorite restaurant. Create your perfect meal and setting in your mind.
- Imagine yourself winning any kind of race. See yourself competing, winning and accepting the adoration of the crowd.
- Imagine your favorite actor or actress professing their undying love for you and begging you to marry them.
- Imagine being very wealthy. See yourself playing with all your big boy/big girl toys.
- Imagine winning a Nobel prize. For what achievement did you win it? See yourself giving an acceptance speech. What famous people and luminaries are in the audience to watch and listen to you speak?
- Imagine finding a great treasure. What is it? Picture it in vivid detail. Completely visualize the adventure you had to go on to find and obtain it.

The Great Bullfrog Race

Here's one of my favorite imagination exercises. Take a look at the photo of the large American Bullfrog below.

1. Now close your eyes and see the same image in your mind. Repeat as many times as necessary, until you can clearly see the image of the bullfrog in your mind when you close your eyes.
2. Once you have succeeded in easily picturing the bullfrog in your mind, close your eyes and picture

Clairvoyance

     the same bullfrog as red instead of green.
3. Open and close your eyes again and picture him blue.
4. Open and close your eyes once more and picture him pumpkin orange.
5. Do it again and see the frog as royal purple.
6. You now have seen 5 frogs, green, red, blue, orange and purple in color.
7. Close your eyes again and picture a medium-size pond where you can see all around the perimeter. It is mostly clear on the surface but has lily pads in clusters around some of the edges. In your imagination, line your frogs up side by side on a pond shore. Expand your imagination to create a festive race scene with as much pomp and circumstance as you can visualize. You can even imagine sounds such as the shrill of a whistle or pop of a starters gun to begin the race to the far shore of the pond.
8. Now comes the real fun. Holding the images of the 5 different colored frogs in your mind, see them frantically swimming, racing one another, pushing each other under, and doing everything they can to win the race. Finally, one leaps up onto the far shore as the winner. Which color frog won in your imagination?

Crystal & Gemstone Assistance

If you are having challenges jump starting your imagination and becoming receptive to clairvoyant images, you may wish to try using specific gemstones to assist you. There are several that have proven to be effective with both myself and others.

Clear quartz crystal that is sceptered or double-terminated, placed on your forehead at the point of the third eye, which is located slightly above the point between your eyebrows has proven effective for many people. If you have an amethyst scepter, where the shaft is clear or white quartz and the head of the scepter is amethyst, it is a very potent amplifying tool for clairvoyance. The most amazing crystal if you can get one is a naturally double-terminated quartz crystal about 2 inches in length with a phantom inside. Wow! Even if you have never had much imagination, you will be astounded at the vivid, detailed, wild images that quickly start flowing into your mind when you use this unusual crystal.

Lapis Luzuli is equally as helpful *if* it has good amounts of pyrite in

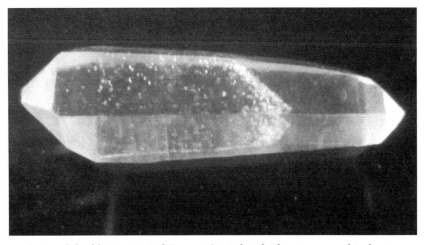

Natural double-terminated Quartz Crystal with phantom crystal inclusion

Unleash Your Psychic Powers

Lapis Luzuli with Pyrite

it. However, it is currently difficult to find items made with recently mined Lapis that contain even a few specks of pyrite, if any. Here's a picture of an ideal piece with lots of pyrite.

Lapis by itself, void of pyrite, seems no more helpful than a plain quartz crystal by itself. But when both blue lapis and golden pyrite are present, there is a power that is grounded in earth (pyrite) and extends to the heavens (blue lapis). This power is very useful for aiding several paranormal powers and psychic abilities. Look for some of the old lapis with pyrite in new-age stores and at Rock and Gem shows. You'll be happily surprised with the results when you start experimenting with it as a psychic and paranormal aid. The lapis can be raw, in a cabochon, or a pyramid. If you can find a small pyramid with lots of pyrite and blue lapis together, you'll have a little treasure and a very powerful tool.

Clear quartz with inclusions of silver hematite and lepidocrocite is also very helpful, particularly when combined with Lapis. Combining multiple gems on the third eye is potently powerful and effective! If you can find one crystal that combines all the quartz variants, you have a very rare and special tool that also has many additional uses.

Evaluating Yourself

How easy was it for you to see the examples presented in this chapter in your imagination? Did you see them in even greater detail than described, in vivid color and action? For some people, their imagination is nothing more than an

Quartz scepter with silver hematite and lepidocrocite inclusions. Red is from lepidocrocite. Sparkles of light are from silver hematite.

imaginary muscle they have seldom exercised. If you have challenges seeing the imagery in your imagination and expanding upon it don't despair. Like any muscle or ability, practice improves your skill level.

If instead you just have little interest in imagination, then clairvoyance is probably not an ability you should seek. Not to worry, other psychic abilities and paranormal powers do not require the same strength of imagination. Many require no imagination at all. Seek out those that you are the most comfortable with. In them you will find the greatest resonance and success.

Learn How to Ask Specifically

One of the complaints against many forms of psychic abilities, such as card readings and clairvoyance, is the information revealed is often general enough in nature that it can apply to a myriad of situations and people. How can you test the validity of a psychic who tells you, "I see a man coming into your life in the near future who will cause you to change direction?" It would be so much better for the person receiving psychic advice if they could be told something more like, " I see a man named Thomas. He is tall and slender, in his mid-20's, and dresses nicely. You will encounter him sometime in the next 2 weeks on a bright sunny day. You will first notice each other when he asks for directions after he drives up next to you in his small, red, open top sports car. He is not a romantic connection, but it is important that you have the opportunity to speak with him about more than just driving directions. He has information that can help you make a very beneficial change in your life."

If someone received the first lame description, they would probably find it interesting, but soon forget about it. If they received the second, more specific description, it is unlikely they would be able to forget about it. They would vigilantly be on the lookout for Thomas in his red sports car during the next 2 weeks.

The interesting thing is, the psychic who gave the first description, if they were truly exhibiting psychic abilities, could easily have given the second more detailed description if they had merely asked a more specific question, or reworded the question of the person inquiring, to be more specific.

When attempting to see a clairvoyant vision, ask a specific question. For example, if you want to find your Soul Mate, don't say, "Let me see my Soul Mate." Ask more specifically, "Let me see the first meeting between me and my Soul Mate, with enough detail to know the time and place, as well as a clear vision of my future love." The more specific your questions, the more specific your visions and answers.

Closed Eyes or Open Eyes?

When you are practiced and proficient with clairvoyance, you will be able to see visions both in your mind and as mirages in the space before your body, with your eyes wide open.

Unleash Your Psychic Powers

You can even be in activities or talking with other people at the time. However, when you are fist learning and becoming proficient, you will probably find it is much easier to receive your visions and insights when your eyes are closed and you are in a quiet undisturbed place.

Focus on Your Third Eye

I like to be laying down in a bath or on a bed when I seek a clairvoyant vision. Wherever you choose, it should be comfortable and a place you will be undisturbed. Before beginning make sure you are in a calm place inside of yourself. For the moment, release all other thoughts and any anxieties. Just find that place of calm and peace inside you. When your mind is clear of outside thoughts and your breathing is slow and calm, you have adjusted your aura into the resonance in which to begin.

Now put a light focus on the area of your third eye, on your forehead right above the space between your eyebrows. Imagine pictures forming there, but don't try to imagine any specific images. Just be open to what appears in answer to your specific question. This is the most ideal spot to see your vision and why it is the location of the spot known as the 'third eye', or 'clairvoyant eye.' You'll know when your third eye becomes activated and ready to receive a vision. You will feel a wave of auric peace wash through your body. It may be a tingle to just a delicious feeling. But there will be no doubt you are primed and ready to receive.

Be Blank but Observant

Train yourself not to allow your own thought pictures to form. Set your intention to see the answer to your specific question, but don't be tempted to answer it yourself. Just let your mind be a blank slate, open to whatever images want to write upon it. You may see single pictures appear or dream-like sequences that show action over a time frame. Your pictures may be in black & white or color. If you didn't grow up watching B&W TV, you'll most likely see in color. The movies or solitary pictures may appear as visions in front of you, or may appear only as pictures or movies in your mind's eye.

If you asked a specific question, you will see the specifics involved in that question. If you asked a more open ended question, the images you see might not even seem related to your question. They may even be cartoons, or images or paintings you have seen elsewhere at other times in your life.

Demand More Detail

Never forget, *you are the master*. You control what can be seen in your vision, either by commission (setting the specific intention and parameters) or by omission (being open ended and vague in your questions and intentions). As the master, once you begin to see your visions or pictures, in your mind's eye, or even out loud with your voice, command them to become clearer and more detailed if they are not yet showing you a level of clarity and detail that is

Clairvoyance

helpful. As you command, so it shall be.

If You're Unsure of What You are Seeing, Revisit Your Methods

There is no reason to be satisfied with seeing images or visions that are not clear enough or sufficiently detailed to help you easily understand the message they are conveying. If you see images that are hazy, convoluted or lack detail, remind yourself that *you are the master*. Demand more detail and clarity and your visions will oblige. If you ever find yourself asking, "what do these images mean?", then you were either not specific enough in your original question or not demanding enough in seeking a detailed vision.

Leadbeater Techniques

Charles W. Leadbeater (1854-1934) resigned his priesthood in the Church of England and become a prominent member of the Theosophical Society and a prolific writer on Spiritualism. The ten exercises he presented for improving psychic abilities, specifically clairvoyance, are just as helpful today as they were 100 years ago.

1. When the telephone rings, pause. Before doing anything, try to visualize the person calling. Before answering the doorbell, try to guess who it will be. Accuracy in intuition and precognition will improve dramatically through practice.

2. At a queue, visualize the teller who will serve you. This exercise is done to develop intuition and ability to psychically connect with those who are in close proximity.

3. At sporting events, guess the outcome before the event begins. To develop this skill, expand to predicting more statistics, such as scores.

4. Practice during a dice roll by calling "even" or "odd" before the dice is thrown; your accuracy will increase with practice. Expand to call the number the dice will land on.

5. With a friend and a deck of cards, predict if it will be black or red. When accuracy is at 80% or better, expand to predict the suit and later the face of the cards.

6. When in an elevator, if another passenger joins you, guess the button that they will press.

7. First thing in the morning, write down the names of those you will have important interactions with that day. Instead of relying on logic, clear the mind and allow faces or names to come to you naturally. Doing this regularly will improve your accuracy.

8. Guess another's intentions. This exercise helps you improve your intuition concerning the intentions, preferences, and actions of others, and it can lead to developing telepathy and empathy.

9. Before a meeting or appointment, guess the color of clothing the other person will be wearing before you meet. This improves your clairvoyant abilities and develops remote-viewing skills as well. Or, see if you can guess the mood of the people you will meet today.

10. Among three friends of yours, ask a friend to lie to you (decided among them earlier). Write down the name of the person you feel will lie to you. After asking the question and listening to their reply, show them the paper. This helps you develop intuition, precognition, and can lead to developing telepathy. This skill is especially valuable in life; the ability to recognize deception, and even predict it, can make your life and the lives of many others much smoother.

Remember, clairvoyance isn't an aimless dream of the night. One of the great advantages clairvoyance can have over nighttime dreams, is your conscious mind is fully available and can help guide you to achieve very clear, unmistakable answers. This is a great power. It's not everyone's cup of tea, but if you are willing to invest time, practice regularly and continue to strive for greater clarity and detail, using your clairvoyant abilities can be very fulfilling and rewarding.

Chapter 26
INSIGHT CARDS

In the early 80's I read a series of books by prolific novelist Piers Anthony, entitled *The Gods of Tarot*. Prior to this, I knew nothing about Tarot or any card reading system. However, after reading Mr. Anthony's books I became quite intrigued with the concept. I was not interested in learning how to interpret Tarot cards or even to own any, but the idea of being able to use cards or other devices to facilitate connecting to higher-self /universal energies excited my curiosity. I did not believe that the cards had the ability to be a medium for communication from outside sources, but rather were a means to help connect the higher-self of the reader to the energies of the person having a reading and other energies that might be influencing that person.

At the time, I actually disdained psychics and card readers in general as I thought they were all charlatans and simply keyed in on subtle cues given by the person being read, from words to body language, and then gave a reading that contained themes that generally affected most people's lives at any time, such as love and money.

My biggest gripe was I felt if there was any validity to psychic readings of any type they could not come from items such as cards, which had fixed meanings. They would have to be more free-flowing and perceived by someone very sensitive to auras and energy fields.

With that in mind, I decided to create my own set of cards to facilitate "readings," as an experiment in this possibility. I called them "Insight Cards" and they were designed to have no set meanings. To create my cards I asked my friends to give me all of their old magazines. I ended up with a pile of well over 100 magazines. I flipped through every single page of every magazine, looking for images that impacted me, simply pictures that had images I really liked. Cutting out the pictures, I laminated them onto 4x6 file cards and ended up making a deck that varied from 50-70 cards as the whim hit me. Just like I didn't want the cards to have any set meaning, neither did I want the number of cards to have importance.

While I was still in the process of creating the deck and only had about 30 cards created, my very religious wife was preparing to go on a trip back to France with our 3 children, as her father had just had an operation for cancer and was very ill. The day before she left I asked if I could give her a reading with my partially completed deck. She objected, feeling things like that were not of God and she didn't want to have anything to do with it. I laughed and told her it was just a game. I assured her we couldn't take anything like that seriously, but I really needed to do a test reading to get a better handle on how I wanted to use the cards.

Reluctantly she agreed. I asked her to draw 9 cards without looking at them, and I turned them over in rows of 3. As I looked at the cards, a psychic hit came into my mind that I knew was impossible, something I had never considered in, what I thought were 9 wonderful years of marriage. I looked again at each card and the message in each one supported the theme of all of them. I glanced up at my wife and laughed a big laugh telling her the cards were definitely a joke and I picked them off the table and put them away.

As I got up to go back to my chores, she asked me what I thought the cards said. I told her again they were just a joke, a game, and were meaningless. And besides I reminded her, she didn't believe in that kind of stuff anyway and neither did I. She still wanted to know what I thought the message of the cards was, so I reluctantly told her. "They said you were going to go to France and never come back, and that today is the end of our life together." I laughed again as I said it and we both agreed that was proof the cards were nothing but nonsense.

The only problem was, she went to France the next day and never came back. And that was the end of our life together. I was devastated. For 2 years afterward I could hardly function. I missed my children so much. It was almost worse than if they had died. At least then I would be able to have some closure, but they were 8,000 miles away. I could not see them, could only rarely speak with them on the telephone, and they were too young to write. As the years passed I couldn't even communicate with my youngest at all, as she only learned to speak French and I was never very adept with French.

I tried to understand what could have precipitated this, as it had hit me out of the blue. I had thought we were the perfect family with the perfect marriage. I understood that I had broken her trust by expressing a love for her sister years earlier, but I had earnestly endeavored to make amends. Then I realized that no matter how wonderfully I had treated my wife, no matter how good a husband or father I had been, I was simply too strange for someone who belonged to a conservative Christian religion and just wanted a normal life. Nor could the trust I had lost ever be regained in her eyes. Understanding this, I did not begrudge her the actions she had taken; they were necessary for her own happiness.

The first real card reading I did with a full deck of Insight Cards almost made me never want to do another one. I am a very optimistic and positive person, so I designed the Insight Cards to have images that by and large brought forth the optimistic and positive aspects of someone's life. There is so much negativity in the world. I wanted the Insight Cards to let people know about the positive energies that were in their lives.

Skye had an aunt in her 70's who had cancer about 15 years earlier. Una's cancer was in remission, but she still needed to go in for an annual checkup with tests to make sure there was not a reoccurrence. She knew I had just completed my deck and asked me to do a reading to see if she had cancer before her tests. Una was really asking for a reading to give me the opportunity to practice with my brand new deck of Insight Cards. She had already been to a prominent psychic, a Shiatsu masseuse and her doctor's preliminary check, and all three had seen no sign of cancer.

My card reading was just supposed to be a fourth confirmation of no cancer. As she was just asking one, simple and direct question, I asked her to just draw one card. The card she drew was a forest burning with wildfire.

When I originally put that card in the deck it was with the thought it would come up as a good card showing for instance, someone's business venture taking off like wildfire. But in the context of her question, the card had only one meaning for me. She was filled with cancer and it would quickly consume her. Una and Skye were jovial, asking me what the card meant. I was amazed that it wasn't as obvious to them as it was to me, and like with my ex-wife, I didn't want to tell them, and instead said the cards were just a game and not a reliable way to tell anything.

I put the card back in the deck and turned to just forget about it. But they insisted that I tell them what I thought it meant, so I did. I could see the disappointment on Una's face. I reminded her that the cards were just a game and that she had three other opposite opinions from better sources than me. Unfortunately, when her test results came back the following week, they showed she was being consumed by cancer and she died just a few months later.

I went on to do hundreds of readings for people over the following years and never ceased to be amazed at the unerring accuracy that came using the Insight Cards. I encouraged people to ask very specific questions and they were rewarded with very specific and direct answers. Many people contacted me later to tell me things had transpired exactly as the reading had specified. And to my great relief, unless someone had a serious issue with their health or life, the cards worked as designed, to let people know about the good energies that were swirling around them and how they could benefit from them.

How To Make Your Own Deck Of Insight Cards

1. Gather at least 50 magazines with a wide variety of genres. Some of my best pictures came from gaming magazines, even though those were not magazines I would usually even glance at. You can also find pictures on the Internet as long as they are high resolution.
2. Look through every page and cut out the pictures that you are drawn to. Many of the pictures I liked were parts of advertisements for products.
3. Your deck can be as big or small as you want, but at least 50 cards gives a good selection to insure the most accurate reading.
4. Trim you pictures to fit on 4x6 inch white file cards. 3X5 is too small. It's OK if the

pictures go right up to the edge of the cards. Even then, there may be some pictures you really like which are simply too big to fit on a 4x6 card.

5. Glue your pictures with a glue stick to the file cards and run the edge of a ruler over the picture to insure the glue is uniformly applied with no air bubbles showing under the surface.

6. Call around to print and copy stores to find one that does lamination and can trim the corners with rounded corners.

7. Get your cards laminated and cut to size. Make sure the shop does not trim right to the edge of the 4x6 card. If you leave about 1/8" to 1/4" of lamination margin around the card it will last many years as the lamination is heat welded to itself around the edges of the card. If the trim is right next to the paper card stock, the lamination will soon separate. The other key is to make sure the shop can trim the corners of the laminated cards with **rounded corners**. Square cut corners make cards that catch on other cards and are difficult to shuffle.

What makes Insight Cards different

Once you have created your Insight Card deck, you will be able to establish a psychic connection that will likely be far stronger than any mass produced deck created by someone else. These are your cards, the ones that called out to you pleading, "put me in your deck." Remember Insight Cards have no set meaning. Consider each question and how the card or cards that come up relate to that particular question. Don't think too hard about the cards as you seek to interpret them. Listen to your inner voice. Even if it does not seem to make sense, the answer that pops into your head is likely correct.

The 9 Card General Reading

I've never had a card reading from another person or even seen one, so I have no idea whether the system I use with my Insight Cards is similar or different than is typically used with other types of card readings.

To learn more about the person having the reading, I begin by asking them to first thoroughly shuffle the deck without looking at the cards to imbue the cards with their energy. I then spread the cards out so they are all partially exposed on a large table. I ask the person having the reading to draw 9 cards by tuning out everything around them and tuning into the energy of the cards and the particular card that is calling to them, one at a time. It should not be something they do hastily, but with seriousness and focus.

Before they draw a card I explain what the cards will mean. The first card they draw will be the most important card. I will lay the cards down in 3 rows of 3. The first 3 cards drawn will be the center row and the first card drawn will be the center card of the center row. All 8 of

Insight Cards

the other cards will revolve around it. It's energy and message will directly connect to all of the other cards.

The first 3 cards drawn will be the center of the 3 rows. These cards will show the 3 primary energies that are currently the most powerful in the person's life. They may or may not be aware of these energies, but they influence choices and actions they take in their life, both big and small.

The next 3 cards will be the top row. These will reflect the 3 challenge energies that are currently in the person's life. These are challenges to overcome that are currently holding them back from having greater success with the energies revealed in the 3 cards previously drawn for the center row.

The last 3 cards are for the bottom row, and reflect the energetic promises that will manifest as the challenges shown in the upper row are overcome.

As the person chooses 9 cards, one by one I stack them upside down. The first card drawn is on the bottom and the last card on the top. After the last card is drawn, I flip over the cards and I put the first card drawn down. This will be the center card of the center row. The second card drawn goes to its left and the third card to its right.

The next three cards are laid down left to right 4,5, 6 as the top row.

The last 3 cards are laid down left to right, 7, 8, 9.

This is how I set up a 9 card spread. It works well for me. However, in the spirit of the Insight Cards, where meaning is transitory and variable, you may choose a completely different arrangement or order for setting down the cards. Whatever you are most comfortable with is the method in which you will get the best results.

How The Cards Relate

As I mentioned. All the cards in the 9 card spread relate to the center card of the middle row and the message of that card should be considered when looking at the meaning of all the other cards as you review them one by one.

I begin the reading by explaining each of the three primary energies that are influencing the person at this time. I reveal the meaning of the center card of the center row first and then the cards to its right and left.

Next I look at the challenge cards of the top row. The cards tend to have vertical connections. For example the challenge card on the left will usually directly relate to the

primary energy card on the left and the promise card on the left.

Going from left to right I explain each of the challenges the person is currently facing as revealed by the challenge cards of the top row.

Then I go down to the bottom row, and moving left to right, reveal the rewards the person can expect as they successfully overcome their challenges.

An Example Of How The Connections Work

Perhaps the left center card, depicting a primary energy, shows a wedding ring or a happy couple. Whether the person is single or married, I might feel they are seeking a great marriage. A quick look up at the challenge card should reveal more insight. If the card is of another couple, or two of anything, I would likely feel both the man and the woman are presenting obstacles in their relationship. If it is a card of a woman, or paraphernalia of a woman, it might indicate she is the problem. The card will normally inspire specific understanding of exactly what aspect is the problem. If the card is of a man or manly effects, it might indicate the man is the problem. Maybe there is no man and the woman is single and still looking for Mr. Right. Maybe there is a man, but the marriage has soured because of things he does or has done, and the lady is looking to bring the marriage back to a place of greater bliss.

By themselves the individual cards just give you snippets of insight, but when they are considered together, the messages usually become quite clear. In the current example, a look at the promise card vertically below it might reveal the answer to the puzzle. If it is another picture of a happy couple or two of anything in harmony, then it is likely promising a fulfilling relationship once the challenge is overcome. If it is of a woman alone, particularly a strong woman alone, or anything alone, it likely means Mr. Right is actually Mr. Wrong, and the challenge card will likely require an ending of the relationship to free the woman to find her greater bliss.

Finding The Ones You Love

If I am doing an in-person reading and both the person and myself have sufficient time before I do a 9 card reading, I will ask them to look at every card in the deck. The ones they like the most they put in one pile and the others go in another pile. There's no limit on the number of cards they choose, so some people will end up with two dozen or more. Then I ask them to narrow their cards down to 10. This can be challenging as most people like all of the cards they chose. Then I ask them to narrow it down to their 5 favorite cards, then their 3 favorite cards. Finally I ask them to choose their absolute favorite card.

The purpose of this exercise is for me to learn as much about them as possible before I begin a reading. If I understand what they are drawn to, it helps me psychically tune in more clearly to the meaning of the cards drawn for their subsequent readings and to most accurately answer specific questions they may ask.

Some people will love their cards so much that it may be almost impossible for them to winnow them down to less than 5, or less than 3. If that is the case, it's fine. The fact that they have such strong connections to 1 card, or 3, or 5, is part of who they are. Understanding this is exceptionally helpful in giving them a meaningful reading.

Insight Cards

Answering Single Questions

Once the general 9 card spread reading is finished, I invite them to ask specific questions about anything they wish greater clarity on. It can be about something that came up in the general reading, or something completely unrelated. I ask them to ask the question aloud as that manifests it's energy most clearly. I remind them that the more specific their question is, the more specific the answer will be.

I ask them to draw a single card and often one card is all that is necessary to know the answer to their question. However, if the answer doesn't jump into my mind, I will ask them to draw another card. Looking at the two cards together will usually make the answer clear. If not, I will ask them to draw a third card. Looking at how these 3 cards relate will almost always produce a definitive answer.

Unanswerable Questions

Occasionally a question will be asked that does not have an answer; at least not at that time. If this occurs, no matter how much you tune into your psychic self, or how many cards the person draws, no answer will come forth. Your mind will just be muddled and empty. Don't be tempted to make something up! If the answer is not forthcoming, let the person know that it is a question that cannot be answered at this time, because all of the aspects of the situation have not yet come into play.

Skype For Long-Distance Readings

For some years after I began doing Insight Card readings they were always in person. But as I became more reclusive and Skype became more ubiquitous, it became a way to do readings for people anywhere in the world.

When doing a reading via Skype, with their permission and along with sending their energy to me, I will shuffle and choose the nine cards for them. I hold each card up to the camera so they can clearly see it before I lay it down. This method actually works just as well as an in-person reading.

Pictures of My Insight Cards

To view full color pictures of some of my favorite Insight Cards you can visit one of my websites, **www.mysoulname.com**. I love them and I think you will too!

UNLEASH YOUR PSYCHIC POWERS

Chapter 27

CHANNELING

Channeling is a modern term and a modern slant on what was called mediumship in earlier generations. Mediumship, up into the mid-20th century involved séances through which the medium contacted spirits of the deceased. Needless to say there was a great amount of fraud. It is sad to think that fake mediums preyed upon the bereaved who so desperately wanted to be able to communicate again with their loved ones.

Channeling does not usually involve contacting anyone recently deceased. Channelers tend to connect to either very ancient people who lived thousands of years ago and have progressed to higher planes of existence, or to higher beings or angels who may have never even been in a physical body. Nor do they use séances to make contact. Channelers simply tune in to the energy of the higher being with whom they are communicating.

A Word Of Caution:

If you are an overly emotional person, or currently experiencing emotional trauma, or seem to always have a lot of drama in your life, you should not attempt to channel, do Automatic Writing, or any psychic technique that invites other beings to come into your consciousness, subconscious, or any other part of you. If you are being affected by negative and lower frequency energies in your life, you will tend to end up having lower frequency entities and beings answer your calls. True channeling of higher beings, brings in noble ones who have humor, are gentle, and bring only light. If you experience the opposite, you are not channeling higher beings.

There Are Several Levels Of Channeling Ability

Level 1: The most common is simply a channeler who is not in a trance, but can hear or in some other way, understand the communication of the higher being. In their own voice, with full cognizance, they repeat the teachings of the higher being to others who are present. Once again, there is some fraud at worst, or self-deception at best, at this entry level. However, there are also those who are succeeding and truly connecting. If they start passing on knowledge there is no way they knew themselves, you have a fairly sure foundation of authenticity.

Level 2: In the next level of ability a channeler will go into a deep meditative state. They will enter into a degree of a trance that can be slight or mostly immobilizing. They will become fairly unaware of their surroundings and be clearer in receiving and sharing the wisdom imparted by the higher being. They will still retain enough cognizance to communicate with others present in their own voice.

In both Level 1 and Level 2, because the channeler is still clearly present, there is always the risk that they could hear the words of the higher being but change or alter them according to their own beliefs or biases when they speak them to others present. This is true even for the most sincere of channelers.

Level 3: Is a deeper trance. There is almost no ability to move even a small part of the body other to speak. The channeler will likely have little or no memory of what they said when they were channeling and repeating the words and teachings of the higher being.

Level 4: Is a Full-Trance Channel. Very few channelers achieve this level. With the permission of the channeler, the higher being will speak through their vocal cords. The voice projected by the higher being, will be a voice other than the channelers, usually accompanied by an unusual or foreign accent. The channeler will be oblivious to what is being said.

Level 5: Is a Full-Trance, Full-Body channel. This is seldom seen. The channeler gives permission for the channeled higher being to take over their body during the channel. This allows the higher being to get up, walk around and touch people or objects. The eyes of the channel are usually tightly closed, so the higher being navigates in their movements around the room, by means other than sight. At the conclusion of the session, the channeler is usually physically drained and even exhausted from the experience, with no memory of what was said or occurred.

Level 6: This is the rarest of all. It is the same as Level 5 except the channeler will be able to give up complete body and vocal control to the higher being, but still retain enough presence to hear and remember all that the higher being speaks while in channel through the physical body. Though they can hear and remember the teachings, they are merely a distant spectator and have no ability to change even a single word spoken.

Until I experienced my own enlightenment I thought anyone that believed in channeling had marbles for brains and that everyone that claimed to channel was a total fake. Never in a thousand years would I have believed that I would one day become a Full Body, Full Trance channeler of over 100 different higher beings, each with their own voice, accent and personality. And both male and female!

Channeling

First Visit to a Channeler

Through all of my unusual experiences I was still a contradiction within myself. My training had been in science and the scientific method of evaluation. Even though I was doing many highly verifiable psychic things, I still was uncomfortable and did not accept them in many ways because I could not scientifically explain them. And I was highly skeptical of anyone else's purported psychic abilities.

About this time, Skye asked me to attend a semi-trance channeling with a fairly famous channeler in Seattle named Evelyn Jenkins. Now of all psychic abilities people claimed, I put channeling up there at the top of the least likely.

Reluctantly, I went with Skye to see the "channeler" and devised all types of scientific lines of inquiry to prove her a fraud. The session did not go well at all. I was not even slightly open to the possibility that she could really channel any "higher beings," and my questions obviously disturbed her. Skye was upset when we left wondering why I had treated her friend so badly.

About a week passed when suddenly, out of the blue, I had an overpowering knowing inside my heart and mind that I had to go back to see Evelyn and that she was 100% legitimate. Not only did I have to go back, but it had to be that night! I asked Skye to call Evelyn and see if it was possible. As luck would have it, Evelyn had a last minute cancellation that night as she was usually booked two weeks in advance. But she did not want to see me again. Our first meeting had convinced her that I was as closed as anyone she had ever met and it would be pointless to get together again.

I asked Skye to call her back again and I got on the line and promised her this time would be different, that I wouldn't ask adversarial questions and would be completely open to whatever occurred. She was suspicious that I could have such an about face attitude, but reluctantly agreed to let me and Skye come over for a session.

In the session I didn't ask any questions about myself, which surprised Evelyn. I had questions about myself, but just had no inclination to ask them. My questions were more of a world changing character, about projects I had been formulating for years like the building of a floating city on the ocean.

The Magnificent Blue Beam

We closed the door for complete privacy and were sitting in a room at Evelyn's house, about 10'x10', in a triangle pattern with one of us at each point of the triangle. This wasn't for any special reason, it is just where the chairs were placed so everyone could see the others in the room. We were separated by about 6 feet between each of us.

With Evelyn in a semi-trance state, we were just talking about the same things we had already been speaking about when suddenly a brilliant, electric blue beam of dancing light, about 1 foot in diameter, shot out from my chest into the chest of Evelyn, and from her into the chest of Skye, and from her back to me. It was like a living lightning bolt that never stopped, with an intense, mesmeric, electric blue color. Evelyn looked at me in astonishment, pointed at the beam, and asked incredulously, "Do you see that?" I said, "Big, blue and incredible?" And she nodded her head vigorously, in awestruck wonder. We both looked over at Skye and her mouth was wide open as she looked at us. We both asked simultaneously, "Do you see it?" She replied, "I don't' see anything, but I feel the most amazing energy I have ever felt."

Evelyn and I continued to marvel at the beams connecting the three of us for a couple of minutes, and then continued in an aura of humbled amazement for another few minutes, asking questions and getting channeled answers.

When the session ended, Evelyn was muted and quiet. Then she looked over to me and took my hand and said with deep feeling, "I have been waiting for you. The only reason I have channeled for the last 10 years is I have been waiting for you to come. Now that you are here, I never need to channel again."

I too was overwhelmed by what had happened, but my first reaction was she couldn't stop channeling, as I knew that was her full-time profession. She was married and that was the way she helped support their financial needs, so I told her that for that reason, if for nothing else, to please continue channeling. She said she would if that is what I wished.

Philos

Ten years passed before I would again encounter channeling. Other than Evelyn, I still thought it was pretty hokey, but I had come to a most uncomfortable place in my life and I needed help.

I had been with Skye, the wonderful lady that first introduced me to channeling for the previous 9 years. We had a great relationship and neither of us were looking to end it or change it. But then I met Sumara. Then Skye met Sumara. We both immediately had a powerful attraction to her and knew she was going to be a part of our lives. But how that was going to manifest was a mystery that caused me many fitful night's sleep. In a few short weeks my feelings for Sumara became a powerful love and I knew that we had an unbreakable future together.

Despite all of my deep feelings for Sumara, I couldn't contemplate abandoning Skye, nor could I conceive of not having Sumara in my life every single day and night! The three of us tried to figure a way we could all be together. We considered several relationship scenarios, but none felt right. For three long months I prayed and racked my brain trying to come up with a solution and I just drew a blank, as did Sumara and Skye. In desperation I agreed to go with the ladies to visit a psychic over on the coast.

We came to her house in Coos Bay, Oregon and presented her with our dilemma, hoping for insights. She gave only one: "I see a little man, about 3 feet tall. He is on another planet. His name is Philos. He has the answers you seek." At the time that seemed less than enlightening; a 3 foot tall man on another planet? Named Philos? Could she contact him? "No." How do we

Channeling

contact him? She didn't know. At the time it just seemed like another dead end.

A few nights after that, on December 22, 1995, at the moment of the winter equinox, I couldn't sleep and found myself alone at my desk, still in a fog trying to figure out a resolution to my relationship challenge. In a final act of releasing my ego, and presenting myself unfettered by belief or bias to receive an answer, I pleaded aloud, "If there is any higher being out there anywhere that can help me find an answer to how the relationship between me, Sumara and Skye, can harmoniously

Embrosewyn channeling Philos, circa 1997

work for each of our own happiness and expansion, please let me know. Right now, right here, speak to me." And then someone did!

A voice rushed into my mind, unbidden and uncontrolled was speaking out of my mouth! "Hello, I am Arnosasium." At first I was sure I was in a delusional haze. I thought the words spoken had just seemed to suddenly come out of my mouth; it was still my voice. And I had complete cognizance of the moment.

I turned on a little mini tape recorder and continued to ask questions. An amazing metamorphosis began to occur. As I asked one question after another, the voice of Arnosasium became less and less my own, and more and more some strange fellow with a foreign accent. It was a good thing I was recording the session, because as my questions progressed I was finding it more and more difficult to stay present and even hear the questions or answers. By the time I was finished, after about twenty minutes, Arnosasium was speaking in quite a strong accent and I was almost completely not present in my memory of what was occurring.

Though it was the middle of the night, I rushed to awaken Skye and tell her that I thought

I might have been channeling! At first, knowing my lack of support for what I had previously claimed was psychic nonsense, she thought I was pulling a joke on her. Once she became convinced that I was serious, she still had a hard time believing that I, of all people, would ever be channeling.

The next day we drove out to an isolated location overlooking a large lake nearby to see if I could contact Arnosasium again with Skye present so she could ask questions. She brought our little tape recorder to record the encounter. Because this was still so completely against the grain of my scientific training, I realized I needed to turn off my rational mind to succeed at bringing in an energy that I could in no way explain scientifically. In my mind I pictured a square room with bare walls, a floor and ceiling. I saw my squiggly grooved brain sitting alone in the middle of the floor and there was a single unadorned door on one wall. As I called in Arnosasium and invited him to speak through me, I envisioned my brain sprouting 8 legs and scurrying over to the door. The door opened up, my brain jumped through into the darkness and the door closed. Suddenly Arnosasium was present. I could physically feel a different energy inside of me and Arnosasium was speaking to me in my mind, greeting me.

Then he spoke in his interesting accent to Skye, saying, "I am here." Skye proceeded to ask Arnosasium several questions she had prepared. Here are a few:

Q: "Who are you and why are you here?"

A: "I am a Galactic Energy Being. I am a member of the Celestine Order of Light (COOL), a group of 397 Galactic Energy Beings that assist the people of worlds on the verge of either catastrophic destruction or peaceful, bountiful unification."

Q: "How do you do that?"

A: "Each of our members have a specialty to assist. My specialty is to be the first Galactic to contact people when they begin to channel. I have a gentle energy that is easy to receive. The specialties of the others cover every known aspect of your existence, from longevity specialists to business specialists.

We speak through a single advanced Channel on each planet; one who has the capabilities to channel all 397 of our members in the fullness of their personalities, some of which have very alien energies. On your earth it is Embrosewyn. He has been chosen because he has the ability and he has a powerful previous life relationship with one of our members named Philos."

Shortly after saying that, Arnosasium asked us to invite Philos to come in his place henceforth, beginning at that moment. Arnosasium departed. I invited Philos to come in and soon we were greeted by a playful Scottish baroque accent. And my life has never been the same!

Not long after Philos came in that day I slipped into a Full-Trance, Full-Body channel and I had to listen to the tape afterward to know what had transpired.

The information Philos provided from that day forth was astounding, Tips for everything from our everyday life to warnings about upcoming national and world events. First, Philos

Channeling

gave us the answer to how the relationship between me, Sumara and Skye would harmoniously work for all of our happiness, growth and expansion. Eighteen years have passed since that day as I write this and we are still in that wonderful relationship that works and have been such catalysts for each other's growths.

We also understood we needed to share some of the wisdom Philos imparted to us with others. He agreed to come in and speak to the public on specific topics, and to take questions from the audience for a limited time, as long as he felt he had useful information to impart that people were not just listening to, but acting upon. We recorded every public session on audio tape and many on video.

After about a year, Philos informed us that he was giving his last public channeling until further notice. He said he had given everyone a great amount of helpful knowledge and only after he saw the majority of people who had heard his words taking action upon them would he return to give more knowledge. There have been no public channelings since that day. However, we have been blessed to continue to have Philos as our personal adviser, uninterrupted during all the years since we first met him.

During the first year or so after I connected with Philos, I had the opportunity to channel many other Galactics of the Celestine Order of Light. With only two exceptions, I was able to contain their energies in my body and act as a Full-Trance, Full-Body Channel for them.

As Arnosasium had mentioned, some had very alien energies and there were two that wanted to come through that I simply couldn't connect with. It was like I was a radio station broadcasting on one frequency and they were trying to broadcast through me from a frequency on the other end of the spectrum. Even some of the ones I was able to connect to and channel for were quite difficult. Skye and Sumara were present for all of the channeled sessions involving other COOL members and they told me that in addition to some very strange voices, there were times my body would contort into very strange positions, positions that I could never do on my own. Occasionally I would come out of a session and have very sore muscles the next day from the physical workout my body went through during the session.

I had to keep reminding myself that it was as difficult for some of the alien COOL members to endure my energy as it was for me to tolerate theirs. I was just as alien to them as they were to me. But channeling such a diverse group of individuals, from so many different species and both sexes, gave me a lot of hope for the future of our Earth. If such a divergent group of aliens could come together in harmony with common goals to help us, then surely we, as the human race of this planet, with all of us being the same species, can come together with harmonious goals for our mutual benefit and prosperity.

How Can You Begin To Channel?

Though channeling came to me in a moment of desperation, it doesn't have to be that way for you, if you would like to connect to higher beings in direct communication. People have been praying to the God of their belief since the dawn of time. Sadly, it is usually a one-way connection -- they speak, but their God doesn't answer directly in clear words and answers. Channeling solves this age old conundrum.

Though the Gods of religions seem to be mute to communicating directly with their supplicants, there is actually a neat scripture in the Christian New Testament that promises the contrary. "Ask and it will be given to you; seek and you will find; knock and the door will be opened to you." Matthew 7:7 Interestingly, if you take the first letter of each of the key words- ask, seek and knock, they once again spell ASK.

Asking, seeking and exploring new possibilities (knocking), are certainly true keys to getting into direct communication with higher beings. Many people will tell you that faith is also necessary, but my own experience has shown this not to be true. I am a very spiritual person and I have a lot of faith, but none of it was evident on the night I first began channeling with Arnosasium. I did not have a belief, or even much of a hope that anyone would answer my cry for help. It was a plea of last resort. When Arnosasium did respond, he was met with incredulity on my part at first.

Here Are Some Keys That I Have Found That Are Helpful:

1. Though you may not need faith, you do need desire in great abundance. It is not enough simply to want to communicate with higher beings. You have to really, really want it. In my case, I came to a point where I was willing to ask for help from a new source, because I had already exhausted every other possibility I knew of in my life. I had a life-altering problem that absolutely had to be fixed and I wanted an answer very, very much.

2. Speak aloud and clearly, even boldly with passion and emotion. Show them that communicating with them is something you deeply desire.

3. At the very beginning of your asking, be sure to specify that you want to communicate with **higher beings**. There truly are a great number of devilish lower beings that can come to you like a wolf in sheep's clothing and lead you down paths you will be sorry you traveled. Eliminate the possibility of encountering these masqueraders by specifically asking only for contact with higher beings right from the start.

4. When the higher being that answers your call arrives within you, you may or may not physically feel their presence, but you will hear them speaking to you in your mind *if you listen*. Right now silently say "*I love you.*" Though no words came out of your mouth you *heard* the words in your mind, but not in your ears. It is the same when a higher being first speaks to you.

5. When you first hear those words in your mind, speak them aloud. Do not worry that it probably just comes out in your own voice. You may even think it is just you speaking your own thoughts aloud in your own voice. Follow through anyway.

Channeling

6. Continue asking questions, or even better, have another person present to ask questions. With each question and answer, tune in closer and more harmoniously to the higher being that is speaking to you and through you. Give up your own ego. Be open to letting the higher being fill you. Turn off your mind. Don't allow yourself to interject your thoughts into the answers. Just let the answers flow out of your mouth unbidden and uncontrolled. Before you know it you will be trance channeling!

7. It is very helpful to have a specific higher being you are desiring to communicate with. Think about a room full of thousands of people. If a person you didn't know stood up on the stage and yelled out, "Is there someone here that wants to talk with me?" Chances are that if you were in the crowd, you wouldn't pay that person much attention. But if that same unknown person went up on the stage and specifically called out your name and asked you to come and speak with them, you would likely hurry on over. It is the same with higher beings. Whether you are speaking to the God of your religion, or specific angels, or Galactics, or other higher beings you are aware of, calling upon them by name to come to you, and speak directly to you and through you, is far more effective than just randomly calling out for an anonymous higher being to come.

8. Arnosasium of the Celestine Order of Light, the Galactic Energy Being I first spoke with through channeling, and who first spoke through me, is a good higher being to contact if you do not have someone else in mind. His specialty is first contact with new channelers and he is an easy harmonious energy to receive.

Chapter 28
AUTOMATIC WRITING

I actually never tried Automatic Writing until sometime after I had begun trance channeling, but for most people it is a far easier way to tune into both the wisdom of their Higher Self, as well as the guidance of Higher Beings. It is also used by some to make contact with the deceased, particularly to get information or confirm something from the recently departed.

Automatic Writing has been around as a type of divination since writing materials have been readily available. Everything from simple one sentence answers, to complete songs and novels have come through Automatic Writing by practitioners of this psychic ability.

When you are automatically writing, your hand writes messages your mind is unaware of. You may be in a trance state, or a semi-trance state, or not in a trance at all. You may be aware of everything around you, but you will not be thinking about, or focusing in any way on what your hand is writing.

Many people in the modern era use a computer to do their Automatic Writing. If you are a good typist, using a computer can be an excellent tool for getting into the flow of the writing without filtering or thinking about the message. Because of its mechanical nature, it easily allows you to write without interjecting your thoughts into what you are writing.

Probably every person in the world that can take a pen or pencil to a piece of paper has already done Automatic Writing many times, every time they doodle. Most doodles have geometric shapes. Some are angular and many are various forms of curves and spirals. My entire life I have tended to draw a flower in a flower pot. Rather than being just aimless wanderings of your writing instrument, the very fact that you are drawing recognizable shapes without any thought to what you are drawing is significant. From crude forms of sacred geometry, to insight into your inner motivations, such as my flower in a pot, doodles are a simple manifestation of Automatic Writing.

Automatic Writing has been used as a tool in writer's workshops and psychological therapy for many years. When you use it for higher purposes it can be employed to access the wisdom and knowledge of your higher self, or to act as a means of channeling the answers, information and recommendations of other beings. Because you are always vulnerable when channeling from sources outside of yourself, the same cautions I mentioned in the Channeling chapter apply to Automatic Writing as well.

Of all the forms of psychic abilities and paranormal powers detailed in this book, Automatic Writing is perhaps the easiest to first accomplish, and succeed at accessing higher information. Because writing and doodling are actions you have probably done almost every day of your life since you entered school, your mind does not have conscious mental impediments to it as some strange new action. Mental inhibitions and defensive barricades are often stout stumbling blocks to first time use of other psychic and paranormal powers.

For years, even while I was experiencing multiple psychic abilities, my conscious, rational, scientific mind fought against me. Your mind tends to not want to have anything to do with things it can't understand and explain. This is a primitive protective instinct that can be helpful in certain situations in life. But it is an encumbrance to first time and early use of psychic abilities and paranormal powers.

When you are fist exploring your psychic and paranormal powers, one part of you is curious and hopeful. However, it is not uncommon for another part to be trepidatious and even a bit fearful. This is partly a primal self-defense mechanism of your body to be cautious with the unknown. It may also be motivated by injections of lingering residue of your personal cultural or religious beliefs that condemn anything to do with psychic powers.

Herein is the beauty of Automatic Writing. Because writing is one of the most everyday actions you do, your body has zero defense barriers against it. If you just sat down and tried to channel, to allow another being's presence inside you, to speak in a different voice through you, your mind becomes a powerful obstruction saying, "No, no no, not on my watch!" Your mind wants to keep everything you do entirely in the physical reality. It naturally rebels against your attempts to go to the unknown elsewhere, especially if 'elsewhere' seems ludicrous, incomprehensible, or is contrary to your previous or current beliefs or culture. Writing, on the other hand is normal. When you start typing on your computer or take a pen to paper, your mind opens the gate, because that is just an ordinary, everyday action. It is certainly the easiest path to allowing spiritual and other higher beings to speak to you and through you, and to receive valuable insights from your Higher Self.

My Experiences Automatic Writing

When I completed revelating the Oracles of Celestine Light , I thought that after that monumental 800 page project, the Celestine's and the Elohim might be done with me. But I discovered I have a lifetime calling. Since the completion of the Oracles, I have had hundreds of pages of subsequent communication in the form of Automatic Writing with the Elohim and their representatives.

Automatic Writing

Not nearly as thrilling as revelating, my communications with the Elohim and Celestine's are pretty simple.

1. I sit down in front of my computer
2. I say a prayer and ask for whichever Celestine of Elohim wishes to speak with me to come in.
3. Immediately I hear their voice speaking silently in my mind. I can mentally hear the words clearly, just like the example I gave earlier of saying "I love you" to yourself.
4. After a few words of greetings, whoever is present quickly begins to dictate. I am but a scribe. Normally, I am not a very fast typist, perhaps 25 WPM. However, when I am acting as the scribe for higher beings I need to type as fast as they speak, which gives me no time at all to even think about what they are actually saying. I just type as fast as my fingers will fly, without interruption until they are done. I correct typos later.
5. It is also while I am looking for typos that I first have the opportunity to actually study the words that came in so rapidly and learn about the subject that was being taught.

The Experiences Of Others

I've only known one other person that used Automatic Writing on a regular and consistent basis and her experience was quite different from mine. Connie was a middle-age woman I knew about 15 years ago. She also communicated via Automatic Writing with multiple beings, but I don't think they were all higher beings.

Connie would simply sit down with a notepad and pen and invite whomever wanted to communicate with her to come on in and give her advice and insights. She would go into a semi-trance where she just looked straight ahead. She was still somewhat aware of her surroundings, but she didn't focus on anything nearby and never looked down at what she was writing, which was sometimes blazing fast. In a limited form of channeling, she gave control of her writing hand to whatever being wanted to take control.

The amazing thing was to look at the handwriting and compare it to the messages when she was finished. Beings of light, that came in with upbeat messages, produced a beautiful flowing script. But beings of lesser light, bearing dark, often frightening messages, wrote in a barely legible scrawl. None of the writing styles Connie exhibited in her Automatic Writing appeared similar to her own handwriting.

How You Can Automatic Write

Set aside 15 minutes to an hour where you can be undisturbed by anyone or anything. Turn off phones, radios, TV's, etc. Not only do you desire no distractions from your task, but you also don't want anyone nearby that might make light of your efforts or in any way send you negative energy. Knowing you are in complete privacy also allows you to shed your inhibitions and more easily access your psychic abilities.

Sit comfortably at a desk or table, in front of your computer or with a pad and pen.

Before beginning, clear your mind of any mundane thoughts or anxieties. Focus on thinking about nothing.

Decide who you are going to receive a message from: your Higher self, your Spirit Guide, your Guardian Angel, your deceased Loved One, or any other spiritual or Higher Being you desire to contact. Write on your computer or pad, "A message from _____ is:" and put in your Higher Self or whomever it is you wish to contact in the blank.

If you are connecting to an angel, your Spirit Guide, or any Higher Being, it is helpful to raise your own vibrations to them and away from the mundane world, just as you are prepared for them to write to you. Picture a paradise somewhere above you where they reside. See yourself going up to greet them and ask them to help you with some insight into a specific problem or just give you some loving general guidance.

Stay out of your mind. Try not to consciously write anything beyond the intro of "A message from _____ is:"

If you are using a computer and can type without looking at the keyboard or screen, that is best. If you are using a pad and pen, just hold your pen resting on the pad, but don't look down when you are writing or at anything you have already written once you begin.

Everything is significant from a doodle to random letters, to symbols, punctuation or lack of it.

If your mind is just drawing a blank, that's fine. Don't worry about it. Let the writing, doodling or typing begin whenever it does. Automatic writing should just flow easily and effortlessly, without input or control from your conscious mind. Don't force it or worry about the time. Some people don't have success on their first endeavor. Some need 2-3 attempts at different times. Just be patient and keep your mind unfocused on writing or thinking.

A good way to stay unfocused, if you are drawing blanks after some time, is to turn on the TV to the most boring show you can find and watch it while keeping your hand holding your pen on the paper or fingers resting lightly on your keyboard. This gets you out of your left brain logical thinking and unfetters your right brain intuitive mind and psychic abilities.

When your Automatic Writing session is finished, examine what was written. It may just seem like gibberish or nonsense, but if it was true communication from realms beyond, there will be meaning. Consider the letters, words, symbols, doodles, phrases all in the light of your own life and current challenges. Find how what was written can apply to your situations in life.

Once you are successful you should begin asking more focused and specific questions to get clearer answers. Questions directed to particular higher beings, rather than anyone that wants to answer, will always give the best response.

If you have more than one specific question, it can be helpful to set a timer of say 5 minutes per question. This actually keeps your mind at bay so it doesn't try to interject itself into the answer, and allows your psychic energy to focus in the specific time frame for the task at hand.

Be aware that if you are not calling in your own Higher Self or a specific Higher Being known to you, you may end up with strange, sometimes scary messages, in handwriting you don't recognize and signed by someone unknown. Once again, I highly advise you to only attempt Automatic Writing to yourself, or to a Higher Being whom you are specifically seeking to communicate. If you have ANY uncomfortable feelings while Automatic Writing, STOP!

Auto Writing Only, Or Being A Scribe?

While traditional Automatic Writing is described in the steps above, you can also do it as I have; as a scribe, where you hear a voice in your mind dictating what to write. If this is a true higher source, the messages will always be helpful, uplifting and full of light, even at times they may be talking about a particular challenging situation. When you are channeling through a voice in your head, if it is real, it will not sound like your voice. You will hear a different accent and it will come through with confidence and authority. After all, this is a Higher Being, they are not timid or unconfident. True communication also tends to be easy to understand and directly stated. It will leave you feeling good, not bad.

Verify That You Are Really Automatic Writing

It is possible to verify that the doodles, scribbles and written messages that came in are actually true communications from higher sources. Whether it is a message from your Higher Self or from angels, Spirit guides or other Higher Beings, true channeled messages coming in from higher sources will be positive, helpful and full of light. If you are receiving dark, negative and heavy feeling messages, you are likely not actually channeling with Automatic Writing, or you are tapping into your own emotional state, which at that time may not be in the best mood, or maybe you are being contacted by negative entities of one type or another that never bring light, only darkness.

Why You Sometimes Know What Will Be Written

At times you may find that whether you are just letting your hand write what it will, or receiving dictation from a Higher Being, you may know what is going to be communicated a second before it is actually written or spoken. This is not uncommon and is a manifestation of your psychic abilities of clairaudience and/or claircognizance. These are both frequently developed in tandem with the growth of other psychic abilities.

Don't Let Your Conscious Mind Make You Doubt

When you are first beginning, once you have completed your session and are looking at what may be fairly indecipherable scribbles on the paper, you may laugh at yourself and just discard it as a failed experiment. Don't act too quickly. Because your conscious mind was uninvolved and closed off during your Automatic Writing session, it is not unexpected that it might rebel and try to convince you it's all nonsense when you let it back in to help analyze what you have written. Continue for some more sessions. You will soon be able to know by how you feel inside, inspired and uplifted, or down and confused, as to whether you are enjoying the success you hoped for and expected.

Chapter 29
TELEPATHY

The word telepathy has Greek origins. 'Tele' means distant and 'pathe' means feeling or perceptions. It is a trendy psychic ability in the public awareness and is often depicted in movies and books as people being able to communicate, mind to mind, without speaking, or even being present together. The likely reason it is so popular, is many people can relate to it, feeling they have also experienced telepathy multiple times in their lives.

It frequently occurs between people who are bonded from many shared life experiences, such as a husband and wife. For those who are close friends or family, it is not uncommon for one to bring up an obscure subject that is usually never thought about, and that neither had been speaking about, only to have the other immediately say, "I was just thinking about that!" I know it happens with my wife and I quite often.

For such a commonly experienced ability, it is quite a super power. Mind to mind communication, works over any distance and is unhindered by any barrier. Obstacles that would prevent the use of any of the normal 5 senses are not impediments to telepathy.

The Only Purple Person?
One thing I learned early on from looking at the auras of every person I met, was there was nobody like me. With all other people I could easily discern major areas of their auras that were quite similar to the auras of many other people. But I never met a single person whose aura even vaguely resembled mine in colors or other characteristics. I came to think of myself as a purple person. At least the only purple person on Earth. Don't misunderstand, I did not think I *was* from another planet, just that it seemed as if I must be, as I was so different aurically than every other person I had ever met. I thought of myself this way for several years and was totally shocked one day when I met another purple person in a place I absolutely least expected it.

My Strongest Experience With Telepathy

While I am going to keep the real facts and details of this account, I am going to change the names and alter the setting, as the real life person involved still desires complete anonymity.

Before I was ever married I always had an infatuation with foreign women. My first wife was French and she was not the first French girl I dated. I was very enraptured of that sexy, soft Parisian accent.

Once I met a charming French girl while she was on vacation in the United States and pined away for her after she returned to France. Finally, I couldn't take the separation any longer and after about 5 months I decided to hop a flight to France, navigate to her house and surprise her at her doorstep. Accordingly, I made the journey, and not speaking French had some difficulty negotiating the right train to her town and getting directions to her house.

Arriving, full of excitement and expectation at meeting the love of my heart, I rang the doorbell at her doorstep. Susanne, her younger sister by sixteen months, opened the door. I introduced myself, although we both knew who the other was from pictures her sister and I had exchanged in correspondence. In broken English, she said her sister was in another town and would be back later that day. There was some awkward silence as we both just stared at each other somewhat perplexed and very surprised. Looking at our energy centers, one by one, I was shocked to see that they were connecting and resonating on every one, something I had never before experienced with anyone. There was an exceptionally powerful channel between our psychic centers. The other centers, though firmly joined, did not have the same intense connection. I was stunned to realize I was looking at the only other purple person I had ever met up until that time.

Susanne invited me in and we both kept staring at each other, not in a romantic way, but with an utter fascination to be seeing someone we had never expected to see, and in my case did not even think existed.

It was extremely awkward for both of us. Here I had traveled half way around the world to surprise her sister and all I wanted to do was to talk with Susanne and learn about her life and what she had experienced. I had to keep silently reminding myself that I was there to see her sister.

Imagine if you had lived your entire life as the only white person or black person in the world, and as far as you knew, you were the only one. You had never heard of another person with your skin color, had never seen a picture of another, or anything else that would make you think that another person with your skin color even existed. Then all of a sudden, out of nowhere, another person who looked just like you, opened a door and was standing before you. I cannot even begin to describe the shock that continued to reverberate inside of me. I was standing and talking with another person who was at least aurically, just like me!

While Susanne and I were falteringly trying to communicate in English, I was silently thinking in my mind that this situation was not good as I had to have all of my attention on the girl I had come across the world to see, not her sister! It was the only right thing to do and

Telepathy

I knew that any other deviation would not have a happy ending. Suddenly, I heard Susanne's voice speaking in my mind saying, "We cannot speak of this to anyone, even to each other." It was in perfect English.

My eyes must have bugged out of my head as I stared at her, cocking my head almost in disbelief. "Did you just speak to me telepathically?" I asked in my mind without speaking. Susanne, continued to stare at me and nodded slowly in acknowledgment. "It's confusing. It's scary. Please stop," she pleaded in my mind.

My first thought reaction was, "You started it." She stood up quickly and fled the room hurrying out the front door. "I'm late for an appointment," she spoke aloud. "My sister will be home later."

"Wait!" I cried out in my mind. "We have to talk. This is incredible. There is so much I want to ask you. You are like me. We are brother and sister."

Her reply in my mind was curt. "No, we cannot speak like this ever again. It would bring shame to me. My family is very religious. My sister would never forgive me if she thought I was coming between you and her, nor would my family." Then she turned me off.

Long after she vanished into the distance, I continued to speak to her in my mind, but she never answered. I was left to wonder if what I thought had happened could really have possibly occurred. Were we really communicating telepathically? Was it my conscious mind to her conscious mind, or, my higher self to hers, or some hybrid in between? So many questions, but no answers!

Left alone in my girlfriend's house, I was in a complete daze by the afternoon's events. Telepathy: actual speaking in your mind; telepathy was real! Even more amazing, I had met the first person in my life whose aura had many of the same peculiar qualities as mine and we connected on every energy center! It seemed a crime to abandon all of this simply because other people would not understand. Yet Susanne was insistent that is how it must be.

Later that day I had a warm and loving reunion with my girlfriend. That night her parents came over for dinner. Susanne was also there and it was difficult for both of us to not glance up and stare at the other. But even one intense look would have been misunderstood by anyone who witnessed it. Nobody would have believeed or accepted that it was a psychic connection. They would assume it was romantic and there would have been a big, unnecessary blowup. It was certainly one of the more frustrating situations I have ever been in.

More Than Just Hearing A Voice

Over the next few years Susanne and I had little contact, while her sister, who became my wife, and I continued our committed relationship. Nevertheless, about once a month or so I found myself seeing everything that was transpiring in her life at that moment through Susanne's eyes. In my mind, I also clearly heard her voice, as well as anyone that was speaking to her. Though this was a psychic ability I had never heard of, I considered that it must be a higher form of telepathy, possible only because of the energetic similarities between my aura and Susanne's.

I first told her about seeing through her eyes and hearing through her ears when she came to visit me and her sister for two weeks one Christmas. She seemed amazed when I told her. Though she knew we had an inexplicable, unique connection, I don't think she believed me at first. So I related some of the private events in her life I had witnessed while she was living 2000 miles away. I knew some of the events I had seen were things she would never have told anyone else. After I recalled one event in particular that she had never spoken of to another person, she knew that as inexplicable as it was, our psychic connection was true and real.

Susanne attended a religiously affiliated college with strict moral standards. Being from Europe, it was a common occurrence for girls and women to walk arm in arm or hand in hand with their close friends who were female. But such actions were shocking to her prudish university. I was watching and listening as she and her best friend were called into an administrators office and chastised for their behavior, walking hand in hand on campus. Though the administrator consoled them that their behavior might be innocuous, there were many who would think they were lesbians and that it was necessary to avoid even the appearance of 'evil.' Susanne was ashamed and kept it a big secret from her other friends and family, so she was wide-eyed in amazement when I first recounted the event to her in detail.

Animals Have Strong Telepathy

Just this week I saw something that reminded me how strong telepathy can be between animals. Telepathy is a wonderful ability because it overcomes the language barrier. Though I have no idea how, when a person speaking one language communicates by telepathy with a person speaking a different language, it comes out in the language understood by the receiver! It seems to be exactly the same for animals.

We have a little toy poodle named Little Bit. She is about 30% overweight and hence has recently had a cutback in her food quantity. Since then she has scrounged around looking for any little tidbit someone may have dropped to help alleviate her calorie loss.

I also have parrots. One pair of Sun Conures are in a big cage in the house as they are a nesting pair, while the others are outside in a large aviary. I was sitting at my desk last week typing on this manuscript when I happened to look over toward the conure cage. Little Bit was standing up on her hind legs with her front paws resting on the bottom of the parrot cage, mournfully looking at the dish of food that was behind the bars just inches beyond her reach.

The male Sun Conure came down to the food dish. I thought he was going to nip at the Little Bit's paws to get her away from the cage. Instead he just cocked his head intelligently and the two animals looked at each other in silence for about 10 seconds. Suddenly the Sun Conure began furiously swinging his head back and forth in the food dish. He ended up throwing almost all the food in the dish out of the cage, which Little Bit quickly ate up.

The first time I saw it I just chuckled. But when I saw the same thing the next day I realized the

Telepathy

two animals, one a bird and the other a mammal, must be communicating and understanding one another with telepathy. Body language alone would not account for the generous actions of the male Sun Conure to give up his and his mates food, even though I'm sure they knew I would soon resupply it.

How You Can Develop Telepathy

Type in "Zener Cards" on a Amazon search and you'll find several vendors selling what are also known as "ESP Cards." These cards were originally created by perceptual psychologist, Karl Zenner in the early 1930's to use with experiments on ESP.

Regardless of how you test out, continued practice with the Zener cards will improve results for most people fairly quickly.

A variant of the test is once you have tested with casual friends as the holder, do the test again with a close friend. The fact that you are close friends indicates you are probably fairly similar in your auras and can more easily tune into one another than to other less similar people.

Still another variant is to have a sibling or parent be the holder. I think you'll find the results interesting.

Telephone Telepathy

Certainly the most fun way to test and improve your telepathic powers is by playing telephone telepathy. For this game you will need 7 participants. Everyone in the group should know one another, and the closer friends you are the better the results are likely to be.

There are three positions: 5 Callers, 1 Callee and 1 Statistician. The 5 Callers sit together in one room or house. The Callee and the Statistician sit together in a distant room in the house.

Each of the Callers chooses a number between 1 and 5 that is their unique number. A dice is rolled and whichever number comes up, the Caller represented by that number rings the Callee in the distant room on the same phone that will be used by all the Callers.

Once the Callee answers the phone and vocally says, "hello," the Caller **answers in their mind only** by saying, "Hello, this is _name of Caller_. They then hang up the phone.

The Callee then tells the Statistician who their telepathic insight tells them was the caller. The Statistician marks down the name under Call #1. The group of Callers also marks on an identical sheet who the Caller was for Call #1.

Continue calling until at least 10 calls have been made, marking Caller #2, Caller # 3 and so on. If you go past 10 calls, continue on until 20 so it is easy to calculate the accuracy percentage.

As there are 5 Callers, just guessing would produce a probability accuracy of 2 out of 10, or 20%. To get none correct, or 4 or more, is statistically significant.

Once one person has gone through a cycle as the Callee, they become the Statistician for the next round and the Statistician moves into the Caller group, while 1 person from the Caller group becomes the new Callee.

As with the Zener cards, practice tends to increase your abilities and improve your results.

Chapter 30
TELEKINESIS

If you think about fantasy shows like Harry Potter; telekinesis, the ability to move and manipulate objects with the strength of your mind or auric field, is one of the most exciting and desired paranormal powers. Perhaps the greatest real life example of astounding telekinesis power, and likely the inspiration for many modern depictions, is the account of Miriam (Mary Magdalene) saving Salome in the Oracles of Celestine Light: Vivus, Chapter 58. Here's a short excerpt:

19 While they were in the water, seven men appeared on the opposite riverbank and called out to the women with obscene words and immediately began to wade into the water toward them, spreading out as if to encircle them.

20 Salome cried out to the women, saying, "These men are drunk. We must flee now!" Immediately, the other women began moving as quickly as they could through the heavy, impeding water to the nearer bank, all except Miriam, who stood calmly in the middle of the river, facing the drunken men who were moving rapidly toward her, some walking in water waist deep.

21 Looking up the embankment to the road where their husbands were, Salome shouted out, "Yeshua, Cephas! Come now to us, for we are attacked."

22 Hearing her cry, the men moved at once to descend to the river and protect the women, but standing upon the road's edge, looking down upon the scene before them, Yeshua held out his arms and bade them to stop for a moment, saying, "It is in times of greatest challenge that the true person of light and power can emerge from within the shell in which they are usually held by everyday life. Let us watch for a moment to see if Miriam discovers who she really is."

23 Looking at the crazed men rushing toward her, Miriam muttered to herself, "These men are more than drunk. They are possessed by devils to act as they do."

24 Seizing upon that realization, she said in a loud voice, "In the name of Elohim, I command the devils within you to depart!" Her forceful words were heard by all, even by the men up on the road.

25 But the possessed men approaching her only laughed, and now they were almost upon her.

26 Salome turned when she heard Miriam's voice, and seeing the demented men coming upon her from three directions, Salome quickly moved back to help defend the one she loved.

27 Miriam did not see Salome turn to come back toward her. Even as the attackers were almost upon her, she stood somewhat dazed and bewildered, not understanding why the devils had not departed when she had so commanded in the name of Elohim.

28 She was awakened from her momentarily disconnected thought by a scream from Salome as she was grabbed by two of the men as she was almost to Miriam.

29 Miriam turned quickly and her eyes were wide and her brows creased with anger. Without uttering a word, she forcefully threw her right hand forward with her palm slightly raised and fingers widely spread pointing at the men holding Salome. Immediately, they released her and fell into the water, screaming in pain and agony and holding both hands to their eyes.

30 Still in a fury, still speaking no words, Miriam turned toward the remaining five men and in quick succession, with forceful movements of both her right and left hands held in the same manner, she called up the power of Celestine Light within her soul with her righteous anger. The attackers were hurled violently out of the water and flung far across the river, landing with bone-crushing impact on rocks and trees.

31 Standing on the road looking down onto the river, the men gazed in amazement at what they had just seen, and even having seen it, they could scarcely believe that which their eyes testified of.

32 The women in the river huddled together, uncomprehending of what they had just witnessed and unsure if they should be grateful to Miriam or fear her.

My own experience with telekinesis is much tamer but still noteworthy. I have had good success with several experiments. They are shared below and I encourage you to try them and practice them at home. If done under controlled conditions to ensure your breath or movement are not affecting the test object, they are a great way to help you realize you have this potent ability and exercise your mind and aura to increase its power. I know I am!

College Experiment (Telekinesis Exercise # 1)

My first exposure to actual telekinesis was in a college physics class. The professor asked us if anyone believed in the psychic power of telekinesis. Because it was a science class and that was considered a pseudoscience, most people chuckled and no one but me was foolish enough to raise their hand. But as I was the only one, the professor gave me the opportunity to design an experiment that the entire class could participate in, limited to 5 minutes, to test whether an object could be caused to move without physical touching, or any obvious physical motivating force. For telekinesis to be a viable possibility, there could not be any other more likely cause.

Thinking quickly, I split the class in two and had them stand in a group on opposite sides of a large wooden table, about 10' x 5', we used for big experiments. Half the class stood on one side and the other on the opposite side. There was a 1 foot gap left between students and the table to

Telekinesis

insure nobody touched it. No active participants stood on the ends, but I asked two students to stand on the ends to monitor each side to insure the table remained untouched.

I placed a single pencil right in the middle of the table parallel to the long side, equally between the two sides of students. The experiment was to see if either side could move the pencil even a little bit. I hoped that the competitive team spirit would heighten any psychic abilities and be more likely to manifest a reaction. Plus, everyone focused on the same task, should amplify any telekinetic power.

After 4 minutes absolutely nothing had happened. Entering the last minute allotted for the experiment, it wasn't looking promising. Suddenly the pencil started to roll toward one side of the table! It was moving at a steady, undeniable clip and nobody was moving or blowing it! After it had rolled about 2 feet and was getting close to the edge, it started to spin around in place. That lasted for about 5 seconds and then it took off even more rapidly for the other side!

As it neared the other side it suddenly stopped before it fell off the edge. After about 10 seconds the pencil started rolling again back in the other direction. When it was in the center of the table the 5 minute buzzer went off and the experiment ended. The professor called it a draw.

Most people were trying to act cool, that it was no big deal, just another science experiment. A few were wide-eyed in wonder and expressing amazement, including me. I couldn't think of any other explanation except telekinesis. The professor asked the class to propose possible motivating forces other than telekinesis, but not one person came up with any theories that weren't even more far-fetched. It was left as a test needing further experimenting to determine the motivating force, but we never revisited the subject. However, I did get extra points for designing a good experiment on a moment's notice.

The Other Name

Telekinesis is an old-fashioned term and has somewhat of a sullied history because of prominent and suspected frauds through the years. The more modern name for this ability is Psychokinesis, which also encompasses more than just moving or affecting physical objects. Psychokinesis is a big basket including teleportation, transmutation of matter, energy healing of biological tissue, magnetism, shape-shifting and control of light.

I've never liked the appellation Psychokinesis, as the preface 'psycho', is a slang term used to malign someone as crazy. Psychic abilities get defamed enough without adding fuel to the fire with words that can be used to insinuate people that believe in them are a few connections short upstairs. Plus, I prefer the abilities to be considered separately rather than all lumped together under Psychokinesis. They are each astounding powers in their own right and deserve undivided attention.

The Science Behind Telekinesis

Telekinesis is certainly one of the more dramatic and magical appearing paranormal powers. You'll have a challenge convincing many people that it's not magic. The reality is it is a biological manifestation of the *First Law of Thermodynamics*, a law of physics, as are many other paranormal powers. Understanding this aspect helps me to get more excited and confident in achieving results.

Stated simply, the first law of Thermodynamics establishes that ***energy cannot be created or destroyed. But it can be changed from one form of energy into another, or transferred from one storage vessel to another***. Heat, light, magnetism, chemical, kinetic, and electrical are all forms of energy that can be transferred or changed.

Most of the energy we receive as humans comes from the food we eat. Food energy is a chemical form of energy and is measured in calories. Our bodies only use about 40% of the energy taken in by eating food to maintain the body systems. The other 60% is available to be changed into another form of energy and used for work or transferred to something or someone else.

For instance, when you exercise, you are changing the chemical energy stored in your body into kinetic (motion) energy. When you do an energy or spiritual healing of someone that is sick, you are transferring multiple forms of energy from you to them, and channeling energy from beyond yourself as well. The energy transfer enters into them revitalizing and repairing their ailing body.

Pilot Rock Unveils Positive Energy Vortex And Much More

One of the more amazing experiences I have had occurred on a beautiful spring day when Sumara and I went for a hike up to Pilot Rock, on the Oregon-California border, to visit two Positive Energy Vortexes and two Dimensional Doorways we had located remotely and now wanted to pinpoint.

It was early May and this was our first hike of the year since the snows had receded and the trails were clear. The combination of amazing scenic views and the opportunity to discover four powerful paranormal energy locations made it a trip we were really looking forward to.

Pilot Rock, as its name implies has been a guidepost for north-south travelers since pioneer days and certainly by Native Americans before that. Strategically located very close to Siskiyou Pass, right on the border of Oregon and California.

The rock is a columnar basalt monolith, the remnants of an ancient volcano. When you are standing on the rock you are actually standing inside an old volcano. This was the throat of the volcano, where the magma and ash rose up and were blasted out. When the volcano was young it had the familiar conical shaped slopes of a volcano that you see with Mt. Shasta or Black Butte. However, the flanks of the volcano were of softer material and over the years they eroded away leaving only the hard basalt magma throat still standing in what is today Pilot Rock.

Telekinesis

Pilot Rock

On the day of our fateful hike, the days were getting longer so we were not in a hurry to get going, so we did not arrive to the vicinity of Pilot Rock until around 2:00 in the afternoon. After leaving the highway, we drove a couple of miles on a very rough, unimproved dirt road to reach the parking area at an old quarry. We left the parking area, about 1 mile below the base of Pilot Rock, and began an easy ascent up toward the base of the monolith. The entire monolithic rock is engulfed in a big and powerful Positive Energy Vortex that extends outward at least 50 feet from the base. The most intense energy concentration is at the very top of the monolith. The rush of energy at the top is astounding, but care has to be taken not to let the swirling vortex energy move you right off the edge, as it's a vertical drop down for almost 600 feet and there's not a lot of room at the pointy top of the rock!

We had only walked about 100 feet from the car when Sumara asked if she could borrow the carabineer that I carried my keys on so she could hook her water bottle onto her belt loop and not have to carry it. I unzipped the coat pocket that my keys were in, removed the carabineer and handed it to her, then put my keys back in my jacket pocket and zipped it up.

We decided to save the ascent of Pilot Rock for later in the day, and first look for an ancient

Dimensional Doorway just a short hike down the Pacific Crest Trail (PCT), which intersected the lower portion of the Pilot Rock trail. After a short distance, while seeking the dimensional energy disruption, we located it in a small, well hidden cave, less than 100 feet off the PCT. Though the view of snow-capped Mt. McLoughlin from the location was beautiful, the energy at the doorway was somewhat dark. It was obvious this was a passage that had not been opened for a very long time.

We lingered but a few minutes, then turned our sights toward the monolith. We needed to return the way we came to get back on the trail leading up to Pilot Rock. But I had the not too brilliant idea to take a shortcut and bushwhack straight up the slope above us, assuming we could intersect the Pilot Rock trail at some point. So off we went through the bush. It ended up being a lot more challenging than I anticipated. The slope was quite steep with many spots of loose talus where it was all we could do to not slip and slide down the mountain. Whenever we did reach a substantial bushy area where we had firm footing, we needed to be very careful about what bushes we touched or even allowed to brush against our clothes, as Poison Oak was everywhere!

Finally, after a lot more effort than a shortcut warranted, we intersected the Pilot Rock trail and headed up toward the monolith. The trail up from that point was very steep, dry and dusty, with numerous loose pebbles constantly underfoot making traction treacherous. It was a relief to finally reach the base of the rock itself and have firm footing. The climb up the rock is through a narrow fault fracture that splits the monolith. Other than two 10 foot vertical spots with little for handholds, the 600 foot hand and foot scramble from the base was fairly easy. From the summit, the 360 degree view was one of the most memorable I have ever seen. Majestic Mt. Shasta towered over 14,000 feet due south and the valley in between, over 2000 feet below, took your breath away with its spectacular beauty. Standing within the very center of the Positive Energy Vortex, right at the peak of the monolith, was also an unforgettable experience.

Coming down was fairly easy, but by the bottom of the hill we were looking forward to getting home and taking a nice hot shower, eating a delicious meal and a getting a really sound night's sleep. But the day was not over and our most interesting adventure of the day was just about to begin.

Out of habit, I reached into my right pants pocket to get my keys to open the Jeep, but they weren't there. Just a little worried, I tried my other pants pocket without success. Then I recollected the history of the keys during our travels that day. After giving Sumara the carabineer for her water bottle at the beginning of our trek, I zipped my keys into a pocket of the light jacket I was wearing.

Before we reached the PCT the day had warmed up and I had taken my jacket off and tied it around my waist. When we were passing through a shady area beneath some large pine trees, Sumara asked to wear my jacket as she was getting a little chilled. I passed it to her and over the next several hours the jacket went back and forth between us multiple times depending upon who was cold or hot. Most of the afternoon we were in the sun ascending Pilot Rock and the

Telekinesis

jacket was tied around my waist. On the way back down, once we were back under the forest canopy and the air was cooler, I put it back on.

Happily remembering that my keys were in my jacket pocket I reached in to get them so we could be on our way. However, they were not in the right pocket, which I was dismayed to find was no longer zipped shut. A serious rush of worry flashed over me as I reached into my left pocket, the only remaining pocket. I looked at Sumara sheepishly, because the keys were not in the left pocket either. Worse, both pocket zippers were open. It became instantly obvious that in passing the jacket back and forth through the day, sometimes wearing it and sometimes tying it around my waist, the zipper had worked open and the keys had fallen out.

I apologized to Sumara. Though I knew she was looking forward to the comforts of home, I told her we were going to need to retrace our steps until we found the keys. I was pretty sure we would find them quickly on the old dirt road that led from the parking area to the Pilot Rock Trail. It was on that road we had the most movement of the jacket, both going up and coming down.

Before we left to look for the keys we said a short prayer then began retracing our steps. Spaced out on either side of the road we walked slowly scanning the ground for the keys. If they still had the bright red carabineer attached that I had given Sumara for her water bottle they would have been easy to spot. But without that, their mostly dull bronze color would be hard to spot on the rocky, road.

We reached the trail head for Pilot Rock without finding the keys. It was getting late, but I realized we would need to backtrack our entire hike of the day until we found the keys. We were the only ones up in the area, a part of the Siskiyou Wilderness, and it was a long walk back home. Resolute, we retraced our steps back to the first dimensional doorway. On the trail under the forest canopy it was much darker and we really had to walk slow and bend down as close as we could to scan for the keys. Unfortunately, after looking just as hard on the way back, we still came up empty-handed.

Now the really daunting challenge was before us. We needed to retrace our steps up the Pilot Rock trail and if necessary scale the monolith again. There was no way we could backtrack through the area we had bushwhacked a shortcut, so we just had to hope the keys had not fallen out there and put all of our focus on the Pilot Rock ascent.

Climbing up the steep talus slope of the Pilot Rock trail was tiring for both of us. One trip like that in a day was great; two trips, not so great. But we had to go on until it was dark. We didn't feel we had a choice. We had our cell phone, but had no reception, even if there had been anyone to call for assistance.

By the time we neared the base of Pilot Rock Sumara said she was sorry, but she just couldn't take one more step up. I told her to wait for me and I would climb the monolith again by myself. About a half hour later, I met up with her at the same spot I had left her, but once again, no keys.

We still had hope and carefully scrutinizing the ground we had already traversed going up, we slowly, on increasingly overworked, shaky legs, made our way back down. When we arrived at the Jeep again it was almost dark and getting colder. I pulled out my wallet where luckily I was smart enough to keep a spare key to open the door. On Jeeps, the key that opens the door is normally the same key that starts the ignition, but a couple of years earlier I had to rekey the ignition when it broke. So now I needed two keys: the old one for the door and the new one for the ignition. Unfortunately, I only had a spare door key.

The first thing we did after getting in the Jeep was to buoy our spirits with one of Sumara's famous raw desserts, which we had stashed in the car as a rewarding treat to share at the conclusion of our hike. It melted in our mouths as we discussed the options for getting out of our predicament. While we were talking, Sumara completely forgetting our predicament for a moment, reached over to where the keys should be hanging from the steering column ignition, to flip them on to see what time it was on the digital clock. She pulled back her hand in disappointment when it reached the empty space where the keys should be dangling, because of course there were no keys there.

We wondered what we were going to do. If our phone worked I could at the very least call a tow truck to come and get us. I let out a sigh thinking about the hike I was going to need to take on the very rocky, unimproved road, hungry, in the dark, for two miles, to get close enough to the highway to get cell reception. I put my head down and cradled it in my hand as I contemplated one more effort my exhausted body was going to need to endure. Moving my hand off my forehead, I was staring right at the empty spot on the steering column where the keys belonged. To my utter amazement, they were swinging slowly back and forth in the ignition, motivated by some unseen force! I quickly looked over at Sumara and pointed at the swinging keys. We were both shocked and incredulous. We realized something momentous had just happened.

At first glance it would seem that this account would be better suited in the Divine Intervention chapter, and we certainly did give our thanks to God after the keys appeared, but the more I thought about it, the more I realized finding the keys back where they belonged, was not a gift from God. The gift from God was our paranormal powers, which God gave us, to teleport the keys from wherever they had fallen on the mountain, back into the Jeep when we needed them most.

Whether we did it or God did it, one way or the other the keys were teleported. I believe it was us, and that this is God's true gift of love to all of us: not to answer our prayers by doing things for us, but gifting us upon our creation with great paranormal abilities to work our own miracles, if we are willing to live in the light and discover and embrace our power.

Most psychic and paranormal gifts work easier and more powerfully when they are exercised with focus and passion. This is especially true with the greater powers. In our quest to find our missing keys, we had total focus and an escalating passion to discover them before the darkness of the night overtook us.

An interesting twist worth noting is what we were focused upon. The thought of teleporting our keys sadly never entered our minds. Instead we trekked off like a couple of Mundanes

Telekinesis

to find them searching with our eyes. Nevertheless, once we had backtracked our hike and returned to the Jeep empty-handed, teleportation was the only viable means for us to have the keys when we needed them. Unconsciously we called upon a hidden paranormal power. Though we were at a loss as to "how," when we sat in our Jeep contemplating a plan to get home, we were at our peak passion and focus of wanting to find our keys. And Voila! They appeared. Though we didn't focus on teleporting them, our passion and desire to have them manifested them for us, as that was the power which provided the most viable way to achieve our goal. It was the instinctual action necessary to produce the required result; little different than unconsciously moving your hand rapidly up to catch an object flying at you unexpectedly. Only this unconscious action gave us an inspiring and motivating glimpse of the vast potential that slumbers inside of us, waiting for us to awaken and call it out.

How You Can Practice And Expand Your Telekinetic Ability

In addition to doing your own variety of the pencil experiment from my college physics class, here are some additional exercises that I enjoy and have found helpful. Be patient and practice regularly and often to discover and increase your own telekinetic ability.

I encourage you to begin with very light objects. The less dense an object is, the more space there is between molecules. That creates more surface area for you to more easily affect the object with telekinesis.

Telekinesis is one of those paranormal abilities greatly enhanced by focus and concentration. Spoon bending, a form of telekinesis, is an exception, as it works best if you are unfocused. Remember, you are creating a beam of energy between you and the object. The object is moved by the force of the focused energy you apply to it. It's no different than if you were shooting an arrow at a distant target. If you didn't focus on the bulls-eye and concentrate on taking careful aim, but instead pulled your bow back and shot your arrow while admiring the clouds in the sky, it is highly unlikely your arrow would impact the target. It is the same with the telekinetic beam of energy you are sending. It must have a target and you must have focus and concentration to hit and affect the target.

Chapter 14 has some excellent focus and concentration exercises. For greatest success with telekinesis, be sure to become proficient in these exercises.

Telekinesis Exercise # 2

This exercise will be conducted with what is known as a 'PSI Wheel.' You can easily make one at home from a sheet of paper or a piece of aluminum foil. Or, if you prefer, you can buy one from many metaphysical stores.

If you would like to build your own, you'll just need 3 items: a 2 inch long sewing needle, a 2x2 inch square of typing paper or foil, and a small piece of clay or a cork 1-1 ½ inches in diameter.

1. Cut the paper into a 2-3 inch square; or you can use a 3x3 inch 'Post It' note.

Unleash Your Psychic Powers

2. Fold the square of paper in half, creating a rectangle and a strong crease line.

3. Unfold the paper, but not so much that you press the crease out. Now fold it in half the opposite direction. You should end up with a cross shape pattern formed by the creases.

4. Now make a diagonal fold through the cross pattern. You are folding the paper into a triangle.

5. Make one more diagonal fold of a diagonal from the other side.

6. Partially unfold your folded paper. You should have a square showing four crease lines, equal distance apart, creating 8 end points at the edge of the paper.

7. The next two steps create the 3 dimensional PSI Wheel. Hold the paper so one of the long crease lines that goes from one side of the paper to the other is sandwiched between your thumb and forefinger, with one hand sandwiching the crease on one side of the paper and the other hand sandwiching the crease on the other side. Now gently press the thumb and forefingers toward each other and simultaneously press the two hands on opposite sides towards each other.

8. Repeat this for the other linear crease. As you do so, you can alternate back and forth to the other crease and form your paper into a 3 dimensional PSI Wheel. You should end up with a paper with a sharp center point and four slightly angled vanes.

9. Make a small ball of clay and stick the needle upright into the clay with the pointy end up.

10. Gently set your PSI Wheel on top of the

Telekinesis

needle tip with an even balance. It is now ready for you to move it with the power of your auric field.

11. Sit in a chair at a table with the PSI Wheel on the table in front of you. Place your hands on either side of the PSI Wheel, 6-12 inches apart, palms facing each other.

12. Envision a spinning ball of energy swirling between your hands. Very quickly the PSI Wheel should begin to move. It may vacillate directions for a moment, then continuously begin spinning in one direction. And it may speed up considerably.

Advanced Practice

Find a glass bowl, a bell jar, or a sufficiently large glass that you can put over the PSI Wheel to insure there are no breezes from breathing or movement, or hot air emanating from your hands, that could be affecting the PSI Wheel. Place your hands on either side, without touching the glass and move the PSI Wheel with your auric field.

More Advanced Practice

Sit back 3 to 6 feet from the PSI Wheel still under a glass. Hold up your right hand with your palm facing the PSI Wheel but at least 3 feet away. Swirl and concentrate your auric energy inside of you, then shoot it down your arm, out your hand and move the PSI Wheel with the stream of force.

Even More Advanced Practice

Sit back at least 6 feet from the PSI Wheel still under a glass. Keep your hands at your side. Swirl and concentrate your auric energy inside of you, then focus it purely through the intention of your mind and move the PSI Wheel with the stream of force. Hint: Imagine yourself 'one' with the PSI Wheel. The molecules that form the PSI Wheel are part of the molecules that form your body. The PSI Wheel is as much an extension of you as your finger. Just like your finger, you can move it anytime you will it to be so.

Telekinesis Exercise # 3

In this exercise you will move a toothpick floating on water.
1. Set up the toothpick floating in a bowl of water on a table.
2. Sit nearby in a comfortable chair. Be sure not to touch the table with any part of your body during the exercise. Allow the water to become perfectly still and calm before you begin moving the toothpick.
3. Swirl and concentrate your auric energy inside of you, then focus it purely through the intention of your mind and move the toothpick with the stream of force. **Hint:** Imagine yourself 'one' with the toothpick. The molecules that form the toothpick are part of the molecules that form your body. The toothpick is as much of an extension of you as your finger is. Just like your finger, you can move it anytime you will it to be so.
4. Once you have movement of the toothpick, focus on controlling the movement by willing it to move to the right, then to the left, then forward, then backwards.

Advanced Practice

To insure there are no breezes, heat emanations, or table movements affecting the toothpick, place it in the bowl with the water and toothpick underneath a larger bowl turned upside down.

Telekinesis Exercise # 4

In this advanced exercise you will float a feather. Take a clean dry jar with a lid and place a feather inside. It should be a good size but still small enough that it does not touch any sides of the jar. Smaller feathers are OK as well.
1. Seal the lid on the jar with the feather inside.
2. Set the jar on a table and sit nearby in a comfortable chair. Be sure not to touch the table in any way.
3. Swirl and concentrate your auric energy inside of you, then focus it purely through the intention of your mind and move the feather with the stream of force. **Hint:** Imagine yourself 'one' with the feather. The molecules that form the feather are part of the molecules that form your body. The feather is as much of an extension of you as your finger is. Just like your finger you can move it anytime you will it to be so.
4. Move the feather. Once you have movement, lift the feather up so it is floating free inside the sealed jar.
5. Once the feather is freely floating, focus on moving it up and down and side to side as you will it to be so, rather than just aimlessly moving around inside the jar.

Telekinesis Exercise # 5

In this exercise you will learn to control fire. Control of fire is one of the more exciting

Telekinesis

aspects of telekinesis and this experiment is just the beginning of what you can do.
1. Light a candle of ½-1 inch in diameter, that stands 6-12 inches tall and set it on a table.
2. Remove all distractions from the room. You should be alone and insure you will be undisturbed.
3. Sit down comfortably about 2 feet from the candle, far enough away that neither your breath or any slight movement will reach and move the flame.
4. Look closely at the flame; notice the different parts, colors and translucencies.
5. Observe the tip and how it tapers and undulates.
6. Become one with the flame. Encompass it in your aura. Though you are too far away to physically feel its warmth, feel it with your aura.
7. Now focus on bending the flame in one direction or other; not just flickering, which is a movement that could be caused by a passing movement of air from any source. This is a focus to physically bend the flame at a sharp angle and keep it bent for a period of time far longer than a flicker.
8. You may be helped by holding up one or both hands with palms facing the candle and sending a concentrated beam of your aura through your hands at the flame.

Advanced Practice

Conduct the same exercise but eliminate any possibility of your breath or movement affecting the flame by putting the candle inside a glass cylinder with an open top for the smoke to vent.

More Advanced Practice

With the candle still inside the glass cylinder, sit in a comfortable chair far enough away from the table that you cannot touch it with any part of your body. Swirl and concentrate your auric energy inside of you, then focus it purely through the intention of your mind and bend the flame with the stream of force. Hint: Imagine yourself 'one' with the flame. The molecules that form the flame are part of the molecules that form your body. The flame is as much of an extension of you as your finger is; just like your finger you can move it or bend it anytime you will it to be so.

Spoon Bending

I'm happy to be able to end this odyssey of a book with a really fun form of telekinesis -- spoon bending. You may have heard of spoon bending. It was made famous back in the 70's by Israeli psychic, Uri Geller. There is some dispute, even among psychics, as to whether Geller was legitimately bending spoons with psychic powers or merely using magicians tricks. But from my own experience I know that spoon, fork and knife bending is a real phenomenon. I became a big believer when I watched my daughter bend them like they were made of clay when she was only 6 years old, including the stiff tines of forks and the thick bowls of spoons!

The concept behind psychically bending metal utensils is to inject psychic energy into the

Unleash Your Psychic Powers

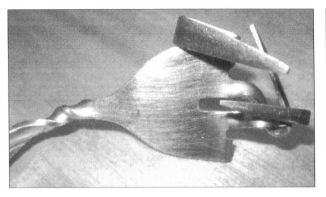

Forks and spoons bent our family when our youngest daughter was 6 years old.

utensil until it becomes soft like a stiff Tootsie Roll. Once at that point you can pretty much bend them into any shape you desire with little effort. Areas on the utensil where it is narrow and thin are easy to bend with just a little physical effort and no psychic energy, so you can't count bends at those locations, unless they include sharp twists. But when you start almost effortlessly bending the rigid tines of forks and the thick bowls of spoons, you know you are doing something supernatural.

How To Use Psychic Energy To Bend Utensils

In 2003, when my youngest daughter Angel was 6 years old, we had read a little about spoon bending parties they were having in San Francisco. My wife Sumara and I decided to give it a try ourselves. We went down to the local Good Will and purchased a couple of dozen used forks, knives and spoons from their basket of old utensils. We had a mixture of cheap thin ones and expensive thick, heavy ones.

When we got home we first began as is typical with psychic endeavors, by focusing on bending the utensils as we held them in our hands and applied light pressure at various spots. We both succeed in bending both forks and spoons right at the narrowest part of the neck but that was it. And we both agreed that was just done using our strength, because it didn't require

Telekinesis

much. While we were laser beam focused on our psychic task, Angel had picked up a spoon off the pile on the table and was playing with it. Neither of us paid attention to her because we wanted to remain focused on our own spoon bending projects.

After about 5 minutes and a couple of additional sacrificial utensils, neither Sumara or I had any success bending anything more than the narrow neck of the utensils. Taking a break we looked for the first time over at Angel. She was playing with a utensil in her hand and she had 2 laying on the table in front of her that were convoluted like pretzels!

"How did you do that Angel?" I asked curiously with a little awe.

"It's easy," she replied. "I just played with the spoon while I watched TV and it bent."

I had completely forgotten about the TV being on. It was out of my view from where I had been sitting at the table and I had asked Angel to turn off the sound when we began our bending experiments because we didn't want any distractions.

"Did you tell the spoon to bend?" I wondered.

"At first," she replied simply. "Then I just played with it in my hands while I watched TV. I thought you were bending them too."

"Yeah, we were." I answered. Just not with as much success as you had."

Then it dawned on me. Perhaps spoon bending was an anomaly in the realm of psychic powers. Instead of requiring focus, maybe it needed disinterest. That was a fairly radical thought in my mind, but the scientist in me decided it would only be fair to test the theory. So we turned up the volume and all watched TV while we "played" with another round of utensils. Like Angel had taught us, we did command them to "bend" before we forgot about them and began watching TV.

The results were beyond our expectations. The utensils bent so easily after just a couple of minutes that we could literally manipulate them into any shape we desired. It became a friendly challenge to see who could bend their utensil into the most interesting piece of art. Angel won every time. It was amazing all the twists turns and bends she could make the thickest points of the utensils do.

We also discovered in later experiments that you do not need to watch TV. The ***simple key is disinterest.*** We could sit and chat about school, or where we were going on our next hike, or relive our last adventure. The more disinterest we had, the easier the utensil ended up bending. The only other key was to focus for a brief moment right at the beginning, before becoming ***disinterested***, and command the utensil to "bend."

FINAL THOUGHTS

All of our lives we are programed to be dependent, not independent. How many of us depend upon the financial, and other material support of our parents long after we are adults? How many of us seek or accept government "assistance?" Not just obvious support like food assistance, but all types of subsidies, including special tax breaks, or even just standard permits and permissions for every aspect of our lives? Do you want to build a house? Don't forget the two dozen different people and agencies that will need to give you permission to build, continue construction and finally move in. You need government permission to move into your own house! Ninety-nine percent of us need approval of a bank to finance the house.

If you think about it, the list of actions you might like to take that require permission or assistance is ubiquitous and very long. They encompass nearly every aspect of our lives. We are not trained by parents, schools, work, religion or government to take unilateral action or be able to stand up on our own two feet and thrive. Nor are we even allowed to do so, even if we can. You may be financially independent, but there remains a bevy of government and society rules, taxes, regulations and oversights that require you to live within the box someone else created. At every point of our lives, in every direction we look, we are taught to ask some other party; be it parent, religious leader, teacher, employer, or government agency, for permission or assistance to do just about anything, and often just for basic necessities of life and living.

Religion often sets the foundation for a life of dependency. Most teach that man is nothing and God is everything. Subservience to the unseen, all powerful God, pleas through prayers for assistance in life, and obedience to the dictates and commandments of God are integral foundations of most religions. If a man or woman does succeed in any way in life, religions tend to teach that it is not because of their efforts as noteworthy as they might have seemed, but because God had mercy on them and allowed or facilitated their success. Therefore, they need to humble themselves to realize they did nothing themselves, but it was the unseen God who did all the work. All praise to God.

Please do not think I am bashing religion; I am not. I admire and appreciate how well religions of all persuasions help their members to be better people; more loving, more compassionate, more helpful and good neighborly. Religion has played an important and pivotal part in my own life. I am thankful for the life lessons I have learned, the better person I have become, and the greater closeness I have gained to "God" because of the teachings and examples of the religions and religious people I have been associated with. But my epiphany is that the entire nature of the relationship between God and man taught in religion of all faiths is an impediment to the true divine nature of men and women.

Religions have set the dependency template that all governments and institutions follow in one form or another. The relationship of God to man as taught by most religions, is one of a parent to a child. But unlike a real parent-child relationship, in a religious context the child never grows up. I don't believe that is the true intention of God any more than it would be the desire of any parent.

One of the greatest joys and fulfillment of a parent is to see all of their years of teaching by precept and example, of hard work and sacrifice for the benefit of their children, produce happy, empowered, self-sufficient adults. I know it is the same for every and any higher being people call God.

Understanding that makes all the difference in comprehending and accepting how and why we all have psychic abilities and paranormal powers. And why, because of the dependency template, our supernatural abilities are so challenging to learn and erratic to manifest, as well as why they tend to come out most powerfully and spontaneously in moments of crisis or passion, when there is no one to call for help and a person must save themselves.

I believe with all of my heart that each one of us has astounding paranormal gifts, given to us when the mold was cast that created us. They are as much a part of us as our eyes to see, or our mouths to eat or speak. With your eyes, you can choose to keep them shut despite all the distractions around. But if suddenly you are thrust into a crisis, they open up without thought, to take in the situation and aid you. Likewise you may choose to keep your mouth closed and not speak. However, when danger threatens, your mouth will open involuntarily to call for help, or say what needs to be said to overcome the crisis.

It is the same for the vast untapped psychic and paranormal powers that abide quietly inside of all of us, ready and waiting to rush out in great power at the times we need them most. Countless examples of real people in real situations have shown this to be so. But most people will go through life never experiencing a situation dire enough that their psychic or paranormal abilities spontaneously manifest to help them. Never realizing they actually have great power stirring within them, they give no thought to their most divine potential.

Our challenge is to not only realize that we are endowed with higher, advanced, untapped abilities, but to learn to call out and use our supernatural capabilities on a regular basis, not just in a crisis. I hope this book will help you to understand the amazing person you really are, and to unleash the great powers that dwell within you.

Thank you for giving me the opportunity to share some of my life's adventures with you and provide some suggestions that might help you have some more adventures of your own. I have a few more stories to tell, but they will need to wait for another book. Until then my friend and fellow paranormal seeker, it has been a pleasure to share with you. May you have great success in all of your endeavors.

Final Thoughts

Namaste,

Embrosewyn Tazkuvel

PS If you have enjoyed and benefited from this book, please be so kind to leave a nice review for it on Amazon to let others know of your experience.

May I conclude by sharing with you three of my favorite poems that never cease to uplift me and remind me of who we are, and the wonder that awaits our deeper discovery of ourselves.

Our birth is but a sleep and a forgetting:
The Soul the rises with us, our life's star,
hath had elsewhere its setting,
and cometh from afar:
Not in entire foregetfulness,
and not in utter nakedness.
But trailing clouds of glory do we come...
~William Wordsworth

Our deepest fear is not that we are inadequate. Our deepest fear is that we are powerful beyond measure. It is our light, not our darkness that most frightens us. We ask ourselves, Who am I to be brilliant, gorgeous, talented, and fabulous? Actually, who are you not to be? You are a child of God. Your playing small does not serve the world. There is nothing enlightened about shrinking so that other people will not feel insecure around you. We are all meant to shine, as children do. We were born to make manifest the glory of God that is within us. It is not just in some of us; it is in everyone and as we let our own light shine, we unconsciously give others permission to do the same. As we are liberated from our own fear, our presence automatically liberates others.
~Marianne Williamson

"I shall be telling this story with a sigh,
Somewhere ages and ages hence:
Two roads diverged in a wood -- and I...
I took the road less travelled by,
and that made all the difference."
~Robert Frost

UNLEASH YOUR PSYCHIC POWERS

Appendix A
CELESTINE LIGHT

The teachings of Celestine Light have helped to manifest and magnify my psychic and paranormal abilites far more than everything else I have learned combined. Below are a few of my favorite quotes from the **Oracles of Celestine Light** that have motivated and inspired me. Perhaps they will you as well.

"You are founded upon Celestine Light. You live, move and have your Soul filled with divine light, whether you know it or not." Genesis 11:101

"The masterpiece is not outside of you, it is inside of you." Genesis 11:55

"You were endowed with gifts of Celestine Light before you were born into this life- the power to hear when others have not spoken, the power to travel from one place to another without traveling, the power to levitate objects and yourself, the power to make fire by calling the aeon and focusing it in your hands. And many, many other powers of Celestine Light have you been gifted with." Vivus 99:84

"You are the master of the Celestine Light that dwells within you. If you choose to embrace the light, there is no darkness deep enough to overcome you." Vivus 27:10

"The people of the world understand that they are affected by mysterious aeons, but to them, the cause is unknown. Among the Children of Light, let those mysterious aeons be known and understood that they may be called upon as needed." Vivus 51:6

"It is in times of greatest challenge that the true person of light and power can emerge from within the shell in which they are usually held by everyday life." Vivus 58:22

"Never forget amidst the travails of mortality that you are sons and daughters of the divine Father and Mother and are connected in spirit to all living things both on Earth and beyond. You are radiant rays of light that can illuminate the deepest darkness." Genesis 11:49

"Now you are cast with the others into the darkness and forgetfulness of mortality for a lifetime. How can you best fulfill the purpose of this life? By reaching through the darkness and discovering yourself, the divinity from which you have come, and living the greater light which is revealed." Genesis 11:51

"There are those that say the Kingdom of God is outside of you; that it is in the sky and in the sea and in the temple built by man of great stones and precious woods. But I say unto you, that the greater Kingdom is inside of you, for you are the temple of light, built by God. When you come to know yourselves in purity, forgetting the conceptions of the world and the teachings of men, then you will realize that you are true sons and daughters of the living Father and Mother in Heaven and are inheritors of all that your parents have..." Nexus 24:2-3

"Even among the honest of heart, it is the nature of man to see and hear that which he wishes to see and hear; and to the contrary, he is blind and deaf. How many times have you held the answer to your question in your hand, but have not seen the truth because you were not seeking it?" Nexus 24:14

"If you will not listen to your heart, which speaks the truth your mind does not know, then you do not know yourselves, and you will dwell in poverty, and it is you who are that poverty, no matter the riches of the world which you may possess." Nexus 24:40

"Therefore take heed about what your eyes see and what your ears hear. Seek things that uplift and inspire rather than belittle and disparage. Seek things that warm your heart and calm your mind; not things that cause fear or anxiety. Seek association with situations, places and people that make you want to become more than you are, not encourage you to be less. Seek out that which is light and calls you to your greatness. And turn away from everyone and everything that does not." Vivus 99:55 – 99:59

"Marvel not at these things, for nothing is impossible to the Children of Light if they have virtue, faith, love, focus, knowledge, and a passion for that which they desire to occur." Vivus 72:9

Appendix B
THE INQUISITION

To understand and appreciate the freedom most people enjoy today to discover and expand their paranormal gifts, it's helpful to look at times in history where just the opposite was true. Things mean more to you, they have more value, from your possessions to your life, to your abilities, when you have some experience and understanding of what it is like to be denied your possessions, abilities and life you would like to lead.

When I was going into my senior year in High School, 72-73, my family moved to Spain. Prior to that time I had taken the social, cultural and political freedom in the United States, my home country, for granted. If anything I thought it was insufficient and had some degree of oppression. After I lived in Spain, which at the time was still under the fascist dictatorship of Generalissimo Francisco Franco, I came to appreciate far more the freedoms I had grown up with and taken for granted.

In Spain at the time, Franco ruled with an iron fist. Everywhere you looked there were quasi-police called the Guardia Civil (Civil Guards) that were Franco's enforcers on the local level. If they were not so deadly they would have seemed like characters out of a B grade comedy movie. They wore shiny black hats, rounded and flat on top, brimless in the front, with the wide brim in the back permanently upturned at a ninety degree angle. They traveled together in pairs on tiny 49cc motorcycles. It looked like they were riding around on children's toys. However, they were well armed, sometimes with machine guns strapped across their backs, and you knew they were not cartoon characters come to life.

The first six weeks we lived in a hotel as our house was not yet ready to occupy. One night after we had been there about a month we heard a horrendous, continuous outburst of gunfire. There were hundreds and hundreds of rounds fired, near enough that we could clearly hear them. As quickly as the onslaught had begun it suddenly ended. We all wondered "what in the hell was going on." My Dad, a naval commanding officer, was highly agitated and thought maybe the town was under military assault.

Guardia Civil

The next day as we had the opportunity to talk with others we heard a horrifying story. I cannot verify its veracity. But neither can I attribute the enormous, concentrated gunfire we heard that night to any other cause. According to the locals, there had been a gypsy encampment of about 150 men women and children about a kilometer from our hotel. Sometime during that night, two Guardia Civil were supposedly ambushed and killed by two men who were assumed by the Guardia Civil to be gypsies. Retribution according to the locals was swift and final. A large group of Guardia Civil grabbed machine guns from the armory and quickly went to the gypsy camp and formed a half circle around it. They ruthlessly proceeded to fire into the camp until every man, woman and child had been killed.

Though that was by far the worst fascist/dictator incident I had any experience with, there were many other minor, but still extremely irritating rules and regulations we had to obey. During my almost two year stay in Spain, my whole perspective on the freedom allotted in my own country changed drastically and I came to appreciate the freedoms I had always had, but never understood or appreciated before.

During the subsequent decades that followed my time in Spain, I have sadly watched the freedoms, personal privacy, rights and liberties Americans enjoyed slowly erode; inch by inch, so it is really not noticed as it is happening. The continually new status quo just seems normal to many people because the change was so gradual and not suddenly thrust upon them. But looking at the USA of today compared to the one I came to appreciate in 1973 - personal privacy, freedom and rights are definitely much less. And government intrusion into our lives with the subsequent dictates of what we can and cannot do, are certainly much more.

In this review of the Inquisition and the Salem witch trials, I hope you come to appreciate the freedoms you still have to explorer your psychic gifts, by comparing the laws of today with those of not so long ago. The mistakes of history tend to repeat themselves if the citizens do not learn from the mistakes and the lessons are not retained by subsequent generations.

The rise and spread of Christianity with its later prohibition and persecution of 'witchcraft,' brought an end to open displays of psychic gifts in most places in Europe by the 1400's.

Interestingly, Christianity did not always persecute those with paranormal gifts. In the very

The Inquisition

earliest days of Christianity, during the 1st through 3rd centuries, the Christians took a mixed view of psychic abilities. Many of the new converts had formerly been Pagans and still had affection for the old ways. Other converts, especially those coming from existing religions with strict guidelines, tended to condemn paranormal gifts based upon two ancient scriptures: Exodus 22:18 "You shall suffer not a witch to live," and Leviticus 20:27 "A man or a woman that has a familiar spirit, or is a wizard, shall surely be put to death: they shall stone them with stones: their blood shall be upon them."

By the early 400's Catholicism had been declared the only and official Christian religion and so it remained until the Protestant Reformation begun by Martin Luther in 1517 with the posting of his Ninety-five Theses. Around 420 AD a very influential theologian of the Catholic church, Saint Augustine of Hippo, presented his learned belief that only God could suspend or alter the natural laws of the world that every man lived within. He stated emphatically that neither Satan, nor self-proclaimed or imagined witches, had ability to invoke any type of magic or supernatural powers. He urged the church to simply ignore those who claimed paranormal gifts, saying it was merely a relic belief of the pagans who falsely attributed supernatural powers to someone other than the one God of Christianity. For nearly 800 years thereafter witches, wizards and paranormal practitioners were not overtly persecuted..

The treatment of practitioners of paranormal gifts began to change in 1208 AD when Pope Innocent III promulgated a new view of Satan by endeavoring to condemn the Cathar sect as heretics because of their belief that both God and Satan had supernatural powers. Prior to that time Christians thought of Satan as mischievous but powerless, in a similar way as the Norse demigod Loki was viewed.

In 1273, a whole army of supernatural beings were created by Thomas Aquinas, a Dominican monk. In his dissertation Summa Theologian, which quickly became foundational orthodoxy in the church, Aquinas contended that evil demons lurked everywhere in the world lusting to bring down mankind. One of his most ardent arguments was that demons led men into temptation and were able to extract the sperm of men and have sexual relations and impregnate women. Thus began an enduring association of witchcraft and sex.

By the mid 1400's, adherents of Catharism, a heretical Christian sect in disharmony with the Catholic church because of its dualistic and gnostic beliefs, began to be openly persecuted and many fled to Germany seeking protection with more liberal rulers from the spreading Papal inquisition. But many Cathars were caught in various lands, and the church decreed it was perfectly acceptable to torture them by any means to extract confessions. In the face of hideous torture that caused men and women to beg for death, of course they would say anything to get relief from the scorching pain. Many admitted to flying on poles to attend gatherings where Satan would appear as a goat and everyone would kiss his anus to show their loyalty. Others before they gasped their last breath from the never-ending torture admitted to having sex with demons or demons in the form of animals, causing storms, ruining crops and casting spells on neighbors. From these early inquisitions and torture the clear crime of witchcraft was formed.

In 1484, Pope Innocent VIII escalated the persecution of witches and practitioners of the paranormal by attesting as God's Pope that Satanists in Germany were meeting in secret sexual trysts with demons, casting spells to destroy crops and lives and causing the unborn infants of women to abort. The Pope charged two friars, Heinrich Kramer, an esteemed Inquisitor of sorcerers, and Jacob Sprenger, to investigate the extent of witchcraft in Germany and report back with recommendations on how to deal with them. Two years later they produced the Malleus Maleficarum. Unlike the old orthodoxy, this document identified witchcraft as the most serious problem facing the world. It became the gospel of persecution for the church and the dictionary for defining witchcraft. It attested that witches did in fact have supernatural powers and that it was the duty of every good Catholic to hunt them down and punish them severely or kill them as their actions warranted.

The Malleus instigated a pervading fear of witches and the paranormal as it related horrifying stories of witches that freely had sex with many demons, and who wantonly killed human babies and stole penises right off the bodies of men. Even worse, the penises would become individual living entities. As the friars explained, "What is to be thought of those witches who collect...as many as twenty or thirty (penises) together, and put them in a bird's nest or shut them up in a box, where they move themselves like living members and eat oats and corn?"

The Malleus Maleficarum was reprinted thirteen times during the next forty years and ushered in the height of the Inquisition. A good portion of the book gave hints and recommendations to judges and prosecutors when dealing with witches. Accused practitioners of the supernatural were women verses men about 4 to 1. This might account for why one of the recommendations in the Malleus when investigating possible witchcraft was to strip the suspect completely naked and then closely examine their body searching for a telltale moles that would be a sure sign they consorted with demons. They also encouraged judges to make sure defendants were required to walk backwards into courtrooms so they would be unable to cast spells on the judges and prosecutors.

It wasn't until the early to mid 1500's that convicted witches began to be executed in large numbers. This was propelled by outbreaks in various regions of witchcraft hysteria. In Geneva, Switzerland approximately 500 convicted witches were burned at the stake in 1515. With witchcraft charges flying, in 1524 authorities in Como, Italy executed over 1000 accused witches.

Though the Catholics created the definitions and procedures for dealing with witches, after the Reformation the Protestants adopted them with gusto. Protestant Germany, was swept by many underflowing tensions and strifes that had nothing to do with witchcraft. But accusing people of being a witch became a popular way to hurt an enemy. More accused witches came to be executed in Germany than in all the other countries of Europe combined.

One of the greatest outbreaks of witch hysteria was in France in 1571when an accused Sorcerer proclaimed at his trial that he had over 100,000 fellow witches and Sorcerers roaming the countryside. A countrywide panic ensued. To abate the panic and expedite the killing of witches, judges proclaimed that the usual protections of the law enjoyed by defendants did not

The Inquisition

apply to accused witches. This allowed them to be executed quickly before they could do more harm.

In 1580, Jean Bodin published On the Demon-Mania of Sorcerers which heralded the widespread use of children to inform against their witch parents, the necessity of acquiring skills of entrapment to catch witches, and the various instruments of torture that were found to be most effective in coaxing confessions.

According to historians, between 40,000 to 80,000 accused witches were executed in Europe during the 160 year period between 1500 to 1660. Many of them were burned alive tied to a stake, but others were drowned and some just tortured until they expired. The number of executions varied widely from one country to another with a high in Germany of about 26,000 executions and a low in Ireland of only four. England also had a relatively low estimate of 1,000 witch executions, with France recording about 10,000 during the same period. England and Ireland had stronger laws in place to protect the rights of defendants and greater requirements for proof of guilt, which is thought to have been the major reason their execution numbers were so much lower than the countries of the continent.

Scotland did experience half a dozen years of intense persecution of accused witches when King James, who had paid scant attention to them before, had an abrupt change of opinion after storms and calamities encountered traveling to and from his wedding to Princess Anne of Denmark.

Princess Anne had set sail from Denmark with a small fleet of ships intending to arrive in Scotland to formerly wed King James. (She had already had a proxy wedding in Denmark with a Scottish nobleman standing in for King James). From the beginning the trip was beset by calamities. While at Elsinore a cannon aboard a naval vessel exploded blowing out the thick metal back and killing two gunners. The following day another cannon suffered a similar failure when being shot to commemorate the visit of two Scottish noblemen. A gunner was killed and another nine were injured. As the flotilla departed the coast and headed out to sea they were beset by a fierce storm. Anne's ship, the 'Gideon', became separated from the fleet. It sprung a significant leak and sought refuge in Gammel Sellohe in Norway for repairs. The remaining ships of the fleet found her there having suffered another two deaths while at sea in the storm when two ships collided.

After repairs, the Danish fleet set sail once again for Scotland but Anne's ship quickly began leaking once again and was deemed unseaworthy. The fleet retreated once again to the safety of land and ported at Flekkero, Norway. Anne decided to return to Denmark by coach as winter was setting in making travel by sea very hazardous.

Once he heard of the events James traveled to Denmark to formerly wed his bride and they honeymooned for some months in Scandinavia before setting sail in March of 1590 for Scotland in the patched up Gideon. In a deja vu encounter for Anne, their fleet was once again assailed by a fierce storm. The Captain was confident in his ship and crew and pushed the ship through, successfully arriving at their destination in Scotland. But the Captain confided to King James that their storm was far from ordinary and surely was the diabolical work of witches.

Subsequently, six Danish women confessed to casting spells to create the storm. Having had his own life and his brides threatened by professed witches, King James became paranoid about the cursed beings that could command the elements and set out to rid Scotland of suspected witches. Beginning in 1591, he authorized extremes of torture to be used to extract confessions from suspected witches, and the penalty of being burned alive at the stake if found guilty. The North Berwick area became a hotbed for the witch hunters and dozens of accused witches were burned alive in the largest witch hunt in the history of the United Kingdom.

King Jame's fear and wrath lasted a half a dozen years. By 1597 he seemed to have realized he had overreacted, as his witch hunts were causing a greater disruption to his kingdom than the supposed witches. He ordered the prosecutors to require firmer evidence, backed by multiple witnesses and allowance of greater evidence to the contrary by the defendants, before guilty verdicts could be rendered. Thereafter the witch hysteria in Scotland settled down.

The height of the witch hysteria in England occurred between 1618–1648 during the Thirty Year War. The conflict was fueled by religious zealots stemming from a failed rebellion by Protestants on the continent trying to break free of the Roman Catholic Hapsburg empire. The civil unrest based upon religious differences made a ripe setting for accusations of witchcraft.

Across the channel in France there was a nationwide witch hunt between 1643 – 1645, with uncounted numbers of suspected witches being tortured and killed. The Provence of Languedoc alone accounted for 650 arrests. Arrest and persecution for witch craft began to abate by the late 1640's in most places in Europe. By 1648, Holland had already nullified all laws regarding punishment for witch craft.

The last witch executed in England was in 1682, when a senile woman named Temperance Lloyd, of Bideford, was executed. According to her defenders such as Sir Francis North, she ended up in the end confessing to the most fanciful things simply to put an end to her suffering.

The Enlightenment began blossoming in the late 1680's. Superstition, dogmatic religious views, and torture were replaced by empirical reasoning, skepticism and humanitarianism. The enlightened presented the argument that there simply was no empirical evidence that accused witches actually caused harm to anyone or anything, and that confessions extracted under unimaginably painful torture could not be construed as valid evidence. People from nobles to commoners began to take pride in being among the enlightened, and the era of prosecution for witch craft quietly ended in Europe. While Europe's witch persecutions were ending, across the ocean in the American colonies the final act was still waiting to take place in Salem, Massachusetts.

Appendix C
SALEM WITCH TRIALS

The witch hysteria in Salem, Massachusetts, lasted for just four months from June to September in 1692. But that was long enough to execute nineteen accused witches and wizards by hanging. Among them was the former minister of the town, who had been living in Maine. A twentieth accused witch, a well-respected farmer in his eighties, was executed by crushing beneath heavy boulders for his refusal to take part in his witch trial. Hundreds of additional citizens languished in jail for months awaiting their trials for witchcraft. When the educated elite of Salem finally began to question how so many respected citizens could suddenly all become witches and wizards, the paranoid hysteria and lust for blood ended quite suddenly. By May of 1693, the last of the accused witches had been quietly released from jail without prejudice.

It all began during the extremely cold winter of 1692. Young Betty Parris, the ten year old daughter of the Reverend Samuel Parris and his wife Elizabeth, began to act very irrationally. Throwing herself on the floor in a fit, hurling the Bible across the room, contorting in pain, diving under furniture and barking like a dog were among her several symptoms.

Soon, several of Betty's playmates including Elizabeth Hubbard, Susannah Sheldon, Mary Warren and Ann Putnam Jr., daughter of a prominent town family prone to quarrels with other villagers, began exhibiting the same frightening symptoms.

With each passing week the girls exhibited rabid new symptoms. One of the additional afflictions were claims of spectral visits by certain Salem citizens intent on attacking them in their spectral form. Three of the girls accused Dorcas Good, a four year old girl, of having attacked and bitten them while in spectral form. The tiny, young girl was imprisoned in the filthy jail for eight months and had to watch while her mother Sarah was led away to the gallows to be hung as a witch.

Attacks upon the cabal of young girls by spectral forms, became one of the primary evidences used to convict other citizens of being witches and wizards during their trials. The band of young accusers became like polished actresses when testifying in court, including antics of fainting upon seeing the accused paranormal practitioners, and being struck dumb and unable to give further testimony. The court considered the fainting and being struck dumb to be damning evidence on their own merit.

Imprisoned in jail for months on end, the women torn from their children, the men unable to work at their professions and earn a livelihood to feed their families, many of the imprisoned began to confess to the crimes they were accused of, with all the sordid details people imagined, in hopes of a less severe sentence and escape from the gallows.

The second woman to confess to her sins was Deliverance Hobbs who admitted to obeying the Devil's command to pinch three girls and later flying on a pole to an open field to attend a witch's Sabbath. So many men, women and children were being accused and imprisoned awaiting trial that the colony "teetered on the brink of chaos" and the overcrowded, highly unsanitary jails came close to standing room only.

During this time Governor Phips had been away on a trip to England. When he returned to the chaos, he quickly instituted procedures to move pending trials to conclusion. Normal rules of evidence were discarded and judges with little or no training in the law, heard cases where hearsay, gossip, unsupported assertions and surmises were accepted as facts, and fanciful testimonies of malevolent visits by "specters" of the accused became expected.

Judges also allowed wtches touching to be admitted as evidence. The scene was set when one of the young girl accusers would start thrashing about in convulsions in the court and the accused witch or wizard was ordered by the judge to touch the afflicted girl. If the girl ceased her flailing about upon touch of the accused, it was considered firm proof that they were guilty. Judges also admitted body moles as proof of a person being a Devil's minion, as it was assumed that witches familiars, supernatural beings that assisted witches and wizards, would suckle on witches moles. Both men and women had clothing opened and were physically inspected in the puritanical court to confirm evidence of moles, which were more commonly known as "witches marks." Those unfortunate enough to be accused of witchcraft were not allowed to have the aid of legal counsel, or call favorable witnesses to testify that they were not practitioners of the dark arts, or had not done any of the actions they were accused of doing. If they were found guilty, no appeal of the sentence was permitted.

The first person brought to trial for witchcraft was the sixty year old owner of two taverns named Bridget Bishop. She was an easy target because of her outwardly displayed disdain for her puritanical neighbors. The fact that her taverns not only served cider ale, but also allowed patrons to play the 'Devil's game of shuffleboard', even on the Sabbath, left many of the towns citizens with axes to grind against her and accusations of witchcraft as the perfect format to attack her.

Testimony against her included a field hand who claimed to have seen her specter stealing eggs and then transform into a cat. Probably hoping to be saved from the gallows by incriminating another, Deliverance Hobbs and Mary Warren, both who had already confessed to being witches, testified that Bridget was also a witch. Several of the girls from the gang of young accusers, testified that Bridget had visited them as a specter and terrified and afflicted them. A local townsman, Samuel Grey, claimed that the accused had appeared at his bedside at night as a specter and tormented him. One of the guards that had been riding on the coach transporting her claimed a part of the Salem meeting house broke off and fell to the ground as they passed it and she gazed upon it. Her jury delivered a quick judgment of guilty and she was hanged on Gallows Hill on June 10, 1692.

Hanging of Bridget Bishop, June 10, 1692

A conclusion can be drawn that many of the people bearing false witness of spectral visits by the accused were doing so simply to protect themselves from accusations. In Salem, life for many during those four months came down to either being one of the accused or one of the accusers.

The pace of trials picked up as the summer of 1692 progressed and many perfectly respectable citizens, especially those who criticized the witch trials, were rounded up, jailed and tried as accused witches or wizards. One particularly egregious case to modern sensibilities was the trial of a pious, respected, elderly woman named Rebecca Nurse. She was a member of the extended Topsfield family which had been having quarrels with the prominent Putnam family over some time. Along with two of her sisters she had been accused of witchcraft by multiple members of the Putnam family, including the child Ann Putnam Jr, and the matriarch Ann Putnam, Sr., who testified that Rebecca had attacked her and a friend, pinched them and demanded that they sign her Devil's book.

Apart from testimony of the Putnams and their friends, the most damaging evidence against Rebecca was the fact that one of her neighbors had died shortly after she had lectured him about his hogs trampling through her garden and rooting up all of her plants. Despite the accusations against her the jury returned a verdict of "not guilty." This verdict did not sit well with Chief Justice Stoughton. He demanded that the jury reconvene to deliberate and reconsider a statement by Rebecca that could be construed as an admission of guilt. In all likelihood, Rebecca who was 71 years old and almost entirely deaf, had not understood the question. Upon returning the jury reversed the previous decision and found the elderly lady "guilty of witchcraft." On July 19, 1692, Rebecca was hung on barren Gallows Hill along with three other convicted witches.

Some historians have concluded that young Ann Putnam Jr. was coerced to give false testimony by her parents at many of the trials, to help them punish people with whom they had quarrels or sought revenge against for past feuds. Credence is lent to this line of reasoning as one of the prime motivators of the Salem witch trials, by the statement of Ann Putnam Jr. years later in 1706, when she admitted giving false testimony and publicly apologized.

"I desire to be humbled before God for that sad and humbling providence that befell my father's family in the year about ninety-two; that I, then being in my childhood, should, by such a providence of God, be made an instrument for the accusing of serveral people for grievous crimes, whereby their lives was taken away from them, whom, now I have just grounds and good reason to believe they were innocent persons; and that it was a great delusion of Satan that deceived me in that sad time, whereby I justly fear I have been instrumental, with others, though ignorantly and unwittingly, to bring upon myself and this land the guilt of innocent blood; though, what was said or done by me against any person, I can truly and uprightly say, before God and man, I did it not out of any anger, malice, or ill will to any person, for I had no such thing against one of them; but what I did was ignorantly, being deluded by Satan.

And particularly, as I was a chief instrument of accusing Goodwife Nurse and her two sisters, I desire to lie in the dust, and to be humble for it, in that I was a cause, with others, of so sad a calamity to them and their families; for which cause I desire to lie in the dust, and earnestly beg forgiveness of God, and from all those unto whom I have given just cause of sorrow and offense, whose relations were taken away or accused."

Ann Putnam's parents both died in 1699, 7 years after the Salem witch trials. She was left with the responsibility of raising nine siblings between the ages of 7 months to 16 years. She never married.

The trial of George Burroghs, the former minister of the village, was one of the turning points in swaying public opinion to at least consider that they might be acting in haste or even in error. Reverend Burroughs had graduated from Harvard College in 1670 and had chosen a spiritual path as a non-ordained minister for his profession. After ministering in Maine he moved to Salem in 1680, but abruptly returned to Maine after just two years, following a bitter dispute with John Putnam, an uncle of his later accusers, over money.

Having been the well-respected minister of Wells, Maine, for nine years, his placid life was violently interrupted when authorities from Salem barged into his house while he was eating dinner with his family. They accused him of witchcraft from his days in Salem, hauled him back to the village and imprisoned him on May 4th. He remained in the squalid jail unto his trial on August 5th.

At his trial and after his execution, dozens of people gave testimony that he was not just a wizard, but far more, a Sorcerer and a Conjurer! In addition to the now expected testimony of the cabal of young girls flailing and convulsing about and the testimonies of spectral visits, Reverend Burroughs was accused of feats that no ordinary wizard could possibly perform. It was said that though small in stature he carried a heavy barrel of mollases, something no man his size should have been able to do. It was also testified that he could run faster than a horse,

Salem Witch Trials

and would often appear at a location far distant from where he had been but a short time before. The gang of young girls went into such violent convulsions in his presence that the judge ordered them removed from the courtroom for their own safety.

Though the Putnam's and their allies gave numerous testimonies against him, many people also stood up for him, even though they risked being accused of being fellow witches and wizards by so doing. It was testified that, "he was self-denying, generous, and public spirited, laboring with humility and with zeal." Another defender said that Reverend Burroughs was, "an able, intelligent, true-minded man; ingenious, sincere, humble in spirit, faithful and devoted as a minister, and active, generous and interested as a citizen." Historical papers in the Maine statehouse show he was highly regarded with great confidence by his neighbors and counted as a friend and counsler by many. All traits highly unlikely to be imbued in a minion of Satan. In Salem, thirty-two upstanding citizens signed a petition proclaiming his innocence. Before he was executed one of his accusers recanted her testimony saying she had made it out of fear and that it was groundless. Nevertheless, on August 19th he was brought to Gallows Hill to be executed along with three other men and one woman that had also been convicted of being wizards and a witch.

Waiting for his turn to be hung, Reverend Burroughs once again proclaimed his complete innocence and suddenly began to recite the Lord's Prayer in a strong voice that carried to the ears of all in attendance. He said it perfectly without hesitation or error. The crowd was stunned, as this was a feat thought to be impossible for any minion of Satan. Most of those in attendance were deeply moved and agitated that he was about to be unjustly hung. They cried out for his sentence to be commuted as he could not possibly be a Sorcerer. Those in charge of the execution refused, saying he had his day in court and lost. They hung him quickly before the crowd could organize in his defense. Many of the depositions in the court record against Reverend Burroughs were actually obtained after his trial and hanging to help counter the rising unease among the populace concerning his execution. Just twenty years later, the government admitted the wrongful execution and gave financial compensation to his surviving children.

One of the last trials and worst travesties of justice, was of a properous farmer named Giles Corey. Mr. Corey was a member in good standing of the village church and well-liked and respected by many in the village, but it did not help him. He was aligned with the Porter faction at church, which was in heated theological disagreement with the Putnam faction at the same church. In April of 1692, he was accused by three of the young girls from the cabal of young accusers of visiting them in spectral form and asking them to write in his Devil's book.

All three young girls were under the strong influence of Ann Putnam Sr. and her husband. Daughter, Ann Putnam Jr., was the first accuser, followed by Mercy Lewis, a serving girl that lived in her household, and Abigail Williams, who was living with her uncle, the current town minister and ally of the Putnams. Ann Putnam subsequently added another accusation that an unnamed ghost had appeared to her and said he had been murdered by Giles Corey. More girls from the gang of young accusers came forward recounting assaults by the specter of the "dreadful wizard."

Mr. Corey was eighty years old, a considerable age for the late 1600's. He had prospered and was known as a hard, stubborn man who wasn't afraid to voice his opinion, including condemnation of the witchcraft proceedings.

Both Giles and his wife Martha were arrested and left to languish, chained in the jail for five months until their trial in September. Corey refused to participate in the proceedings where nearly a dozen accusers gave depositions that he was a wizard, including one that said he had seen Mr. Corey serving bread and wine at an unholy Sacrament of witches.

Mr. Corey knew his conviction was a foregone conclusion. Historians feel his main motivation in refusing to participate in his trial, besides disdain and contempt for the court, was the hope that by not being present he would avoid a conviction and loss of his farm to state seizure upon his death. He had recently deeded the farm to his two son-in-laws and he hoped his actions would keep all that he had worked a lifetime for, with his family.

But the court did not take kindly to Mr. Corey's affront to their proceedings. They invoked the punishment of peine et fort also known as Pressing, which had never before been used in the colony of Massachusetts. Stripped naked while his neighbors watched, Corey was laid on the ground on September 19th, and a large board was placed on top of his body. Heavy boulders were then stacked on the board slowly crushing him beneath their weight, eventually suffocating him when he could no longer expand his lungs to take even the slightest breath. Wanting his ordeal to be over Giles yelled out to his executioners ordering them to add more weight and to do it quicker.

Corey's punishment had previously been declared illegal. There was no law that permitted it and it violated the Massachusetts Body of Liberties which forbid cruel and torturous punishments. Giles Corey is the only person ever executed by Pressing by order of a court, in the entire history of the United States. His gruesome execution certainly played a part in the rising opposition to the Salem witch trials and their subsequent quick end. He is often remembered as a martyr who "gave back fortitude and courage rather than spite and bewilderment." On September 22, three days after Corey's Pressing, eight additional convicted witches and wizards were executed, including Giles wife Martha. They were the final victims of the Salem witch hunts.

Appendix D
THE ADVENTURES OF MARVELOUS MARGERY

Despite her detractors, one of the more enigmatic Spirit Mediums ever tested by the Scientific America investigators was Mina "Margery" Stinson Crandon (1888-1941). Houdini seemed to have a particular vendetta against Margery and even wrote a pamphlet denouncing her and detailing his explanation of her paranormal feats. Though some of the phenomena she manifested could be duplicated by magicians such as Houdini, looking at the full picture of her examination by the Scientific America committee shows many unexplained and baffling phenomena.

Mina was an unlikely medium and a less likely fraud. She was the wife of a wealthy Boston surgeon who was a respected instructor at Harvard Medical School. He was considered part of an original American family as his ancestors had come over on the Mayflower. Mina was known for her sharp mind and quick wit. She had no reported paranormal experiences growing up and nor any interest in Spirtualism until the first manifestations of her abilities in 1923.

It all began when her husband invited some of their friends over for a dinner party to experiment and see if they could contact the dead in a seance. Several paranormal manifestations occurred. By a process of asking each person one by one, to leave

Mina "Margery" Stinson Crandon

Unleash Your Psychic Powers

the room while the manifestations were occurring, it was determined that the paranormal activity came about because of Mina.

Despite the fact that she was an unknown amateur who had been manifesting paranormal abilities less than a year, when the committee heard about the astounding array of manifestations that had suddenly sprung up out of nowhere from the upper class wife of a respected doctor, they invited her to sit and be tested. J. Malcolm Bird, secretary of the committee, gave her the pseudonym "Margery" to protect her identity because of her husbands position at Harvard.

Mina stated right up front that she would not accept any prize money. According to J. Malcolm Bird, secretary of the committee, confident in her ability, she cheerfully allowed herself to be tested at least 90 times to very exacting procedures! Can you imagine sitting for 90 different seances with the dubious committee members devising new challenges with each one to try to disprove your abilities? Modern skeptics make their negative conclusions after just a single test of a psychic. Part of the testers challenge with Margery was she produced so many effects that they could not explain by scientific or magician trick means, they felt the need to persist in testing her. Rather than announce her authentic and a winner of their contest, they were sure if they just tested her enough times, in a wide variety of ways they would eventually find a way to prove she was a fraud.

Because seances most often happened in darkened rooms, Margery and other mediums were searched prior to a séance to prevent the possibility of aids hidden on their body. However, considering she was an upper class lady, Margery's husband did not allow an invasive physical search of her body. Despite that restriction or perhaps because of it, every effort was made to insure that she was immobilized and unable to physically move or affect anything in the room. Immobilization methods included locking her in a coffin-like box that only allowed her head, hands and feet to stick out, with separate committee members holding onto each foot and hand for the entire time of the séance. On multiple occasions, they wound her entire body, mummy-like, in several layers of adhesive tape, completely immobilizing her.

More commonly they would form a séance circle around a table with every member continuously holding hands and touching calves to calves and ankles to ankles, to insure nobody in the room including the medium could in any way physically move to influence any object. Despite all these precautions, the spirit Margery called in, easily produced telekinetic and paranormal effects throughout the room including ringing bells, snuffing out candles, breezes, raps, spirit writing in several languages, apports of various objects, several different spiritual voices from all around the room and making a rocking chair on the other side of the room begin to rock.

Margery brought in the spirit of her deceased brother Walter, who died in a train crash in 1911. While Margery was always pleasant and co-operative, Walter had disdain for the testers, particularly Houdini. Her brother's spirit had made it clear from the time he had first spoken through Margery that he was not interested in giving inspirational messages as many other deceased people did through mediums. Rather, in his down-to-earth, profanity enhanced

The Adventures of Marvelous Margery

speaking style, Walter explained he was there to make it clear that there was life after death by demonstrating physical phenomena from the other side.

From the beginning of the tests in 1924, very strict controls were created to insure that the results demonstrated by the medium would be completely free from fraud of any kind, conscious or unconscious. If any tricks were employed by Margery to create paranormal effects, the committee felt confident their procedures would detect them.

Margery with Houdini on her left, at a Seance test

Because their controls were so exacting and Margery so confined, yet still able to easily produce a wide array of paranormal effects, Houdini seemed to see her as his ultimate challenge to reveal as a fake. After she had undergone many tests he was outspoken in denouncing her and giving his explanation of how she produced telekinetic movements and other paranormal effects. Among students of the paranormal, Margery is famous to this day, and Houdini's claim to have unveiled her as a fraud is said by believers to be the greatest myth perpetuated by the skeptics and completely unfounded based upon the facts.

Houdini seemed to be willing to resort to any means to disprove Margery's psychic abilities. During one long night of tests, while Margery was physically confined as was normal, Houdini brought an electric doorbell into the room and challenged Walter, the spirit entity, to ring the doorbell placed on the middle of the table, which everyone sat around.

When the doorbell remained silent, Houdini smirked. But then Walter's voice spoke loud and clear, taunting Houdini, "Still trying to get some publicity by haunting seance rooms, eh?" Walter told the committee that Houdini had rigged the doorbell so it could not ring. He told Malcolm Bird to take the bell out of the room and examine it. Bird was dubious, but did finally take the bell out of the séance room. He was not happy when he returned and reported he had found pieces of rubber affixed inside the bell preventing the ringer from ringing. Houdini did not admit guilt, but was chastised that the committee was not served in any way by dishonesty in the testing procedures.

No sooner had the admonishment been given than the electric bell began to ring in vigorous spurts followed by Walter's mocking voice booming through the room, "How does that suit you Mr. Houdini?" Walter, Margery's all-seeing spirit brother, continued to methodically reveal

Houdini's tricks whenever he tried to skewer the testing results as he was discovered to have done on other occasions.

One of the other notable instances of Houdini using disreputable means to try and falsify the test results came from the placement of a ruler. Houdini had designed the tight fitting, coffin-like box that Margery was encased within, with just her hands, feet and head sticking out with each of her limbs being firmly held by a committee member. During the séance, the spirit of Walter accused Houdini of surreptitiously placing a ruler inside of Margery's box so he could accuse her of cheating by using the ruler as an extension tool to move objects. After the séance ended the box was inspected and as Walter had revealed, there was a ruler inside. Subsequently, one of Houdini's assistants admitted that he had placed the ruler in the box before the séance at Houdini's instruction, so the master conjurer would have something to prove Margery a fraud in case he could not disprove her other manifestations.

Houdini had also boasted he could duplicate any effect Margery produced. But when the committee pressed him to prove the claim for all of Margery's effects, he deferred, saying he had no time as he had to leave town on business.

One of the physical manifestations Houdini was initially at a loss to explain was the flying megaphone. Margery was sitting in a chair. Houdini was on her left, tightly holding her hand and with his bare calf and ankle pressed tightly against hers. Another committee member was on her right holding on to her in a similar manner. The remaining committee members formed a circle, all joined at their hands and lower legs in the same way. When a megaphone suddenly appeared in the air above them, Walter called out "Where would you like me to put the megaphone," Houdini responded, "Here between my feet." Obligingly the megaphone suddenly flew through the air and came to rest right between Houdini's feet. Somewhere either before or after the megaphone appeared, the screen behind Margery fell over. Supporters said the screen fell over after the appearance of the megaphone. Opponents, including Houdini, claimed it fell over before.

When he met with the committee members at a hotel afterward the master magician confessed that how the megaphone had flown through the air and landed between his feet as he requested left him completely baffled. Though he felt he could explain the other manifestations, he told the committee members, "One thing puzzles me. I don't see how she did that megaphone trick." Upon more pondering however, Houdini came up with a theory of how it was accomplished that is laughable when you realize the lengths he would go to to try and explain her manifestations. Here's a diagram from the pamphlet Houdini later printed to denounce Margery by giving his explanation of her feat.

He claimed that she first fooled everyone into thinking they were holding onto her hands and feet when they really were not on the right side. Thus freed up on her right he imagined she must have stretched back with her right foot and tipped over the screen behind her chair, then leaned far back to reach down and grab the trumpet on the floor that had been laying on the floor behind the screen. Of course it had conveniently not moved when the screen fell backwards

The Adventures of Marvelous Margery

and she was easily able to locate it simply by touch while she was stretched out backwards in the dark room. According to Houdini, Margery then stuck it on top of her head so it would appear to those in the darkened room to be floating. Then when given instructions to make it appear between Houdini's legs she jerked her head with exactly the correct amount of velocity and whipping action for it to fly through the air and accurately reach its target. Of course all this being done without those holding her left hand and foot detecting any movement on her part, in fact still thinking they were holding both of her hands and feet! I'm sorry, Houdini's explanation that an upper  class lady, who was not a professional medium, magician, contortionist or gymnast, could go through all those very physical convolutions at all, let alone undetected, strains credulity far more than to just accept that the spiritual manifestation was real. Nor do I think Houdini himself could have pulled off the feat the way he described Margery supposedly doing it.

Another unlikely act Houdini thought up as a way to explain tables tipping during Margery's seances was that she bent forward and lifted the table with the back of her head as he diagrammed in the drawing below in his pamphlet denouncing her. Although this would certainly be a possible method it seems unlikely that her movement bending forward to lift a table with her head could have been done without making a sound or movement detectable by those holding her hands and feet, even if she had been willing to do it.

With such a co-operative and remarkably patient psychic, the Scientific America testing committee continued to come up with more and more strenuous tests to challenge Margery's paranormal abilities. In one arduous test, colored water was carefully measured and put into Margery's mouth to insure she could not open her mouth during the séance and speak in Walter's voice. But as Margery was not trance channeling Walter, but merely acting as the psychic bridge to physically bring his spirit to the room, the fact that she had a mouth full of water was irrelevant. Walter and several other spirit entities continued to freely speak during the seance. When the séance was finished, the testers carefully removed the colored water from Margery's mouth. They were more than surprised when after measuring the quantity they found it had diminished by less than a teaspoon.

However, because a small amount of the colored liquid was missing, some of the testers insisted on a more full-proof test. While the next séance was in progress, they inserted a balloon into Margery's mouth and inflated it to open her mouth wide and completely block her ability to speak. They were dumbfounded when Walter and his spirit friends continued to clearly talk back and forth with one another. Several of the spirit entities derided the committee members for putting Margery through such ordeals and scoffed at their attempts to prevent them from speaking.

One of the more unexplainable paranormal manifestations by Margery was of spirit ecotoplasm. This was a white substance that would issue out of the medium, usually from the nose or mouth. Many fake mediums commonly produced it by using surgical gauze dipped in phosphorescent paint or some other goop to make it appear to have an otherworldly quality. The ectoplasm that issued from Margery often seemed different to observers. Sometimes it had a distinct ethereal nature yet still seemed to have substance. It also sometimes, but not always, had an eerie luminescence in the darkened room, similar to the ectoplasm last seen with the medium Eva Carriere. However, where Eva's ectoplasm would extend from hand to hand and could conceivably be artificially created by something she was holding, the luminescent ectoplasm issuing from Margery was recorded as originating from her on one end, but freely moving and expanding on the other end without physical connection to her or any other person.

Because the ectoplasm was purported to be from the spiritual realm but physically connected to Margery, before the committee first began testing his wife, her physician husband, fearing potential harm, insisted that committee members each sign an affidavit that they would never touch the ectoplasm. In one séance however, an overzealous member disregarded his signed affidavit, with disastrous results for Margery. As the ectoplasm spread out from Margery and passed over his hand, he reached out to touch it. Like almost every event with Margery there are two accounts of what happened next. Supporters claim the ectoplasm instantly

Eva Carriere producing Ectoplasm in 1912

The Adventures of Marvelous Margery

vanished and Margery let out a bloodcurdling scream of pain. The session quickly ended and she was ill and hemorrhaging for several days. Opponents claim the session ended without incident and that Margery only fainted later when told someone had touched the ectoplasm while she was in a trance.

On another occasion, while Margery was in a deep trance, a committee member decided to see if she was faking by sticking a large, thick needle into her hand. To his disappointment she did not flinch, but she suffered great pain upon coming out of her trance and ended up with an infected wound.

During another séance, a committee member had devised an experiment that used caustic chemicals. During his fumbling around while Margery was in a trance, he spilled the corrosive chemical on her, severely burning her skin where it made contact.

After Margery had been exhaustively tested for a six week period, the committee was split about whether what they had observed was real or tricks they had simply not been able to uncover. J. Malcolm Bird for one, was enthusiastic in his belief in Margery's abilities and began publishing multiple articles praising her. As more and more committee members began to agree they had found a person with true paranormal abilities, Houdini became furious that they could draw such a conclusion. As he had publicly and vocally staked the position that all mediums were fake, if the Scientific America committee deemed her authentic Houdini might have felt it threatened his own credibility and standing as a master magician.

Houdini published a booklet in 1924 entitled, Houdini Exposes the Tricks Used by the Boston Medium Margery, to stake his position and reasons for calling her a fraud. He continued to be incensed at members of the committee that had opposite opinions. He vented his anger to the point of accusing fellow committee members Carrington and Bird of being collaborators helping Margery to perpetrate paranormal frauds.

In fact, Hereward Carrington went publicly on record saying that after over 40 seances with Margery, he had come to the "definite conclusion that genuine supernormal would frequently occur. Many of the observed manifestations might well have been produced fraudulently… however, there remains a number of instances when phenomena were produced and observed under practically perfect control."

Due to the many paranormal occurrences they could not explain, the committee in all likelihood would have declared Margery an authentic medium despite the doubts they had about the authenticity of some of her manifestations. But a single incident of what seemed to be undeniable fraud, tainted the entire body of her 90+ demonstrations.

One of the spirit manifestations sometimes left behind after a séance, would be a piece of paraffin wax with one or more spirit fingerprints embedded in it, laying in a bowl of water on the table. One such artifact, supposedly left by the spirit of Walter, proved to be the fingerprint of a dentist from Boston who admitted to giving Margery a small piece of wax with the imprint of his fingers. Following this revelation the majority of the committee members concluded that despite all the unexplained phenomena Margery manifested, the one incident of proven fraud was enough to disqualify her.

Considering she was not a performer or a professional medium and had just in the last year discovered her ability, did not act as a medium for money, refused to accept prize money, wasn't doing it for fame, as her true identity was originally kept secret, allowed herself to be physically constrained in a number of exceptionally confining manners, allowed herself to be tested over 90 times, and consistently despite every physical constraint continued to produce a wide variety of paranormal effects, some that even Houdini could not explain, one can only wonder how despite the single case of proven deception, the Scientific America committee could have denied declaring her authentic.

Why if she was an authentic medium did Margery stoop to hiding fake fingerprints in wax to delude her investigators? It is not likely we will ever know the answer as Margery never revealed more about the incident. But neither should that be the accepted conclusion to the matter. Just like there was no proof or admission by Houdini that he was the one that put the rubber in the bell to silence it, so too there was no proof that Margery was the one who left the wax fingerprint impressions in the room. It just as easily could have been Houdini or another member of the committee seeking to discredit her after she had successfully passed the extreme gauntlet of tests they had given her during a grueling six weeks. Even if she had obtained the wax imprints from the Boston dentist that does not irrefutably lead to the conclusion that she placed them in the séance room. Houdini was a master magician, which would include being a master at sleight-of-hand. It is not out of the realm of possibility that Houdini may have acquired the wax imprints from Margery by dubious means and placed them in the room to discredit her. Considering he had been caught setting up other items like the bell that wouldn't ring to discredit her, and the ruler to insinuate the use of aids to simulate telekinetic movement, it has to be considered that the wax imprints were just another attempt on his part.

Appendix E
MISTRESS OF LEVITATION EUSAPIA PALLADINO

Another medium famous for the telekinetic and paranormal effects she manifested, but also for accusations by skeptics that she cheated, was Eusapia Palladino (1854-1918), the Italian woman whose spirit, after her death, was claimed to be brought in by Nino Pecoraro, the medium who failed to produce any spiritual manifestations once Houdini had securely tied him to a chair.

While she was alive Eusapia was considered one of the most amazing and authentic spiritual mediums, despite multiple instances when she was accused of cheating in her seances. Is it possible for a medium to be both authentic in some instances and a cheat in others? Most who believed in Eusapia's abilities vocally exclaimed, "yes!" Many supporters also suspected interference with the intention to discredit Eusapia, on the part of some of the investigators.

What cannot be disputed is that for 28 years, from 1890 to 1918, dozens of eminent scientists, including multiple Nobel prize winners, in Italy, Russia, Poland, England, America, Germany and France, subjected her to scientific tests in rigorously controlled conditions, in light good enough for them to observe her every movement and action. Though many had come hoping to be able to

Eusapia Palladino

prove her a fraud, most left as converted skeptics, forced to conclude that her phenomena and manifestations were genuine, when no other explanation of science or magicians tricks could account for them.

As Margery, the well-educated wife of a respected doctor and a member of the 'high society,' was an unlikely person to become a spirit medium, Eusapia was just as unlikely, but from the other end of the social spectrum. A coarse, uneducated, Italian peasant, her mother died shortly after she gave birth to Eusapia in 1854. Her father was later murdered when she was twelve, leaving her a parentless, poverty stricken orphan.

After the death of her father, friends and relatives hired Eusapia out as a nursemaid to a family living in Naples. From the beginning it was a fractious relationship. Eusapia was a stubborn and willful child. She caused the family repeated upset by not only refusing to bathe, but her flippant disdain to even comb her hair. The family sought to help her in life by arranging for her to learn to read, but she steadfastly refused that kindness as well. Even later in life she was barely capable of signing her name. In exasperation the family dismissed her.

Her psychic gifts began to manifest after she sought shelter with some friends who had an interest in Spiritualism. One night while friends of the family were visiting they tried having a séance to see if they could get the table to tilt. They had no success and someone suggested adding the young orphan to the group to see if one more person added to the circle would make a difference. And what a difference she made! Almost as soon as she sat in on the circle the table began not just to tilt but to levitate! But that wasn't all! Bottles and glasses throughout the room began to jitter and clank, bells started ringing and curtains in the house began to blow vigorously. Eusapia was reportedly frightened by her abilities and deferred from using them until it seemed the family was going to send her to a convent. Once she agreed to sit in on more seances the family agreed to keep her. But Eusapia seemed to chafe even living under the roof of friends who admired her for her paranormal abilities. She soon moved out and took a position as a laundress, which allowed her to live independently at a young age.

Some time afterward she married Raphael Delgaiz a small-time merchant, and worked for some years with him during the day, while continuing to hold seances at night for friends and to further discover her own abilities. When she felt confident, she began charging for her seances.

Word of the unusual manifestations that were witnessed during her seances brought her to the attention of a wealthy couple named Damiani, who were influential in Italian Spiritualist circles. Realizing she was special in her gifts, they offered to help improve her social skills and integrate her into a higher level of society where more well-to-do Spiritualists could give her career and finances a boost. Eusapia rudely declined and expressed no interest in fraternizing with a higher social class.

Dr. Ercole Chiaia's Report On Palladino

Her uneducated, coarse and rude demeanor would have condemned her to a life unknown outside of a small circle of followers in Naples had she not had a visit in 1886 from Ercole Chiaia, a well-to-do doctor and researcher of the occult. After witnessing her paranormal feats during a séance, Dr. Chiaia wrote a public letter to Cesare Lombroso, a famous Italian criminologist and psychiatrist.

Writing as if he were recounting his observations of a patient, Dr. Chiaia made a case for the famed detective to come and help ascertain whether Eusapia was demonstrating the actions of an unknown force. Though at the time Lombroso declined, the open letter publicly spread word of Eusapia's abilities far and wide. She saw an immediate increase in the number of people seeking to be a part of her seances, as well as a greater amount of money they were willing to pay.

Dr. Chiaia wrote: *"She is 30 years old and very ignorant; her appearance is neither fascinating nor endowed with the power which modern criminologists call irresistible; but when she wishes, be it day or night, she can divert a curious group for an hour or so with the most surprising phenomena. Either bound to a seat or firmly held by the hands of the curious, she attracts to her the articles of furniture which surround her, lifts them up, holds them suspended in the air like Mahomet's coffin, and makes them come down again with undulatory movements, as if they were obeying her will. She increases their height or lessens it according to her pleasure. She raps or taps upon the walls, the ceiling, the floor, with fine rhythm and cadence. In response to the requests of the spectators something like flashes of electricity shoots forth from her body, and envelops her or enwraps the spectators of her marvelous scenes. She draws upon cards that you hold out, everything that you want --- figures, signatures, numbers, sentences, by just stretching out her hand toward the indicated place.*

If you place in the corner of the room a vessel containing a layer of soft clay, you will find after some moments the imprint in it of a small or large hand, the image of a face (front view or profile) from which a plaster cast can be taken. In this way portraits of a face at different angles have been preserved, and those who desire so can thus make serious and important studies.

This woman rises in the air, no matter what hands tie her down. She seems to lie upon empty air, as on a couch, contrary to all the laws of gravity; she plays on musical instruments --- organs, bells, tambourines --- as if they had been touched by her hands or moved by the breath of invisible gnomes. This woman at times can increase her stature by more than four inches.

She is like an India rubber doll, like an automaton of a new kind; she takes strange forms. How many legs and arms has she? We do not know. While her limbs are being held by incredulous spectators, we see other limbs coming into view, without her knowing where they come from. Her shoes are too small to fit these witch-feet of hers, and this particular circumstance gives rise to the intervention of a mysterious power."

After this letter and subsequent visits during the next few months by prominent Spiritualists at her seances, Eusapia's fame spread quickly. Many of her manifestations such as raps on the table and walls and bells ringing, were common at seances conducted by any competent medium. But several others, such as her entire body rising in the air; drawing any figure or words desired on paper others held without touching it; the facial or hand imprints left in bowls of clay far across the room; and the ghostly hands and feet that reached out all around her in addition to her own that were all being held by "controllers" at the séance, were either very rare manifestations or had never before been seen, and they greatly buttressed her reputation.

Investigation of Palladino in Milan, Italy in 1892

Invited to visit Milan, Italy in 1892 for a series of controlled, scientific investigations of her phenomena, Eusapia conducted seventeen seances for Professor Schiaparelli, director of the Observatory of Milan, Professor Gerosa, G. B. Ermacora, Alexander Aksakof, Baron Carl du Prel, Charles Richet and others in attendance that were part of the Milan Commission. Excerpts from their report observed: *"It is impossible to count the number of times that a hand appeared and was touched by one of us. Suffice it to say that doubt was no longer possible. It was indeed a living human hand which we saw and touched, while at the same time the bust and the arms of the medium remained visible, and her hands were held by those on either side of her."*

After the completion of all of her seances, the report made particular note of those conducted in bright light, concluding, *"In the circumstances given, none of the phenomena obtained in more or less intense light could have been produced by the aid of any artifice whatever."*

Eusapia Palladino's Amazing Table Levitations

For a 28 year period, Eusapia Pallidino was rigorously tested by scientific experts, professional psychic investigation committees, Nobel Prize laureates, magicians and professional criminologists from several countries. Sometimes they concluded that a few of the common Spiritualist phenomena she demonstrated were created fraudulently. Eusapia even admitted that she often played with the investigators at first when she was tested by cheating just to bother them. But when she got serious, amazing manifestations began to happen that defied explanation. Some phenomena were suspected of being fraudulent by the investigators, but they admitted to not being able to discern the method.

However many paranormal phenomena Eusapia produced completely baffled the investigators. They seemed to not only be impossible to the known laws of physics, but impossible to be fraudulent, as the investigators subjected her to pre-seance search, secured her hands and feet during the séance, conducted the séance under fully lighted conditions and personally checked above and under the table during the séance to insure there were no hidden wires or other devices being used to create the effects. In most instances, how Eusapia manifested the phenomena she did remained an unsolved mystery.

One of the most dramatic phenomena manifested by Eusapia and one of the most difficult to try to explain as cheating, was her levitation of tables. Though tilting tables on two legs was common at seances by other mediums and could easily be done by cheating, Eusapia levitated all four legs of the tables far off the ground under fully lighted conditions, even bright sunlight.

Mistress of Levitation Eusapia Palladino

Investigators would crawl under the tables while they were levitating trying to figure out how it was being done. They never did. Following below are some pictures of Eusapia's levitating tables in various locations from private homes to strict scientific settings.

As you view these pictures please keep in mind that purely from a physics standpoint, even if she was somehow using some part of her body to exert a lifting force on the table, it would be entirely beyond the capabilities of even a strong man to lift all four legs of a table entirely off the ground and hold it at shoulder height from a position sitting at the end of the table. The amount of functional

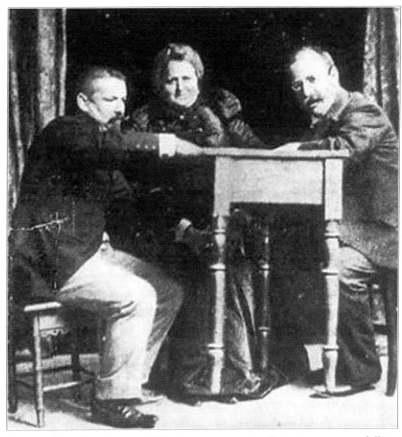

It seems from the picture as if the two men are actually trying unsuccessfully to push the table down. There were multiple reports from Eusapia's séances that no amount of force even from multiple people applied together, could push down tables she was levitating.

weight increases with the distance an object is away from the body. If you want to try your own simple experiment to prove this point, take a large push broom, hold it with one hand placed in the middle of the handle and the broom standing vertically with the brush portion at the top and the end of the handle resting on the ground. Now lift it vertically. As the entire broom only weighs a couple of pounds a 4 year old child could do it. Now stretch the broom handle out horizontally with the brush end on the floor and your hand grasping the very end of the handle. Now try to lift it up and hold it in a horizontal position perpendicular to your body. Though it only weighs a couple of pounds, with the weight positioned a few feet away from your body, lifting and holding the broom perpendicular from your body will be an impossible task. Now try to imagine doing it with a table that weighs 15 to 20 pounds.

Magicians can do marvelous tricks, but they also require elaborate setup before the event and specially constructed equipment and props to pull off their illusion. When mediums were tested by

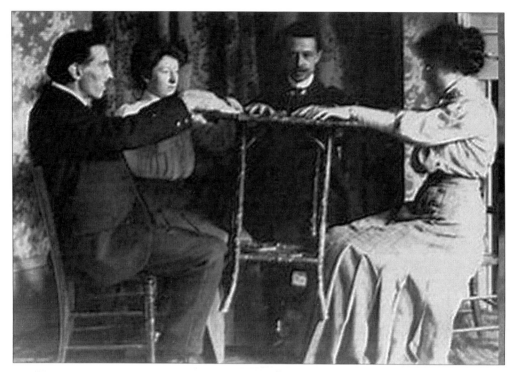
Excellent picture clearly showing the table is not in contact with any part of the bodies of any of the four participants, other than the palms of their hands lightly resting on top of the table. And the table is at least one foot off the ground.

scientific committees there was no possibility of hidden mechanical devices, confederates to assist them, or anything preset and prepared to aid them in the room. And unlike magicians performing on a stage set some distance from the audience, Spirit Mediums held hands and joined feet with the investigators that sat right next to them, searched them before the séance, and were constantly on an eagle-eye lookout for any indication of trickery. A challenge I would give to any skeptic and particularly modern magicians and illusionists is to duplicate Eusapia's feats of levitating tables under the same conditions.

Palladino in Paris

In 1905, Eusapia visited Paris, where Nobel laureates Pierre and Marie Curie, along with future Nobel prize winner Charles Richet investigated her, accompanied by several other prominent scientists including William Crookes and future Nobel laureate Jean Perrin.

The Curies were exacting scientists. They were keen observers and took scrupulous notes of the seances which were conducted in full light. Just as they had discovered the mysterious radioactive element Radium, they approached the séances as a scientific experiment to determine if there was some unknown force of physics at work in the paranormal manifestations.

Mistress of Levitation Eusapia Palladino

This picture clearly shows the man who is the "control" ensuring that Eusapia could not be using trickery to levitate the table. She is using her raised right hand to initiate the paranormal force to lift the table upward. Even if she had a rope attached from her right hand to the table top neither she, nor even a strong man, could lift it to the height it is, from the angle she sits, just using the strength of one arm. Meanwhile the "control" is ensuring that no other parts of her body can be employed to aid the table in lifting. His left hand is covering both of her knees and his right foot is covering both of her feet, while his right hand is securely holding on to her left hand.

On July 24, 1905, Pierre wrote to his friend Gouy the results of their first experiments with Pallidino. *"We have had a series of séances with Eusapia Palladino. It was very interesting, and really the phenomena that we saw appeared inexplicable as trickery; tables raised from all four legs, movement of objects from a distance, hands that pinch or caress you, luminous apparitions. All in a [setting] prepared by us with a small number of spectators*

Notable about this picture, is that in addition to Eusapia and the five participants sitting around the table holding hands, there are two additional observers standing right beside the table intently observing, with one of them apparently taking notes. The male participant at the end of the table is stooping down so he can see under the table to insure no trickery taking place. The bright light reflecting in the large mirror in the background shows a fully exposed window at the opposite end of the room with accent curtains at the top, bathing the entire scene in very bright sunlight.

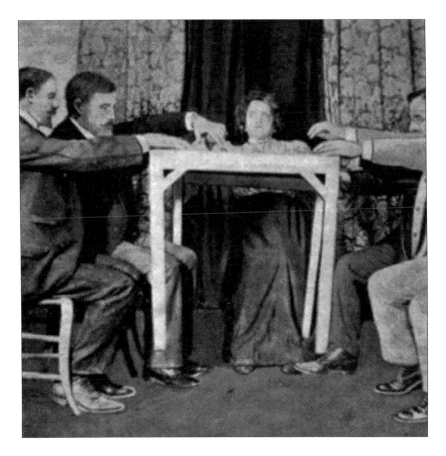

This is another picture taken in full light that seems to show all participants just lightly resting their palms on the table top, with all feet firmly on the ground and no part of their bodies touching the table. Eusapia's left foot is covered by the foot of the man on her left. While her right foot appears uncovered by the foot of the man on her right, we can clearly see the projecting points of both of her knees through her dress so she is not using her legs to somehow surreptitiously lift the table.

all known to us and without a possible accomplice. The only trick possible is that which could result from an extraordinary facility of the medium as a magician. But how do you explain the phenomena when one is holding her hands and feet and when the light is sufficient so that one can see everything that happens?"

In subsequent letters to Guoy, including one he sent just five days before his accidental death, Pierre Curie wrote, *"I hope that we will be able to convince you of the reality of the phenomena or at least some of them."* Pierre explained he was planning on continuing experiments *"in a methodical fashion."* He concluded, *"There is here, in my opinion, a whole domain of entirely new facts and physical states in space of which we have no conception."*

One of the participants in some of the seances with Eusapia and the Curies was Charles Richet who would become a Nobel Laureate in 1913 in physiology. He left the following account of one séance he attended. *"It took place at the Psychological Institute at Paris. There were present only Mme. Curie, Mme. X., a Polish friend of hers, and P. Courtier, the secretary of the Institute. Mme Curie was on Eusapia's left, myself on her right, Mme. X, a little farther off, taking notes, and M. Courtier still farther, at the end of the table. Courtier had arranged a double curtain behind Eusapia; the light was weak but sufficient. On the table Mme. Curie's hand holding*

Mistress of Levitation Eusapia Palladino

Eusapia's could be distinctly seen, likewise mine also holding the right hand... We saw the curtain swell out as if pushed by some large object... I asked to touch it... I felt the resistance and seized a real hand which I took in mine. Even through the curtain I could feel the fingers ... I held it firmly and counted twenty-nine seconds, during all which time I had leisure to observe both of Eusapia's hands on the table, to ask Mme. Curie if she was sure of her control ... After the twenty-nine seconds I said, 'I want something more, I want uno anello [a ring].' At once the hand made me feel a ring ... It seems hard to imagine a more convincing experiment ... In this case there was not only the materialization of a hand, but also of a ring."

Another attendee, Jules Courtier, struck down the frequently asserted belief of skeptics that some type of mass hypnosis was taking place during seances, making participants imagine they were seeing phenomena that were in their imaginations. Courtier reported that in experiments conducted in bright light, with Palladino's upper body in full view and her hands and feet secured and also in full view, automatic recording instruments in the room recorded molecular vibrations and movement of objects some distance from Palladino.

1908 investigation of Palladino by the Society for Psychical Research

In 1908, the Society for Psychical Research of London, England, which had examined Eusapia some years earlier with inconclusive results, decided to test her once more with three expert and skeptical investigators, two of which thrived on exposing fraudulent mediums. The three formidable investigators included, W. W. Baggally, a practicing magician; Hereward Carrington, an amateur conjurer, whose expose book, *The Physical Phenomena of Spiritualism* (1907) is still considered a reliable source to discover the tricks of fraudulent spiritual performances; and Everard Feilding, a lawyer and psychic researcher who had exposed many fraudulent mediums. They held eleven seances in November and December in a room at the Hotel Victoria in Naples, occupied by a member of the committee.

Their highly anticipated report, published as Part 59 of the Proceedings of the Society for Psychical Research, concluded that the paranormal phenomena they witnessed were not only genuine, but inexplicable by means of fraud or any magical conjuring. Even Frank Podmore, an ardent opponent of Spiritualism, and member of the society, admitted Palladino might be genuine. Commenting on the report he said, *"Here, for the first time perhaps in the history of modern spiritualism, we seem to find the issue put fairly and squarely before us. It is difficult for any man who reads the Committee's report to dismiss the whole business as mere vulgar cheating."*

After the sixth séance, Everard Fielding, renounced his skepticism. *"For the first time I have absolute conviction that our observation is not mistaken. I realise as an appreciable fact in life that, from an empty curtain, I have seen hands and heads come forth, and that behind the empty curtain I have been seized by living fingers, the existence and position of the nails of which were perceptible. I have seen this extraordinary woman, sitting outside the curtain, held hand and foot, visible to myself, by my colleagues, immobile, except for the occasional straining of a limb while some entity within the curtain has over and over again pressed my hand in a position clearly beyond her reach. I refuse to entertain the possibility of a doubt that it could be anything else, and, remembering my own belief of a very short time ago, I shall not be able to complain, though I shall unquestionably be annoyed when I find that to be the case."*

Following the Society report, Richert summarized twenty years of investigations into Palladino's telekinetic abilities: *"There have perhaps never been so many different, skeptical and scrupulous investigators into the work of any medium or more minute investigations. During twenty years, from 1888 to 1908, she submitted, at the hands of the most skilled European and American experimentalists, to tests of the most rigorous and decisive kind, and during all this time men of science, [who] resolved not to be deceived, have verified that even very large and massive objects were displaced without contact."*

Concerning her spiritual materializations he added, *"More than thirty very skeptical scientific men were convinced, after long testing, that there proceeded from her body material forms having the appearances of life."*

Palladino in the United States

Palladino visited the United States for 7 months beginning in November of 1909. It was the scene of both one of her greatest condemnations of fraud and one of her most ringing endorsements of authenticity.

After having conducted at least twenty seances at various locations with good reports, Eusapia sat for investigators at Columbia University. Both there and at the house of Professor Lord, observers claimed to have caught her in numerous tricks. The US press raked Palladino over the coals as an exposed fraud, but Hereward Carrington one of her investigators back in Europe, scorned the US newspaper accounts as sensationalism and inaccurate.

It would seem in Eusapia's case, from records of many observers over the years, that she was occasionally a cheat for small manifestations, while almost always being credited with being authentic for the great ones. Does that make any sense? How can that be and why would she bother to cheat with small things like pretending to make flowers apport that she had had hidden on her person, but then levitate a table with all four legs over a foot off the ground, in bright light, with the investigators checking over and under, undeniably assuring it was a real phenomena? Her actions left almost every scientific investigation group split between those who thought one trick proved that everything must be a trick, and those who were adamant that her great manifestations were authentic.

One of her defenders, Camille Flammarion, while admitting Palladino sometimes cheated, gave her opinion as to why: *"She is frequently ill on the following day, [of a séance] sometimes even on the second day following, and is incapable of taking any nourishment without immediately vomiting. One can readily conceive, then, that when she is able to perform certain wonders without any expenditure of force and merely by a more or less skillful piece of deception, she prefers the second procedure to the first. It does not exhaust her at all, and may even amuse her."*

It would appear from contemporary accounts that she had three reasons for occasionally cheating on the small phenomena. First, she was very playful and enjoyed the reactions of her scientific, high society observers who would first be smug when they thought they had caught her cheating, and then be dumbstruck when she would manifest the larger, inexplicable phenomena. Second, and this was especially true as she became older, manifesting the greater paranormal phenomena was very tiring and draining of her energy. She would often be lethargic and exhausted after a powerful séance. It would seem on at least some occasions, she hoped that smaller tricks, if undetected, would be sufficient to satisfy those in attendance and save her the effort required to manifest the authentic phenomena. Lastly, as she told a newspaper reporter during her tour of the United States, that she was just giving the skeptics what they wanted. *"Some people are at the table who expect tricks—in fact they want them. I am in a trance. Nothing happens. They get impatient. They think of the tricks—nothing but tricks. They put their minds on the tricks and I automatically respond. But it is not often. They merely will me to do them. That is all."*

Eusapia would have returned to Europe disgraced if not for a séance she held for Howard Thurston (1869-1936), who was at the time the foremost magician in the world. When he traveled from city to city on tour his entourage included 8 railroad cars. He investigated Eusapia as a skeptic, certain he would be able to prove her a fraud as he had done with previous mediums. He came away an awed believer. Here is his account in his own words:

"I witnessed in person the table levitations of Madame Eusapia Palladino ... and am thoroughly convinced that the phenomena I saw were not due to fraud and were not performed by the aid of her feet, knees or hands."

On another occasion he elaborated with a more detailed account of his observations.

"I do not believe that ever before in the history of the world had a magician and a sceptic been privileged to behold what I then looked upon. I saw Eusapia place her hands on that table I had examined so carefully. I saw it lift up and float, unsupported in the air; and while it remained there I got down on my knees and crawled around it, seeking in vain for some natural explanation. There was none. No wires, no body supports, no iron shoes, nothing—but some occult power I could not fathom. ... I demanded more proof, and with bewildering willingness the strange old lady agreed. Mrs. [Grace] Thurston held her feet, I held her arms. And even then, thus guarded and a prisoner, the table rose again!

When it finally crashed back to the floor again before my very eyes I was a defeated sceptic. Palladino had convinced me! There was no fake in what she had showed me. ... If after reading what I have said of this adventure into the realm where my magic cannot penetrate, the reader doubts, not my word, but my observation, let me say this: My career has been devoted consistently to magic and illusions. I believe I understand the principles governing every known trick. ... In all my seance examinations I train all my faculties against the Medium, watching for the slightest evidence of trickery. I am willing to stake my reputation as a magician that what this Medium showed me was genuine. I do insist that woman showed genuine levitation, not by trickery but by some baffling, intangible, invisible force that radiated through her body and over which she exercised a temporary and thoroughly exhausting control."

Modern Aberrations

Despite modern scientists disdain for claims of ESP, there is undeniable evidence of the paranormal that continues to pop up in scientific inquiries of non-related research and observation. This is particularly true in the field of psychology. Psychologists continue to be fascinated by the unexplained manner in which the human body sometimes seems aware of unpredictable or harmful events before they occur; kind of like the comic book character Spiderman's "spidey sense." These visceral, internal warning alarms are documented to exceed the laws of chance. That very conclusion was drawn by Julia Mossbridge who led a trio of researchers from Northwestern University that reviewed 49 previous professional articles noting the unexplained ability of humans to have a sixth sense. This was demonstrated by physiological responses such as increased heart rate or change in skin conductance, to portending danger or something that would cause them discomfort.

An example of a test from the articles would be to have participants shown a series of images with a short time lapse in between. Most of the images would be benign, like a flower or a child blowing bubbles. But every now and then there would be a threatening picture like a coiled rattlesnake preparing to strike. Test subjects were hooked up to multiple pieces of equipment to monitor their heart rate and other physiological norms.

The fact that they knew that somewhere in the pictures they would be shown frightening ones, did not create an apprehensive response as one benign picture after another was shown. But in far more cases than expected by statistical norm, many participants showed a reliable ability to know that the next picture coming was going to be a scary one. Just before they would see the picture their heart rate increased along with measurable and immediate changes in all their other physiological measurements.

To ensure the most conservative results the investigation team put aside 23 articles that did not meet their exacting standards. According to Ms. Mossbridge, the remaining articles clearly showed, "...remarkably significant and homogenous results of this meta-analysis suggest that the unexplained anticipatory effect is relatively consistent..."

To date, no scientist or researcher has been able to explain how test subjects are able to show by measurable physiological responses, that they are aware of what will be occurring before it happens. Astutely, rather than attributing the cause to some supernatural ability, the Mossbridge trio concluded it was caused by an unknown aspect of normal senses. They related, "The cause of this anticipatory activity, which undoubtedly lies within the realm of natural physical processes (as opposed to supernatural or paranormal ones), remains to be determined."

One interesting and unique idea came from the Mossbridge trio. They suggested that because most people are not very attuned to the subtly of their senses, and because the body gives physiological indications warning of things to come, that an app could be created that monitored the body indicators and send a warning alarm to their smart phone whenever the body signs suddenly started changing, warning of impending danger that they were not recognizing from their usual perceptions.

Challenges in Creating Tests of Psychic Abilities

There are two big challenges to proving paranormal powers to skeptics, disbelievers and investigators such as Randi. First is the challenge to design tests that can take into account the subtly of many psychic gifts and the unique forms of energy associated with them, that may not be measurable by standard methods and equipment. Metaphysics literally means beyond physics. Though I firmly believe that all psychic and paranormal abilities are rooted in functions of our bodies that we all possess, I also believe these abilities transcend and are more comprehensive than can be measured by scientific equipment designed to measure far more mundane energies.

Second, investigators must have enough patience to wait out the fickleness of psychic gifts and to create testing environments that lend themselves to producing rather than retarding manifestations. Most psychics, with most paranormal gifts, cannot simply call them out on demand unless they are very practiced. I imagine at least 70% of all valid paranormal gifts ever manifested occurred spontaneously, without warning, and often times without any understanding of what had just occurred by the person whom experienced it. Even professional psychics, if they were honest, would admit that their gift is not always present when they want it to be. Even more so if they are in a situation that makes them nervous, or in an energetically hostile environment.

Certainly the unpredictable fickleness of these abilities may account for why famous mediums such as Margery and Eusapia sometimes resorted to little acts of cheating. It is certainly not a stretch to consider they may have sometimes manufactured the results their impatient investigators were seeking, when after sitting in séance for an hour or more nothing real was manifesting on its own. Most of the time, most true psychic gifts are not like a light switch. You cannot just flip a switch and have them suddenly come on and go off.

As an example, I sometimes am asked to discover the Soul Name for various individuals. This is the name they gave themselves before they were ever born on this world, but they no longer remember it. Though it can be spelled various ways, the sounds of each syllable are vitally important. In those sounds are special resonances, unique to the individual, as no two Soul Names are alike. Hearing each sound, especially if by their own voice, triggers an energy inside the person that contains a unique ability to propel them toward special character and accomplishment goals they called upon themselves to achieve in this life. Discovering this special name and the meaning of each of the sound syllables, often takes me 2-3 hours of psychic reflection and inquiry. I would like to be able to just sit down for a few minutes and have the name come to me, but it is never that easy. Often times I'll be seeking for an hour and just draw a complete blank. When the name finally comes, it is a often in a flood, with the name and the meaning of the sounds coming suddenly and unexpectedly.

Appendix F

MASTERING YOUR BRAIN WAVES OF POWER

"The power to move the world is in your subconscious mind." William James

As I look back on my life and how easily psychic and paranormal gifts have come to me, of course I feel blessed. But I also owe a large part of the ease to an aspect of my being that was frowned upon by my parents, my teachers, my first wife and others who have known or worked with me. The cause of their displeasure was that I frequently drifted into an Alpha state of mind, often at the most inopportune times.

I have always been a vacant viewer. I could glance at a wall, or a person, or a scene outside and be as if spellbound; looking but not seeing; my thoughts completely empty. I wasn't a very good student in high school because I would look out the window for a moment at the sun dappled trees and luscious green grass and in the blink of an eye I would just be vacantly staring out the window as if I was hypnotized. Whatever the teacher was talking about would instantly be tuned out to unintelligible background noise, if I heard it at all. Most of the time I wasn't daydreaming or thinking about anything. I was just gazing out the window in a daze. And no, I wasn't on drugs. I have never used or even tried, any type of mind or mood altering drug in my entire life. With the natural euphoria I have for life and the calming peace of the blissful alpha state so easy to reach, drugs were never even considered.

Both those with psychic and paranormal abilities and those who research them, tend to agree that reaching an Alpha State in your brain is very helpful in achieving successful supernatural experiences. The brain is the master organ of the body and all other functions, including the manifestation of psychic or paranormal abilities, are directly or indirectly connected to brain activity.

Unleash Your Psychic Powers

Neuroscientists, who study the brain as a profession, use EEG (electroencephalograph) machines to measure brain waves, which are the pulses of bio-electrical energy moving through the intricate neural network of the brain. The "frequency" in which the brain waves move refers to how fast the brain wave is traveling. This is recorded on the EEG machines with a sine wave of peaks and valleys The Hertz (Hz) refers to how many wave tops (cycles) occur in one second on the EEG.

Until recently, brain waves were categorized with 5 frequency levels, with some slight variations in opinions regarding the transition points from one level to another:

Delta Wave: 0.1 – 4 Hz

Theta Wave: 4 – 8 Hz

Alpha Wave: 8 – 12 Hz

Mu Wave: 8 – 13 Hz

Beta Wave: 12 – 30 Hz

You'll notice that one wave category ends where the next one begins except with the Mu Wave, which overlaps both the Alphas and Beta waves. Mu Waves are a different type of brain wave that are seen simultaneously with either the Alpha or Beta waves, but only in a narrow specific area of the brain that controls voluntary motion. They are usually not considered when looking at the frequency step progression of the other brain waves.

Brain Waves, Frequencies & Functions

Unconscious			Conscious	
Delta	**Theta**	**Alpha**	**Beta**	**Gamma**
0.1 – 4 Hz	4 – 8 Hz	8 – 12 Hz	12 – 30 Hz	25 – 100 Hz
Instinct	**Emotion**	**Connection**	**Action**	**Power**
Survival	Drives	Body Awareness	Perception	Lucid Dreams
Deep Sleep	Feelings	Heart-Mind Integration	Concentration	Extreme Focus
Rapid Healing	Trance	Calm Clarity	Physical Activity	Ecstasy
Coma	Metaphysical	Relaxation	Mental Activity	High Energy
Anti-Aging	Dreams	Imagination	Higher IQ	Euphoria
Bliss	Intuition	Inspiration		
	Super Learning	Creativity		
	OBE's	"In the zone"		

Mastering Your Brain Waves of Power

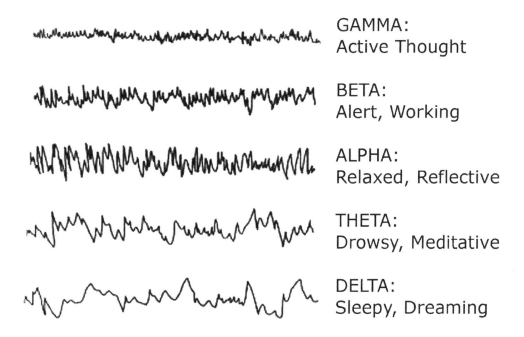

Recently there has been widespread, but not complete acceptance by scientists, of a sixth brain wave called Gamma, in the 25 – 100 Hz range, with 40 Hz being typical. Though the word is the same, Gamma Waves are not the same thing as Gamma Radiation. Gamma also overlaps into the Beta range, but activates large swaths of the brain, so it is not considered a narrow specialty band like the Mu Wave. Gamma waves were overlooked prior to the development of digital electroencephalography. The analog EEG machines that preceded the digital era were usually only capable of measuring waves less than 25 Hz.

Delta Waves are generated in the brain during times of extremely deep sleep or unconsciousness. As a point of reference, if your brain had 0 Hz you would be dead. During Delta there is an extreme lack of awareness and no conscious thoughts.

The Delta state produces some very special affects on the human body. With brain activity at an almost negligible point, body activity such as pulse and large muscle movements, slow correspondingly. This is the most common state for Coma patients. For other people it is almost like going into hibernation. Because the energies of the body are not needed for physical or mental activity they are more fully available for healing and recuperation. Rapid healing and rejuvenation of both the body and mind of patients in Delta states has been noted for some time. On numerous occasions it has also been documented that a skilled hypnotist can bring a patient into a Delta state just prior to an operation and no anesthesia will be required.

While most aspects of the mind and body drastically decrease during Delta, some significant functions affecting anti-aging beneficially increase. Delta stimulates the release of extra melatonin and DHEA, two potent anti-aging hormones. In some individuals the Delta state has been observed to also increase the amount of Human Growth Hormone (H.G.H), another contributor to anti-aging and rapid healing. While these helpful increases are occurring, Delta states simultaneously decrease cortisol, a hormone noted for contributing to stress and rapid aging. Even in regards to simple day-to-day health, the Delta state combined with the mix of increased and decreased hormones it creates, tends to produce a potent boost to the immune system.

You may drift into Delta while you are sleeping or purposefully seek it out during a deep meditation. Those who experience a greater than normal amount of Delta states, will be calmer and have a greater empathy for others. Those who are not empathetic and are noted for their ability to irritate and disrespect others, probably never attain the Delta state.

Another outward indicator of someone that likely experiences greater than normal Delta, is one who besides being very calm and peaceful, has a sincere smile as they look into your eyes and often conveys an intangible inner state of bliss.

Though the conclusion is controversial, it is likely that most people who have Near Death Experiences (N.D.E), do so while in a dominant Delta brainwave pattern.

How to Induce & Increase Your Time in Delta

For most people this is an easy path. Simply get a good night's sleep. Go to bed as much in harmony with the cycles of the Earth as possible. Arise within an hour of sunrise in the dark winter months and within 1 hour of sunrise during the long days of summer. Sleep on a comfortable bed. Do not eat anything including snacks within 4 hours of retiring to insure your stomach is not active and requiring energy while you are sleeping. Do not drink anything within 2 hours of retiring so you will not need to arise in the middle of the night to use the bathroom. For adults, get at least 7 hours of sleep and 8 hours is usually better. Teenagers and children need more. If you do not fall asleep within minutes of retiring, then add however minutes it usually takes you to reach sleep to the 7-8 hours of sleep you need. A good nights sleep will usually take you into Delta at multiple points during the night. You will awake with both body and mind deeply refreshed, rejuvenated and energized for the new day.

Theta Waves are a wonderful place to be! Theta is an extremely rejuvenating time of unconsciousness most beneficially experienced during the twilight/dawn state between waking and sleep, although it can certainly occur at other times too. It is a state of primarily unconsciousness, but it sometimes does have a bit of consciousness in it. Remember times, often in the morning, as you were beginning to transition from sleep to awake? You could simultaneously be dreaming and consciously hearing voices of people talking in the house or noises in the room. Often times the real noises and voices from around you were incorporated into your dreams. Those were times you were in transition between Theta and Alpha. The more in your dream and the less conscious of background voices and sounds, the more in Theta you are. The more aware of the voices and sounds with the dream just holding on tenuously, the more in Alpha you are.

Whether you are falling asleep, succumbing to hypnosis, or consciously meditating into a very quiet place inside yourself, as you become calmer and more relaxed, then drift into unaware drowsiness, your brain waves shift into Theta. It's time for the fun to begin! Vivid, memorable dreams, including sexual dreams, most often occur in the Theta state just before awakening.

Theta is a magical land in your mind filled with vivid imagery, light bulb flashing creative ideas and insights, prophetic visions, deep spiritual enlightenment, relationship resolutions and moving connections to powerful emotions. It is a particularly beneficial state for connecting emotionally to other people, especially personal relationships. As you go deeper into the Theta state your emotions will also deepen and become more profoundly felt.

One of the most helpful benefits of being in the Theta state is the ability to clearly know the correct choice to make, in decisions that may have stumped you while in your normal awake Beta state. During your regular awake day 'mental blocks' more easily occur. Trying to make decisions can be challenging because there is so much mental and physical activity occurring every minute you are awake. The brain can easily get mental overload and become confused and undecided even making relatively simple choices and decisions.

Choices become much clearer in Theta. The clutter falls away and the answers seem so obvious and simple that you'll shake your head when you awake wondering why you didn't think of it before. Often the clearest answers you'll receive to any question, from relationships, to finance, to work, to creative endeavors, school or politics, will come as one of your first conscious thoughts in the first minute or two after you awaken from a nights sleep. This is your transition into Alpha, which is quickly followed by the awake Beta state. But before your mind gets cluttered with all the thoughts of things you need to do that day, at the very moment it transitions from Theta to Alpha, it processes all the clear thoughts and ideas you had through the night in Theta and presents your conscious mind with the conclusions and answers you may not even have known you sought.

The Theta state is also the place where your physical body meets your spiritual. Deeper, more profound spiritual awareness is easier to reach in Theta. As your consciousness departs another part of you awakens that is intimately connected to all the world, all life, and the vast universe beyond. Enhanced spiritual experiences are common in Theta.

Paranormal experiences, particularly out-of-body experiences (OBE's) are most easily experienced for the first times while in a high Theta state after just transitioning down from Alpha. In the calm Theta state psychic phenomena are also much easier to manifest and be noticed.

The Theta state has been associated with "super learning" with as much as a 300% increase in learning ability and memory retention. As I spoke about in greater detail in **Chapter 23 Dreams & Dream Interpretation** , this certainly worked for me in college. I was not the greatest student. But I found the way to ace every test was to speak out loud and record all of my notes and anything I read before a test, then put it on a delayed playback on a tape deck next to my bed while I slept. The tape would begin playing 1 hour after I laid down to sleep. When the tape was finished it would rewind and play again, over and over through the night. As an experiment I did this multiple times and then other times slept without listening to a recording. I always got an "A" on tests with recordings at night and very seldom got an "A" and sometimes was lucky to get a "C" without them.

The brain is extremely open to suggestion, facts and new ideas during Theta. If you are trying to make any changes in your life from quitting a bad habit, to excelling at school, to improving your personality, playing a quiet recording of positive affirmations, or the life changes you want to make, while you are in Theta sleep can quickly and profoundly reprogram your brain and change your life.

Another benefit of Theta is to initiate a state of hyper-focus that can be maintained when you transition into Alpha. The ability to maintain intense focus is often the key attribute of people with ADD or ADHD when they have success in certain endeavors. Hyper-focus seems to be a unique ability generated by the Theta state and is oftentimes one of the goals of some meditation experts.

Theta, like Delta and Alpha, is a beneficial healing and rejuvenation state because both the mental and the physical are slowed down and have time to heal. Being in Theta has been documented to restore the sodium / potassium ion ratios in your brain to healthier levels. These chemical ions are often thrown out of balance during the anxieties and challenges of day to day life in the fast paced Beta state. A short trip into Theta is always an invigorating experience, helping both the body and mind to be restored and refreshed after tough mental or physical exertions.

When Theta Is Too Much Of A Good Thing

As invigorating and pleasant as being in a Theta state for a short time can be, it has definite drawbacks if you find yourself in this state often while you are awake. Too much time in any of the brainwaves will cause overload in one or more functions of your body. If you already experience frequent times in Theta, it would be inappropriate and unhelpful to add more. People under continual extreme stress for prolonged periods will sometimes fall into a dominant Theta state due to overload of their central nervous system. This leads to Theta brainwave patterns that are unsynchronized and not helpful for healing.

Even under normal circumstances too frequent trips into Theta while awake can lead to a persistent inability to focus, mental fogginess, disconnected random thoughts and aimless daydreaming. This is one of the challenges of people with ADD. If you already consider yourself to be unfocused, adding more Theta time would not be a good choice.

Most people with clinical depression are frequently too often in a Theta state. Clinical depression benefits from more time in Beta not Theta. However, someone experiencing short-term depression from mental or physical over stimulation would benefit from some short, rejuvenating trips into Theta.

Other common symptoms of people spending too much time in the Theta state include a lack of excitement or enthusiasm about virtually anything, persistent drowsiness and sleepiness, and extreme impulsiveness. Because Theta is technically an unconscious state (even if you are awake), people experiencing it too often can act impulsively without thinking or considering the consequences.

Many of the depression related negative effects cause a disruption in the brain chemicals, particularly serotonin. If you or anyone you know suffers from prolonged depression or anxiety, help can be found to restore healthy brain chemical balance, in my multimedia book, Depression Free!

Interestingly, while too much Theta can lead to drowsiness and sleepiness, it can also contribute to periods of hyperactivity. Someone in a frequent Theta state uses far less energy for both their mind and body during their listless, sloth periods. But they often still consume normal intakes of food during meals. All the energy in the food has to go somewhere. Some of it will be stored as fat and may contribute to weight gain. But other times an internal trigger may be pulled that sends the person into hyperactivity to burn up some of the excess energy.

A person in a Theta state is exceptionally open to acting on the suggestions of others. This is a state hypnotherapists strive to get patients into when they want to reprogram them with new habits. The same techniques have been used for nefarious purposes by governments, individuals, religious cults and others, to erase or erect inhibitions while altering old beliefs and implanting new ones into unsuspecting minds.

How to Induce & Increase Your Time in Theta

You go into Theta every night when you sleep. Great ideas and answers to vexing questions and challenges frequently pop into your mind in the first minute or two that you are awake. But usually they are quickly forgotten as you zoom through Alpha and into Beta and start your hurried morning routine. To not lose your nights genius or spiritual insights, simply keep a pad of paper by your bed to write down brilliant ideas and answers as they miraculously occur, either when you first awaken, or even if you are roused from sleep in the middle of the night.

Another great time to consciously drift into Theta and have a stream of clear thoughts and bright ideas pop into your head is while you are taking a shower or enjoying a quiet, hot bath. To achieve Theta you'll need to be in a bubble of one, undisturbed by distracting noise, so it's best to take your shower or bath after everyone else has gone to bed, the pets are down for the night, the TV's off and the phone disconnected. You should have the water deliciously hot, but not overly hot that it becomes a distraction. Don't think of anything. Just relax in the hot water, either standing in the gentle rain of the shower or soaking in the wonderful warmth of the tub. Don't think of the day that has just passed or the day that is coming. Don't think of the challenges of work, school or relationships. Just clear your thoughts and think of nothing. Let your mind just go blank. Take a deep breath and exhale deeply letting all thoughts vanish. Quietly stay there and relax. As you do, you will transition from Beta down into Alpha and then down into the upper end of Theta where you still have whispers of consciousness.

In the shower or bath, especially in a bath where you don't have to exert any effort to stand, you can reach a prolonged state of upper Theta that lasts several minutes. This is the zone between Alpha and Theta that brilliant ideas and answers to previously vexing questions will suddenly pop into your mind from the ethers. If you are trying to find those answers or thinking about those questions, you will not be able to achieve the upper Theta state. But if you completely relax and tune out the world, including any thoughts in your own mind, and let the hot water release all the tensions and anxieties built up in your body, then you will be blessed with astounding insights from time to time.

It likely will not happen every day or even every week. But the more often you seek Theta in a hot bath or shower, the more often you will have amazing insights for your life and answers to questions you may not have even been asking. Even when you do not succeed in reaching a Theta state, simply seeking it in a hot bath or shower, in peace and solitude, with a mind cleared of thoughts, is always a calming and rejuvenating pleasure for body, mind and spirit and well worth experiencing every day.

Certain tones are also exceptionally helpful to rapidly bring you into a Theta state. There are multiple free sites on the Internet, especially Youtube, where you can listen to a Theta tone and other frequencies too). Just type Theta tone in your Internet or Youtube search and you'll be offered a list of choices. Here's a link to one as an example. This is called Brainwave entrainment by some. When your ears hear a Theta tone your brain quickly shifts into a harmonic resonance to match the tone, naturally and safely putting you into a Theta state. The link above is a good example of a healthy dose for most people. It plays for 10 minutes.

Similar to tones, listening to harmonious music in most genres except Classical, (which is more helpful to reach Alpha states), are another useful method of calmly drifting into a Theta state. The other exception would be discordant, grating sounds that pass as music with some people. Emotions run deep and close to the surface when you are in a Theta state. Because music often brings us into Theta it also can bring deep emotions to the surface as your brain naturally transitions into a Theta state.

The calming serenity of Yoga is another excellent choice for entering both Alpha and Theta states. There are many variations and types of Yoga. Practice of any of the more meditative forms will definitely help transition you into Theta states of mind, helping you to achieve a higher sense of awareness and greater insight.

Alpha Waves produce a calm state of balance in your body, heart and mind. Have you ever become so enraptured reading a book that you were nearly unaware of noises and actions of people, even in the same room? You were in Alpha. Have you ever been driving down the road with little traffic on a beautiful day and become so blissful that several miles passed before you realized you had completely missed your turn off? You were in Alpha. Have you ever just sat back in a comfortable chair, taken a deep breath, exhaled and just zoned out, perhaps with a light daydream, without either your mind or emotions nagging at you? You were in Alpha. Most people drift into an Alpha state multiple times a day, including within one minute of sitting down to watch the TV. Even if you watch an action show, you are quickly zoned into Alpha.

Alpha is a highly beneficial state of light relaxation and freedom for the moment, from emotional, physical or mental stress. Children naturally experience Alpha states far more often than adults. Most often if viewed on an EEG machine, Alpha waves exhibit a good balance with a synchronized pattern between both the left and right hemispheres of the brain. People exhibiting Alpha waves are considered to be in a state of clear, reasonable thinking and calm, appropriate, emotional reaction with excellent ability to think creatively. If you are not experiencing enough periods of Alpha, you will feel very refreshed and invigorated if you take the simple actions needed to increase your time in that realm.

Boosting your time in the Alpha state has many benefits besides a release of tensions and worries. When your body is calm, relaxed and free of anxiety, it helps your thought process to be clear and focused. Your brain processing slows down, becoming less harried, enabling you to think more clearly about any subject you choose to ponder.

Your ability to be inspired creatively is also enhanced when you are in an Alpha state. Scientific testing has shown that highly creative individuals such as artists, musicians and business problem solvers, function with different brainwaves than non-creative people and have an abundance of time in Alpha. During inspired moments of creativity there are bursts of Alpha brainwaves in the left hemisphere of the brain. This actually dampens left brain activity and enhances the right hemisphere, which is the location for creativity and new ideas.

Stable and balanced emotions and clear mental thought processes are another benefit of the Alpha state. Being able to maintain an Alpha state even during stressful situations, allows an individual to always think clearly and reasonably despite the chaos that may be going on around them and to make decisions without being moved by overactive emotions. Anyone that has challenges being overanxious, hyperactive or emotionally unstable, would benefit from increasing their time in an Alpha state. And it's easy to do!

"Mental blocks" are also most easily vanquished in an Alpha state. The boost to creativity and tendency for the brain to have excellent interconnectivity during Alpha make projects flow easily.

In fact, the Alpha state is often referred to as the "peak performance brainwave" or the "in the zone" or "in the flow" brainwave. *The Beta state is often one of over thinking. The Theta state is one of under thinking. The Alpha is the fine balance in the middle that produces optimum performance and great results.* This has been proven conclusively with studies conducted on active basketball players and golfers. Just before sinking a free throw or hitting a great golf shot, Alpha brainwaves shoot up in the left brain hemisphere. By comparison, those who miss the basket or shank the golf ball are found to have been overactive in Beta. Professional marksmen have also been noted to have a burst of Alpha waves before perfect shots, while novices are recorded to have no Alpha waves at all and far less accuracy!

As Alpha states are noted for lack of stress and anxiety with calm, balanced emotions, being in one is a natural boost to the immune system. Stress and anxiety are both known to weaken the immune system by causing the body to release an overabundance of the hormones adrenaline and cortisol.

"Super learning" has also been noted in the Alpha state. This is the ability to absorb and retain a great amount of knowledge and information and easily bring it to the forefront when needed. It certainly worked for me in college when I would make an audio tape of my class notes the night before a test and have it quietly play back through the night on a repeating loop beside my bed. It's likely I benefited both in Alpha and Theta sleep periods. There was no doubt I did better on tests the next day compared to taking tests without the listening to recorded notes the night before while I slept. Without exaggeration the results were phenomenal! Information I didn't have a clue about the day before, I answered to perfection on tests the next day. Even while I was answering the questions on the tests I had to chuckle to myself as I thought, "I didn't know I knew that."

As the Alpha state is a relaxed, low anxiety time, it lends itself to helping you maintain a positive mood and outlook, with feelings of contentment and hope. Obviously **anything that is counter to relaxation such as caffeine, should be avoided** if you are seeking an Alpha state.

Brain activity in the Alpha range has also been linked to a greater release of the brain chemical serotonin. Medical researchers have concluded that too little serotonin can be a major contributor to depression. Though I've never been personally affected by depression, someone I know, a very sweet and caring lady, one day suddenly just jumped off the deep end without a life preserver.

It came out of nowhere and for a couple of months it was as if she had been transformed into a living nightmare. She went days without sleeping a wink, hallucinated fairies everywhere, became rabidly paranoid that people who loved and cared for her were out to hurt her. One day while alone at her sisters house she physically ripped up a bunch of the carpet and threw it out the front door along with all the lamps! She was wildly crazy in every way and it just kept going on and on every day. Finally, she was diagnosed with low serotonin levels and became her normal, sweet, considerate and intelligent self after just a short time on a serotonin increasing medication. Perhaps the entire prolonged episode could have been avoided if in the months before she snapped she had purposefully taken a few minutes each day to seek out and immerse herself in the Alpha state. The increased levels of serotonin the Alpha state induced might have prevented her entire crazy episode from ever occurring.

Alpha brain waves also contribute to beneficial introspection, promoting heightened awareness of how you feel and self-analysis of your own thoughts and actions.

When Alpha Is Too Much Of A Good Thing

Too much of almost anything can have negative repercussions and this is also true of a person who spends too much time in the Alpha state. Inability to focus and shift into a Beta action state, frequent fatigue without a cause from physical exertion, monotone speaking, lack of excitement about anything, very unobservant of things occurring around them, an inordinate amount of time spent daydreaming, and passively going along with the suggestions of others, are all common signs of a person who is out of balance with too much time in Alpha.

While a good amount of time in Alpha lends itself to countering depression with naturally increased levels of serotonin and great moods, too much time in Alpha can have the opposite affect and contribute to states of depression. A person whose depression is contributed to by over stimulation of senses and nerves would benefit from more time in Alpha. But a person whose depression is contributed to by under stimulation of senses and nerves should seek to have more time in Beta and less in Alpha.

How to Induce & Increase Your Time in Alpha

Visit Youtube and type in "Brianwave Entrainment" or "Alpha Brain Wave tone" in the search box. You'll find several clips to listen to that will play a monotone audio tone matching the brain wave frequency you wish to attain for the moment. Brainwave audios are available for Delta, Theta, Alpha and Gamma. When you hear the sounds in the audio your brain quickly synchronizes to the same frequency, very rapidly putting you into the state of mind you desire. This is especially beneficial when combined with meditation. Here is an Alpha Brainwave Entrainment tone from Youtube as an example.

Closed Eyes Visualization is another excellent way to quickly enter an Alpha state. Though you can do it anywhere from a cramped subway to sitting atop a mountain peak, the easiest place for most people is simply a room or place you can be alone and undisturbed for a short time. Lay or sit comfortably. Close your eyes and visualize anything that brings you peace. It can be carefree peace like a walk in a meadow of flowers, or creative peace like designing your new kitchen or creative project in your mind. As you imagine and picture scenes in your mind, with your eyes closed so you are not visually stimulated by things that may be happening around you, you begin to relax and your brain waves dip into the Alpha frequencies.

Deep Breathing for a few breaths is an excellent prelude to your Closed Eyes Visualization and any of the other techniques you may choose to use to help attain an Alpha state. Deep breathing beneficially increases oxygen levels in both the body and the brain, which helps you relax and transition from the active Beta state to the calmer, less mentally cluttered Alpha state.

All forms of no or low physical activity relaxation are helpful to putting you in an Alpha state. These include, meditation, self-hypnosis, steamy saunas, laying on the beach as the warm sun soaks into your body, soothing hot tubs, gentle massages and even watching TV. Though yoga involves a level of physical activity, it is a very calming gentle form that also lends itself to putting you in an Alpha state.

Reprogram and Reorient Your Life with Alpha: Alpha is an important mental state where a lot of reprogramming can take place in your mind. Think of your mind as a sparkling clear spring bubbling up out of the ground. It's full of potential and promise. But since your childhood people have been intentionally and unintentionally dumping mud in your spring. Every negative comment made by parents, friends, clergy, teachers and anyone else is recorded in your subconscious and whether you realize it or not often has a profound dampening affect on your own attitudes and demeanor.

Consciously going into an Alpha state allows you to purge yourself of old, unhelpful mental programming, much of it a burden weighing you down since childhood, and to replace it with new positive programming. *This can be an almost miraculous transformation of your life.* You are throwing out the old attitudes that have weighted you down and stopped you from reaching your potential and replacing them with new positive attitudes that will propel you to a happier, more fulfilling life. As icing on the cake, you'll be able to tap into your psychic abilities far more easily as well! Following are some easy steps to make it so. Insert your own positive affirmations in place of those in this example.

Step 1: Enter the Alpha state by simply relaxing. Get in a comfortable chair with your feet on the floor, or lay slightly propped up on a bed or couch as long as you can do so without falling asleep. Make sure it is at a time and place where you are assured of at least 15 minutes completely undisturbed by people intruding, cell phones ringing, or distracting noises of any kind in the back ground. For 15 minutes find a place to tune out the world. Check that you are comfortable in the room temperature. If not raise the temperature, or add some clothing, or cover yourself with a blanket. Lower the lights; loosen any tight-fitting clothing, from the belt around the waist to the tie around the neck. Close your eyes as you are sitting or laying comfortably. Take a deep breath in through your nose and slowly and fully exhale through your mouth.

Silently speak to yourself in your mind and affirm that *"I am quiet and relaxed; I am free of all tensions."* Settle into a calm, regular breathing. Be conscious of your physical body. If you are feeling any tension or muscle tightness take a deep breath and release it. Feel yourself letting go of the thoughts of the day and just relaxing. Silently remind yourself "I am serene and relaxed. I am calm and tranquil." If you have any challenge getting to Alpha with these relaxation steps, simply play a brainwave audio of an Alpha tone from You Tube while you are going through the relaxation steps. Your mind quickly wants to slip into a resonate frequency with the tone

Step 2: Purge your doubts and insecurities: Og Mandino, the author of a valuable self-help book entitled *The Greatest Salesman in the World*, taught in his book that you cannot just stop a bad habit. You need to fill the void with a new and better habit to affect a permanent change. Think about your 3 most bothersome self-limitations, fears or concerns. If you want to bring out your psychic powers and doubt your ability to succeed, this is the perfect way to banish the

Mastering Your Brain Waves of Power

doubts and replace them with convictions.

Encapsulate your three choices into concise definitions of one to three words. Find a smooth fist-size rock and write the personal limitation you are getting rid of on the rock with an indelible marker. Now go outside and throw the rock far into the woods, into a lake or bury it in the ground where it will never be seen again.

Step 3: Replace What Has Been Erased: Remember to affect permanent change you must replace the negative old with a positive new. Choose appropriate affirmations to replace the negative thoughts and habits erased in Step 2. You can say as many as you want that you feel are helpful in creating the new you. Say each affirmation of your choice three times and always proceed it with the words, "I am empowered." Here are some examples:

I am empowered. I have great psychic abilities

I am empowered. I am clairvoyant (or whatever psychic abilities you desire)

I am empowered. I am confident

I am empowered. I am self-assured

I am empowered. I am always calm, cool and collected

I am empowered. I attract positive people

I am empowered. I believe in my abilities

I am empowered. I am lucky

I am empowered. My life is good

I am empowered. My relationship with ____ gets better everyday

I am empowered. I have abiding inner peace

I am empowered. I think good thoughts

I am empowered. My future is bright and prosperous

I am empowered. I have unlimited potential

Every time you do this exercise you will permanently improve yourself and get closer to the ideal you seek in every area you affirm. You can dramatically change your life and your abilities with Alpha Affirmations.

Beta Waves are the frequency range you are in during normal, eyes-open activities during the day. Beta activities require alertness and concentration. While in Beta you are fully aware of arousal, upset, and all forms of cognition. Beta waves are particularly strong during times of stress or intense logical thinking. Many if not most people spend too much time in the Beta state, particularly the higher frequencies and this can lead to hypertension, increased heart rate, blood flow, glucose and cortisone production, all of which can be detrimental to your health in overabundance.

There really are no psychic or paranormal benefits to the Beta state. The benefits are derived from insuring you make efforts to spend adequate time in the other brainwave states - Delta, Theta, Alpha and Gamma, which each have aspects that enhance psychic and paranormal abilities.

There are some people that do not have enough time in the Beta state and they are often lethargic, unmotivated, insomniac, pessimistic, anxious, tense and embroiled in addictive behaviors. While more time in Beta will not bring out their psychic or paranormal abilities it will vastly improve how they feel mentally and physically. Anyone deficient in Beta time who corrects the imbalance will feel like thy have been reborn!

How to Induce & Increase Your Time in Beta

There are several good to excellent brain wave entrainment audios available for free on http://youtube.com. These are very helpful for quickly putting you into a Beta state if you feel you need it. The nice thing about brain wave entrainment with Beta is you can listen to the audio relaxed with your eyes closed or while your eyes are open and you are actively involved in an activity.

Reading short stories, novels, doing puzzles and even homework that requires logical thinking such as math, are all good ways to maintain a Beta brain wave pattern.

Any mental games from solitaire to Big Brain Academy on the Nintendo Wii are also excellent choices for stimulating Beta.

Detrimental Methods To Increase Beta

There are several chemical ways you can induce Beta. I don't recommend any of them. They are mentioned here to advise you to avoid them. Even one time is one time too many, as they all have addictive qualities as well as cause unhealthy and detrimental affects to many parts of your body and brain. These include, cocaine, diet pills, tobacco products, Redbull and other energy drinks, and coffee.

Gamma Waves

Gamma brain waves have only recently been positively identified with modern digital analysis equipment. There have been many surprises as this higher frequency of brain waves has been studied! Before scientists had the ability to accurately measure Gamma waves Lucid Dreaming was somewhat of a mystery. One assumption was that Lucid Dreaming occurred in Theta where most other dreaming takes place. But feedback from experiment volunteers correlated to measurements on the scientific instruments did not verify this presumption.

Scientists next looked at Beta as a possible location for Lucid Dreaming as it is somewhat like being consciously asleep. But they couldn't find it there either.

It wasn't until a 2009 study at the Neurological Laboratory in Frankfurt, Germany that the mystery location was finally revealed. Lucid dreamers were not in Theta or in Beta. They were Lucid Dreaming at 40 Hz, a far higher frequency than Theta and higher even than the top range of Beta. They were in Gamma. And Lucid Dreaming is only the tip of the proverbial iceberg. There are many exciting psychic and paranormal abilities that are triggered and unleashed in Gamma!

With more studies concluded in recent years, many scientists now consider Gamma to be the optimal frequency for enhanced human functioning. Observations of test subjects have found the highest levels of compassion, feelings of happiness, acute awareness of reality, and maximum speed of thought and brain processing when the test subjects were in Gamma.

Gamma waves have been discovered racing around in virtually every part of the brain helping to connect the diverse parts together, enhancing memory and perception, while uniting feelings and thoughts.

Many scientists now consider Gamma brainwave activity an essential to optimum performance. Gamma when induced after Alpha has been attributed to peak performance in multiple fields of both mental and physical activity. More than one brainwave training program suggest sports performers tune their brain into Alpha at 10 Hz while visualizing their event for several hours before it occurs, then switch to Gamma at 40 Hz for an hour before the event. The combination of Alpha visualization followed by Gamma activation is claimed to be very invigorating and perception enhancing, jump starting both the brain and the body for peak performance.

From a paranormal perspective, speaking from personal experience, whenever I successfully call upon any paranormal ability it is always when I am in a Gamma version of being 'in the zone.' I am aware of everything more fully, from the subtlest energies to the tiniest sounds and movements around me. It is almost an out-of-body experience. Gamma enhances my perception of both the physical world around me and the unseen world as well. I am quite aware that all of my senses are simultaneously more acute by far than normal. My powers of observation take in every detail around me. My mind is unified with great clarity, processes with astounding speed, and is in unison and perfect harmony with my feelings and emotions. If I have to think or act, there's no hesitation, only instant recognition of the correct course and immediate action to fulfill the choice.

I also find being in Gamma to be an exceptionally spiritual state. I effortlessly without thought, feel energetically connected to all life around me, one with them, sensing the exhale of their breath, feeling the beat of their heart. There is a profound and penetratingly deep connection in every fiber of my being to a God energy of a source far above and beyond this world. When I am in Gamma I truly feel "in the world but not of it." My mind, my body and my paranormal abilities all feel super charged and invigorated.

Additional Benefits Of The Brain Wave State Of Gamma

There are many additional and very helpful benefits to the Gamma state, including:

- **Enhanced perception:** Because Gamma brainwaves circulate through almost every part of the brain they help connect the many divergent inputs from sight to sound, to other senses. Combined with boosting memory and the thought processes, high Gamma helps weave all the incoming information into a clear perception and understanding. The brain operates more rapidly and efficiently. As an example, people with low Gamma can usually only focus on the input from one sense at a time, such as what they are hearing, or what they are tasting, or what they are seeing. People with high Gamma simultaneously receive and process the signals from all senses for higher perception.
- **Enhanced Focus:** Most people are easily distracted and this leads to less efficiency when they are trying to learn something or accomplish a task. The problem is worse for people with learning disabilities. High levels of Gamma allow a person to have laser focus on a single task, which has been a noted hallmark of success in every field of endeavor. Sustaining high levels of focus is greatly aided by the 40 Hz range of Gamma. If you have trouble focusing take periodic breaks to listen to a 40 Hz soundtrack for a few minutes of meditation to insure you maintain high Gamma throughout your task.
- Enhanced memory: The 40 Hz frequency in particular has been noted to increase the ability to recall past events and boost all facets of memory.
- Enhanced understanding: The more active Gamma is in the brain the more efficient the mind seems to be processing information at a high and rapid level. Incoming sensory information is processed more rapidly and the mind is able to easily absorb and clearly understand a higher amount of information.
- Enhanced Sustained Energy Levels: Anyone with high Gamma is a powerhouse of energy, without the need for a jolt of caffeine or other drug induced stimulant. This is true for high Beta as well. When powered by Gamma the high energy levels are sustained and apply to both mental and physical activities.
- Depression Suppression: Abundant Gamma brain waves are considered an effective natural antidepressant. Not only are people with high Gamma happier overall, but those suffering from depression have noted relief and often elimination of the depressive bout by meditating while listening to an audio of Brainwave Entrainment at 40 Hz.
- Increased Energy Levels: Both Beta and Gamma are noted for increased mental clarity and higher more sustained physical energy. Gamma being a higher frequency than Beta seems to exhibit this tendency even stronger.

Mastering Your Brain Waves of Power

- Enhanced Positive Attitude: Observations of test subjects hooked up to EEG machines that measure brain wave activity, have shown that people reporting a positive, happy attitude have levels of Gamma. On the opposite end, those with negative attitudes and low levels of happiness show very little activity in the Gamma range.
- Enhanced Learning Ability: New information and knowledge is absorbed more quickly and thoroughly by people with high Gamma. On the opposite end, individuals experiencing high stress levels or ADD have considerably less Gamma activity.
- Elevated Levels of Compassion: Though increased mind power is most often associated with Gamma brain waves, a greater depth of compassion has also been demonstrated. A sympathetic, empathetic level of compassion far exceeding the norm was verified by tests at the University of Wisconsin Madison when experienced meditation practitioners were measured on E.E.G. Machines. Data showed that the more experienced the meditation practitioner was, the higher levels of compassion and Gamma brain waves they demonstrated.

How to Induce & Increase Your Time in Gamma

A sound, long, good night's sleep: Many, if not most people, have sleep deprivation. This is not merely inadequate number of hours sleeping each night. It is more about the quality of the sleep, plus, the number of hours, plus, when those hours occur. After tens of thousands of years of evolution the human body is genetically programmed from birth to sleep deeply for an adequate period to revitalize itself during the night. Many people's work schedules or personal habits do not allow a good night's sleep to occur. But if it does, sleep is a free and powerful method to increase your time in Gamma. If you wake rested and refreshed during the day you are much more likely to have increased Gamma while you are awake and involved in your daily activities and challenges. If you have a disturbed sleep pattern where you sleep fitfully or get up during the night one or more times, or go to bed late and sleep late into the morning, you are not getting a restorative sleep.

To help you sleep better, if possible with your work schedule, try to sleep during the hours of darkness and be awake during the hours of light. Don't eat or drink anything at least 3 hours before retiring to help your sleep be sounder and less disturbed. If you live in an area with fairly good air, leave a window in your room cracked, even on cold nights, to keep a continuous circulation of fresh air in your room.

Listen to Brain Wave Tones: If you want to quickly zip into an invigorating Gamma state just listen to a Gamma frequency tone. Your brain rapidly syncs in resonance with the sound. 40 Hz seems to be an optimum frequency to promote activation of Gamma and the many beneficial effects associated with it. Just type "gamma brain waves" on a You Tube search and you'll have many free choices of Gamma audio tones to listen while you work or meditate.

Detrimental Activities That Decrease Gamma

It should be noted that if you are trying to increase your time in Gamma you need to decrease or eliminate activities and actions that inhibit Gamma waves. Anything that is detrimental to your mental health will also suppress Gamma wave activity. This includes stress, alcohol and mind and mood altering drugs. When Gamma activity decreases, depression, anxiety, physical illness, increased stress, unfocused mental haze and poorly reasoned and harmful impulsive actions often increase.

Brain Wave Power Summary

Understanding the different frequencies of brain waves and which are helpful when and for what, is a valuable tool in revealing and expanding your psychic and paranormal abilities. If you want to unleash your supernatural self, take the time to purposefully and consciously seek out each of these mental states for the hidden powers they can give you. If you would like greater understanding or additional techniques on how to reach any of the brain wave states there are many excellent, free resources available on the Internet.

OTHER CAPTIVATING, THOUGHT-PROVOKING BOOKS BY EMBROSEWYN

CELESTINE LIGHT MAGICKAL SIGILS OF HEAVEN AND EARTH

What would happen if you could call upon the blessings of angels and amplify their miracles with the pure essence of spiritual magick?

Miracles manifest! That is the exciting reality that awaits you in *Celestine Light Magickal Sigils of Heaven and Earth*.

Calling upon the higher realm power of angels, through intentional summoning using specific magickal sigils and incantations, is considered to be the most powerful magick of all. But there is a magickal method even greater. When you combine calling upon a mighty angel with adding synergistic sigils and words of power, the amplification of the magickal energy can be astounding and the results that are manifested truly miraculous. This higher technique of magick is the essence of *Celestine Light Magickal Sigils of Heaven and Earth*.

This is the third book of the Magickal Celestine Light series and is an intermediate level reference book for students and practitioners of Celestine Light Magick. It contains a melding of the sigils and names of 99 of the 144 Angels found in *Angels of Miracles and Manifestation*, coupled with synergistic sigils and magickal incantations found within *Words of Power and Transformation*. To fully be able to implement the potent combination of angel magick and words of power magick revealed in this book, the practitioner should have previously read and have available as references the earlier two books in the series.

When magickal incantations and their sigils are evoked in conjunction with the summoning of an angel for a focused purpose, the magickal results are often exceptional. The potent combination of calling upon angels and amplifying your intent with words of power and sigils of spiritual magick creates an awesome, higher magickal energy that can manifest everyday miracles. Employing this potent form of magick can convert challenges into opportunities, powerfully counter all forms of negative magick, entities, phobias, fears and people, greatly enhance good fortune, and help change ordinary lives into the extraordinary.

ANGELS OF MIRACLES AND MANIFESTATION
144 Names, Sigils and Stewardships To Call the Magickal Angels of Celestine Light

You are not alone. Whatever obstacle or challenge you face, whatever threat or adversary looms before you, whatever ability you seek to gain or mountain of life you want to conquer, divine angelic help is ready to intervene on your behalf. When the unlimited power of magickal angels stand with you, obstacles become opportunities, low times become springboards for better days, relationships blossom, illness becomes wellness, challenges become victories and miracles happen!

In *Angels of Miracles and Manifestation*, best-selling spiritual, magickal and paranormal author Embrosewyn Tazkuvel, reveals the secrets to summoning true magickal angels. And once called, how to use their awesome divine power to transform your compelling needs and desires into manifested reality.

Angel magick is the oldest, most powerful and least understood of all methods of magick. Ancient books of scripture from multiple religions tell of the marvelous power and miracles of angels. But the secrets of the true angel names, who they really are, their hierarchy, their stewardship responsibilities, their sigils, and how to successfully call them and have them work their divine magick for you, was lost to the world as a large part of it descended into the dark ages.

But a covenant was made by the Archangel Maeádael to the Adepts of Magick that as the people of the world evolved to a higher light the knowledge and power of angels would come again to the earth during the time of the Generation of Promise. That time is now. We are the Generation of Promise that has been foretold of for millennium. And all that was lost has been restored.

It doesn't matter what religion or path of enlightenment and empowerment that you travel: Wicca, Christianity, Pagan, Jewish, Buddhist, Occult, Muslim, Kabbalah, Vedic, something else or none at all. Nor does your preferred system of magick from Enochian, Thelemic, Gardnerian, Hermetic, to Tantric matter. Once you know the true names of the mighty angels, their unique sigils, and the simple but specific way to summon them, they will come and they will help you.

This revealing book of the ancient Celestine Light magick gives you immediate access to the divine powers of 14 Archangels, 136 Stewardship Angels, and hundreds of Specialty Angels that serve beneath them. Whether you are a novice or a magickal Adept you will find that when angels are on your side you manifest results that you never imagined possible except in your dreams.

The angel magick of Celestine Light is simple and direct without a lot of ritual, which makes it easy even for the novice to be able to quickly use it and gain benefit. While there is a place and importance to ritual in other types of magickal conjuring it is not necessary with angels. They are supernatural beings of unlimited power and awareness whose stewardship includes responding quickly to people in need who call upon them. You do not need elaborate rituals to get their attention.

If you are ready to have magick come alive in your life; if you are ready for real-life practical results that bring wisdom, happiness, health, love and abundance; if you are ready to unveil your life's purpose and unleash your own great potential, obtain the treasure that is this book. Call upon the magickal angels and they will come. But be prepared. When you summon angels, the magick happens and it is transformative. Your life will improve in ways big and small. But it will never be the same.

Want to know more? Take a moment to click on the Look Inside tab in the upper left of this page to see the full extent of the marvels that await you inside this book!

WORDS OF POWER AND TRANSFORMATION
101+ Magickal Words and Sigils of Celestine Light To Manifest Your Desires

Whatever you seek to achieve or change in your life, big or small, Celestine Light magickal words and sigils can help your sincere desires become reality.

Drawing from an ancient well of magickal power, the same divine source used by acclaimed sorcerers, witches and spiritual masters through the ages, the 101+ magickal words and sigils are revealed to the public for the very first time. They can create quick and often profound improvements in your life.

It doesn't matter what religion you follow or what you believe or do not believe. The magickal words and sigils are like mystical keys that open secret doors regardless of who holds the key. If you put the key in and turn it, the door will open and the magick will swirl around you!

From the beginner to the Adept, the Celestine Light words of power and sigils will expand your world and open up possibilities that may have seemed previously unachievable. Everything from something simple like finding a lost object, to something powerful like repelling a psychic or physical attack, to something of need such as greater income, to something life changing like finding your Soul Mate.

Some may wonder how a few spoken words combined with looking for just a moment at a peculiar image could have such immediate and often profound effects. The secret is these are ancient magick words of compelling power and the sigils are the embodiment of their magickal essence. Speaking or even thinking the words, or looking at or even picturing the sigil in your mind, rapidly draws angelic and magickal energies to you like iron to a magnet to fulfill the worthy purpose you desire.

This is a book of potent white magick of the light. Without a lot of training or ritual, it gives you the ability to overcome darkness threatening you from inside or out. For what is darkness except absence of the light? When light shines, darkness fades and disappears, not with a roar, but with a whimper.

Use the words and sigils to call in the magickal energies to transform and improve your life in every aspect. In this comprehensive book you will find activators to propel your personal growth, help you excel in school, succeed in your own business, or launch you to new heights in your profession. It will give you fast acting keys to improve your relationships, change your luck, revitalize your health, and develop and expand your psychic abilities.

Embrosewyn Tazkuvel is an Adept of the highest order in Celestine Light. After six decades of using magick and teaching it to others he is now sharing some of the secrets of what he knows with you. Knowledge that will instantly connect you to divine and powerful universal forces that with harmonic resonance, will unleash the magickal you!

Inside you will discover:

- 101 word combinations that call in magickal forces like a whirlwind of light.

- 177 magickal words in total.
- 101 sigils to go with each magickal word combination to amplify the magickal results you seek.
- 101 audio files you can listen to; helping you have perfect pronunciation of the Words of Power regardless of your native language. Available directly from the eBook and with a link in the paperback edition.

AURAS
How To See, Feel & Know

***Auras: How to See, Feel & Know*, is like three books in one!**

1. It's an information packed, full color, complete training manual with 17 time tested exercises and 47 photos and illustrations to help you quickly be able to see Auras in vibrant color! It is the only full color book on auras available.

2. An entertaining read as Embrosewyn recalls his early childhood and high school experiences seeing auras, and the often humorous reactions by everyone from his mother to his friends when he told them what he saw.

3. Plus, a fascinating chapter on body language. Embrosewyn teaches in his workshops to not just rely on your interpretation of the aura alone, but to confirm it with another indicator such as body language. *Auras: How to See, Feel & Know*, goes in depth with thorough explanations and great pictures to show you all the common body language indicators used to confirm what someone's aura is showing you.

Auras includes:
- 17 dynamic eye exercises to help you rapidly begin to see the beautiful world of auras!
- 47 full color pictures and illustrations (in the Kindle or Full Color print edition).

Anyone with vision in both eyes can begin seeing vividly colored auras around any person with just 5 minutes of practice!

Learn how to:
- See the 7 layers of the aura using Embrosewyn's pioneering technique
- Understand the meaning of the patterns and shadows observed in the layers
- Train your eyes to instantly switch back and forth from aura to normal vision
- Understand the meaning and nuances of every color of the rainbow in an aura
- Use your aura as a shield against negative energy or people
- Power up your aura to have greater achievement in any endeavor
- Interpret body language to confirm observations of the aura
- Cut negative energy cords to disharmonious people
- Understand health conditions and ailments through the aura

The secret to aura sight is to retrain the focusing parts of your eyes to see things that have always been there, but you have never been able to see before. It's really not complicated. Anyone can do it using Embrosewyn's proven techniques and eye exercises. The author has been seeing brightly colored auras for over 60 years and teaching others to begin seeing auras within 5 minutes for the last 22 years. *Auras: How to See, Feel & Know*, includes all the power techniques, tools and Full Color eye exercises from his popular workshops.

For those who already have experience seeing auras, the deeper auric layers and subtle auric nuances and the special ways to focus your eyes to see them, are explained in detail, with Full Color pictures andillustrations to show you how the deeper layers and auric aberrations appear. It is also a complete training manual to help you quickly be able to see Auras in vibrant color. It includes 17 eye exercises and dozens of Full Color pictures, enabling anyone with vision in both eyes to begin seeing vividly colored auras around any person. The secret is in retraining the focusing parts of your eyes to see things that have always been there, but you have never been able to see before. *Auras: How to See, Feel & Know*, includes all the power techniques, tools and Full Color eye exercises from Embrosewyn's popular workshops.

Additionally, there is a fascinating chapter on body language. Embrosewyn teaches in his workshops to not just rely on your interpretation of the aura alone, but to confirm it with another indicator such as body language. *Auras: How to See, Feel & Know* goes in depth with thorough explanations and great pictures to show you all the common body language indicators used to confirm what someone's aura is showing you.

For those who already have experience seeing auras, the deeper auric layers and subtle auric nuances and the special ways to focus your eyes to see them, are explained in detail, with accompanying Full Color pictures to show you how the deeper layers and auric aberrations appear.

SOUL MATE AURAS
How To Find Your Soul Mate & "Happily Ever After"

The romantic dream of finding your Soul Mate, the person with whom you resonate on every level of your being, is more than a wishful notion. It is a deeply embedded, primal desire that persists on some level despite what may have been years of quiet, inner frustration and included relationships that while fulfilling on some levels, still fell short of the completeness of a Soul Mate.

Once found, your relationship with your Soul Mate can almost seem like a dream at times. It will be all you expected and probably much more. Having never previously had a relationship that resonated in harmony and expansiveness on every level of your being, you will have had nothing to prepare you for its wonder. Having never stood atop a mountain that tall with an expansiveness so exhilarating, once experienced, a committed relationship with your Soul Mate will give you a bliss and fulfillment such as you probably only imagined in fairy tales.

But how to find your Soul Mate? That is the million dollar question. The vast majority of people believe finding your Soul Mate is like a magnetic attraction, it will somehow just happen; in some manner you'll just be inevitably drawn to each other. The harsh reality is, 99% of people realize by their old age that it never happened. Or, if it did occur they didn't recognize their Soul Mate at the time, because they were looking for a different ideal.

Soul Mate Auras: How To Find Your Soul Mate & Happily Ever After gives you the master keys to unlock the passageway to discovering your Soul Mate using the certainty of your auric connections. Every person has a unique aura and auric field generated by their seven energy centers and their vitality. Find the person that you resonate strongly with on all seven energy centers and you'll find your Soul Mate!

Everyone can sense and see auras. In *Soul Mate Auras* full color eye and energy exercises will help you learn how to see and feel auras and how to use that ability to identify where in the great big world your Soul Mate is living. Once you are physically in the presence of your prospective Soul Mate, you will know how to use your aura to energetically confirm that they are the one. The same methods can be used to discover multiple people that are Twin Flames with you; not quite seven auric connection Soul Mates, but still deep and expansive connections to you on five to six energy centers.

Soul Mate Auras also includes an in-depth procedure to determine if someone is a Twin Flame or Soul Mate, not by using your aura, but by honestly and rationally evaluating your connections on all seven of your energy centers. This is an invaluable tool for anyone contemplating marriage or entering a long-term committed relationship. It also serves as a useful second opinion confirmation for anyone that has used their aura to find their Soul Mate.

To help inspire and motivate you to create your own "happily ever after," *Soul Mate Auras* is richly accentuated with dozens of full color photos of loving couples along with profound quotes from famous to anonymous people about the wonder of Soul Mates.

Treat yourself to the reality of finding your Soul Mate or confirming the one that you have already found! Scroll to the upper left of the page and click on Look Inside to find out more about what's inside this book!

Secret Earth Series

INCEPTION
BOOK 1

Could it be possible that there is a man alive on the Earth today that has been here for two thousand years? How has he lived so long? And why? What secrets does he know? Can his knowledge save the Earth or is it doomed?

Continuing the epic historical saga begun in the *Oracles of Celestine Light*, but written as a novel rather than a chronicle, *Inception* unveils the life and adventures of Lazarus of Bethany and his powerful and mysterious sister Miriam of Magdala.

The first book of the Secret Earth series, *Inception*, reveals the hidden beginnings of the strange, secret life of Lazarus. From his comfortable position as the master of caravans to Egypt he is swept into a web of intrigue involving his enigmatic sister Miriam and a myriad of challenging dangers that never seem to end and spans both space and time.

Some say Miriam is an angel, while others are vehement that she is a witch. Lazarus learns the improbable truth about his sister, and along with twenty-three other courageous men and women, is endowed with the secrets of immortality. But he learns that living the secrets is not as easy as knowing them. And living them comes at a price; one that needs to be paid in unwavering courage, stained with blood, built with toil, and endured with millenniums of sacrifice, defending the Earth from all the horrors that might have been. *Inception* is just the beginning of their odyssey.

DESTINY
BOOK 2

In preparation, before beginning their training as immortal Guardians of the Earth, Lazarus of Bethany and his wife Hannah were asked to go on a short visit to a world in another dimension. "Just to look around a bit and get a feel for the differences," Lazarus's mysterious sister, Miriam of Magdala assured them.

She neglected to mention the ravenous monstrous birds, the ferocious fire-breathing dragons, the impossibly perfect people with sinister ulterior motives, and the fact that they would end up being naked almost all the time! And that was just the beginning of the challenges!

22 STEPS TO THE LIGHT OF YOUR SOUL

A Treasured Book That Will Help You Unleash The Greatness Within

What would it be like if you could reach through space and time to query the accumulated wisdom of the ages and get an answer? 22 Steps to the Light of Your Soul, reveals such treasured insights, eloquently expounding upon the foundational principles of 22 timeless subjects of universal interest and appeal, to help each reader grow and expand into their fullest potential.

In a thought-provoking, poetic writing style, answers to questions we all ponder upon, such as love, happiness, success and friendship, are explored and illuminated in short, concise chapters, perfect for a thought to ponder through the day or contemplate as your eyes close for sleep.

Each paragraph tells a story and virtually every sentence could stand alone as an inspiring quote on your wall.

These are the 22 steps of the Light of My Soul
Step 1: The Purpose of Life
Step 2: Balance
Step 3: Character
Step 4: Habits
Step 5: Friendship
Step 6: True Love
Step 7: Marriage
Step 8: Children
Step 9: Happiness
Step 10: Play & Relaxation
Step 11: Health
Step 12: Success
Step 13: Knowledge
Step 14: Passion & Serenity
Step 15: Imagination & Vision
Step 16: Creativity & Art
Step 17: Adversity
Step 18: Respect
Step 19: Freedom & Responsibility
Step 20: Stewardship
Step 21: Faith
Step 22: Love Yourself - the Alpha and the Omega

ALSO AVAILABLE AS AN AUDIO BOOK! You can listen as you commute to work or travel on vacation, or even listen and read together!

PSYCHIC SELF DEFENSE

A Complete Guide to Protecting Yourself Against Psychic & Paranormal Attack (and just plain irksome people)

Felt a negative energy come over you for no apparent reason when you are near someone or around certain places? Had a curse hurled at you? Spooked by a ghost in a building? Imperiled by demonic forces? Being drained and discombobulated by an energy vampire? Or, do you encounter more mundane but still disruptive negative energies like an over demanding boss, the local bully, hurtful gossip, a physically or mentally abusive spouse, or life in a dangerous neighborhood threatened by thieves and violence? Whatever your source of negative energy, danger or threat, you'll find effective, proven, psychic and magickal countermeasures within this book.

Psychic Self Defense draws upon Embrosewyn's six decades of personal experience using psychic abilities and magickal defenses to thwart, counter and send back to sender, any and all hostile paranormal threats. Everything from unsupportive and dismissive family and friends, to ghosts, demons and exorcisms. The same practical and easy to learn Magickal techniques can be mastered by anyone serious enough to give it some time and practice, and can aid you immensely with a host of material world challenges as well.

17 psychic and paranormal threats are covered with exact, effective counter measures, including many real life examples from Embrosewyn's comprehensive personal experiences with the paranormal, devising what works and what doesn't from hard won trial and error.

Whether you are a medium needing to keep foul spirits away, or simply someone desiring to know that you, your family and property are safe and protected, you will find the means to insure peace and security with the proven methods outlined in *Psychic Self Defense*

You will learn how to:
- Create your own Magick spells tailored to your particular situation and need
- Call upon specific angels to aid you
- Create Crystal Energy Shields
- Protect yourself when in a channeling or spirit medium trance
- Use your Aura to create ASP's (Auric Shields of Power)
- Empower Wards for protection against specific threats
- Recognize and counter Energy Vampires
- Cleanse a home of negative energy
- Cut negative energy cords to disharmonious people
- Counter Black Magick
- Detect alien presence
- Banish malicious entities or demons

Though dealing with numerous and sometimes dangerous other-worldly and material world threats, the entire approach of this book is from a position of personal empowerment, no fear, and divine white light. Whether you are religious or an atheist, an experienced practitioner of the psychic and magickal arts or a neophyte, someone living in a haunted house or just an employee wanting to have a nicer boss, there will be hundreds of ways you can use the information in this book to help you in your life. And you will learn to do it in ways that are uplifting and empowering, producing results that are peaceful, safe and harmonious.

Psychic Self Defense is also available as an AUDIO BOOK.

LOVE YOURSELF
The Secret Key to Transforming Your Life

Loving yourself is all about energy

As humans we devote a great deal of our energy through our time, thoughts and emotions to love. We read about it, watch movies and shows about it, dream about it, hope for it to bless our lives, feel like something critically important is lacking when it doesn't, and at the very least keep a sharp eye out for it when its missing.

Too often we look to someone else to fulfill our love and crash and burn when relationships end, or fail to live up to our fantasies of what we thought they should be. When we seek love from another person or source greater than the love we give to ourselves, we set ourselves up to an inevitable hard landing when the other person or source ceases to provide the level of fulfillment we desire.

Loving yourself is a precious gift from you to you. It is an incredibly powerful energy that not only enhances your ability to give love more fully to others, it also creates a positive energy of expanding reverberation that brings more love, friendship and appreciation to you from all directions. It is the inner light that illuminates your life empowering you to create the kind of life you desire and dream.

The relationship you have with yourself is the most important one in your life. Happiness will forever be fleeting if you do not have peace, respect and love for yourself. It's not selfish. It's not vain. It is in fact the key to transforming your life. Inward reflection and appreciation will open up clearer channels to the divine. Relationships with everyone will be enhanced as your relationship with yourself expands and is uplifted.

All other relationships are only mirrors of the one you have within. As you love yourself, are kind to yourself, respect yourself, so too will you be able to give those and so many other good qualities to others in equal measure to that which you give to yourself.

This is a short, but very sweet book to help you discover your inner glow of love. Within its covers are two great keys you will find no other place. These two keys will proactively bring you to the serenity of self-love regardless of whether you are currently near or far from that place of peace.

Are you familiar with the infinity symbol? It looks pretty much like the number 8 turned on its side. As love for yourself should be now and forever, in the last chapter you will find 88 reasons why loving yourself is vitally important to your joy, personal growth and expansion, and the happiness of everyone whose lives you touch. Most people have never considered that there could be a list that long just about loving yourself! But with each short phrase you read your mind begins to understand to a greater depth how important loving yourself is for all aspects of your life and relationships. As your mind understands your life follows.

This book leaves you with a special gift Inside you'll find two short, but very valuable multimedia flash presentations. One is entitled "Forgive Yourself". The other is "Love Yourself"

These are not normal flash presentations. They are self-hypnosis, positive affirmations that will rapidly help you achieve greater self-love and more fulfilling love-filled realities in your life. As soft repetitive music plays in the background, images reinforcing the theme will flash by on your screen about three per second, accompanied by short phrases superimposed on a portion of the image. In a quick 7-10 minute session, sitting at home in front of your computer, you will find the flash presentations buoy and motivate you. Repeat them twice a day for several days and you will find they are transformative.

    Special Bonus: *Love Yourself* is ALSO AVAILABLE AS AN AUDIO BOOK! This allows you to listen and read at the same time!

ORACLES OF CELESTINE LIGHT
Complete Trilogy Of Genesis, Nexus & Vivus

Once in a lifetime comes a book that can dramatically change your life for the better - forever. This is it!

WHAT WAS LOST...HAS BEEN FOUND

This is the complete 808 page trilogy of the Celestine books of Light: Genesis, Nexus and Vivus.

The controversial *Oracles of Celestine Light*, is a portal in time to the days of Yeshua of Nazareth, over 2000 years ago, revealed in fulfilling detail to the world by the reclusive Embrosewyn Tazkuvel. It includes 155 chapters of sacred wisdom, miracles and mysteries revealing life-changing knowledge about health, longevity, happiness and spiritual expansion that reverberates into your life today.

Learn the startling, never before understood truth:

About aliens, other dimensions, Atlantis, Adam & Eve, the Garden of Eden, Noah and the ark, giants, the empowerment of women, dreams, angels, Yeshua of Nazareth (Jesus), his crucifixion & resurrection, his wife Miriam of Magdala (Mary Magdala), Yudas Iscariot (Judas), the afterlife, reincarnation, energy vortexes, witches, magic, miracles, paranormal abilities, and you!

The **Or***acles of Celestine Light* turns accepted religious history and traditional teachings on their head. But page by page, it makes more sense than anything you´ve ever read and shares simple yet profound truths to make your life better today and help you to understand and unleash your miraculous potential.

The *Oracles of Celestine Light* explains who you are, why you are here, and your divine destiny. It is a must-read for anyone interested in spirituality, personal growth and thought-provoking answers to the unknown.

"You are a child of God, a Child of Light, literally a priceless son or daughter of divinity. Even through the fog of mortal upheavals and the tumults and tribulations, always remember you are still a child of God and shall inherit joy and kingdoms beyond measure, as you remain true to your light."

Genesis 11:99

Psychic Awakening Series
CLAIRVOYANCE

Would it be helpful if you could gain hidden knowledge about a person, place, thing, event, or concept, not by any of your five physical senses, but with visions and "knowing?"

Are you ready to supercharge your intuition? Clairvoyance, takes you on a quest of self-discovery and personal empowerment, helping you unlock this potent ESP ability in your life. It includes riveting stories from Embrosewyn's six decades of psychic and paranormal adventures, plus fascinating accounts of others as they discovered and cultivated their supernatural abilities.

Clearly written, step-by-step practice exercises will help you to expand and benefit from your own psychic and clairvoyant abilities. This can make a HUGE improvement in your relationships, career and creativity. As Embrosewyn has proven from over twenty years helping thousands of students to find and develop their psychic and paranormal abilities, EVERYONE, has one or more supernatural gifts. Clairvoyance will help you discover and unleash yours!

If you are interested in helping yourself to achieve more happiness, better health, greater knowledge, increased wealth and a deeper spirituality, unlocking your power of clairvoyance can be the key. Hidden knowledge revealed becomes paths unseen unveiled.

Unleashing your psychic gifts does more than just give you advantage in life challenges. It is a safe, ethical, even spiritual and essential part of you that makes you whole, once you accept that you have these special psychic abilities and begin to use them.

TELEKINESIS

Easy, comprehensive guide for anyone wanting to develop the supernatural ability of Telekinesis

Telekinesis, also known as psychokinesis, is the ability to move or influence the properties of objects without physical contact. Typically it is ascribed as a power of the mind. But as Embrosewyn explains, based upon his sixty years of personal experience, the actual physical force that moves and influences objects emanates from a person's auric field. It initiates with a mental thought, but the secret to the power is in your aura!

Telekinesis is the second book in the Psychic Awakening series by popular paranormal writer Embrosewyn Tazkuvel. The series was specifically created to offer short, inexpensive, information filled handbooks to help you quickly learn and develop specific psychic and paranormal abilities.

Clearly written, *Telekinesis* is filled with step-by-step practice exercises and training techniques proven to help you unlock this formidable paranormal ability. Spiced with riveting accounts of real-life psychic experiences and paranormal adventures, you'll be entertained while you learn. But along the way you will begin to unleash the potent power of Telekinesis in your own life!

As Embrosewyn has proven from over twenty years helping thousands of students to find and develop their psychic and paranormal abilities. EVERYONE, has one or more supernatural gifts. Is Telekinesis one of yours? Perhaps it's time to find out.

DREAMS

Awaken in the world of your sleep

In *Dreams*, the third book of the Psychic awakening series, renowned psychic/paranormal practitioner Embrosewyn Tazkuvel reveals some of his personal experiences with the transformational effect of dreams, while sharing time-tested techniques and insights that will help you unlock the power of your own night travels.

Lucid Dreaming

An expanded section on Lucid Dreaming gives you proven methods to induce and develop your innate ability to control your dreams. It explores the astonishing hidden world of your dream state that can reveal higher knowledge, greatly boost your creativity, improve your memory, and help you solve vexing problems of everyday life that previously seemed to have no solution.

Nine Types of Dreams

Detailing the nine types of dreams will help you to understand which dreams are irrelevant and which you should pay close attention to, especially when they reoccur. You'll gain insight into how to interpret the various types of dreams to understand which are warnings and which are gems of inspiration that can change your life from the moment you awaken and begin to act upon that which you dreamed.

Become the master of your dreams

Sleeping and dreaming are a part of your daily life that cumulatively accounts for dozens of years of your total life. It is a valuable time of far more than just rest. Become the master of your dreams and your entire life can become more than you ever imagined possible. Your dreams are the secret key to your future.

Additional Services Offered by Embrosewyn
~ on a limited basis ~

I am honored to be able to be of further service to you by offering multiple paranormal abilities for your enlightenment and life assistance. On a limited basis as my time allows I can: discover your Soul Name and the meaning and powers of the sounds; custom craft and imbue enchantments upon a piece of your jewelry for a wide beneficial range of purposes; discover the name of your Guardian Angel; have an in-depth psychic consultation and Insight Card reading with you via a Skype video call. My wife Sumara can also create a beautiful piece of collage art on 20"x30" internally framed canvas, representing all of the meanings and powers of the sounds of your Soul Name.

If you are interested in learning more about any of these additional services please visit my website, *www.embrosewyn.com* and click on the link at the top for SERVICES.

NOTES

Made in the USA
San Bernardino, CA
27 January 2019